Where the Acorns Fall

*To Mary
Enjoy the Tale!
[signature]*

WILLIAM E. SHELTON

Copyright © 2019 William E. Shelton
All rights reserved
First Edition

PAGE PUBLISHING, INC.
New York, NY

First originally published by Page Publishing, Inc. 2019

ISBN 978-1-64462-951-2 (Paperback)
ISBN 978-1-64462-952-9 (Digital)

Printed in the United States of America

I would like to dedicate this book to my wife, Barb. Without her love and support this book would have been left in a shoebox under our bed. She has been the best editor any writer could ever want.

PROLOGUE

"Oh my! Barb, come look what we got last night!" I exclaimed, remembering that the weather forecast from the previous evening showed a possibility of eight to twelve inches of snow. It had been a relatively nice winter, but now it was late winter. Things were drastically changing and not for the better! Luckily, it was Sunday morning and my day off.

Smiling broadly, I began thinking of spending the day hunting and walking in the woods. I thought it was a good day to try out my ten-shot .22 Marlin rifle that Barb had bought for me as a Christmas gift just this past Christmas. I loved the woods and couldn't pass up a chance to get out there. Before I could turn from the window, small arms and legs were going ninety miles an hour trying to climb up to my neck with an excited "Let me see, let me see!"

"Get up here, son, and look at that!" I said to the three-year-old boy.

"Mom, come see! Snow is everywhere, it's covering the window. I want to go out in it," he said.

Eric was just like me, always up early and ready to go. Barb was still in bed resting and recouping from a bout of morning sickness. She informed both her men that neither of us were going anywhere until we had our breakfast. Knowing how bad she felt, I yelled, "You stay in bed. I'll fix us a bowl of cereal! We will be back after you are up. I won't keep Eric out very long."

We lived just west of the city limits of the town of Farmington, Missouri. It was a great place to be living. The small duplex apartment we rented sat just off Bray Road on the Pogue Farm. Gene Pogue gave his son, Jerry, eighty-three acres of land to build his house. Just as the basement was done, Jerry was transferred to another state to work. So for the time being, they put a flat roof on the basement and made a duplex apartment. For a young couple with a young child and another on the way, this was the perfect place to be. The Bray Farm bordered the north side of the property with its homemade "Keep Out" signs posted on the fence. The best part of the Bray Farm was the west side that bordered thousands of wooded acres owned by the St. Joe Mining Company. The acreage stretched from our back door, north to the mining town of Flat River, to the city of Elvins to the west, and to the town of Doe Run to the south. In this vast expanse of land were tailing ponds, ridge roads, fire trails, logging roads, hills, valleys, and just about anything a wanderer, adventurer, or hunter could ever want.

After our bowl of cereal, we dressed for the morning's adventure of making a snowman and playing with Blue, our mixed-breed mutt and Eric's faithful companion. Stepping out from under the awning, Eric was laughing, hollering, and having what seemed to be the time of his life. "Dad! Let's build a snowman!" he yelled. "Look how deep the snow is! It's so much fun!" I couldn't tell who was having the better time, Eric or Blue, as they were falling over each other.

"Where do you want the snowman built?" I asked.

"Here in front, where Mom can see from the front door," he replied.

"Okay, but start rolling the snow at the end of the house and go downhill so we can make a big snowman."

As we roll the first ball for the body, I see Barb standing at the front door laughing with her Instamatic camera in hand, taking pictures of Eric—and Blue knocking him down just about every step he took. After about an hour and a half, we had what I thought was a good-looking snowman. Barb came out with one of my high school ball caps, an old crocheted scarf, some gloves, and a carrot we had in the fridge.

"Great, Mom, now he will look real, like Frosty!" Eric exclaimed.

I broke off some limbs for arms and dug in the driveway for rocks to make eyes, a mouth, and buttons on his belly. Feeling proud,

Barb took some family pictures. Noticing how Eric was looking totally worn out, his teeth chattering, Barb said, "Time to go in and warm up, okay?"

"No! I'm not tired!" he shouted through his chattering teeth.

"We will make hot chocolate and turn on cartoons. We can come back out later and play some more," Barb promised.

It's now my turn to play, I thought as I reached for my rifle to head to the woods. Eric began to cry as he wanted to go to the woods too. I convinced him the snow was too deep and he needed to stay and look out for his mom. I wiped his tears then out the door I went, telling Barb, "I won't be gone long. I'm just going over the Bray's fence line. Maybe I'll get a squirrel or rabbit!" She rolled her eyes and gave me that "Oh, please don't!" look. I knew she didn't like the taste of wild meat and wouldn't eat it even if I got one.

With a kiss on the cheek, she said, "Don't be gone long."

"I won't," I said as I head to the corner of the house and toward the backyard.

The backyard was small, and it didn't take me long to get to the fence line separating the yard from the woods. I thought Blue would follow me, but I guess he thought Eric was coming back out, or maybe they gave him something to eat. Crossing the fence proved no easy chore with a lot of clothes on and slick footing, but I got over and was on my way.

It's a strange feeling to be in the woods when there is no breeze blowing, the snow falling so fast, and you can't hear a single flake hit the ground. The sound of absolute silence while there is so much movement in the woods makes a man's mind wander. As the crunch of the snow breaks the silence through the dense hardwood forest, my mind runs wild with images of myself as a great trapper in the towering Rocky Mountains. I began to feel as though I was the first man to step in this part of the world. I stopped to wonder what it would really be like. *What would I eat? Could I survive?* I walked about a hundred yards through the woods to a field on the back side of the Bray Farm and hoped to see a deer. Walking slowly and being careful not to spook anything, I veered off to the left feeling like something was drawing me that way. I spotted a colossal mammoth of a tree just on the other side of the fence. It stood out like the grandfather of all trees. The limbs were as big as most trees in the woods. My thoughts of hunting ceased as I headed straight for the giant sentinel. Just as I was trying to cross the fence, I heard a noise coming from across the field, and I froze.

Staring intently through the thick falling snow, I finally saw it. Crossing the field was a man slowly prodding through the snow, talking to a single cow while driving her across the field. Hoping he hadn't spotted me, I laid my rifle up against the mighty oak and walked into the open field.

Being raised on a farm, I knew not to yell or come to them at an angle as to spook the cow and scare her off, so I just talked a normal greeting and fell in behind him.

Mr. Bray, as we all called him, was a farmer who made his living from the farm. He and his wife lived on the farm with their two children. They moved to this farm that was given to them by Mrs. Bray's uncle, Mr. Jennings, who lived in St. Louis and wanted nothing to do with farming. With a firm handshake and a love for his niece, he told Mr. Bray if any of his family was alive, the place would be theirs. So they put down roots and built a small house to raise his family. The house was heated with the wood from the farm, and they got their water from a spring that was behind their house. Mrs. Bray later got a job at the state hospital just south of where they lived, but Mr. Bray sold vegetables all spring and summer long from a mule-drawn wagon. Everyone in town knew the Brays, especially the cry of "Fresh vegetables, no finer vegetables anywhere!" The kids would all want to go see the mule with his long ears poking through holes in a hat he wore, and a red neckerchief tied around his neck. Their moms would come out to say "Be careful," and that would be Mr. Bray's chance to hold up some vegetables or fruits and say, "No finer vegetables around." He made his living that way plus selling a few cattle each year. Mr. and Mrs. Bray had three children, two sons—John and Sonny—and a daughter, Wilma, whom we called Jeannie.

Mr. Bray seemed surprised to see me, and I couldn't blame him, but I gave him a neighborly "Hello" and asked if things were okay. He quickly snapped, "Yes, they are, and *you* are trespassing!"

I halfway held up my hands and said, "Sorry, but if you need any help with the young heifer, I'll help drive her down the hill. I can tell she is getting ready to calf."

Surprised, he stopped dead in his tracks, looked at me, and said, "I'm afraid I'm going to lose them both, and the vet said there is no way he could make it out here today."

I told him I'd helped my dad deliver calves before, and I would be willing to help. In my mind, I was thinking, *Dad always delivered, and I watched and was his gofer. Go get this, hand him that and whatever else he needed.*

Mr. Bray looked at me hard in the eyes, took a half step toward me, and softly said, "I could really use your help." We had little over quarter of a mile to get her to the shed. Mr. Bray put a rope on her halter to lead her home, and I drove from behind.

Watching the heifer, I wondered if she would make it, and I was thinking, *What would I do when I get there?* Bloody mucous was hanging from her rear end, and every so often, she would stop for a contraction. I could see the calf move in her side. He would coax her on, and I would think, *Oh please, don't lay down now.* A little less than a half hour later, we made it. There to meet us were Jeannie, Sonny, and Mrs. Bray. We all knew each other kind of well because we all went to the same Baptist Church, but not well enough, so I just said, "Wow, what do you think of all the snow?"

Jeannie and Sonny greeted me while busily preparing the shed for the delivery while Mrs. Bray stood by with her stern and majestic Queen Elizabeth look that required very few words to insinuate "Don't mess up!"

While helping Mr. Bray spread straw out on the floor, I couldn't help but notice that theirs wasn't your ordinary farmer's shed with an overall size of approximately twelve feet wide by maybe fourteen or fifteen feet long and made of logs on all sides. On the outside of the back was a partial rock chimney that stood no higher than the wall. The front had a window by the doorway. The oak doorframe was in good shape and had woven wire fencing tacked up to keep the cattle out of the hay they had stored inside. Jeannie noticed that I was looking at the chinking between the logs and told me this was the original house on the farm. The porch had rotted away, revealing a large flat rock, but on the inside, the floor was in decent shape where we had spread the straw in the first room. Hay was stacked full in the back room. It kind of looked as though the hay was holding that side of the small house up. Jeannie also pointed out a loft on the back side of the front room and said, "That's where the children slept. Right here is where the girls must have carved their names."

I strained to make out the girls' names on the homemade bunk but quickly turned my attention back to the young heifer because Mr. Bray was pulling her head through the front door while Sonny was pushing. She came in easy, and I could tell she had been treated like a pet. Each one of their cows had a name, and this one's name was Miss Pretty Girl.

"You never know how these things will go with heifers being so young and small," Mr. Bray told us.

Her water broke just before I saw Mr. Bray in the upper field. It really was a wonder we made it to this house. As we were watching Miss Pretty Girl having contractions, she knelt on her front knees and just rolled on her side. With a pitiful bawl and stiffened legs, she tried the best she could to push the baby out.

Nervously wringing her hands and her eyes full of tears, Jeannie weakly said, "She is not going to have this baby by herself. We've got to help her."

Mr. Bray asked, "Can you check her out and see if the calf is lined up right?"

My heart started pounding in my chest as I thought this wouldn't go this far. I didn't say yes, and I didn't say no, probably because I was afraid my voice wouldn't sound normal. I just turned toward Mrs. Bray, who was holding a towel and some Joy dishwashing liquid. A bucket of warm water was in front of her feet. I took my coat off and threw it in the corner and rolled up my sleeves. Mrs. Bray squirted some Joy into my hands. As hard as my hands were shaking, I don't know how it ever landed in my palms. Mrs. Bray gave me a look as though she was saying, "These are our babies, save them!" I told Jeannie to sit down by Miss Pretty Girl's head and hold the halter.

This felt very strange to me. It even startled me a bit. I sounded just like my dad when he was telling me to hold the halter for our cows. I told myself it was okay, I could do this, as I regained my composure and reached for more Joy. Getting down on my hip and elbow, I told Jeannie to talk to Miss Pretty Girl. I asked Sonny to get me three pieces of balers twine off the hay and not to cut them. I needed them to slip over the calf's front hooves and head to help pull the baby out. I waited until she quit straining, and just as she became relaxed, I slid my hand in just past my wrist. I could feel the calf's head. I worked my hand under the head toward the neck and quickly glanced at Mrs. Bray and said, "The umbilical cord is around its neck."

Jeannie gave a helpless moan and held Miss Pretty Girl's head up and laid it in her lap. With both arms around her head, she started rocking her back and forth.

I told them the only thing I knew to do was to push the calf back in and try to get the cord off. Just as I was pushing the calf's neck and chest area in, I discovered something else. Only one hoof was positioned in the right place. I informed them this may be what caused the problem with the umbilical cord. Pushing the calf back farther, the heifer tried to get up. Mr. Bray and Sonny held her down, and she let out a god-awful bawl of pure agony. I felt for the shoulders and followed it down to the knee and noticed I was as far as I could go. "Don't let her move!" I shouted. "I'm pulling the leg forward!" I instructed Sonny to make loops in the twine and get ready to hand it to me. I slid my arm back and got the hoof placed by the other one just under the calf's chin. I let go and grabbed the umbilical cord and moved it down under the front legs. "There!" I explained just as the heifer strained again and pooped all over my neck and shoulder.

Mrs. Bray never said a word and reached down for the towel and wiped me off. No one missed a beat. Sonny handed me the twine, Jeannie rocked and talked to Miss Pretty Girl, and Mr. Bray held her down all the while Mrs. Bray kept wiping me off. I slipped the twine over the hooves and one over the head, imagining my dad was there helping me.

I informed them the baby had not moved one time. Through falling tears, Jeannie said, "Please save Miss Pretty Girl!"

I told Mr. Bray and Sonny, "On the next contraction, we need to pull the calf out. If we can't, we will have to go get the tractor and pull with that!" I don't think they liked hearing that, and I didn't like saying it, but I had seen my dad use the tractor before in an emergency such as this.

The contractions came, and we all pulled. The head and front hooves seemed to pop out, but nothing more. Noticing a very purple nose and no movement, I yelled through gritted teeth, "Harder! Again, pull harder!" The calf slid right into my lap as we all fell backward.

The three of us scrambled up and grabbed rags and straw, wiping the mucous off. Mr. Bray was pushing on the calf's sides trying to get it to breathe and get its heart pumping. Nothing seemed to work. I cupped my hands over the calf's open mouth and slowly filled the young tender lungs full of air just as I had watched my dad do. Mr. Bray kept pressing on the calf's sides.

Looking around the room at nothing and at everything, feeling lost and moving in slow motion, a whisper came to me, "Son, hand me that piece of straw." I slowly reached down and picked up a single piece of straw. I looked up and saw Mrs. Bray watching me. I turned and pushed the straw in the calf's nostril and shoved until it seemed to be up to its eyeballs. To all our surprise, the calf jerked its head. I quickly breathed some more air in its lungs and shoved the straw in the other nostril. The baby calf shook its head hard enough to sling mucous out of his mouth. We grabbed rags and started rubbing all over the calf to get its circulation working. After a few minutes, we had him standing. Miss Pretty Girl let out a better sounding bawl, and Jeannie said, "Well, you're welcome Miss Pretty Girl!"

Mr. Bray said, "We all need to stand back and see if she will get up."

We all moved over toward the doorway when Sonny said, "It's a little bull."

A solid-black stiff-legged and shaking calf fell to the ground. The young heifer turned her head and looked straight at her new baby. With a couple of tries, she soon got up and began cleaning her new baby boy.

As Sonny and I back out of the doorway, Mr. Bray said, "Get some feed and water. We will keep them here for a day."

They all thanked me, and I could tell I had made new close friends. Jeannie asked if I would come to the house and have something to eat.

I said, "I'd like to, but Barb has no idea where I am, and I have been gone way too long."

After saying thank you and telling some recent family history stories, I said, "Would it be okay if I bring Barb and Eric down to see the baby calf?"

"Oh yes! Come by anytime!" they replied in unison.

I said, "Thanks, I'll bring them down," and started to walk away. Before I could take a step, I looked back, and without asking anyone, I said, "Did you know the people who lived in the log house?" Mr. Bray kept walking away, and Jeannie and Sonny just stopped and looked at their mom as she turned and walked toward me. With a long, lonely stare past me, through the falling snow, and up the hill past the corner of the woods, she said, "No, we don't." After a silent pause, she looked at me and said, "There's three girls buried under that big oak tree by the woods. They were part of the family that lived in the log house." She looked back up the hill and then turned and walked away.

I looked at Jeannie and Sonny, raised my hand to wave goodbye, and walked home. I never turned to look back at the family, I just looked at our steps in the snow that were disappearing due to new falling snow. I got a good way, stopped by a pond that was just about to the corner of the woods where the gap was to the small back field. Going uphill with a deep snow on proved to me that I was not in the best of shape, or maybe it had been an exhausting morning, and just a bowl of cereal had not done its job. I caught my breath, headed through the gap, and walked the edge of the fence line toward the big oak tree. Walking on this side of the woods, I felt a breeze with a bit of a cold bite starting to pick up. I looked up at the sky and thought to myself, *The warm front has moved through, and now the cold north winds will come through for the rest of the day.* That meant the moisture was moving out, and the snow would soon end. Knowing I must work tomorrow, I figured the break in the snow would give the snowplows a chance to clear the roads off. But then again, if it kept snowing, maybe I wouldn't be able to go to work, and we would all stay home. With an exhausted sigh, I thought, *I need to go to work.*

Getting closer to the big oak tree, I saw my .22 rifle leaning against the tree as I closed in on it. I kind of surveyed the ground to see if I could tell where the graves might be. With all the snow, I couldn't really tell a thing except for what my imagination was making up. I picked up my rifle and backed up a few steps and really looked at the tree. It was strange that it was not in the woods but here on this property all by itself. Why would someone leave this one tree? For the girls? I walked back up to the tree, put my gun down again, and spread my arms out and started measuring the base of the tree. "Let's see, one, two, three, and if my arm spread is at least five feet, that would make the tree about fifteen feet around! Wow!" I said softly as the cold frost flowed from my mouth. *I bet Indians have climbed this tree*, I thought to myself.

Again, I imagined I was the first white man in these parts of the woods. I looked up at the limbs wondering if I could climb the tree, but the first limbs were fifteen to twenty feet up the massive trunk. No way I could shimmy up a tree that big around. There was one limb that came straight out about ten feet and bowed down and then straight out again. It could have been a "hanging tree." I wondered if any man was ever hung here. I even checked the tree for rope marks. I saw my rifle out of the corner of my eye, picked it up, and heard myself say, "Goodbye, girls," and waved.

Crossing the fence, the same way I came, I headed into the woods toward home. Just like before, the woods offered a sanctuary to silence. I thought, *How wonderful it is to be out here.* Taking deliberate steps so I didn't trip over down trees or broken limbs, I came to the center of this section of woods and noticed an old road. Perhaps a logging road or old fire trail from days past. It led toward the Pogue farm and north toward the Bray farm. No sooner had I looked that way than five deer had come out of some cedar trees and had stopped in the road about thirty yards away from me. I loved seeing deer in the woods, especially when they were not bounding away waving a big white flag at me. They saw me but really couldn't tell what I was as I held perfectly still, hoping they didn't see my breath. At that moment, they froze, I froze, and it became a stare-down. The big doe stomped her feet at me, but I didn't move. After what seemed to be an hour, she turned those big ears toward the other deer. I assumed they decided I was not a threat, and the deer move on into the woods, looking back at me every few steps. I took a big breath and yelled, "I win!"

Feeling like I needed a little rest, I kicked the snow off a stump next to the old road and sat down. Without thinking, I placed my rifle in my lap, took off my gloves, and pulled my coat hood off my head. It was just about done snowing. The temperature was getting colder, and I just stared at the pure white beauty of the frozen woods. Without thinking of any of the past morning's events, I put my hands together and bowed my head to my knees and said, "Thank You, Lord. Thank You for allowing me to be here, here at this place and at this time. I don't have much, but I am so happy." I thanked God for my family, our health, my job.

I was on a roll thanking God for all my blessings and felt closer to my Creator as I neared to the "Amen." I stopped short and got down on my knees in the snow, placed my hands on the stump, and bowed my head into my hands. With tears in my eyes, I prayed, "If it could ever be possible, Lord, I would like to own some of these woods and build my home here someday." I was silent for a minute, wiped my face with cold hands, and said, "Amen."

With a big smile, I lay on my back in the snow, laid my rifle on my chest, and made a snow angel. Staring straight up into the clouds past the bare treetops and past the falling snow, I imagined angels shearing their sheep. I smiled a half-cocked grin remembering that was something my mom always said. When I was done, I did the best I could to get up without messing up the snow angel. Still in my same footprints, I turned my head toward the big oak tree and shouted as though they could hear me, "That's for you girls!" I turned back around and looked to see if anyone else was in the woods to hear me. I laughed to myself and started walking home. Home to where it was warm and there was food. I thought out loud, "I'm starving!"

Chapter 1

A few weeks after a record-breaking snowfall of 15.5 inches, March came in like a gentle lamb. The snow had melted away, and the usual March winds were beginning to dry the very soggy ground. That evening, Barb asked, "Which is it, in like a lamb or out like a lion?"

I said, "I think since it came in like a lamb, it will go out like a lion." I'm always glad to see warm weather come. As a matter fact, I'm always glad to see winter come too. That's the thing about Missouri weather, if you don't like it, just wait a day or two, and you'll get something else.

The small two-bedroom basement apartment with all the land a guy could hunt on was the perfect place for a young family to start out. Even though there were just a few things Barb didn't like. Basements drew humidity and could cause mold problems. Missouri is kind of famous for its humidity. She also thought Eric and I were in the woods too much, and she always had to honk the car horn to get us to come home. It was a good home.

It was, for us, a great summer. I worked at a local florist shop as a designer and wasn't half bad at it. The pay wasn't great, but we made ends meet. Which meant we couldn't save enough money to buy our own place. Barb was always looking at houses on weekends. We would drive around looking at trailers. She got a job as a personal secretary for Western-Southern Life Insurance Company. Now I needed to stay home more and help. The Bray family became good friends, and Mr. Bray would come up now and then on his new tractor and give Eric a ride. What days off we had together, we would go tent camping at Sam A. Baker State Park. It was cheap and a lot of fun.

As summer made way for fall and the leaves began to turn, Barb informed me that time was getting very close for our second child. She told me I needed to stay close to home or near a phone. I let her know that bow hunting for deer started October 1, and she was the one who bought me a new bow for my birthday in June.

"Fine," she said, "I'll just have my sister Dolores come and stay while you're out."

"Well, no, don't do that, I'll just stay in the woods between here and the Bray Farm."

On October 25, Barb informed me, "It's time to get the suitcase."

Doing this once before, it should be a breeze, so why isn't anything where it should be? I thought. "Who moved my car keys?" I yelled as Eric came and picked them up off the floor by the table where I had laid them.

Barb rolled her eyes and said, "Take the suitcase to the car. Dolores is on her way to watch Eric, and I'll call our parents."

"Okay," I said, remembering the conversation when I called my mom when Eric was born. To say the least, I do get emotional. Mom picked up the phone, and I didn't know why, but I started to cry and said, "Mom, Mom, Mom, Barb, Barb, Barb."

She said, "Is Barbara going to have the baby now?"

I said, "Yes, yes, yes." Weirdest thing ever. So I let Barb do the talking.

Danielle Christine Shelton was born that morning, and I am proud as ever. While Barb and Danielle are in the hospital, Eric and I set up the baby bed, and I see there is very little room in our bedroom. I sort of mumbled to myself, "I see what you mean. This is a small two-bedroom apartment with no storage space." I knew Barb would want to move soon.

November rolled in, and I started getting excited for deer season and finally worked up the nerve to ask the Brays if I could hunt on their property. With reluctance in their eyes and speech, Jeannie said very slowly, "Well, I guess so." As it turned out, I saw one deer on the last day of deer season.

On that last day when I sat up in bed to get ready to go, I told Barb, "I'm really tired. I don't feel very well. I think I'll just go later." A couple of hours later, Barb got up with Danielle, and I got the whole bed to myself and slept till 10:00 a.m. Feeling better, I got up, messed around some, and decided to get ready to go out. It was an abnormally warm day for November, and the sun was shining very bright. I walked through the patch of woods and came to the big oak tree. As I always did when I passed by here, I looked to see where the girls might be buried. I couldn't tell anything, and without stopping, I gave a half wave and said, "Morning, girls."

I kept going across the field, climbed the fence, and stepped into the big woods—as I called them because they go on for miles behind the Bray farm. After stepping over the fence, I reached down to pick up my rifle. As soon as I stood up straight, I saw a glisten about one hundred yards to my right up the hill. It was kind of far. It seemed to look like someone flashing the sun at me with a mirror. Quietly but quickly, I went about twenty-five yards up the hill toward the flash, thinking I would see someone leaving after they watched me cross the fence to this part of the woods. Trespassers were rare, but not uncommon. I saw it again, and this time, I saw what it was. With his head going up in the air then back to the ground and a flash of red slick antlers, I could tell this was a very nice buck. The way he was acting, I knew he was trailing a doe in heat, and fortunately for me, he had no interest in anything else. To get a clear shot, I had to walk parallel to him and try to get closer. With my 30-30 open-sight rifle held up, I finally got an opening. I stopped, took aim, and squeezed the trigger. One shot, and the buck turned and bounced back from the way he came.

In woods like these, there was no second shot. A few seconds later, I heard it—a loud crash in dry leaves. I knew I hit my mark. I took my time walking up the hill with my rifle ready, just in case he was only injured. The closer I got, the more nervous I became and had to tell myself to slow down and breathe. There he was, a perfect ten-point buck. I couldn't believe it. It was the biggest deer I'd ever seen!

After regaining my composure, I thanked God for such a great hunt. I thanked the old-timers for their wisdom: keep the sun at your back and your nose in the wind. Sleeping late seemed to bring me a little luck too. I just couldn't believe it. Seeing the reflection of the sun on his antler that far away. Would anyone believe it? After rolling the deer on his back, I got him field dressed and started pulling him down the hill. I suppose the Brays heard my shot because when I got to the fence, I could see Mr. Bray getting on his tractor. After crossing the fence and pulling the deer under, I sat down and rested while Mr. Bray drove up my way. As warm as it was, it was good to see him—or so I thought. We tied the deer to a boom on the back of the tractor and hoisted him off the ground. I rode on the fender and held onto his seat while heading down the hill. All the Brays came out when we got to their backyard and came to see the deer.

Sonny said, "My, that's the biggest buck I've ever seen!" Mrs. Bray gave a look that said, "That's been our baby for several years." Then I went weak in the knees when Jeannie pet the deer's head and said, "Look at those beautiful, big brown eyes." I was thinking this wasn't a good idea coming here. I told them that when I got him butchered, I'd bring them some meat. That satisfied everyone but Jeanie, who kept petting the deer's head.

I got back on the tractor, and Mr. Bray took me home. My pride swelled again when Eric came running toward us thinking he was going to get a ride on the tractor. When he got near, he saw the deer and started hollering for his mom. Barb came out with the baby and simply said, "Well I'll be."

Thanksgiving came and went, then we started preparing for Christmas, which is my favorite holiday. I got one and one-half extra days off work—without pay, but off nonetheless. With two kids, a tree in the living room, and presents under the tree, we really started feeling the pressure of living in a small apartment. Especially when one of us had to look through the Christmas tree to see the TV.

As luck would have it, that spring, Barb's mom called her to let us know the house on the street behind her house had been put up for sale. They were friends of Barb's family and were even at our wedding. So we knew what the place was like. It was a small house of just over a thousand square feet of living area. The house had three bedrooms, a nice kitchen, and a detached garage. It was a great starter house, but there was only one problem. We needed a down payment. My dad, who is a carpenter by trade, farmer for the love of it, and a building trades teacher, checked the house out and said it was well worth the price. So he put my name on a section of his farm that I could use for collateral for the down payment. Everyone was happy, but I knew I was going to miss the great hunting spot I had in my backyard. After moving everything out of the apartment, I told Barb to go with the truck, and I'd be there in a bit. I just wanted to take one last walk in the woods behind the apartment.

I crossed the fence and got on the old logging road and walked into the cool woods. All the trees fully leafed-out in their dark-green canopies made it hard to see very far. This time of year brought on the tunes of many birds calling their mates or challenging fellow birds. Squirrels were checking on one another, and woodpeckers were tapping on the hardwood trees for a bite to eat. This reminded me that this was also the time for ticks. I couldn't see anything anyway, so I turned to head back; and as I did, I caught a view in an opening of the dense woods and saw the giant oak tree. At that same time, the whole woods became eerily quiet. So quiet that the hairs on the back of my neck tingled. I stared at the giant oak and thought of the girls buried there. For some reason, my attention was drawn back to the trail; and as I looked down it, I saw the tree stump. The silent woods became alive again, and I got the feeling that all was well. As I took a deep breath, I turned to go back, raised my hand slightly, and softly said, "'Bye."

Chapter 2

Returning

Time passed as it always did, but not without wonderful joyous times and very sad, heartbreaking times. I got a new job at the glass factory in Flat River, and we got health insurance for the first time. Our third child, Brooke Elizabeth, joined our family; and after a while, Barb got a new job at the local Walmart as a pharmacy technician.

In the winter of 1984, my dad died of lung cancer at the age of fifty-two. Mom decided to sell all their cattle and the farm they had in East Bonne Terre. The buyer told my mom that he wanted the land that had been deeded to me for the collateral for my house. I knew my dad wanted me to have that property because he had given my sister's property to build their homes. That was where he wanted me to build my home when that time came. This was so hard, but the wisdom of my wife said to me, "Which would hurt the most, losing that piece of property or losing the joy and company of a mother who just lost her husband?"

"That's not fair!" I said and thought it was never really mine to begin with. We went to the bank the next day, and I signed the paper without saying a word.

Once back in the car, I drove the family out to the property I just signed away. With a small lunch of bologna sandwiches, chips, and a cooler of soda and carrying a playpen for Brooke, we walked down to the river that bordered the east side of the farm. Once there, we let the kids swim, and Barb and I just sat on the gravel bar, watching. I reached down, took her hand, and brought it up to my lips, whispering into her palm, "Nothing is forever, is it?"

She lay her head on my shoulder and told me, "Just you and me." With tears in my eyes, I pressed her hand tightly to my lips and agreed.

The years passed by, and now and then, we would drive by the farm in East Bonne Terre on Big River just for the memories, and they were good ones.

Feeling the pressure of a growing family and the accumulation of a lot of stuff, Barb showed me some plans of moving the garage up toward the side of the house and building a breezeway between them. The living room would be enlarged, and we would add a dining room to the front side of the kitchen. I liked the idea and the challenge. We drew up some plans ourselves and took them to the local lumber company for estimates on materials. Planning to get an estimate from a local contractor to do the whole job, we would figure to show the bank the savings of doing it ourselves.

"Kids! Breakfast is ready, Mom made pancakes!" I exclaimed as they were all huddled around the TV watching Saturday morning cartoons. I could smell the bacon frying through the screened-in door as I entered the house. As I was washing my hands, my oldest daughter yelled, "Dad! Someone is at the front door and wants to talk to you!" Thinking it was the neighbor down the street, I yelled back, "Tell him to come in!"

As I reached around for a towel, she ran up to the kitchen doorway and said, "I don't know who it is!" Laying the towel down, I followed her to the front door. A sandy-headed stranger greeted me as I opened the door, and he shook my hand. He introduced himself as a realtor and wanted to give us a free appraisal of our home. I shook his hand and asked him to come on in. Knowing that we were going to the bank to see about a loan to build onto the house, I thought it might be a good idea. The realtor, Barb, and I sat down and talked. We explained that we were thinking about building an addition to the house. He suggested that selling and buying something larger might be the way to go. Barb said, "This may be another option. What do we need to do?" That reply shocked me as I knew Barb liked living by her parents. He explained the listing procedure, and we talked about a fair price. We agreed to put the house on the market. Before he left, I told him I would give him just six months to sell the house because if it didn't sell, I didn't want to be remodeling in the winter. He agreed.

The following Monday, the realtor put a "For Sale" sign in the front yard and told us it might be a couple of weeks before it was in the real estate books. He said it would be in the local paper in a few days. That really got us excited and talking about looking at other houses.

For the next few weeks, we would pile in my red Datsun King Cab truck and drive around to look at other homes with "For Sale" signs. Eric and Danielle would sit in the jump seats in the back, and Brooke would sit between Barb and me or on Barb's lap. After a month of weekends of this and not one person showing any interest at looking at our house, the excitement quickly wore off. As a matter of fact, for the whole six months, we only had one couple that called about the house, and that was a relative of one of our relatives.

I suppose the one good thing that had come out of this was that I finally admitted the Datsun truck was too small for all five of us. Thinking we weren't moving, I traded the truck off for a new 1986 Mercury Cougar.

Renewing our efforts to remodel our home, we called to make an appointment to get a loan to add on and remodel. "No problem, come in next Tuesday," said the banker. Barb told me I needed to take off work that day. Seeing her excitement, I asked, "Do you want to go out and eat? After all, it may be the last time we can afford it!"

She furrowed her eyes at me and said, "You need to really decide if this is what you want to do!"

"No, no!" I said and walked over and gave her a big hug. "I just hope we can."

Before we could decide where to eat, the phone rang. I heard Barb say, "Let me talk to Will, and I'll call you right back." Hanging up the phone, she walked over to me and said with a grin on her face, "That was a realtor who says a young couple is interested in looking at our house. Would you be willing to do a one-time showing tomorrow?"

I tried to read the expression on her face; her eyes were asking me, "Well…yes or no?"

"Well…" I said, "one time! That is it. If they want it, I want to walk away with $15,000 in my hand after everything is done!"

Barb laughed and said, "That's just about what we bought the house for!"

I said, "Yes, sixteen years ago. I know it is high, but we can't find anything else we like, especially since I gave up the land by Mom and Dad's farm. We will do one time, but I would just as soon add on. We are happy here!"

Barb called the realtor back and agreed to the one-time showing and explained the conditions that I had spelled out. She agreed and said that we should be out of the house at 10:00 a.m.

The next day, we left and went to town. We ate breakfast out and did some shopping. After a couple of hours, we headed back home with not much concern about the house selling.

That same afternoon. I was outside mowing when Barb came to the front porch. She had a funny look on her face and waved at me to stop mowing and come to the porch. "What!" I yelled from the mower.

"They want to buy our house!" she exclaimed.

"Oh crap! What do we do now?" I said. I turned off the mower and repeated those words in my head, over and over again.

"Yeah, that's right. The realtor called and said they loved the house and absolutely no question about the price!" Barb rattled on. "Only one problem, they want it as soon as possible."

"Whoa, hold on a minute, let me put the mower away and I'll be right in. We need to talk about this," I said about to bust with excitement. I hurried to the garage and gave the mower a shove. Turning toward the house, I could see Barb already at the back door smiling from ear to ear, just like me. "What will we do, where will we go?" I asked as I jogged up the porch steps and entered the house while she held the door open for me.

All three of the kids were standing in the kitchen with the same look on their faces as Barb and I walked in. "Are we moving?" Eric asked sheepishly, and Danielle abruptly cut him off and said, "Where are we moving?"

"I don't know. Whatever we do, we have one month to move, if possible. That's what they would like," Barb said to all of us.

"Oh, good!" I said. "That gives us some time. We'll find something—I hope."

Three weeks into the month, and we went to the bank to close on our house. I did not see the new owners, but I could hear them all talking in a different room. "I think they are more excited than we are," I whispered to Barb.

"Yeah," she said, "but we need to find something, or we will have to rent."

The realtor came in with a check in her hand and some papers for us to sign. We looked over the papers as best as we could while she explained what they mean. "The bank paid your home loan off, and this check is the rest of it. Have you found anything?" she asked.

Barb said, "You've shown us some nice places, and we have been looking everywhere in the Farmington school district but haven't found anything that suits the both of us."

"Well," said the realtor, "I have an option for you. My husband has been transferred to Elko, Nevada. We traded our home in Holiday Park for a home on KREI Boulevard. They're moving into our house, and we are going to sell their house. If you'd like, we would like for you to move into the house on KREI while it is on the market. A house does sell better if someone is living there, and I really like the way you keep your home so clean. If it sells before you are ready to move, I would give you ninety days to move."

I couldn't believe what I was hearing as Barb said, "When can we move in?"

"Tomorrow, if you'd like. The house is empty now, and nothing has been turned off. You can have everything turned off in your home and transfer your name to the utilities on this one. You just move in. Let me finish up here, and I'll meet you there. It's right across from the radio station."

We took the kids to Barb's mom and headed across town to see the house. It was a newer single-story brick home and looked very nice from the road. I told Barb, "Look, the garage is connected to the house!"

She laughed and said, "I think ours was the only one that wasn't."

The realtor pulled into the driveway behind us and as she got out, asked, "What do you think so far?"

"Nice," I said as she got her keys out to unlock the front door. We went in and looked the place over. The house was a three-bedroom home with two baths, a nice living room and kitchen, and it had a large dining room and a large screened-in back porch. "This is great," I said. "We have plenty of spare room to store all the stuff we've accumulated in the last sixteen years."

My friend, Denny Franklin, let us use his big trailer, and my brother-in-law had a large utility truck that he used for his carpet business. That helped make moving everything go easy. The boys and I moved everything in, and the girls set the furniture in the right place. Most of the stuff stayed in boxes in hopes we would move again soon.

Moving in went smoothly except for one thing. The previous owner had dogs and left fleas behind. The realtor had the place sprayed then the carpets cleaned and then sprayed it again. The fleas were gone, and we were happy.

As the days went by, we looked at several homes and even some lots where we could build. I liked several, but Barb was never quite thrilled enough. There was always something just not quite right, whether it be price, layout, location—always something. On the last Sunday in August as we were leaving church, Barb suggested we all go for a Sunday drive. The girls got all excited, but Eric grumbled, "I've got things to do."

I looked in the rearview mirror at Eric and said, "Just a short drive, it won't hurt you." Glancing back to the road, I told Barb, "Hey, why don't we go out to where we used to live? You know, out by the Bray farm."

"That sounds good," she answered. "We haven't been out that way in a long time."

We traveled down Maple Street, one of the few streets that go all the way through town and out to the country. When we crossed Highway 67, Maple Street makes a sharp left and turns into Bray Road. Bray Road runs parallel with Highway 67 for a couple of miles then comes back to Highway 67, crosses over an overpass, and back into town on the southside.

As we made a left turn, I showed the kids where I killed the big ten-point buck up on the hill and back in the woods. We passed by the Bray home and Eric said, "I remember that blue tractor Mr. Bray used to give me a ride on. How are they doing?"

"He passed away a couple years ago. The rest of the family is doing fine. I see them in church sometimes," I told him, and then I said, "What is that?" Someone had put in a gravel road right through the center of the field that lay between the duplex basement we lived in and the Bray farm. Barb and I both stare as we drove by really slowly. "Let's turn around and go see what's going on there," I tell them all as I pull in the driveway where we used to live. I drove back to the gravel road, pulled in, and stopped.

Barb and I got out, and she said, "Kids, stay in the car."

Halfway up the hill and in the small field on the right side of the road, we could see a two-story cedar-sided house being built. I said, "Look, there is a 'For Sale' sign in the yard!"

"Well, let's go look," Barb said.

We both got in the car, and I could feel some adrenaline pumping through my veins. As we top the knoll, I could the road went farther up the hill, right up to the woods.

Barb said, "I'm not sure, but I think someone is going to build a small subdivision here."

I drove right by the house and slowly pulled up to a dead end by the woods. This time, we all got out to look around. I blurted out, "This is the perfect place. We are back in the country and close to town. The high school is just on the other side of the highway!"

"We need to find out who owns this and see if any of the land is for sale," Barb stated.

"I agree!" I said enthusiastically.

"Where are you going?" Barb shouted to me as I began to walk up the hill.

"Stay there. I'll be right back—and no, you guys can't go! It's too thick, and ticks will be everywhere!"

I walked up the hill about fifty yards, then I stopped and stared. Goose bumps rose on my arms, and a cold feeling went up my back making the hairs on the nape of my neck stand on end. In a silent whisper, I said, "Oh, Lord, please let this be so." I was standing in the same fire trail by the same stump, looking at the same giant oak as I did sixteen years ago.

Racing back to the car, I told Barb, "Let's drive up the road and find out from Gene Pogue what's going on here." We all piled back into the car and drive on south past the same duplex basement we used to live in next to the Pogue's farm.

Seeing his car in the driveway, I pulled in right behind it and told Barb either they were eating or getting ready for their Sunday meal. "Well, we will all wait here in the car, and you go knock on the door," Barb told me.

Walking up the steps, I could see that the front door was open and could hear the TV. Before I could knock on the door, a low manly voice bellowed, "Well, would you look who's here! Come on in!"

I opened the screen door and stepped inside, asking, "How have you been?"

Gene invited me in, and I had a seat. "Lorna is in the kitchen fixing dinner, and we are doing great," he said. "Crappie aren't biting, or we would be down at Clearwater. What brings you out this way?"

I explained that we were out for a Sunday drive and were showing the kids where we used to live.

"Boy, it's been a long time since then," Gene said. "How many kids you got now? I remember the boy."

I told him about my two daughters, "Danielle is now fourteen, and Brooke just turned eleven." Being as polite as I could, I asked about his son Jerry and the duplex basement and about the house being built in the field.

Gene said, "Jerry still owns the basement and most of the land, but he sold fifteen acres to a contractor who is building the house."

I asked, "Is he going to build more houses there?"

"Yeah," he said. "He plans on building five houses. Tom is a contractor and is going to build a small country subdivision."

I absolutely couldn't believe what I was hearing. I almost felt a little light-headed. I explained to Gene that we were looking for a place to build and asked if all the lots were sold.

About that time, Lorna came in and greeted me, "How are you doing?"

"Doing great!" I said.

"Well, come on back to the kitchen. I have dinner on the table."

"Barb and the kids are in the car and I really should go so you can eat. They are probably wondering what happened to me, and I don't want your dinner getting cold."

Gene replied with a drawn out, "Well...don't be strangers and come back again! By the way, I don't think any of the lots have been sold. The way I understand it, he will build a house and sell it. When that one sells, he will build another one until they are all built. His number is in the book. He lives on Highway 32 on the right side just before you get to Doe Run."

We shook hands, and I went back toward the door, telling them how good it was to see them. I hit only one of the five porch steps and double-timed to the car.

Once in the car, I turned around in their driveway and headed back to Bray Road. The kids were all hanging over the front seat in anticipation, and Barb asked, "Well? What did they say? You were gone forever!"

I told them what Gene had said and asked, "Do you want to drive out to Doe Run?"

"Yes, but it's getting late. Maybe we can make a call and come out here tomorrow to check this out," said Barb.

I told Barb, "I just can't believe it. It's like I'm living in a dream!"

That night, I could not sleep for thinking about the property on Bray Road. I got up that morning so excited that the first thing I said to Barb was "Are you going to call the contractor today?"

"Yes, I will call later. It is too early right now," she replied.

"Are you okay with this?" I asked Barb.

"Yes, it's the right place. Hope it's the right price and the right house. It seems perfect. Just hope it works out for us," she said.

I grabbed my lunch box and gave Barb a kiss. "It will work out fine," I said. "Things don't work out like this by accident."

The day at work dragged on. I caught myself talking to God a lot. "Please, Lord. Please, Lord!" The day's work was finally over, and I went to pick Barb up from work.

Finally, she said, "I called this morning, and Mr. Corcoran's wife said she would talk to him about selling us a lot when he arrives home from work this evening."

"Can we go out there?" I asked.

Barb said, "She took my phone number and said he would call around 5:00 p.m. We just need to wait. Patience, dear!"

When we arrived home, Danielle said, "Some lady called and said we could go out to that house around 5:30 p.m."

On the drive across town, you could feel the excitement. Even the radio seemed to be playing happy, upbeat songs, and we seemed to avoid every red light.

As we turned onto Bray Road, Barb pointed up the hill and said, "That must be his truck parked in front of the new house."

Tom opened the front door and waved his hand to come on in. As we stepped inside, Tom said, "Watch your step. We are drywalling, and it is a little nasty in here."

Barb said, "We will stay right here."

"You don't want to see the rest of the house?" he asked. "My wife said you were interested in buying this home."

"Well, no, not this one, but we may be interested in one of the other lots if you are going to sell them," I said.

"Sure," Tom said, "let me show you what we have going."

"I hope he has other house plans. This one seems small," Barb said.

"This is the first house of five lots in the subdivision. Each lot is at least three acres," he said as he pulled out a layout map of the subdivision.

We looked the map over as he said, "I plan to build one house, and with the profit, I will build another, but if you would like to pick out a lot, we would be more than happy to build a home on it for you."

Barb asked how much the lots were being sold for. Tom said, "Eighteen thousand dollars. This is a great location, and part of the money will go toward a paved road when all the lots are sold."

"How many lots are left, and do you have to build the house?" she asked.

"Well, I did plan to build all the homes. Do you have a plan in mind?" he asked.

Barb replied, "We would like to have the house framed out and do everything else ourselves to save some money."

"We could work something out, but there would be restrictions on the type and style and size of the house you wanted to build. By the way, none of the lots have been sold," Tom informed us.

I think I showed every tooth in my head with the broadest smile aimed at him. I could see Barb mirroring my smile. "We would like to buy the wooded lot at the end of the road," I said.

"Well, maybe I misspoke," he told me. "That is where I wanted to build my home."

My breath caught in my throat, and I got a queasy feeling in my stomach. I couldn't think of what to say next.

"Yeah," he said, "as soon as I sell the other lots, I'll put my house up for sale. We both just fell in love with that place and location. It is why we bought the whole place."

I guess he could see the expression on my face because his smile faded as fast as mine did. I explained that we used to live in the basement house next door and how that place was kind of special to us. We really wouldn't be interested in any of the other lots. I couldn't think of anything else to say, so I finally said, "I'm sorry to waste your time" and extended my hand out to shake his.

The silence in the air was deafening, and the crunch of the gravel under the tires sounded like a funeral procession, which brought tears to my eyes.

Barb asked, "Are you sure you wouldn't want one of the other lots?"

"No," I said. "I don't even like them." It was complete silence the rest of the drive home. I thought of how I would always be looking to those woods and somehow resent the area if we lived on one of the other lots. It was just wrong.

The rest of the week greeted us with the same routine as always: we got up, went to work, and looked at another house we didn't like and wished we had never looked at the property we so desperately wanted.

Friday brought a better day because it was payday and the start of the weekend. When I arrived home, Barb announced that it was a bad week and maybe she and I should go on a "date." "What? You want to all go get pizza?" I asked.

"No, let's go to the city and eat at Red Lobster and maybe take in the new *Indiana Jones* movie. I know you are bummed. We need to lift our spirits," she said.

"All right!" I exclaimed. "Get a sitter, and we can be on our way!"

The sitter arrived, and we drove an hour to South County to Red Lobster. We both love Red Lobster. We enjoyed the *Indiana Jones* movie and then headed back home. The evening was relaxing, and it felt good to have some tension melt away and just enjoy each other's company.

When we got home, the sitter had the kids in bed, but they were not yet asleep. They bounced out of bed knowing we brought them something back for a treat. The sitter left, and Eric, who was out with friends, came in. He headed for his room and then said, "Oh, some guy by the name of Corcoran called and wants you to call him back."

I was stunned to the point that I couldn't get any words out of my mouth. Barb said, "Did he leave a number?"

"Yeah, it is by the phone in the kitchen," Eric replied.

"We will call first thing in the morning," Barb said.

"I wonder what he wants? Probably wants to come down on the price of one of the other lots," I remarked. "Maybe he just wants to build a house for us if we find somewhere to build."

That night, lying in a room as dark as the space between the stars, I reached over to Barb and asked, "You asleep?"

"No," she said.

"Well, why not?" I asked.

"Just lying here thinking how such a wonderful evening could turn into such a night of anxiety," she said.

The next thing I heard was "Mom, I'm hungry!" Brooke was yelling as she came bounding into our room first thing in the morning. "You and Dad need to get up. Danielle won't let me watch *Scooby Doo*."

"Okay, okay!" Barb said to calm her down. "We will get up. Tell Danielle to share." Barb then looked at me and said, "I guess you want bacon and eggs."

"Oh yeah! I'm starving to death," I said with a big grin.

I got up and watched cartoons with the girls while Barb fixed breakfast. She yelled to me, "Are you going to call Mr. Corcoran?"

"Yes, get me the number, and I'll call right now," I said. I found the number and made the call while I silently watched Barb fry the eggs. Linda answered the phone, and I said, "Hello, this is Will Shelton. Tom left a message for me to call him. Sure, we can do that…in about an hour? That will be great. I'll tell Barb. We will both be there. Thanks, I really appreciate it."

"What will be great?" she inquired as she put the plates on the table.

"That was Linda, and she said Tom wants to meet us at the property on Bray Road. They are going to let us buy the lot at the end of the road!" I exclaimed.

"The one they were going to build on?" she asked as she poured some milk into my glass.

"Yes," I said as we stared at each other. "Hurry with breakfast, we need to get ready and go. He will be waiting on us."

We all joined hands for the morning blessing and thanked God for our food—and threw in a "Please, God, help us get that lot." Everyone said, "Amen."

On our way, I said, "Seems like we've been down this road before. Maybe I ought to come in the other direction for a change of luck. These highs and lows can really wear on a man's soul."

We pulled into the gravel road and didn't see anyone around until we drove over the knoll and saw Tom's truck at the end of the road. I parked next to his truck. Barb and I got out, and there was no one around. Out of the woods, we heard Tom yell, "I'm up here! Be right there!" In just a couple of minutes, he came walking out with little red flags in his hand. "I was trying to mark off the boundary lines from the surveyor's pins. Do you still want this end lot?"

Without hesitation, Barb said, "Yes!" and I agreed.

"Linda and I talked it over, and we both like where we are living now and thought we would give you guys first shot at buying it, but I want to be the contractor on building your house," he said.

With a long drawn out "Well..." I said, "I really wanted to build my own house."

"Oh, I didn't know you were a carpenter," he said with a shocked look on his face and a bit of skepticism. "I thought you said you worked at the glass plant."

"That's right, I do," I explained, "but my dad was a self-employed carpenter during the summer. He was the building trades instructor, and every summer, he would build a house and sell it or build one for someone else. He's built several in the Desloge area, and I have helped him ever since I was old enough to climb a ladder."

"So you want him to build your house," Tom said. I could see by the look on his face that he might back out of selling me the lot.

"No," Barb said, "he died five years ago." She explained that we were hoping we could save some money doing it ourselves since the lot was expensive.

"Well, that is the going price nowadays, and part of the money will go to pave the road once all the lots have been sold," he stated as though he had been offended. Staring at us and with a look of deep thought, he finally said, "Tell you what, if you let me do the concrete work and frame the house up to the rafters, I'll turn it over to you to finish the inside."

Letting him do the concrete work sounded great to me because I knew nothing about it, but I really wanted to frame the house. Then I looked at Barb and said, "That sounds okay to me as long as you can cover it to keep it dry if it rains."

"I won't start if there is a chance of rain, and it shouldn't take a week, maybe two, to frame it to where you could put the roof on," he told me.

I gave him a hard look straight in his eyes; I could tell he was sincere, and we could do this. I held out my hand, and everyone smiled as he gripped my hand and we shook on it.

"Have you an idea of the type of house you want?" he asked.

"We have one picked out of a book, but all we have is the floor plan. We can send off for the building plans as soon as we get home," Barb replied.

"Why don't you guys bring what you have out to my house. If it's not too difficult, I can draw the plans out myself. That way, I can give you a copy of the restrictions and make sure the house meets them."

"That would be great!" I replied. "That will give us something to take to the bank. As far as I'm concerned, the sooner we get started, the less I'll be working in the winter."

That evening, we met Tom and Linda at their home and showed them the house plan we were considering. Barb told Tom of some of the modifications to the floor plan that she would like, add a bay window, open up the stairwell, etc. Tom drew a sketch for us.

"Yes, that's just what we wanted," Barb and I said in unison.

"I'll have a full floor plan for you Monday, and you can take it to the bank. I'll also give you a copy of the restrictions," Tom said.

On the ride home, I told Barb, "I can't believe this is finally happening. I'm going to bust with joy!"

Barb called the bank on Monday morning, and they told her to get quotes on the cost of materials and bring them with us to our appointment.

We arrived at the bank, and the lender told us since we have enough cash, we can purchase the land and then use the land as collateral for the house. That way, we could get started a little sooner.

We purchased the property, and I told Barb, "It has been sixteen and one-half years. My prayers have finally been answered. Let's go stand on our property!"

When we arrived at the property, we sat on the car and pointed out where we would like the house to be and where to put the driveway. We discussed what color we would like and how we would want the yard. There were so many trees we would have to cut down, but I was ready to start. We were so excited.

As we were dreaming, we heard a car coming up the gravel road. Tom got out and said, "Getting excited, are you?"

"Yeah," I said, "thought we would come out and try to find the right spot to build the house. We would like for the driveway to start right here between these two big oak trees."

"That's what I wanted to do this evening," Tom said as he pulled out a handful of red flags from the back seat of his car. "Tell you what, I'll start here at the drive that you want, and you let me know the layout of the house. I know where the septic tank should go, and you will have to decide which trees to cut down and which to keep."

"Just make sure we are back off the road some," Barb said.

I said, "Make sure we have a great backyard."

With a laugh, he said, "I know, I know, just let me do this, and we can go from there!"

That night while lying in bed, Barb said, "I can't wait until this is all done! I'm already tired of living out of boxes."

"I know what you mean. Just have patience and bear with me. I haven't worked on a house since Dad died," I said, praying I would be able to do all this work myself.

The next morning, I woke up before daylight and asked Barb if she was awake. "No!" she said and gave a jerk of the covers, indicating to shut up and leave her alone.

"I'm getting up and going to the property," I whispered in her ear.

"Why?" she asked and turned her head to look my way.

"I can't sleep. I'll change the alarm and make my lunch for work," I said as I slipped out of the bed. "I hope there is some cereal. I'm hungry."

I leaned over and gave her a kiss on the cheek as she gave me a big hug and said, "Love you, see you this evening."

As I got out of my car, I took a deep breath and smelled the hardwood forest of oak and hickory trees, thinking to myself, *Sure has been a long time*. It was still too dark to go into the woods even though it was light enough to see back down the gravel road toward the open field. So for a few minutes, I just sat on the hood of my car and listened to the morning symphony of birds coming to life and hickory nuts falling to the ground from the feeding squirrels. I laughed when I thought, if I had a gun and was out here hunting, there wouldn't be a squirrel anywhere. Suddenly, I heard a cow bawl for her calf over on the Bray Farm. After a few minutes, I thought it was light enough to go into the woods. I noticed there were no more stars in the sky but a clear turquoise sky above the twin peaks to the west and a yellow glow chasing the pink sky away back in the east. Walking between the two big oaks, I figured this to be my starting point and headed straight back toward the direction of the giant oak that was on the back of the three-acre lot.

Once in the thick woods, I had to stop to let my eyes adjust because the ground was too dark to see where I was stepping. It didn't take but a couple of minutes of adjusting, and with the rising sun bringing in more light, I could see really well and sidestep some low poison oak brush. About forty yards in, I saw the spot where Tom had cleared some brush and put some flags in the ground. Walking around in a bit of a circle, I noticed the sun rising over the town of Farmington in the east; and as I looked to the west, I noticed the twin peaks with the giant oak tree due west, directly between the two hills. With a smile on my face, I said, "Good morning, girls, it's been a while." Then I looked down. I made a sudden stop and just about started crying when I noticed that I was standing in the old logging road, right next to the stump where sixteen and a half years ago, I had knelt on this very spot and prayed that someday I might be able to own a piece of this land.

With tears coming down my cheeks, I dropped to my knees and lifted my eyes to the sky. "Thank You, Lord. This is the most perfect place for our home." After saying "Amen" with my knee on the ground and sitting on my heels, I just looked around thinking of God's awesomeness and looked toward the great oak tree. With a really big smile, I pointed toward the tree and said, "Thank you, girls. I know you are there with our Savior, and you will be smiling down at me."

I got up and started to walk back to the car, but then turned around and pointed again at the tree and whispered, "Now go tell my dad I'll need his help. I'll listen this time."

Chapter 3

I've had several people tell me that the sign of a good marriage is if the couple is still together after building a house. Not only are we still together, but I can honestly say we had fun. With the help of our brother-in-law Greg, who worked for a flooring company, and installed our carpet and flooring and helped with the plumbing, and brother-in-law Byron, who knew how to do electrical work and guided me in how to run the electric, we finished the house and moved in.

That evening after the last piece of furniture had been moved and clothing had been placed in the closet and the many helpers had gone home to rest, I decided to take a walk in the woods just before dark. The weather was a little cold and the sky was cloudy, and there was a slight breeze that made it feel colder than it already was. Stepping out the back door and onto a log for a makeshift step until concrete could get poured, I walk just a few steps, and I was in the dense woods. Thinking out loud, I said, "Wow! It is going to take a long time to make a yard out of this!" Walking toward the big oak, I was thinking I needed to start pretty soon before the small trees would leaf out and the ticks came to life. "That gives me about three months of good ole outside work," I said to myself as I came to the fence and the old oak tree. This was where the Brays said the three girls were buried.

I heard Barb calling my name and hollered back, "I'm back by the fence!"

"Supper is ready!" she hollered back.

"Be right there!" I said with a wave and turned back around to soak up the scenery. Even though there were no leaves on the trees, there was still a red tint to the sky casting sunrays behind the mountains on the right. "I guess you girls get to watch the sun travel from one mountain to another," I spoke out loud as though the girls were standing there watching me and listening to me talk. *I wonder how long you have been here,* I thought. How lonely it must be where no one comes but the birds and the animals to remember the three little babes in the woods.

"Well, girls," I said with a cheerful voice and a smile on my face, "it is my understanding that the Good Book says those who have gone before us are in heaven watching down on those left behind. Thanks for watching and taking that message to my dad because I really don't know how we ever got this place and built this house except by the help of some unseen forces." I turned to leave to go eat, but then stopped before turning all the way, and slightly raised my hand to wave as I said, "You are going to like us living here. My girls want a tire swing in this tree, and I'd like to build a tree house."

Clearing the woods to make a yard proved to be quite a task. With no chain saw and only a hatchet, an ax, and a bow saw, I chopped away at it every day after work and on weekends. Lucky for me, I liked to be outside; and on cool nights, Barb and the kids enjoyed making bonfires out of the wood I had cut.

I borrowed a friend's tractor to disc the ground that we got cleared. I sowed grass seed and fertilized the ground. I spread straw to keep it all in place. A few weeks before Easter, we began to see a tint of green across the yard.

Easter was cool but cloudy. The redbud trees were in full bloom, and the dogwood trees were starting to show some white from their blooms. The gooseberry bushes back by the big oak were fully leafed out, and there just happened to be three Easter eggs under the oak tree. Danielle and Brooke loved looking for Easter eggs, and I wanted them to enjoy our first holiday in our new home.

As the weather continued to warm and the days became longer, my girls and I would spend most of the time outdoors. We would keep clearing brush to make the yard bigger, and I soon had to say, "I think we've done enough! I don't want to spend all my time mowing the yard. Besides, where would the deer hide if we cleared everything away?"

It was a fun summer for all of us. We found out there would be another addition to our family in the fall. Danielle and Brooke accepted the fact that they were going to be big sisters, especially when we all found out it would be a boy. Eric was excited to have a brother. The summer consisted of Eric playing baseball and spending time with his girlfriend, Brianna. Brooke was taking dancing lessons a couple of times a week that never ended until it was time for her to go to bed. Danielle was always in the yard by the fence and loving every minute being around the Bray's cows and horses. I would go out after dark and just sit under the big oak tree and look up at the stars. Every so often, I asked the girls on the other side of the fence, "Well, what do you think? Do you like having neighbors?"

But this night while looking at the stars, I said in a soft voice, "I guess you guys heard the news. Yep, we're going to be having a baby boy." Just as I found the Big Dipper and traced the end of the cup out to find the north star, I told the girls, "He will be your little brother too. You will get to watch him grow. And if you don't mind, I'd like to build him a tree house to go along with the swing."

I sat there in the lawn chair looking at the black sky dotted with twinkling diamonds, thinking how sad for the girls to die so young and to be buried in a field under an oak tree where no one would come to visit or place flowers on their graves. I looked back to the dark, and I could almost imagine on this moonless night, three little girls standing there looking back at me, a girl of about fifteen with sisters of about eleven and eight, holding their big sister's hand, smiling at me.

As tears filled my eyes, my mind drifted to a time long ago. "What's your story, girls? I'd like to know your names and how this all came to be."

BOOK TWO

The Other Side of the Fence

I feel safe when he's there
The sun shines, and it is warm
Laughter fills the air though we are poor
The rain gives the ground a drink
Lightning and thunder make the flowers grow
We work hard and love the life we have
But there is a different cloud coming
It doesn't let the sun through
I can see it in the distance
It is dark and ugly and getting darker
The days drag by and become black
So black I can't see anymore
I cry for the hope of one speck of light
Will I ever find it?

Chapter 1

Millie slipped out of bed to greet the new day. The dark moonless night still held its grip as her eyes tried to adjust to the only light of the morning stars. Lightly landing on her feet, she looked back up on the bunk to make sure she didn't wake either of her younger sisters. Mother and Father were still sleeping in the back room of the three-room cabin they called home. Slipping through the gathering room, she grabbed her shoes at the door and gritted her teeth as she lifted the handle on the heavy oak door, hoping the iron hinges didn't squeak and awake anyone.

Almost out the door, she tilted her head and pointed her ears toward the back room to make sure everyone was still sleeping. Suddenly, she gasped for air and almost screamed as Rusty, the family dog, stuck his cold nose against her calf. Millie took her hand with her shoes in it and pointed at the half-heeler and half-pointer bird dog and shushed the dog back. Rusty sat and then cocked his head. He waited for Millie to come out when she reached back in and grabbed a jacket that was hanging on a nail. Dropping the shoes and jacket down on the flat rock porch, she grabbed the door with both hands and gently pulled it shut.

"Whew!" she said to the dog. "I hope you have all the snakes run off so's I can sit here!" She pushed his head out of her face and said, "Let me get my shoes on." Once ready, she made her way to the outhouse and then back to the front of the house and went about thirty yards to the spring. Gulping down fresh cold water brings her wide awake as she looked to the east toward the town of Farmington and saw a soft amber hue in the sky. She said to Rusty, "Let's go, it will be light soon, and Mother and Father will be getting up."

Walking up the hill, she could see the pond about a quarter of a mile to the west where it was still dark, and the stars were shining. "I guess they're all in the back field staying where the frost isn't so heavy," she said to Rusty. It didn't take long, and they were both standing on the dam of the pond still looking to the west for the sheep. Millie heard Rusty bark. Looking at the dog to see what he was barking at, she followed his line of sight back down to the small homestead. There, standing on the rock porch with her hands on her hips, was her mother. Millie raised her hand high in the air and said to Rusty, "I guess we weren't that sneaky." Mother waved back with a white dishrag and turned to go back into the cabin.

"Well, Rusty," she said, "let's find the sheep and see if we have any new babies!" About a hundred yards farther up the hill, Millie came to the corner of their neighbor Mrs. Tennessee Bell's woods and the fence that separated the back five-acre field from the rest of their farm. Millie and Rusty walked down the fence that separated Mrs. Bell's woods from Millie's farm and stopped at the big oak tree that was left when this part of the woods was logged and cleared. "Why they left it there, I don't know. Maybe for shelter or because it was the king of the woods, but I'm glad they did," she whispered to herself as she patted her leg to call Rusty to her side. "This is my most favorite spot in the world!" she said as she scratched her dog behind the ears.

Turning her head to look behind her, she could see red rays of the morning sun shining through the woods just before rising for the new day. "Might be a rain coming as red as that sky is," she said, and Rusty nuzzled her hand with his nose for another scratch. Looking back across the white frosted field toward the big wood where no logging had been done, she asked Rusty, "Well, where are they? They should be coming soon. Are they on the hill on the left, or did they sleep on the hill on the right? Oh, hear that, Rusty? Listen, I can hear the bell. They are coming!"

The pair started walking across the field toward the big hill on the left near the creek that lay at the bottom of the hill when Millie saw white spots coming down a trail toward the creek. "We'll meet them there. Come on, Rusty!" It's a race to the creek, and Rusty beats Millie by only a few seconds. The sheep stopped and watched the two race across the field, and held back until Millie called them. The sheep recognized her voice and let Rusty circle them and drive them to the water.

"Hold still, will ya!" Millie said, scolding the sheep. She pointed a finger at Rusty and said "Sit!" in a soft determined voice. Rusty sat with a grin and tongue hanging out the side of his mouth. "Now let's see," Millie was talking out loud to herself, "one, two, three..." all the way to twenty-seven. "Who's missing?" she asked. As the sheep and their babies started leaving the watering hole and moving toward the gap in the fence by the larger pasture, Millie counted again. "Yep! Twenty-seven!" Millie looked at Rusty, who was shaking with anticipation to heel the sheep but wouldn't move until told. When she pointed up the wooded hill and said "Sheep," Rusty took off up the hill with Millie right behind him. The trees were not quite fully leafed out, and it was hard to see Rusty after he made a cut to the left. Millie lost sight of him in the thick brush.

Out of breath from the steep climb, she heard the friendly "Woof!" of Rusty, and she knew he had found the sheep. Without seeing Rusty, she yelled out, "Sit, Rusty, stay!" hoping he wouldn't try to bring the sheep down off the hill. After a couple of minutes, she could see Rusty sitting about twenty yards from the sheep and her brand-new baby lying just a few feet from its mother. "Oh my!" Millie exclaimed, bursting with joy. "Thank you, Jesus," she said in a prayerful way and bent down to pick up some leaves for the new mother to eat and keep her calm. "You're the first I've ever found by myself," she said in a soft calming voice, taking one step at a time to reach the mother. "Father will be so proud, yes, he will. You're a good girl. There now," she said, stretching her hand out with some leaves for the sheep to eat. The sheep ate the leaves and took a step toward Millie. She bobbed her head up and down, chewing the dry leaves in an accepting way.

Finally, Millie pet the mother and moved very slowly toward the new baby as not to scare either one. With her calming voice and slow movement, Millie squatted down and gently touched the baby lamb. "Yes, you are a tiny thing," she said. The mother baaed to indicate, "That's my baby." The baby struggled to get up on his feet. Rusty's ears perked up watching every movement, but he did not move from his spot. Millie bent down and helped the little lamb steady itself while its mother and Rusty watched every move. "You are a beautiful baby, but it is time for us to go." She put one arm under the lamb's rump and the other arm under its chest. "Let's take you home where you belong." Millie pulled the tiny lamb up under her chin and started walking down the hill. Looking back at Rusty, Millie said "Let's go!" They started their walk back down the hill toward the creek.

The walk down the hill was fairly easy, but Millie was dreading the walk back up the back field and said to the baby, "We may have to stop halfway and rest a bit." About a quarter of the way, Millie took a deep breath and raised her head to look at the pass just past the big oak tree. She could see someone she couldn't quite make out, standing right in front of the rising sun. She stopped, squinting her eyes, and heard a voice yell down to her, "Stay there, honey, I'll be right there."

"Father?" Millie replied in a soft, out-of-breath voice with a smile as wide as the sun and beaming every bit as bright.

"You did good," he said, walking up to her. "Where did you find them?" He gently took the lamb out of her arms and stood the lamb on the ground. Giving Millie a big hug, Father said, "I'm so proud of you!"

"Rusty found them," she said, pointing to the spot past the creek up on the side of the hill.

"Well, we'll have to give him something extra in his meal today. Are you hungry?" he asked Millie.

Millie replied with a hug of her own and said, "Starved!"

With a really big smile, Millie's father revealed from his jacket pocket something wrapped in a small white cloth and handed it to Millie. "I thought you might be, so Mother wrapped this up for you. Let's sit by the big oak, and you can rest a minute and eat it before we head back."

Veering off toward the big oak instead of the gap in the fence, Millie and Father made their way and found a spot to sit down. Father let the lamb loose when the mother sheep gave a baa for her baby. Millie smiled and unwrapped the cloth to reveal a still warm biscuit with fried apples, cinnamon, and honey layered in the middle of it. "Oh wow! This is good!" she said and closed her eyes to savor the smell and taste.

"Millie, you know there is something we need to talk about," Father said with a serious tone in his voice.

Squinting her eyes and with a stern voice, Millie said, "No, I *don't* want to talk about it. I don't ever want to talk about it! It's not good, and I don't like it at all. Mrs. Bell's husband went, and no one has ever heard what has happened to him. *Please*, Father, no! You don't have to!"

"Listen to me," Father pleaded. Millie turned her back to him. "It's the right thing to do. It's about freedom and slavery and the right to live free and not be separated from family and loved ones."

"We don't have slaves here," Millie said and threw the rest of her biscuit toward Rusty. "I don't even know any Negroes. As a matter of fact, I only know of one, and that's the one Mr. Casey brought with him, and he set her free as soon as they came to Farmington. Besides, all this war does is bring out hate in people. Even around here, some are for the South and their way, and some are for the North on what they believe. Just the other day in town, men were yellin' and pointing guns at each other. I don't like it! Please, Father, stay here, *please*!" she exclaimed and turned her head to look into his eyes with tears coming down her cheeks.

"Listen to me, Millie, just listen this one time. You are wise beyond your years. You understand things. You helped Mother when your sisters were babies. You love the farm and know when something needs fixin' and what to do with the sheep. I know you'll soon be fifteen, but I swear, I've never seen anyone take care of things the way you do. But you've got to listen to me really good and not say a word to a living soul about this, not even your mother."

Silence filled the air for what seemed several minutes. They just stared. Both as serious as any expression could be given with love still attached to it. "Okay!" she said and wiped the tears with her sleeve. "Tell me."

"They are here, and they are coming every day. I hear their stories at night," he said. "It chills me to the bone. You know that big house on Columbia Street right before you get to the funeral home on the other side of the street?"

With a questioning look on her face, Millie said with a slow drawl, "Yes, I know."

"Well," Father continued, "there are several stables behind the house, and under the stables are some small caves that have been dug out about the size of two of our cabins. The slaves that escape from the South make it to here from other places. It's called the underground railroad. They eventually get to Illinois, a free state. We feed them and give them a place to rest. There are a lot of people that help late at night when it is safe. We help them go along their way. I've heard some of the most awful stories you could imagine from these slaves."

"How do you know they are true?" she asked. "Maybe they are just running away."

"No. They are not running away just to get away!" he replied. "Tell you what, Millie, I'll take you with me tonight. Then you tell me what you think."

"Okay, I'll go," she said, still frowning, "but I don't think dying for Negroes is worth it!"

With a loving smile, Father said, "You just tell me what you think after tonight. Time for us to go, don't ya think? Mr. Highley is coming today to collect pay for the lease on the farm, and I hope he brings the wagon wheel I had him fix. You know, Mr. Highley will be there tonight. He's a good man, and so is that young fellow who works for him at the livery stable."

Going through the gap in the fence, Millie took in the view of the large pasture where the sheep were feeding on the new spring grass. She reached up to hold Father's hand as they walked along with the lamb and new baby. They passed by the pond. Steam rose off the pond as she looked over to see the smoke coming out of the chimney of their small cabin.

Home was always a good place to come to even when you've just spent the morning just over the hill out of sight. "You go on in and tell your sisters about the lamb," Father said. "I'll put them in the holding pen for a while to make sure they'll be okay."

Millie smiled at her father and turned toward the cabin while Rusty stopped and looked at her then back to Father, trying to figure who he was supposed to follow. The hungry dog decided to go with Millie.

All during breakfast, all the talk was about the new lamb and how Millie and Rusty found them when Mother said, "Okay now, we need to clean up. We are getting company. Mr. Highley is coming by. Mattie, when you are done, get the brush from my room so I can brush yours and Evelyn Rose's hair for school. Hurry!"

The girls all did their jobs and were done in no time. After getting ready for school, they kissed their mother goodbye, and all three headed out the door and straight to Father and the new baby lamb. Mattie and Evelyn Rose tried to reach through the wooden fence to pet the snow-white lamb. Millie stood on the bottom rung to watch how they were doing.

"Girls!" Mother yelled. "You need to go now. I don't want you being late—and come straight home after school!"

Millie jumped down and grabbed Mattie by the hand and told Evelyn Rose, "Let's go!" The three sisters marched off to school.

There were three roads that led into town. At the southern end was Columbia Street, where most of the wealthier folks lived, like the St. Joe Lead Co. owners and other business owners. Liberty Street led past the townspeople's homes and directly in the middle of town. Maple Street was on the northern end of town. Even though they were a few miles apart out in the country, they were parallel to each other and only blocks apart in town. Maple Street was their way into town, and they passed by many farms along the way. By the time the three sisters reached school, several other kids would have joined them on the two-mile walk. Sometimes someone would pull up in a wagon and holler for them to hop on. Occasionally, they would ride, but mostly they would walk just for the fun of it.

The school was one of the best in the county. There were two teachers, and each had a room of their own. Mrs. Rains had the younger children from kindergarten through fifth grade. Mrs. Aller had the older children. There were not as many older children in school as they went to work in the Doe Run or Federal Mines as soon as they were able. Others just simply stayed home to work on the farms. Still others joined the war effort by signing up for the military.

Many of the farms were run by women and what children were still at home. A lot of children would only come to school when all the farm chores were done. So most of the students lived in town. Even though there were two social classes of students, the students all got along. The town kids thought the farm kids were tough, and Millie was as tough as any of the boys. She could outrun, outjump, and outthrow almost all the boys. They never said anything to Millie because they knew she could outpunch them too. Millie skipped two grades because she was just as smart as she was tough. Even though she didn't like school, she would fly through her schoolwork.

Millie's only drawback was her temper. It got her in a lot of trouble. Most people didn't like sheep farmers, and every so often, someone in the back of the class would baa like a sheep, and the rest of the class would laugh. That would make her so mad. Sometimes Mrs. Aller would send her on an errand just to cool her down. If Millie would find out who did it, there would be no stopping her, and someone would pay dearly.

Mattie and Evelyn Rose were quite different. Both girls enjoyed each other's company and always stayed close to home. They loved to follow their mother or Millie when away from the farm. You would think they were twins, but Evelyn Rose was actually older than Mattie. The two girls played with dolls that Mother made for them out of old dishrags and stuffed them with sheep's wool. They liked school and would always do their best for their mother or teacher. Mattie and Evelyn Rose were also shy and at times withdrawn as not to draw attention. Their security was at home.

Arriving early for school as they usually did, the two younger girls would play with the younger kids. Millie and some of the older kids would run a block or two into town to watch the activities that were going on. They would take the trail that ran through Mrs. Aller's yard and wooded lot that led to the corral of horses by the side of Mr. Highley's livery stable. From this point, they could see the courthouse and the jail across the street. The hotel was just to the left where the stagecoach was always letting people off or people getting on. The big church was a block over at the end of the street. This morning was especially busy. There was a lot of activity going on between the courthouse and the hotel. Millie noticed a lot of men dressed in blue in the crowded street. It seemed like a river of blue with waves washing back and forth.

Right in the middle of the street were two men dressed in blue with gold stripes on their shoulders. They were different than the rest of the men wearing blue. They sat at a table with large books in front of them. The one looked in his book, and the other would write in his book and turn it around so the men that were lined up could also write in the book. Millie asked Cecil, one of the older boys in her class, "What are they doing at that table?"

"Don't you know?" Cecil asked. "That's where you go to register to join the Army. The soldier on the right looks your name up to make sure you live in this county, and the other soldier writes when you report, and then you sign your name. My dad told me the president and General Grant are signing as many men they can to keep our state from going to the South."

About that time, the school bell rang, and the kids climbed down off the gate; and just as Millie hit the ground, she dropped her writing tablet and bent down to pick it up. Picking it up and dusting the paper off, she looked between a couple of fence planks at the busy street when their eyes meet. Standing there in line, staring at her, was her father. Millie froze where she was standing. She tried to speak, but nothing came out. She couldn't move when suddenly Cecil grabbed her arm and yelled, "Let's go!"

Millie looked at him and looked back to the line of men, but her father was gone. He had vanished into the river of blue men. Crying and running, she didn't want to go to school but knew she had to for her sisters.

The day was a blur to Millie. She couldn't think and felt like crying all day. She even avoided her friends at lunch. The walk home was fast paced to the point that Mattie would fall down just for a rest. Millie would give her a stern look, and after a minute, through gritted teeth, she would say, "Get up! We have to go now!" Evelyn Rose would help her younger sister up, and they would follow Millie at a distance.

Once home, Millie gave her mother a big, quick hug, ran into her room, and threw her books on a small table. She grabbed her farm clothes off the end of her bunk and changed. She folded her school clothes and placed them at the end of her bunk. She left her shoes in the corner and, in bare feet, she left her room. When she came into the gathering room, she looked at her mother sitting at the eating table with a sister on each side. Mother looked up, and Millie knew her mother knew about Father. Her poor mother must have been crying ever since her father left this morning. Her face didn't look the same, older with lines of sadness and wrinkles of fear. Millie went out the door and stood on the flat rock porch. A voice came through the door, and she could hear her mother say in the most lost and bewildered voice, "I'll need you."

Millie tooke a deep breath, let it out really slow, and replied, "I'll be here." She ran to the pen where the lamb and its mother were lying. She threw in a small bundle of hay and let out a "Hey! If you don't quit sticking your wet nose on my leg! Oh, come on, Rusty, let's go!"

The two of them headed up the hill toward the pond. Halfway up, Millie heard the bell on the lead sheep. She stepped just below the pond and held her hand over her eyes to shade the sun. She could see the herd coming out of the woods to the northwest. "Good," she told Rusty, "they're lining up to walk the path. I'll be able to count them easy as they come to water. Now don't you go and run after them!" Millie kept her left hand over the top of her eyes to shield the sun to get a count before they got in the pond. She counted twenty-six sheep and said to Rusty, "Just like this morning, one is missing." Millie looked at the dog, and he is up on all fours to start the search. Millie started laughing and said, "You're a silly dog, twenty-seven and her baby are down in the pen! They are all here!"

That didn't stop Rusty from prancing around Millie waiting for the command to chase something. So she picked up a rock and threw it on the other side of the pond as not to bother the sheep and yelled "Fetch!" The dog ran after the rock, and Millie headed toward the gap in the fence. Once there, Rusty returned with the rock and figured out he's not going to be herding the sheep; he settled in behind and to the right of Millie, still holding the rock between his teeth. They walked through the gap and to the big oak where she and Father were this morning. Millie found her usual spot where the trunk of the tree had a couple of large exposed roots, just right for Millie to sit between and lean back to snuggle against the giant tree. Rusty dropped his rock and lay next to her leg, his head upon her thigh.

"Peace and quiet," she said, looking at the spring sun heading down toward the hill on the right. She closed her eyes and felt the warmth of the sun warming her body on the cool spring day. Almost drifting into a nap, she felt Rusty jerk his head off her thigh. Without opening her eyes, Millie said, "It's okay, you can round them up later," and stroked his neck and shoulder. Then she heard a low, deep growl, and Millie snapped her eyes open to see what was going on. Looking the field over and not seeing a thing, she asked Rusty, "What is it, boy? What do you see?" Rusty stood on all fours with his hackles standing straight, and the growl in his throat continued.

Millie tried to see where Rusty was looking and put both hands over her eyes to keep the big bright orange sun out of her vision. Through the leafless trees, she caught a glimpse of a figure just as he stepped into the sun and on over the ridge. Millie stroked Rusty's head and said, "Who was that?" Pulling the dog to her, she gave him a big reward of a hug and told him, "Good boy! How did you ever see him? Must be someone hunting, maybe from the mining company just over the ridge. Well, fella, guess we need to head back. Sheep have been counted, and Father will be back soon, if not already."

Waiting until the giant red ball of sun set behind the northwest hill, she scanned the ridge trying to see if anyone was still up there. Seeing nothing, Millie got up, and the two headed home. Sticking to the sheep trail, Millie went through the gap and past the pond. Looking over toward Rusty, she said, "Look at that big full moon. We'll have a heavy frost on in the morning." About that time, a tom turkey let out a big gobble, and Millie and Rusty froze in their tracks. Neither moved while Millie tried to pinpoint where the gobbler might be roosting. Again, the tom let out a gobble.

"Coming from Mrs. Bell's place," she said. "Maybe she'll let Father do a little hunting." She turned around, and they headed down the hill. Even though the sun had just gone down behind the hill, there was plenty of light to see all the goings on at the homestead. One of the sisters was getting a bucket of water from the spring. Off to the left, she could see her father leading his horse into an open end shed that he and Mr. Highley had built last fall to shield the horse and milk cow from rain and weather. *I hate milking cows! But I sure like to drink milk,* she thought to herself. Millie stopped and stared at her father. Rusty returned to her side and sat while she whispered, "Lord, please watch over Father." After a short walk to the cabin and just before going in, Rusty looked up when she said, "Amen."

Millie went in, and Rusty lay on the ground next to the flat rock porch. She closed the door and took in the busy sight of the small gathering room. Her mother was cooking by the fireplace, and Evelyn Rose and Mattie were putting plates and silverware on the table. Mattie pushed a bucket of water toward Millie so she could wash up before supper and asked in a squeaky voice, "Are you still mad at me?" Mother glanced up, surprised at the question. Millie quickly replied, "I wasn't mad at you. It's just that I wasn't feeling so well. I'm sorry. Thanks for the water."

Father came in, and with a loud, happy voice said, "Where's my girls?" Evelyn Rose and Mattie rush over for a hug. Father picked them both up, one in each arm, and spun in a circle.

Mother flipped her dishrag over her shoulder and, without looking at anyone, said, "Put them down before you knock something over, and clean your hands for supper."

Father did as she said, but the two girls hung at his side. Millie could tell that mother knew something by the sad look on her face and the way she didn't look at anyone. Millie stepped to her mother's side, took the ladle from her hand, and said, "I'll stir this while you cut the bread. Smells good. What is in it?"

Wiping her eyes with the dishrag and without looking at Millie, she said, "Some pork fat your father picked up this morning in town. Goes good with the late winter vegetables we have left." Mother gave a nod and turned to the table where father and the younger girls were starting to sit down. Taking her long kitchen knife, Mother sliced the warm bread and placed a slice on each plate. She carried two plates at a time to Millie to ladle out the stew next to the bread. The last plate Millie took from her mother, and after filling it, they both sat at the table with the rest of the family.

Sensing that something was wrong, Evelyn Rose and Mattie became quiet. For what seemed like forever, no one said a word and just looked down at their plates when finally, Mother raised her left hand, and Father took it. Then she raised her right hand, and Millie took hold of it; and around the table, everyone raised their hands until all were holding hands. Mother asked the Creator of Heaven and Earth for his blessing on each of them, their farm, and the food they were about to eat. She then asked God to protect each of them when they were apart, and Millie knew she meant that for her father.

Supper was quiet and stayed that way until Mother got up and went to the old Hoosier cabinet and got out the last jar of her prized apple butter. A smile broke out on Father's face. Evelyn Rose and Mattie oohed and aahed as Mother opened the jar and spooned out a big scoop to each of them while Father cut more bread. "I was saving this for Easter, but I think we'll enjoy it more now," Mother said.

"This is just perfect. Don't you think so, Millie?" Father asked, handing her a big slice of bread. "Did all the sheep come down off the hill this evening?" he asked, trying to cheer everyone up.

"Yeah, they're all accounted for," Millie replied.

"We should have about a dozen new babies in the next two or three weeks. They'll be white dots all over them hills," he said to the younger girls and pinched Mattie on the nose.

Mattie squealed, and Evelyn Rose scooted in and leaned her head to father so she could get a pinch of attention too. With the silence broken and the taste of Mother's apple butter, they all began talking about the baby lamb Millie found and all the new babies to come. Millie could tell Father was doing everything in his power to deliver the happy moments they were having. She noticed Mother making coffee with two cups in her hand, knowing her mother didn't drink coffee. After filling the cups and placing them on the table, she said to the two younger girls, "How about you two come with me, and I'll brush your hair while you study some of your schooling?"

"Aww, it's not all the way dark yet," cried Evelyn Rose. "We wanted to go see the baby lamb before it's all the way dark."

"Well, I think that is a great idea!" Mother said, clapping her hands together. "Grab your coats, and let's go before it's too dark to see."

"Girls," Father said, "can you make sure they have plenty of water?"

"I'll do it," Mattie said as Mother walked over to get the bucket.

"Might as well bring in some fresh water while we are out there," Mother said.

"Mother," Evelyn Rose whispered, pulling on her mother's arm.

"What?" exclaimed Mother.

"Could you take the lantern? I think I might need to use the outhouse. It's really dark over there," Evelyn Rose pleaded.

"Yes," Mother said with a smile. "Once we get in the cold air, we will all be lined up dancing at the outhouse!" They all burst out laughing as they went out the door.

Millie and her father were still chuckling at the outhouse dance when Father slid the extra cup of coffee toward her. "I think you might need this in case we're gone very long. Do you still want to go?" he asked.

Millie answered him, "Yes, I do, if I'm to make any sense of this at all."

"I hope you do," he said. "It's important that we're in some kind of agreement on this. I know you saw me this morning, and it about broke my heart."

Millie sipped her steaming coffee and, looking over her cup, said, "Wasn't you going to tell me?"

"Yes, I was," he said, "but not till after tonight."

"Then let's go," Millie said in a sharp tone. "The sooner we get there, the sooner I'll tell you what you want me to say since you've already signed them papers!"

"Millie, that's not fair," Father said. "Just for your mother's sake and the girls, be kind. Okay?"

"I am! Okay, I will!" she said in a lower voice. "I'm just scared!" She whispered to herself, "And scared you'll be right, and I don't want to give you away."

Father leaned over and kissed Millie on the forehead and said, "Let's see what your mother and the girls are doing. Then we will head out when they come in."

"Father, wait!" Millie said as she grabbed Father's arm. "Does Mother know?"

"Yes, she does," he said. "She's known for a long time. She's been to the house several times while you girls were in school to care for some of the worst ones. They come in with cuts and bruises, wearing hardly nothing at all and no shoes. Some are about to starve to death 'cause they wouldn't stop to eat for fear of being caught. Mother never wanted me to sign up. She only wanted to keep helping the way we are now. We will talk more on the road. If you'll saddle Ole Smokey, I'll get the girls in the house."

"But they will wonder where we are going," said Millie.

"Your mother has a plan," Father said, "and I am letting Rusty go inside until they are asleep."

Millie laughed and said, "He might keep them up all night. He loves playing in the house."

Father laughed too and said, "You're right, but if all goes well, we should be back before the candle your mother places in the window burns out. Be about four hours."

Millie headed toward the open-end shed where the milk cow and the steer she's nursing were penned, and Ole Smokey was tied up. Millie climbed up on the wood fence that separated the animals, and with a low soft voice, she talked to the horse to keep him calm. After some petting, Millie slipped the saddle from the top of the fence right onto Smokey's back. Smokey stomped his hooves some but was used to the routine. Millie waited for Smokey to breathe out to cinch the leather strap good and tight. She then got the bridle and walked to the front of Smokey. Stroking his soft nose with one hand, Millie slipped her other hand to the top of Smokey's head and slipped off his halter; and in one motion, the halter came off his head, and the petting hand brought the bridle up, and the bits slipped in his mouth as it went over his ears. Millie grabbed the last hanging strap and brought it under his jaw to buckle it on the opposite side. "There you go," she said to Smokey and gave the horse a kiss on the nose. Leading him out by the reins, she could see Father standing in the yard watching her.

"Very well done," Father said, smiling with pride. "It's time we go."

Father got up on Ole Smokey and settled into the saddle, making sure it's on tight enough. He reached down with his hand, and Millie took hold of it as Father slipped his foot out of the stirrup. Millie lifted her foot and placed it where her father's foot was, and he pulled Millie up to straddle Ole Smokey to sit right behind him.

"We'll go south till we get to Columbia Street," Father said, "but first, we need to stop at Mrs. Bell's home."

If it weren't for the trees, the neighbors would be in eyesight of one another. They were just far enough apart as not to hear the sounds coming from their homes. Mrs. Bell was from Tennessee, which is why everyone called her by the state's name. She moved here just after the war broke out. She lost her husband fighting for the Union in one of the first battles. Living in a Southern state made it hard on her, so she moved to a so-called neutral state. Missouri provided just what she needed, some kind of peace. After a year, the Northerners made a push for more men. The South retaliated by hiring men to destroy homes and farms to keep men from joining. Lots of men stayed home to protect their homes and families.

Mrs. Bell was hard and tough. She could run the small farm as well as any man. Having no children, she lived alone and pretty much kept to herself. Mrs. Bell prided herself on raising Polled Hereford cattle and made good money selling beef to the townsfolk. Mrs. Bell's farm was probably twice the size as Millie's father's farm. Most people detested sheep farmers, especially on the open range parts of the county. These two neighbors were as close as neighbors could be. She treated Millie's family almost like the family she never had.

Turning in Mrs. Bell's lane, Millie and her father rode in silence until it was broken by a pair of redbone hounds howling like they had a coon treed. Ole Smokey almost reared up, but Millie's father quickly kept the horse's head down, keeping him from rearing back. Mrs. Bell came out the door and called the dogs to her on the porch.

"I hope you're who I think you are!" she yelled out while cradling a double-barrel shotgun in her arms.

"It's your neighbors!" Father yelled back.

Not taking a chance, Mrs. Bell took a couple of steps with the hounds at her side and held a lantern up high to see the riders. Convinced who it was, she told the hounds to get under the large wooden front porch and said, "Well, get yourself down and come on in. Times a-wasting."

Father helped Millie to the ground and then climbed off the horse himself and said, "Sorry we are late, been a big day at home."

"It's okay. I just don't like being out in the dark with these Southern sympathizers burning a person's home or barn to the ground. Now get in here. I got your things all tied up and ready to go."

Millie didn't have to ask what was in the bundle because to her, nothing smelled better than fresh roast beef.

"Must be thirty pounds here," Millie's father said. "You're some special person to have a heart this kind."

"My man gave his life for this cause," said Tennessee, "and if I'm gonna help show them the way, the least I can do is feed them. Now little missy, this is for you and your father. Now you two better be going before it gets too late, and be very careful!"

Without warning, Mrs. Bell gave Millie a hug and opened the door to let them out and on their way. Saying their goodbyes and getting back on the road, the pair headed south toward their destination on Columbia Street. Millie unwrapped the warm gift and exclaimed, "Oh boy!" She and her father shared one of the biggest juicy, tender roasted steaks Millie had every eaten. "She is a nice lady," Millie said. "Shame we don't see her more often."

"Don't think a person could ask for a better neighbor," Father said while wiping the steak juice off his mouth with his sleeve. "It was especially good of her to give us the little steer for fixing her fence. She could have sold that little fella."

"Why didn't she want to keep him?" Millie asked.

"She did want him," Father replied. "For some reason, the calf's mother rejected him and wouldn't let him nurse. She tried bottle-feeding him, but it just became too big a chore. She tried to give him to us. Never was much on handouts, so she hired me to repair the fence around her farm."

Millie asked in a bit of a trembling voice, "Are you going to butcher him?"

"Not for sure," Father said. "I'd kind of like to see you raise him until the fall and maybe enter him in the fair. Might sell him for a good price."

"I'd like that," Millie said, all excited, "but I don't know about selling him."

"He's a steer," Father said. "You either sell high to be butchered or we do it ourselves."

"I know," Millie said, laying her head on her father's back. "Just don't sell him to someone mean. I like beef, but I won't eat him."

Father laughed and said, "You can sell him to anyone you want."

They rode in silence until they came to Columbia Street that led into the southern part of Farmington. Their destination was not quite a mile down the road.

"Millie," Father said, "once we get there, we're never sure how many will be there or how bad a shape they might be in. It can go either way. They might be in good shape and happy or they could be next to dead. Some die on the road and are buried right where they lie. Most of the time, they are just tired and hungry. In any situation, we do all we can, and they go to the next stop. If you want, you can stay off to the side. Just take notice is all I ask, and maybe we can come to an understanding."

"I don't like the sound of someone dying," Millie said. "Just hope it's not that bad, and they can go on their way."

"I just want you to know," Father said in a very soft voice, "sometimes there is worse things than dying."

Millie leaned back away from her father in bewilderment, and he turned a little in the saddle, looked at Millie, and said, "If anything goes wrong, you know the way home. Stay off the road but within sight of it. Go slow and be quiet. If you hear voices, lay low. Don't answer even if you recognize them or their voice. You'll be fine. I know you will." Father looked back at her and tenderly smiled. Millie hugged her father's back as they rode slowly and in silence for the last quarter of a mile as though a drifter was coming to town.

Chapter 2

Once Millie and her father got to the large home, they sat in silence for a short time before going directly to the back of the house. Father told Millie to take the fresh meat in the house while he tied his horse to a hitching post. "Won't we go to the stable?" Millie asked her father.

"No, it's just stables," he answered. "Now do as I say and no talking. We won't be here long."

In the dark, Millie found a set of double doors, and after a bit of trouble, she figured out how to open one while hanging on to the meat. The door opened to a large dark hallway that led to a large kitchen that had very little light. There were three people busy cooking. Without a single word, a large woman walked up to Millie, gave her a smile, patted her on the head, and took the meat out of her arms. Behind the large woman, one of the men started sharpening a large butcher knife, and the two met at a table in the center of the room where she unwrapped the meat and started cutting it up into portions. The third person was taking bread out of a large metal box that was in one of the biggest fireplaces Millie has ever seen. Millie figured this was all for the slaves that were on the run and was amazed at how fast and quietly the three were working. Millie was pondering how amazing all of this was when she was startled by her father's hand on her shoulder. In a soft voice, he said, "Follow me, this way."

Father led Millie back to the dark hallway and slid a large wooden box that had some firewood in it away from the wall. From where she was standing, all she could see was a black floor when to her surprise, her father started going down into the floor. Following her father to the dark spot and looking down where he was going, Millie could see a candle at the bottom of some steps. Just as she took a couple of steps down, a woman grabbed hold of her shoulder and whispered to Millie, "Hand these down to your father, would you, honey?" She handed Millie about a dozen shirts tied up with meat, apples, potatoes, bread, and some with jars of beans and even some with clothes and shoes in them. When handing the last one down, Millie looked back up at the woman and the two men standing behind her and gave them a smile. The woman smiled back, but the sad eyes remained the same, and she gave Millie another pat on the head. Father loudly whispered, "Come on," and Millie went down as the firewood box was slid back over the hole.

"Oh!" Millie said to Father, "It's kinda hard to breathe down here."

"Yeah, it is hard to see too!" Father told Millie. "Just go slow, and you'll get used to it in no time. You gonna be okay?"

"I think so," Millie told her father. "My eyes are getting used to the dark." She took a long, deep breath and said, "Yeah, I'm fine."

"Now your job," Father said, "is to carry these things down the tunnel to the rooms under the stables I was telling you about. There will be some other people you'll hand them to when you get there. Don't be afraid, okay? You don't have to go into the rooms if you don't want to, and I'll be back right after they leave."

"What? Where are you going?" Millie asked in a panicked whisper.

Father told her, "At the far end of these underground rooms, there is another set of steps that go up to the far end of the stables. There is a small hole on the back wall that is hidden by some bushes. They'll go out that way and head into the woods."

"What if they get lost in the woods?" Millie asked.

Father smiled and told her, "Don't worry, there is a guide waiting for them. That's where I went before I came inside. You'll do fine, and when they're gone, I'll come back and meet you at the top of the steps. Okay?"

Millie nodded her head, and they gave each other a hug. Father went back up the steps, and Millie walked down the dirt hallway with a bundle in each hand.

Millie could see the candle at the end of the hallway where the underground rooms started. About halfway down the opening just before she reached the candle, Millie froze in her tracks. Under the candle, a black head popped out. She dropped her bundles when another head pops out right under the first one. The one on the bottom said, "Hi!" Then the one on top shoved the other's head back into the room and stepped out into the light and said, "Hi!"

Millie took a step backward and just stared at a boy that couldn't have been much older than she was. He may have been a couple of inches taller than her. He had very short black hair, twisted in really tight coils. His skin was so dark the candlelight seems to absorb into his skin and disappear. He was wearing a burlap feed sack with holes cut in the top for his head and arms to fit through. The pants were homespun material that looked to be two sizes too big, held up with some grape vine around the waist and tied in a knot. The boy said "Hi!" again.

"Oh!" Millie said. "Hi!"

From behind the boy, a head poked out, smiled at Millie, and said, "Hi!"

Millie smiled at the younger boy, nodded her head, and said, "My name is Millie." I was bringing these things"—she pointed to the bundles on the ground—"to you and whomever is in there."

"My momma and daddy's in there," he said, taking a step toward Millie. "This is my brother George. I'm," he said, pointing to his chest and holding his head and chin up high with pride, "Henry." Looking down at the two bundles on the floor, Henry's pride completely disappeared. Without looking at Millie, Henry picked them up, turned, and almost knocked his little brother down to go back into the room.

"Wait!" Millie shouted. "Don't go!"

Henry stopped and without turning around, he said, "Why for?"

"I could use your help," answered Millie. As Henry turned around, Millie pointed down the hall. "There's more to be carried here."

Henry handed the two bundles to his younger brother, and with a bare foot, he gave him a light shove on the rump toward the large room where their parents and others were resting and preparing for the next leg of their journey. Henry turned back toward Millie and saw her smiling for the first time. He returned the smile and said, "Let's go."

Taking just a few minutes, the pair had all the bundles in the room with the others. Though Millie wouldn't go in the room herself, she could see from the opening several people eating and resting inside. Picking one of the bundles up, Millie said, "This looks nice. I think it will fit you." With a shy look, she said, "At least it won't be as itchy as that feed sack you are wearing."

Blushing himself, Henry took the shirt and with a nod said, "Thanks." He jerked the burlap sack over his head to change.

Millie gasped and let out an "Oh my!" loud enough that some of the people came to the opening to see what was wrong.

Henry quickly put the shirt on and said, "I'm sorry. You shouldn't have seen that," and headed into the room so as not to face Millie anymore.

Millie hurried into the room to find Henry to ask him what happened to his back. Stopping in the middle of the room to search in the dim light, Millie was startled to see about ten or so slaves huddled around the wall. She spotted George smiling at her, and she walked to where he and his family were. "Where's Henry?" she asked George.

George looked behind his parents and nodded toward the floor. Millie, true to her temperamental form, placed her hands on her hips and said in a stern whisper, "Come back out here and let me see that."

Henry looked away from her, and Millie doesn't move one bit. Finally, he got up and without looking at anyone, walked back to the hallway with Millie following.

"What is that?" she asked once they were alone in the hallway.

Through gritted teeth, Henry said, "It's a brand my master gave me. If I'm caught, they take me to my master and gets a reward. We might be free in this state, but if caught, they can take us back. We're their property."

"Does it hurt?" Millie asked.

"Yes," Henry replied.

"Stay here," Millie said, indicating where he was standing, "and don't move." She went into the room where the others were.

When she came back, she said, "Father told me there'd be someone here in case somebody was hurt. So they gave me this salve to put on your back. Turn around, and I'll do it."

Henry just looked at her. Millie said, "Turn around and let me put this on." Henry slowly turned around and lowered his shirt. "Oh my!" she said. "Don't move, I'll be right back." Millie left and returned with the man who gave her the salve and showed him Henry's back. The man looked closely at Henry's back, shook his head, and said, "Son, you've got a bad infection."

"Is he gonna be all right?" Millie asked.

"We'll clean him up and wash those maggots out and see how he feels. It might not be as bad as it looks if the maggots have eaten away the infection," he said. "Are you chilling, son?"

The man looked at Millie and said, "Go get some fresh water and bandages from in there." He pointed into the room. He turned Henry around and said, "This might hurt some, but we've got to clean that out really good. Son, don't be afraid to cry. It will be okay, and we're not here to hurt you on purpose. Do you understand?"

Millie returned with a bucket of water and handed it and some white bandages to the man. Henry turned his back to the man and faced Millie. When the washrag and soap first touched the wound, Millie could see Henry's jaw muscles pop out and hear his teeth grinding together. Sweat beads formed on Henry's forehead, and the man said, "Hang tough, son."

An involuntary groan came from deep within Henry, and when one of his legs started to collapse, Millie grabbed hold of his hand and pulled his arm around her neck to help support him. Finding an inner strength from a simple touch, Henry bore the pain until he finally heard the man's words, "There you go, son, now just let me wrap these bandages around you, and you can put your shirt back on. Then you should get some rest before you leave. I'll leave some salve with your parents, and when you go to Ste. Genevieve, have your shoulder cleaned and reapply the salve. Try to keep it covered so the flies don't get in it."

Millie and Henry went back into the room where everyone else was eating and resting. Henry's parents took over his care and had him rest. Millie took a couple of steps back, and Henry reached out to her. Henry's mother took hold of the hand and pulled it back, turned her head toward Millie, nodded, and gave her a thank-you smile. Millie turned and went back to the hallway and sat by the stairs to wait for her father.

Being startled by a touch on the shoulder, Millie looked up to see her father standing next to her. She looked up the stairs and saw an opening in the floor. Father said, "Time for us to go home."

Millie jumped up and started down the hall, and Father said, "They're not there. They've gone up to the horse stable and are waiting for us to leave."

Father started up the steps, and Millie asked, "Why are they waiting for us? We are not going with them."

"No, we're not. We'll be a diversion," he said. "It will be very late, and everyone will be out to say their goodbyes to us. While all this is going on, the slaves will slip out to the woods and start their way to Ste. Genevieve and on across the Mississippi River to Illinois."

"Will they make it all right?" Millie asked.

"They made it this far," he said. "Now come on. We need to go."

No sooner had Millie and her father placed the firewood box back into place when the heavyset woman and her two male friends began lighting lanterns, talking loudly, and "making merry" as they all went out the double doors. A young boy brought father's horse to them. Millie and her father mounted Ole Smokey, and the pair headed back toward Columbia Street. The heavyset woman and the others followed for about forty to fifty yards. Without making too big a scene, they finally stopped and held their lanterns up high and waved until the pair were almost out of sight and heading out of town.

Millie asked, "What was that all about? You'd think we were related or best friends or at a party."

"That, my dear child, was a,"—and he said in a whisper—"diversion."

"A what?" she asked. "Just what is a *diversion*?" Millie whispered the word back to her father.

"To put it simply," Father explained, "we were making a scene with the lights and all so the slaves could slip out the hole in the last stall and meet up in the dark with a couple of guides and not be noticed."

"Oh, I get it." Millie softly chuckled. "In case someone was watching. Do you think they made it?"

"So far, yes," he told her.

"How do you know?" she asked.

"Well," Father said, "if they didn't, we'd have heard gunshots, people yelling, and even hounds barking. Remember how Mrs. Bell's dogs barked at us and all the noise they made?"

"I see," said Millie. "I hope they make it."

Father told her once they make it to the edge of town, Mr. Highley, from the livery stable, took them on to Ste. Genevieve in his wagon and dropped them off at the Mississippi, picked up a load of supplies, and came back the next day.

"You mean the man we have leased the farm from?" Millie asked.

"Yep, that's why he was at the house," Father said.

"Will Henry be okay?" she asked with a yawn and lay her head on Father's back.

"I believe so," Father replied. "He's young and strong, and I believe his family will take good care of him. Tonight wasn't bad at all. Sometimes it can be so bad they can't travel anymore. Some even die, usually before they get here."

"That's what I heard," Millie said, speaking very softly, and nodded off to sleep hanging on to her father.

Chapter 3

"Millie! Millie! Time to get up if you want some breakfast!" Mother said, lightly shaking Millie's shoulder.

"Oh! How'd I get here?" Millie asked in a daze, looking at her Mother.

"Your father brought you in last night," she explained. "Your sisters have already gone to school, and your father is in the back pasture checking on the sheep. Just you and me, so why don't you come on and eat? We'll talk, and you can tell me about last night."

"If I hurry, I can catch up with the girls before they get to school," Millie told her mother while getting down from the top bunk. "I need to talk to Evelyn Rose anyway. I was kinda mean to her yesterday."

Millie's mother grabbed hold of her arm and said, "Too late for that. I walked with them a ways till they got a ride on a wagon that was heading into town. Evelyn Rose and Mattie really liked that. They said you'd only ride if the weather was looking bad. So it's just you and me for a while. We need to talk."

"I'd like that, Mother," Millie said, and Mother wrapped both arms around her and hugged her until Millie said, "I really need to go outside."

"Yes, yes," Mother said. "While you're dancing to the outhouse, I'll cook you some eggs." Mother laughed as Millie ran out the door waving.

After a few minutes, Millie came out of the small outhouse and breathed in some fresh clean air and said out loud to herself, "Whew, that's much better!" She walked to the sheep corral, guessing

Father must have let the sheep and her baby out to be with the rest of the flock. "Yep, I guess so," she said, "and took Rusty with him." Standing there looking at the hills, Millie smiled and, for a second, thought how she loved the life she had and how lucky she was. The smile faded, and she quickly became sad at the thought of how their whole lives would soon change. She thought of the farm, her mother and sisters, Father leaving soon, and then tears started to fall. The crying became harder, and soon Millie was heaving with great sobs and dropped to her knees. She heard a tender, soft voice behind her say, "It's okay. Get it out."

Millie turned and buried her head in her mother's dress and cried with her mother until neither had any tears left. Getting to her feet, Millie and her mother walked to the house; and just before going in, Millie looked back to the hills and said, "At least we are not running."

Millie looked at her mother smiling at her, and she said, "No, we are not, Millie, and we have a home. Let's go in and eat. You and I will talk about the things to come."

All during breakfast, Millie and her mother talked about the farm, the sheep, her sisters, school, and everything they all could do together while Father was gone. They talked about how Mrs. Bell did the farming all by herself and others who have been alone after sending their fathers and brothers and sons to fight for someone else's freedom. They talked about how so many would never return home.

"Yes, that is so true," Mother said to Millie. "Here in Missouri, we've seen some of the ravages of a civil war, but nothing like to the East and South. Both sides are here, and both sides have their opinions. Both sides want our timber and mostly the lead in the area to make their bullets. Like it or not, those lead bullets have caused many a man to die. The thing is, Millie, most people know the end of the war is near. It's been long, too long. The war isn't about pride anymore. It's just plain about stubbornness. General Grant says our president wants the killing to stop, and he says it won't stop unless those in charge in the South have been utterly defeated. The men fighting can see no way of winning and just quit and go home. I know this is a lot for you to understand, but if a man's freedom isn't won down in the South, that dark cloud of slavery will take over here and our whole nation."

"You're right," Millie said. "It is a lot to understand and makes my head hurt trying to think too much. But the thing I saw last night made me grit my teeth and clinch my hands into fists. To brand a human is not right! I hope it ends soon and Father isn't gone long."

"Me too, Millie," Mother said. "Now why don't you go find your father. Might have a new baby."

Millie got up from the table and started to pick up the plates, but Mother stopped her with a soft touch on the wrist and said, "Go ahead. I'll clean up."

Millie gave her mother a hug and headed outside. Looking up the hill toward the pond, she could see her father coming her way from the back field with a white baby lamb on his shoulder. The mother sheep was trailing behind him, and Rusty looked as though he was driving all three down the hill. Heading up to greet them all, Millie made a sudden stop when she noticed black clouds coming from the hill in the southwest. "Early spring storm coming," Millie said out loud to herself. "Better get the pen ready for the baby." She turned back around to get things ready before her father and the storm came.

While spreading some straw out for the mother and her baby, Millie heard her father calling for her to come to him. Leaving the pen open, Millie took off running toward her father. "Just getting ready," she said. "Is something wrong?"

"Not really. It's just there is another one of the sheep missing. I thought you and Rusty might want to go find her," Father said. "I heard her baaing in the valley between the two hills. There's plenty of time before that front moves in, and I'll get everything done here. I'll get Ole Smokey and come back to get you. It will help a lot if you can find them."

Millie smiled with pride knowing her father was counting on her and trusting her to do the right things. Off she went with a whistle for Rusty to follow her. Up the hill past the pond, Millie stopped just before getting to the gap in the fence that separated the small back field to the much larger grazing pasture and saw the flock of sheep at the far upper end of the pasture. She tried to count, but at that distance, it just couldn't be done. *Oh well,* Millie thought, *Father knows for sure.* She headed through the gap. "Come on, Rusty!" she said while slapping her leg. "Let's go to the big oak so we can see straight through the valley and maybe catch a glimpse of that sheep." Not seeing any white spots, Millie stared toward the valley when movement caught her eye on the hill to the southwest. She stopped and studied the side of the hill where she thought the movement came from. "Maybe not," Millie said out loud. "The woods are really leafing out. After this rain, the hills will be a solid mass of green leaves. Must be those dark clouds playing tricks on me," Millie said to Rusty. "Let's go!"

Crossing the creek at the bottom of the small field, Millie and Rusty made a zigzag run through the valley. Walking from the base of one hill to the base of the other, Millie finally spotted the ewe about fifty yards up ahead in the valley. Smiling, Millie called Rusty to follow her. Suddenly, Millie spotted movement again off to the left of her about halfway up the hill. She called Rusty to her side, and while scratching behind his ear, Millie said, "Let's go up there and see who is up there."

About two hundred yards up the hill, Millie heard Rusty growl, and she slowed down. Taking one step at a time, Millie snapped her fingers to bring Rusty next to her. With his hackles raised, Millie saw Rusty looking in one direction and start barking at whoever was there. Millie saw a pair of raised hands come out from behind a tree, then a head, and a man said, "Don't shoot!"

"Who are you?" Millie asked with a loud and excited voice.

Hearing a girl's voice, the man stepped out but quickly got behind the tree again when Rusty showed his teeth in a snapping snarl. Pleading with Millie, the man said, "Please don't let your dog get me. I mean you no harm."

Keeping her distance and Rusty by her side, she said, "I'll ask you again. Who are you?"

The man stepped out again from behind the tree and said, "Name's Nathan. I don't mean no harm, ma'am."

Millie could see it's no man at all but a boy of about seventeen or eighteen years old and said, "What are you doing here? This is private property! You don't belong here."

"I know. I know," he said, holding his palms open and facing Millie to show he had no weapons or anything in his hands. "If you please, I'll tell you. Just don't sic your dog on me." He leaned back toward the tree.

"Okay. Tell me," Millie said, squatting down on one knee to put one of her arms around Rusty's neck and patting his head with her other hand.

"Like I said, my name is Nathan. Friends call me Nate, and I'm from just south of Cape Girardeau area."

"That doesn't tell me what you are doing here," Millie replied.

"No, no, it doesn't," Nate said. "To make a long story short, I'm just plain hidin' from the war. If you want to know why, can I put my arms down?"

"I guess so. But just so you know, my father is coming soon."

Hoping to play on Millie's immaturity and sympathy, Nate told how he joined the Union forces about a year ago and how he ended up in the Arcadia Valley area and was in the battle at Pilot Knob. "We was in a small fort in the Valley," Nate explained, "a valley almost like this one with a big hill on each side. The enemy set cannons up on them hills and fired on us all night. The next day, the charge came, but we was so dug in we'd just shoot them crossing the moat that was around the dirt walls. I thought they'd stop and turn back. They didn't, and we just keep shooting. It lasted all day." With a shaky voice and working up some tears, Nate continues, "The moat was full of dead men and looked like they had drowned in blood. We left that night and walked right through their camp. After that, I just couldn't take anymore. I left. I just plain ran away and been hidin' in some of the mines back in them hills. I stay there till I can figure out what to do next."

Millie, feeling sorry for the young man, asked, "How do you eat? Don't you get hungry?"

"I manage," Nate said with a grin. "I'm good at living off the land. You know, trapping, and besides when I left, I brung some food with me. Maybe I won't have to stay here for long. I'd like to go to town. Maybe do some work, get some money, and go home to my family. Are there any soldiers in town?"

Thinking she understood and feeling sorry for the young man, Millie told him about the soldiers in town and the recruiting they were doing. How it might not be best to go into town just yet. She offered to bring some food if he needed it.

Nate thanked Millie for the offer, and when he heard Millie's father calling from the valley, he begged Millie not to say anything to anyone.

Millie agreed and started to leave. "That's not a gun under your belt?" she asked.

"No, no, it's not!" Nate said and started to turn to leave.

"If it's not a gun, then what is it?" she questioned, letting her curiosity get the better of her.

"Well, it's this thing I use for hunting," he said, stumbling over his words. "You can open it up and see off into the woods at a far piece. I got it from a dead soldier, and I use it to check on my trap and when I hunt. You better go. Your father's calling."

Millie watched the young man leave, taking long strides to get up the hill, and noticed the very dark clouds just past the top of the hill. Rusty watched too, with raised hair down his back, and he growled low and deep down in his throat. Millie stroked the dog's head and said, "It's okay, sounds like he's been through a lot and scared. We better go, boy. Father will be worried." The pair took off down the hill at an angle toward where the sheep was first spotted.

Almost to the bottom of the hill, Millie heard her father call again, and she let him know where she was when she placed two fingers in her mouth and gave out a loud shrill whistle. Millie and her father met just below where the sheep were grazing near a big brush pile father had made last fall.

"Millie, what were you doing up on the hill? I thought I told you she was down here."

Thinking it best not to tell her father about the boy, she did some quick thinking and said, "Thought I'd just come in from a different direction in case the sheep ran off, she'd go toward the back field instead of farther into the valley."

Lightning struck, and the thunder was so loud you would think the top of the hill was blown off. Ole Smokey threw his head back, but Father hung on to the reins while Rusty kept trying to stay right next to Millie.

"Looks like we're in for a dandy spring storm," Father said, calming Ole Smokey down. Father noticed the sheep and yelled to Millie, "Get Rusty after the sheep. She's gonna get away to the far end of the valley."

"Rusty! Go!" Millie gave the command. Rusty got a few feet away and hunkered his head down, not wanting to get away from his masters. "Go!" Millie commanded again. "Get the sheep!" She points her right hand out in the direction of the sheep. Rusty relented and circled around the sheep to herd her back.

More lightning strikes, and the thunder rumbled. Father told Millie, "We'll never catch her, and she's in labor. When Rusty brings her back, see if you can get her to stop. I'll try to get a rope around her neck."

When Millie looked up, she told her father, "Here they come."

"Spread your arms out, but don't move too much. Just let her see you," he told Millie as the winds started to gust down from both hills right through the valley. Millie spread both her arms out and had to squint her eyes from all the dust and pollen blowing in the air. The sheep and Rusty saw Millie standing right in their path, and both slow down just before getting too close. Suddenly, a colossal streak of lightning hit a tree just off to the left of them. Rusty hunkered down to the ground, and Millie wrapped her outstretched arms around his head just as the sheep raised her front legs to bolt for another run. Just as she lunged forward, the lasso that Father threw went right around her head. Father jerked the rope taut, and the sheep flipped over on her back. Millie kept her head covered but could see between her arms the sheep flailing on the ground. She looked at Father and said, "Wow!"

Father smiled and gave the look of "I meant to do that" and said, "Can you hold her while I try to get Ole Smokey?" The lightning strike startled the horse, and he was acting very skittish. After a few tries of coaxing the horse back to him and before the next lightning strike, Father finally got the reins. "If I can," Father said, "we'll tie the sheep on the saddle, and I'll ride her back to the house."

The wind picked up, and Millie yelled, "Look!" and pointed toward the top of the hill. "The rain's coming. It looks like a wall of water."

Father said, "Help me get the sheep on the horse. She'll weigh a ton if that wool gets wet!"

Millie rushed over but first made Rusty sit in front of Ole Smokey to draw the horse's attention away from Father. Millie and her father lifted the sheep up and threw the tied front legs over the saddle. More lightning and thunder rolled off the hillside as the wall of rain rushed toward them. Father put his foot in the stirrup and took hold of the saddle horn. In one motion, he rose and straddled the horse behind the saddle. Looking at Millie then at the rain coming, he said, "Please try your best to keep up with me, okay? Let's go home."

They made it across the small back field past the big oak tree, and the rain overtook them. Father turned and smiled at Millie. When he turned back, Millie turned and looked to the top the southwest hill. The rain was coming down so hard, and the wind was blowing so fast it made the hill look like a blurred face, lightning coming from its eyes and its voice was thunder. The black clouds looked like hair being tossed in the wind. Rusty nudged Millie with his nose, and the trance was broken. Through the gap, past the pond, and it was homeward bound.

Mother, watching from the window, finally made out why the delay. Grabbing the kitchen wash pan, Mother raced outside. Splashing her way to the holding pen, she did her best to open the gate with one hand while holding the large wash pan over her head with the other. As Father and Ole Smokey trotted up, Mother opened the gate and without hesitation, Father guided Ole Smokey right into the pen. Millie followed the horse into the pen, and Rusty stepped next to Mother as she closed the gate. Millie and her father got the sheep nestled into the manger area where the other sheep was the day before. "I'll put Ole Smokey up if you get some feed for the sheep," Father said. They get their respective jobs done just as the rain began to quit and the clouds started breaking up.

"Wow, what a storm!" Mother said as she walked over to Millie and her husband. "Is that sheep going to be all right? That was a pretty rough ride she had to go through."

"I don't know," Father replied with a very worried look on his face. "Let's give her some peace and quiet for a while and see if she gets up. I'm ready for some coffee. Wouldn't happen to have some made, would you, hon?" Father took the wash pan and said, "I'll fill this with some spring water."

Millie yelled to her father as he started walking over to the spring, "You expect us to do this while you are gone!"

Millie's mother was walking toward the house but stopped dead in her tracks and turned to look at Millie. Father stopped and turned around too, holding the wash pan as though it was completely full of water. The three turned about twenty yards apart in a triangle, just staring at one another.

"Yes! Yes, I do!" Father finally said. "Not only do I expect you to, I know you can. Millie, you've got the grit and determination and the know-how of most anyone I know. What I do expect, young lady, is for you to not venture off the path of your goal."

Millie thought of the troubled young man that had seen his share of war and dropped her head and said, "Yes, I know. It's just that—"

"No," Father said, "it's past and over." He walked toward Millie, and Mother turned back to go in to make coffee. "You'll do fine. Just remember to stick to the task at hand." Father stopped in front of Millie, placed the pan on the ground, and took hold of both her hands. "Do no more and no less than what you know, and I'll be here before you know it. Besides," Father said grinning, "look at all the help you'll have."

Millie rolled her eyes and said, "I'll be fine if them two just stay out of my way!"

Father turned, laughing, and tousled Millie's hair, saying, "No, I mean Rusty. That dog will do anything you say, and nobody will bother you with him at your side. Come on now, we'll have some of your mother's coffee. Then we'll hook the wagon up to Ole Smokey. Since the rain's over, what say we all go to town."

"Oh, yeah! That'll be great!" Millie said. "We can get Evelyn Rose and Mattie from school and all of us go to town."

Millie and her parents had their coffee and talked about the suddenness of spring storms. They all changed into dry clothes. Father got the wagon hitched to Ole Smokey while Millie and Mother prepared for a Friday afternoon in town.

After checking on the mother-to-be sheep one more time, and convinced she would be all right, Millie let them through the gate and told Rusty to stay home. She hopped on the wagon and said, "Let's go!"

Chapter 4

The ride into town was only about two miles. Going around some muddy holes and a couple of creeks that were rushing with the spring rain runoff made it a little longer and adventurous for the three of them. Seeing that all was well at school, Father said, "Why don't we go to the livery stable? I'll get some tack supplies from Mr. Highley. I'm kind of curious to see that he made it back from last night. School should be out soon. Millie, you can get your sisters, and we'll all meet down at the General Store."

Millie jumped off the wagon and took off running to the schoolhouse while her father helped his wife down from the wagon. Giving her a kiss on the forehead, he said, "Why don't you go in while I take care of some business here?"

"And what kind of business might that be?" she said while returning a kiss on his cheek.

Explaining how the wool prices had gone really high because of war, he wanted to get a guarantee now on a set price. The price might be a little lower, but he could use some cash now especially since he would be leaving just after shearing time. With some cash on hand, they might be able to get a line of credit at the mercantile.

"That would be so good," Mother said. "I would really love to see the girls in some new shoes and clothes for Easter."

Father took hold of Mother's hand and said, "Yes, but I'd really love to see you in a new Easter dress." He gave her hand a squeeze. "Go on now, I'll be there soon."

Business in the livery stable didn't take long since Mr. Highley was in no mood to dicker on prices. Looked like he had been up all night, but it was good to see him back safe from the Ste. Genevieve area. The only talk going on was business and not one word about the underground railroad.

Shearers were set up for a future date, and Mr. Highley would take care of the sale of goods at the mercantile exchange. "It may have to wait till Monday," Mr. Highley said. "I'll send a boy down there, so you can open a line of credit till you get your cash." Both men smiled, and Mr. Highley got up and said, "You've done good from what I can see. You might think about buying that place from me. Seems to me you have the right stuff to be a sheep farmer."

Father smiled, and as they shook hands, he said, "We'll see how things are when I get back. I do appreciate all you've done, and if you don't mind, I'd really appreciate it if whenever you are out that way, you would stop by. Just to see how the family is doing."

"I will, but you know better than me that girl of yours can more than take care of that farm. Maybe better than most men. But yes, I will," Mr. Highley replied. The two men make a tighter grip on the handshake, and Mr. Highley patted the back of Father's hand with his other and told him not to worry. With a tip of the hat, the two men said their goodbyes. Father headed toward the General Store.

Meanwhile, back at the school, Millie sat under a tree to wait for her sisters to get out of class. Just as she was about to doze off, someone kicked her feet, and Millie jumped in shock.

"Cecil," she shrieked, "what are you doing? You about scared me half to death!"

Cecil laughed and said, "You a might skittish, aren't you?"

Millie blushed and sat up straight against the tree. Sitting down next to Millie, Cecil said, "I saw you here by yourself, and since Mrs. Aller left early because of the storm, I thought I'd just come out to see how you are doing. Evelyn Rose said you had to help with some farm work. She even said you and your father left last night and didn't come back till late. What was that all about?"

"She's a busybody," Millie said in a brash tone. "Besides, what business is it of yours?"

Cecil waited till Millie looked up, and when their eyes met, he said in a soft whisper, "It really isn't unless you'd let it be. I was just worried about you is all," and he stood back up.

"Oh, sit back down!" Millie explained how she and her father went to Mrs. Bell's house to deliver some beef for her but thought better to not tell about the runaway slaves and the underground railroad. "Besides, it wasn't that late when we got back home. Why would you be worried about me?"

Cecil blushed a little and said as he sat back down, "'Cause I like you."

Putting her hands on the ground and stiffening her arms to raise a little, she leaned her head toward Cecil—who had scooted away to be shielded by the tree—and said, "You *what*!"

Getting back up to his feet but keeping the tree between them, Cecil quickly said, "I know you're only fifteen, but you'll be sixteen next month. I'm gonna be seventeen this summer. When I get back, we'll both be a year older. My father is older than my mother. If we court for a year, you'll be sixteen, and I'll be eighteen and—"

"Cecil!" Millie yelled. "Slow down a minute and catch your breath. Just tell me. Where are you going?"

Cecil shut his mouth and just stared at Millie. Backing away with tears filling her eyes, Millie repeated her question, "I said, where are you going?"

Not a word came out of the tall, lanky boy that always picked on her. Millie turned to walk away but stopped to say, "You're the only friend I have," and then ran. Hearing her name being called, she ran faster and didn't look back.

Running up to the front of Mr. Highley's livery stable and seeing Mr. Highley getting ready to leave, Millie asked, "Is my father still here?"

"No, you just missed him," Mr. Highley told her. "He went to meet your mother down at the General Store." Before he could say anything else, Millie turned on her heels and ran to the heart of Farmington's business area. Getting to the courthouse, Millie slowed down to a walk just so the people in the streets wouldn't be staring at her. Trying to regain her composure, she saw her father standing on the porch of the General Store talking with a man she didn't know. Guessing her mother was inside, she slipped past her father without his knowing and went inside. Walking around the busy store, Millie saw her mother talking with whom she guessed to be a store saleslady. Slowly maneuvering in the aisle next to where her mother was, Millie got her attention and beckoned her to where she was. Giving Millie a stern look of impatience, Mother noticed that her daughter had been crying.

"What is wrong, Millie?" asked Mother.

"I, I can't get the girls. I'm going home," Millie told her mother.

"Slow down a little and tell me what's going on," she said, trying to calm Millie down.

Millie started crying and said, "Cecil's going just like Father," and buried her head in her mother's shoulder.

"Okay now, it's okay. Let's go outside and take a walk. I think we both need some fresh air," she said, leading Millie out the door. Looking back, she waved at the store clerk and mouthed the words, "We'll be back." Walking past Millie's father, she placed a finger over her lips and said, "We are going to get Evelyn Rose and Mattie. Be back soon."

Walking down Liberty Street, Mother took Millie's arm and folded it in with her own and asked, "So Cecil told you he signed up to join the Federal Army?"

Millie told her mother all about his joining and something about waiting till he gets back and their ages and something about his father being older than his mother.

"Oh my!" Mother said, holding her other hand over her mouth. "I think your father needs to have a talk with Cecil."

"Why?" asked Millie.

"Just to find out what his intentions are," she said, patting Millie's arm that's entwined with hers. "You need to calm down a little. We'll get your sisters then go back to the General Store." Mother leaned her head to one side and gave Millie a little bit of a smile.

Just about a half block from the schoolhouse, Millie and her mother heard children playing, and they knew school had been let out. Millie pulled her arm away from her mother and told her to wait there, and she'd run ahead before the girls started walking toward home.

Trying to get a glimpse of Cecil and not seeing him anywhere, Millie called to her sisters. Mattie came running pell-mell, but Evelyn Rose, still a little upset with her older sister, took her time and lollygagged her way toward Millie. Once the three girls were together, they saw their mother walking toward them. Evelyn Rose's attitude changed, and the two younger girls knew they get to spend some time in town. After an afternoon of shopping and ordering material and new shoes, Mother let the girls know it was getting time to go home. They walked toward Columbia Street in search of their father at the feed store getting supplies for the farm.

Usually Friday evening and Saturday morning were busy days in the town of Farmington. Farmers getting their supplies and the womenfolk doing what shopping needed to be done to fill the cupboards. It seemed that springtime was busier because of changing warmer weather and restless people from a long winter. The men were doing their trading and buying and selling while the ladies caught up on the news from neighbors and friends. The children walked around the town from store to store by way of the wooden porches to stay out of the muddy street from the storm. From the very youngest who couldn't stay out of the mudholes to the very oldest who liked to sit in the chairs or rockers on the porches, the town was filled with laughter and a lot of happenings. The one thing on everyone's lips though was the war. The talk of who was going to war and who had come home. Everyone questioned when it would end.

Everyone, whether they supported the North or the South, knew the Confederate forces were on the run and pretty much whipped. However, the rebel pride prevented any kind of surrender just yet. In Missouri, it was scoundrels like Sam Hildebrand that kept the hate strong but beginning to creep back into the shadows. All in all, everyone knew what was, and that's the way Missouri folks liked it especially in this quiet farming town.

"There he is!" yelled Mattie, who took off running toward a man in a wagon and slipped in the mud.

Hearing his youngest daughter hollering, Father looked up and saw his family coming. Giving them a wave and then a wave beckoning them to come faster, he yelled, "I've got some good news!"

"What's the good news?" Millie asked when they all got to the wagon. "Help carry the feed out to you?"

"Hey now, little lady," Mother said, "that wasn't nice. You apologize to your father."

"I'm sorry," Millie said, dropping her chin and slumping her shoulders. "I really didn't mean that."

Father leaned over to the edge of the wagon, placing a hand on Millie's shoulder, and told them all, "We've been invited out to an early evening supper."

Everyone gasped at the surprise, and Mother said, "Oh my! Mattie is covered in mud. What will we do?"

Evelyn Rose asked, "Where we going?"

Father placed his other hand on Millie's other shoulder and told them all, "Do you remember that man I was talking to on the porch of the General Store?"

Mother said, "Yes, but I didn't pay much attention to who he was."

"Oh, you know him, he and his family sit a couple rows in front of us at church," Father said with a great-big-teeth-shining smile on his face.

Millie's head popped up, and her eyes became the size of saucers. A look of terror came on her face, and after a hard swallow, Millie inquired, "You mean Cecil's father?"

"Yep, that's them," Father replied. "He and his wife invited all of us for supper before we head home."

Mother quickly put an arm around Millie and led her to the front of the wagon where Ole Smokey patiently waited. Father just stared and turned back around and asked Evelyn Rose, "What's going on? Do you know?"

"I'm not say nothing!" Evelyn Rose quipped. "Millie will bite my head off. You'll have to ask Mattie."

Father looked at the back of the wagon and saw Mattie playing in a mudhole. He shrugged his shoulders and said, "Never mind, I'll wait."

Meanwhile, Millie and her mother discussed the dilemma that had besieged the young girl. "Maybe it would be best to tell your father now," Mother said. "It's up to you, Millie, but we have been invited to dinner, and it would be rude if we did not go. Besides, Cecil is your friend. No matter what happens, where he goes or what he does, he is still your friend. He is a good person, and it sounds to me he cares about you a lot."

"But, Mother," Millie said, "look at me. I'm a mess. My hair is all kinky from the rain this morning, and I don't even have my school clothes on!"

"Don't worry. I'll fix your hair. I have a brush in my bag, and I might even have a ribbon or two in there," she said holding Millie's shoulders at arm's length. "You look fine. With that blush on your face, you almost look radiant."

"Mother!" Millie squealed and blushed a little more.

"You two have been friends forever," she told her daughter. "Don't let him leave without a reason to come back. What I mean is, his dreams should be of better days and a future to look forward to. Remember, you don't have to do more chin-ups than he can do."

With their spirits better, Father finished loading the wagon while Mother did her best getting the mud off Mattie and keeping her still. Millie and Evelyn Rose talked about the morning storm and how most of the kids in school were afraid and how upset Cecil was that Millie wasn't in school.

After loading the wagon and getting the credit papers signed, Father led Ole Smokey toward the south end of town and the Plank Road that led toward the Fredericktown area. Father explained how the new road system was a great thing. "You can travel all the way from Arcadia Valley to the Farmington area to Mine La Motte and travel to the port in Ste. Genevieve too. The road was made so mining companies could haul their heavy loads of lead and iron ore. It sure makes nice travel for the rest of us too," Father remarked.

Cecil and his family were town folks even though they had some land and lived just on the edge of town. His father was a store clerk and part owner of the General Store. Arriving at their house, Millie and the girls could not believe the beautiful home they would be eating in. Millie turned her head to look at how Mother was trying to brush her hair and said, "I'm not hungry anymore. Mother, I don't want to go. Please don't make me."

"Why, young lady?" Mother asked, laughing. "Please go, Millie. With this yellow ribbon holding your hair up just so, that boy won't be able to talk straight."

Father pulled the reins to slow Ole Smokey down a bit so not to get to the house before he could understand what the two of them were talking about. "You care to let me in on what you just said?" Father asked.

"Yes, I would," Mother said, "and yes, I will. On our way home, we'll have us a nice talk, but right now I'm starved and want to see the inside of that house."

From the back of the wagon, Evelyn Rose yelled, "I hope their outhouse is empty. I can't wait much longer!"

"Thank you, Evelyn Rose!" Mother yelled back and then said to her husband with a smile, "Don't slow down now. I don't want our host to see what kind of dancing we can do at the outhouse."

Millie cracked up laughing, and her father just gave an awkward "This isn't fair" stare at the two of them.

Chapter 5

The early evening dinner was everything Millie's parents had hoped it would be and enjoyed all that it was. With so much tension of everyday farm life and the gloom of the war that had moved into the tiny towns of Missouri, it was nice to just talk with friends about the growing church that both families belonged to.

"Pa?" Cecil said. "Would it be okay if I took Millie and her sisters down to the barn and show them our new colt?"

"Sure, I don't see why not," Cecil's father replied. "Just be still 'cause that mare is really skittish."

"Millie," Father said, "just a short time. I'd like to get through town before it gets dark, especially since its Friday evening."

Once out the door, Evelyn Rose and Mattie ran with Cecil's younger brother and sister to the barn. Millie yelled out to Mattie, "Stay out of the mud!"

With their sisters and brother gone ahead, Cecil told Millie, "I didn't mean to make you mad today when we were at school. I just sometimes get so tongue twisted I even confuse myself. I'm sorry."

"It's okay," Millie said. "I liked the first part about me and you, but you going away scares me. I'll worry about my father, and now I suppose I'll worry about you too."

Cecil stopped, looked at Millie, and said, "I like that. My Pa says it'll make a man out of me."

Looking down and rubbing her shoe over an anthill, Millie said, "Maybe so, if it don't make worm food out of you first."

Not knowing what else to say, Cecil blurted out, "That may be, but I'm not scared!"

"I am," Millie said. "I already told you so." Both Millie and Cecil just stood there. Cecil watched Millie shuffle her feet over the anthill when Millie broke the silence, saying, "Tell me again your plans when you come home."

"Uh, well, I, umm," Cecil stammered. "You know, and I meant it too!"

Millie smiled at Cecil and said, "Meant what?"

"Millie!" Father yelled from the back porch. "Get the girls. We have to go!"

"Okay! We're coming," Millie yelled back then turned to Cecil and said, "I have to get my sisters. Write me a letter." She ran to the barn as the siblings were coming out of the barn.

"We have to hurry," Millie said to Evelyn Rose. "Father is calling for us." She grabbed Mattie's hand and said, "Let's go!"

The three ran back toward the house, and as they got to Cecil, he ran with them. "Wait, Millie, stop! Tell me again what you want me to do," Cecil exclaimed.

She slowed down to a walk and told the girls to go on ahead, and they did as soon as Cecil's brother and sister ran past them. Millie reached up and took hold of Cecil's shirt-sleeve and replied, "Write me a letter."

"Okay, I can do that."

She let go of his sleeve and took off toward the house when Cecil heard her say, "And tell me about me."

Cecil watched Millie run to the house, blinked a couple of times, and slowly, a broad smile spread across his face. As he took off in a brisk walk toward the front of the house to say goodbye, he said to himself out loud, "I'll write you a letter, Millie, and I'll tell you what all I think about you. Yes, I will."

By the time Cecil got to the front of the house, Millie and her family were coming out the front door. Father rushed everyone to get settled in the wagon while he and Mother thanked their host for the meal and the visit. As they waved goodbye and said "Let's do this again sometime," Cecil saw Millie sitting in the back of the wagon on a sack of feed. She smiled at him and raised her hand, softly waving goodbye.

Cecil's Pa looked at him and said, "Son, is there something we need to talk about?"

Generally, like most small towns, a weekend night in Farmington was a great place for families to come for some kind of a social event. Square dancing and music playing attracted people from all around to the county courthouse square. However, the last few months, especially since the weather was getting warmer, miners, loggers, and people usually not associated with or living in the area were flooding the small town on the weekends. Men were drinking, and arguments between the North and the South would heat up. Lucky for the county seat, the Union soldiers stationed there would break up the fights almost as soon as they had begun.

Once through town, Millie and her family relaxed for the rest of the ride home. Songs were sung, and stories were told, but mostly they talked about sheep and work to be done on the farm.

Chapter 6

Farm life was never-ending but always gave a person a sense of self-worth. Whether it was for sheep, cattle, crops, or whatever people depended on farmers. A farmer never depended on an instrument of time but always depended on the one who gave them their time. Days could begin in the middle of the night and not end until the day after next. A farmer could never put a thing off until tomorrow because tomorrow may never come. Millie's father knew these things and enjoyed all that farm life threw at him. This wasn't always so. Like most men, settling down usually didn't come until their own firstborn reached out their small hand and held tight to its father's hand. The bond was sealed. Before Millie was born, Father and Mother moved into the small cabin that was rent-free for logging the small farm. Timber was in great demand for the newly developed Plank Road that centered around the Farmington area.

After the birth of Millie, Father had a determination to make a good life for his family. Recognizing the hard work and determination, Mr. Highley made a deal with Father, which allowed him to farm the land he had cleared. The land was not very good for pasturing cattle, so Father tried his hand at raising a couple of sheep. The farm was just right for raising sheep, and the wool prices brought in a little extra money. The young farmer and his family were doing well enough that Mr. Highley was trading farm goods and supplies for wool. Mr. Highley was so impressed that Father had turned the land into a workable farm.

Mother had heard from Mrs. Bell that Mr. Link, who owned the land northeast of their small sheep farm, had been hurt and was laid up for a while. Millie and Mother walked to the Link home to check on him. They took some canned peaches and fresh bread to give to his wife. Upon arrival, the old man, not being very neighborly, yelled through the open door to just set the stuff on the porch and thank you.

Obliging him, Mother started to set the jar and bread on the porch when she heard Mrs. Link from inside say, "No, no, no, you two come inside. Pay him no never mind!"

"We just came by to see if you all needed any help and brought these to you," Mother said as she looked through the doorway to see Mrs. Link coming from the kitchen area of the house, wiping her hands on a dishrag.

"Now you two come on in and pull up a chair," said Mrs. Link, taking the jar of peaches and bread from Mother. "Warm bread sure does smell good. Don't you think?" she said, looking over her glasses at her husband.

"Don't like sheep," said Mr. Link. "Guess that's all that land over there is good for is sheep herdin', too rocky for anything else."

"Now, dear, they just come to be neighborly, not to talk business," Mrs. Link said and looked at the two neighbors. "He's a crank pot even when he feels good."

"I heard that!" he replied. "And I am not!" Scooting to the edge of his chair, the old man pointed a finger at Millie and said, "Remember, I'm the one who gave you that pup that runs those sheep!"

Millie remembered the day that she and Mother came to visit, and Mr. Link had asked her if she liked dogs. Mr. Link had told Millie to look under the porch. Millie could see a beautiful dog lying on the ground with her back facing Millie. Mr. Link called out to Lady, and she eagerly came out from under the porch. *What a beautiful dog,* Millie thought as she reared her head back to keep from being licked in the face. Mr. Link told Millie that Lady wasn't the dog she needed, and Millie felt very disappointed. Mr. Link got down on his knees and elbows and reached as far back under the porch as he could with one arm and pulled out a white-and-liver-spotted pup by the scruff of his neck. "This right here is the dog you need! What you gonna name him?" Mr. Link asked in his gruffy voice. "Don't you want him?"

"He's mine? Oh yes, I want him! And surely Mother won't mind," Millie recalled the conversation. The pup had brown spots on his side, which reminded her of rust, and she decided to call him Rusty. Thanks to Mr. Link, she had her lifelong friend who helped with the sheep that he so despised. Millie and Mother overlooked Mr. Link's sarcasm because they knew deep down he had a heart of gold.

Mother and Mrs. Link exchange some recipes, and soon it's time to go back home. They said their goodbyes, and Mr. Link gave a wink to Millie and told her to take good care of Rusty.

Chapter 7

As the weather warmed and brought new life to the earth along with the spring rain, the sheep farm exploded with life at every turn. Millie's mother and sisters got the garden planted. The hardwood trees on the hillside were fully leafed out, but the real new life was in the pasture. Fourteen new baby lambs dotted the hillside, running around their mothers. Millie and Rusty kept a close eye on the flock from the back side of the pond. "Sure is going to look different in the pasture soon," she said while scratching her dog behind his ear. "I'll be glad when they get all that wool sheared off of them. When they get wet, they must weigh a lot! Say, fella," Millie said while looking down at her dog, "let's go to the giant oak and see if we can see Father at Mrs. Bell's."

The pair moved toward the gap in the fence and walked down toward the lone giant oak in the back field. Looking as hard as she could, Millie couldn't see a thing through the dense forest. "Well, I don't see him or hear anything," Millie said to the dog while standing on her tiptoes to get a better view. "Can you smell him?" she asked Rusty, looking down at the dog. "Well, look at that, would you?" she said, stepping away from the tree and going to the fence. Millie leaned over the fence and picked a few little green berries, cupped her hands together, and showed them to Rusty. "Gooseberries!" she said laughing. "Go ahead and try one," she said to Rusty, sticking her hands to the dog's nose. Rusty smelled them and turned away, not falling for Millie's trick.

Rusty crawled under the fence and, without any warning, lowered his head into a point and started growling. Millie froze, thinking the dog had found a snake, and said, "What's the matter, boy? I don't see anything over there." At that moment, Millie saw it. "What you got there?" she asked while crawling through the middle of the fence. "I didn't think it was a snake," she said, coming up beside the dog, "or you would be barking your head off. What is this anyway?" Millie bent down and picked up a round white inch-long object. She looked closely at it and said, "Why it's somebody's cigarette! Whose could it be? Maybe it's…nay, Mrs. Bell don't smoke!" while showing the cigarette to Rusty and letting him smell it. "Maybe it belongs to that man we talked to on the hillside," she said, standing up straight and looking to the top of the southwest hill. Rusty started barking insistently, and Millie furrowed her eyes while giving the dog a pat, saying, "I hope you're wrong."

Millie and Rusty began walking back to the pond, but Millie pondered if she should have said something the first time she saw him. *No,* she decided, *some people need to be alone.* On second thought, she wondered about it. *Something just doesn't feel right.* Millie looked down at Rusty, who seemed to have lost all interest in everything but the flock, and said to herself, "No, he's just scared and alone."

About an hour or so later, Millie noticed the lead sheep started heading down the hill toward the spring for water. "Well," she said to her dog, "time to earn your keep. Let's take them home." Just moving in behind the flock got their attention, and all the sheep started moving slowly to the sound of the bell on the lead sheep. The sound of Millie's voice and the precision drive of the dog brought all the sheep to the watering hole. Then they were herded to the holding pen. Evelyn Rose came out to help, followed by Mattie, who just liked to sit on the fence and watch.

"Good job, you two!" someone said over by the horse shed.

Millie looked up as she looped the rope over the gate to keep it closed and secured shut. "There you are," "I've been wondering where you've been." She said to her father as they walked over to him.

"What's wrong with Bessie?" Mattie asked her father and threw an arm around her father's leg to look through the wood plank fence. "Is she gonna have her baby now?"

"No, not that yet," he answered the youngest daughter and picked her up so she could see better. "Bessie got loose this morning and wandered off towards the Link farm—"

"So is she in trouble?" Evelyn Rose interrupted.

"No, little missy. If you give me a minute, I'll tell you. Bessie got loose, like I said, and wandered toward the Link farm. There is a lot of spring clover growing in the field, and poor old Bessie didn't know when to quit eating. She ate so much she got a bad bellyache," he told the girls and pinched Mattie's belly.

Mattie giggled and squirmed in her father's arms. Evelyn Rose said, "Is this why Bessie has the poopies really bad?"

"Sure is," Father answered. "It's called the scours. If it gets too bad, we might have to poke a hole in her belly to let the gas out or she could die."

Both the younger girls made an "O" with their mouths, and Father said, "But I think she is gonna be okay." He looked over at Millie and told her, "But I won't be here when she has her baby."

Millie gave her father a blank look, turned, and walked away saying softly, "I know."

"But tomorrow is a big day, ya know," he told her, and she just kept walking.

Mattie leaned her head next to Father and asked, "All them sheep gonna get a haircut tomorrow?"

"They sure are!" he said. "And you girls are going to help."

Evelyn Rose looked up at Father and asked, "How are we gonna help?"

"Well," he said, "Millie and Rusty will catch the sheep and hold them. Me and the boys from town will do the shearing, and your mother will keep us in vittles for when we take a break."

"Hey!" both girls say in unison.

"Hey what?" Father asked, grinning.

"What are *we* gonna do?" asked Evelyn Rose.

"Yeah," Mattie chimed in, "you said we get to help."

"Oh, yeah, I almost forgot the most important thing," he told them. "You girls get to play in the wool. We'll throw the wool over the fence, and you get to put it all in big bags. Don't that sound like fun?"

Mattie said, "Oh yes, it does!"

Evelyn Rose complained, "Do we have to? I remember last year, and that wool is really itchy!"

Early the next morning, well before daylight, a couple of young men from Mr. Highley's livery stable brought their large flatbed wagon pulled by a pair of giant Belgian horses to a halt at the gate of the sheep farm. There to meet them were Father along with Cecil and Cecil's Pa, a few neighbors, Millie, and her dog, Rusty.

Mother brought out a large skillet of scrambled eggs followed by their neighbor, Mrs. Bell, with a large board piled high with bacon and ham. Off to the side of the table that was set up for the food was a nice warm fire with three iron rods made into a tripod that had a large pot of coffee hanging over the center of the fire. Evelyn Rose followed the two women with an armload of bread with Mattie carrying a couple of jars of apple butter.

"All right," Father said, "roll up one of those large logs to sit on, and we will gather together for grace, and then you can dig in."

There under the morning stars with a big full planter's moon going down over the southwest mountain, Millie watched her father standing beside the crackling fire. As the blue-violet-tinged fire glowed in the morning sky behind him, Millie listened to her Father giving thanks to the Lord above. He asked for blessings upon his family, his friends, those who came to help, and the food. He asked the Creator of all things to give them a good and prosperous day. Just before his "Amen," Millie blurted out, "Keep my father safe!"

Silence filled the air until Father said with a smile, "Yes, He will!"

Everyone at once started talking and filling their plates. Mother and Mrs. Bell carried the crock of milk around so everyone could dip their cup while Evelyn Rose made sure they all had something to eat with. Mattie tried her best to get in her father's lap, and as usual, she made it there. As usual, someone would tell her she's too big and to get down. This time, Father held on tight and whispered in her ear to make her giggle, "You stay right here."

WHERE THE ACORNS FALL

Everyone ate their fill while Rusty ran around the crowd licking up whatever would fall to the ground. Millie made sure he had more than his share.

The deep-blue and violet sky started to turn a more pink and light blue. The moon had disappeared behind the mountain while the stars vanished. Father asked everyone if they've had enough to eat and enough coffee to drink. Father said to Millie, "Are you two ready for a long day?"

"You bet we are!" Millie said while scratching Rusty under the chin. "Ain't we, fella?"

"All right then," Father told everyone, "daylight is cracking, and it's not gonna stop to give us any rest today."

Very few people here had ever witnessed the shearing of sheep. After all, this was cattle and crop-farming country. People from all over the county took a detour on their way to the county seat just to see the sheep get their wool sheared off. Mother, Mrs. Bell, and the two younger girls made money by selling coffee for two cents a cup, and they were kept busy all day. Father and the two young men that Mr. Highley sent out to help had a system worked out that had one holding the sheep while the other would shear, and the other would take a break. After a while, you could see some of the spectators making bets how fast a certain man could shear a sheep or who would shear the fastest. The biggest thrill the visitors got was watching the fifteen-year-old girl and her dog work the sheep with precision and control.

Millie's voice would keep all the sheep calm while at the same time, hand gestures and whistles would send the dog over, under, and around the sheep. Rusty would cut out the exact sheep that Millie wanted and hold it at bay in a corner until the two men could grab it and start their shearing. After the sheep were sheared, Millie would send Rusty in and work the sheared sheep to the gate that Millie would open and close to let it out. Then they would start all over and do it again. The crowd enjoyed the pair working as a team. They would applaud as Millie would have Rusty do tricks, showing off his skills.

The day was hard but rewarding and prosperous for the sheep farmer and his family. What he thought would be a full wagonload of wool ended up doubled that amount. Money was made for the show and from the mercantile exchange set price of wool. Enough money was made at the place from selling coffee and drinks that the two boys were paid on the spot without waiting for Mr. Highley to pay them. Millie's dad even gave them a nice tip for the hard work they did. Everyone talked about the young shepherd girl and her amazing dog.

Chapter 8

Later that evening after everyone had gone home and the itchy wool had been washed off, as the family sat at the table, Father told them all, "We done good, girls. I'm so..." He stopped and swallowed then wiped the tears from his face and started again, "I'm so proud of you all. You all worked so hard. I just couldn't believe at times what I was seeing. So many people came to see what we were doing and going away with a different view of sheep farming. I think we made some friends today." Mattie crawled up onto her father's lap and snuggled into his arms. While he stroked her damp hair, Father continued by saying, "I did some figuring, and with the money we made, we'll definitely be able to pay bills, have some for winter to come, and"—he stopped to make sure everyone was watching and paying attention—"and make a down payment on a place of our own."

Evelyn Rose sat up straight and said, "A place that would be just ours, better than this one?"

"Well, I don't know if it would be better than this one," he said, reaching out to pat her hands that were folded on the table. "But, yes, a place all our own."

Mother stood up and told the girls, "Your father and I were hoping for a long time that the hard work would pay off, and it did. Between the logging and your father working on some of the other farms along with the sale of the wool, it was better than expected. It is time we take a chance." She walked over and held her hands under Mattie's arms and said, "This little one is sound asleep. I'll tuck her into bed. I'm wore out myself. Why don't we talk about this tomorrow?"

Millie finally spoke up and said, "Well, I don't like the idea of moving. I like it here."

Father looked at her and waited for her to look up at him. When she did, he said, "I know. I like it here too. The only problem is, this place isn't ours. We pay a yearly lease, and at the end of the year if Mr. Highley wanted to, he could just tell us to leave. I know he wouldn't. He's a nice man, and we're good friends, but, Millie, what if something happened to him?"

"I know," Millie said. "I understand that, but will a new place have the pasture for the sheep like this place. Will it have a creek and a big pond, and how about the hills with the hardwoods like these and a big oak tree like the one in the back field? We have one of the best springs in all of the west of Farmington."

Father listened and smiled at Millie until she finally said, "And what if something happens to you? We could lose a new place just like we could lose this one."

Walking back into the room, Mother put her hands on her hips and said, "This farm is not ours. Mr. Highley may sell it to us, but, Millie, we have an opportunity to buy something. Why don't we look some?" She looked at her husband and told him, "Why don't you tell the girls about the place we looked at north of here?"

"What?" Millie angrily shouts. "You've already found a place without the rest of us knowing?"

"Yeah," Evelyn Rose said, getting up and standing next to her sister. "We didn't get to go too!"

Millie gave her sister a shove and said, "What's the matter with you?"

"Now, girls, both of you, calm down," Father sternly said. "Your mother and I went a few weeks ago to look at a small farm north of here."

"How far north?" Millie sternly replied to her father.

"Okay," Father said, "let's all calm down. Everyone's tired and a little on edge. Before tempers get a little worse, why don't we all just sleep on it till tomorrow?"

"I'm sorry," Millie said, "I didn't mean that tone of voice." She grabbed Evelyn Rose and pulled her down to sit next to her in the chair. "I do want to hear about this new place."

Father gave both the girls a hard look that quickly softened when Evelyn Rose said, "Please, Father, Millie won't say anything else. Ouch! Why did you poke me for?"

With a smug grin, Millie said to Evelyn Rose, "No, I won't interrupt."

"Well, okay, if you want me to," Father said as he sat back down at the table after Mother joined them. "Like I said, its north of here, about twelve miles. There's a mining town called Bonne Terre."

"Yeah, I know that town," said Millie. "I've heard Mr. Highley say it's about half a day's ride from Farmington. It's—" Millie noticed everyone staring at her with furrowed brows. "Sorry, go ahead."

"If you go north," Father continued, "about twelve miles, you come to Bonne Terre, but you don't turn toward the town. You go right, turning east on the same road going to town, only the other way. If you go about three miles, you come to a river called Big River. The place your mother and I looked at is there on that river. On the left side of the road is a nice farm of about a hundred acres. It has three large fields, more field than here with hardwood trees and some of the tallest, thickest cedar trees you've ever seen. There is a lane that turns off the road before you get to the river. It is lined with some of the nicest mimosa trees you'll ever see anywhere. At the end of the lane is a nice-size one-room cabin that sits by a beautiful spring-fed lake. There is a deep well just to the back of the cabin, and—get this—a two-hole outhouse just forty yards from the cabin with a divide in it with separate doors. The river goes a mile or more along the edge of the property with some bluffs along the back field that overlooks the river and the farms on the other side. When your mother and I were there, the owner let us walk around some, and you'd never believe what we found."

Both girls sat up straight, and Evelyn Rose said, "You found gold in the river!"

"No! No! Nothing like that!" Father said laughing. "But we did find these." He took a tin down from the shelf and dumped on the table some flint and two flint arrowheads and a hide scraper.

"Wow!" said Millie, picking them up. "Are there Indians there?"

"No, not now," Father said, "but at one time, there must have been a tribe there along the river. There was flint in several places."

"I love the place already," said Evelyn Rose. "But we have three rooms here. One room would be too small."

"Well, your mother and I checked into that as well," Father said as he scooted his chair closer to the table and laid both arms one on top of the other with folded hands. "The people who own the farm are some kind of big shots in the mining industry. They actually live in New York. When they come here, they have a big company house in Bonne Terre, but when they want to get away from all the business, they go to this cabin. They like the hunting and fishing and peaceful surroundings. Your mother and I noticed the big sycamore trees just as you go through the gates to enter the place, and we thought what a beautiful place to build a real house. It would overlook the bottom fields as well as the field on the upper end and the beautiful mimosa trees."

"What about the sheep?" Millie asked. "Will it be a good place for them?"

Father leaned over toward the girls, smiled, and placed his hand on Evelyn Rose's head and said to Millie, "You girls will have to see it to really appreciate what it looks like. The fields have topsoil that's about two feet thick and some of the best bottomlands in the whole county. Yes, it would be the most wonderful place for the sheep and that many more if we wanted."

Father got up and walked to the other end of the table to face Millie and Evelyn Rose as their mother came over to stand by his side. Looking at his wife then back at the girls, Father said, "I'd like to sign a note and put some money down to hold this farm in my name till I get back. If this family all agrees to it."

Evelyn Rose shouted, "Oh yes! It all sounds so good." She leaned against Millie and said, "Don't you think?"

Millie gave Evelyn Rose a little shove to back her off then stood up herself. With a concerned look, she said, "It all sounds really nice, and I suppose we'll all dream of a new home and have a lot to look forward to. I do love this place, but I just don't want you gone long." Millie walked toward the door and opened it to go outside. Before she did, she took a deep breath and told her father, "If you promise to come home, I'll move anywhere you want. Just come home."

Chapter 9

The next morning as Father went through to the living area, he had to give all the girls a shake to wake them for Sunday church service. "Time to get ready," he said. "Big day at church today!"

This was the day the church would recognize those going into the armed services for the Federal forces. Nine in all had signed up from the small Baptist church.

Mother had on her new dress and bonnet that she had ordered for Easter. The girls had their dresses on that Mother had made for them. Everyone was wearing new shoes and doing their best to keep Mattie out of the dirt and clean.

The trip into town went quick because everyone laughed and joked how sore Father was from the hard work the day before.

Upon arriving at the church, they were met by several people who had seen them in action the day before. Cecil asked Millie if he could sit with her and her family. Of course, she could not say no as he was one of the nine being honored that day. Cecil's family sat with him and Millie's family. The pews were packed, and the laughter, fellowship, and greetings soon come to a halt when the pastor comes to the pulpit and begins the service with a prayer. The service was dedicated to those who would be leaving their homes, and the message was about a man laying down his life for the freedom of others. At the end of the pastor's sermon, he had the nine enlisted men come to the altar and asked the rest of the church to gather around them. They held hands, and everyone said prayers for the safety of those leaving and the well-being of the families left behind. Hugs were given, and tears were shed. A lot of hand-shaking, and words of encouragement were given; and before everyone left to attend the church-style picnic, the pastor told the men not to worry, that the church would be the guardian and sanctuary for their families.

Almost everyone stayed for the picnic dinner, although most left right after the eating was done. Everyone understood the quick exits because of the few days remaining before their departure.

Cecil walked with Millie and her family to the wagon. While they were finding their seats on the wagon, Cecil slipped Millie a letter and whispered to her, "I hope this is what you wanted, and if it is, send word, so I can see you again before I leave."

Millie held the letter in one hand and pressed it to her chest while touching his cheek with the other hand. With a look of joy and affection, she whispered back, "I'll be watching for you every day."

Father yelled, "If you are going, hop on! We've got a lot to do yet!" He flicked the reins and told Ole Smokey, "Get up there!" With a jerk, the horse started his walk. Millie turned, and in the blink of an eye, she bounded to the wagon, jumped, and in midair, turned her body to sit perfectly on the back of the wagon. With a smile, she held the letter out and waved goodbye to Cecil.

Evelyn Rose scooted in beside Millie. Mattie stood behind Millie with her arms around her neck. The three girls watched Cecil standing there as they rode away. Millie said while patting Mattie's hand, "He's a dandy, don't you think?"

"Ugh!" said Evelyn Rose and stared at Millie.

"I like him," said Mattie. "Are you going to read the letter to us?"

"No!" Millie cried out. "It's mine, and I better not catch you girls trying to find it." Lowering her voice and pointing a finger at Evelyn Rose, she told her, "Don't even think about it!"

The three girls did their petty bickering the rest of the way home as Father kept Ole Smokey heading toward the setting sun and the hills to the west.

Turning off Maple Road and onto the road that led to their home, Father yelled out, "Here comes Rusty! That dog must have smelled us before he saw us! Hope you girls brought him some scraps."

Millie and her sisters carefully made their way up to the front of the wagon and stood behind their parents to watch their dog make his way up the road. "Look at him go!" Mattie said.

"Yeah," said Millie, "we should've took him with us. You'd think, the way he acts, we were gone a week."

Ole Smokey threw his head up and down as if to greet his best friend. Once Rusty reached the horse, the pair trotted in tandem, escorting the family through the gate to their home.

Millie told her father she wanted to go check on the freshly sheared sheep in the back pasture.

"Don't be gone long," he told her, looking to the western hills. "The sun will be down soon and I—"

Millie cut him off, saying, "I know! I'll be right back. I gotta go." She took off up the hill, leaving her shoes by the fence post. For a second, Rusty looked at the food scraps Evelyn Rose was putting on the ground for him. Then without hesitation, he left the food and took off running to catch up with Millie.

"If that girl ain't acting peculiar," Father said, scratching his head. He asked Mother, "What's got into her anyway?"

Mother shushed the girls from giggling and told them to go feed the milk cow and bring in a bucket of fresh water from the spring. "Go on now," she said, "and don't be getting your dresses and shoes dirty. On second thought, Mattie, give me your shoes."

Mattie slipped her shoes off without untying them and handed them to her mother, who said, "Thank you. Now go help your sister."

After the girls were out of hearing distance, Mother reached out to take her husband's hand and said, "We need to sit down and have a little talk."

Father looked at her with a blank, wide-eyed stare, and said, "We do?"

"Yes, we do," she explained with a smile while patting his hand.

Millie jogged past the pond and turned toward the open gap in the fence to the back field. As she stopped, Rusty sat on his haunches next to her, panting. They both took a quick gander over the flock, and all seemed to be in order. Millie took the letter in both hands and held it up to the sun, saying out loud and to herself, "Yep, there's writing inside this envelope. Come on, fella, let's go see what Cecil has to say to me." The two walked down the fence that separated their farm from the Bell farm. About halfway down the fence line, the pair came to what Millie considered her most favorite place on the whole farm. Millie patted the giant oak and sat between a couple of exposed roots and said, "I'm back." Making herself comfortable, she watched the setting sun send out its golden rays from behind the drifting clouds. She took a deep breath. Rusty raised his head and saw her staring at the letter. Since no head rub was coming, he lay his head back down, and finally Millie opens the letter.

She began to read the first sentence after "Dear Millie" when she heard a limb crack and break in the woods just past the fence at the corner of the field. Rusty stood on all fours and watched intently but didn't offer a bark or a growl. "What was that?" she asked, staring as hard as she could into the dark, shaded side of the hill. "I can't see anything, and I bet you can't smell anything either with that breeze blowing the other way." Giving up, Millie patted Rusty's side and said, "Deer don't break dead limbs on the ground unless they smelled you. You stinky dog!" She laughed and gave the dog a shake of the head. Millie settled back into the comfort of the massive oak and dreamed of a future with Cecil as she read the letter of a love that would soon depart, and he begged for her patience until he returned. Cecil wrote of his faithfulness until they were once more together and closed with the prayer of a growing love in his absence, and the Good Lord above will watch over them both. Millie smiled a little and got misty eyed when she read the words, "Always and Forever Yours, Cecil."

Looking at Rusty then wiping her nose on her dress sleeve, Millie mumbled to herself, "This isn't right. Father's too old, and Cecil is just too young for this sort of thing." Looking up through the green leaves of the big oak toward the heavens, Millie wondered why things were the way they were. Catching a glimpse of the bright evening star between the southwest hill and the outstretched arms of the oak that cradled her body, she resigned herself to the fact that it's not her that had control but the One who created all that there is. Millie held the letter in both hands, brought it to her lips, looked up at the evening star, and said, "Please, Lord, watch over them both."

Chapter 10

The next five days seemed to go by so fast that there wasn't enough time for Father to explain all there was to know about the farming. It seemed his favorite phrase was always "I have all the confidence in the world that you'll be fine." He told his family, "I'll write, and make sure you return my letters."

Father went over things to do, and everyone had their jobs to take care of. He even made Millie promise to stay in school, but when the weather was threatening to either stay home or head home. Neighbors, friends, and church family would be their family and protector for maybe the next year or so.

Father explained how if everything went according to plan, the new enlistments would leave Farmington and meet the regular Federal troops and other new enlistments from the Ste. Genevieve and Cape Girardeau area. From there, they would go to St. Louis for training and then on to the lines of engagement.

"Talk is," Father said, "the Confederates are leaving ranks twice the rate as new recruits can join. Single men are going to Texas or out west to the new frontier in hope of not getting caught for desertion. That just leaves the married men to surrender in hopes of getting fed and sent home."

Mother did the best she could to keep from breaking down and totally falling to pieces. Finding her strength in her daughters, especially Millie, Mother coped fairly well. Having Mrs. Bell as a neighbor and within earshot gave her just the source of strength she needed to know that a woman can and will handle the farm life.

The eve of departure brought hugs, kisses, tears, and I love you's. Last minute preparations and instructions were gone over before it was time for bed. Sleep eluded all of them, and the morning had arrived way too soon. Father leaned over Evelyn Rose and Mattie and gave them a farewell kiss. He walked into the gathering room where Mrs. Bell had come to watch over the two girls until Millie and Mother returned from taking Father to town. Tennessee gave a neighborly hug and said, "Don't fret none, deep down it's the right thing to do, and I truly believe the long run will prove that. You just keep your eyes peeled for any of them graybacks hidin' behind a tree." Tennessee patted his hands and gave him a tight-lipped smile.

Without saying anything, he gave her a big hug, turned away, and walked out the door where Millie and Mother were waiting to take him into town. Millie opened the gate and shut it after Father brought Ole Smokey and the wagon through it. Hopping on the seat next to Mother, Millie said, "Guess this is it!"

"Yep," Father replied, "suppose so."

Father brought Ole Smokey around the bend, and just as they got to Maple Road, he brought the wagon to a halt. He told Millie she needed to send Rusty home and tell him not to follow.

As Millie got down off the wagon, Rusty came up to her. Millie knelt on one knee, grabbed hold of his bottom jaw with one hand, and pet him with the other. "Rusty," she said, "go home, Rusty, go home, stay!" The dog obeyed her command and ran toward the cabin. Just as he rounded the bend, Millie noticed a small fire way up on top of the northwest hill. This would have been unnoticeable from the house side of the farm. Millie wondered who could be out in the woods in the early morning hours before daylight.

"Father!" she yelled. "Do you see—?"

"Yes, I do!" he cut her off in mid-sentence. "I saw it when I told you to run the dog back home. That land is on the back side of the Links' place. It belongs to the Woodland Mining Company, I believe."

Millie crawled back on the wagon next to Mother. Father told Ole Smokey to get up. Looking over at Millie and Mother, he said, "I believe it really is maybe some miners looking for some ore samples.

Just keep a close watch back in the wood line and keep that old pistol close at hand. Okay?"

"We'd do that anyway," Mother told him. "But I do think I'll go over to see Mrs. Link and see how she's doing. She hardly ever gets out since her husband has passed on."

"Can I go too?" Millie asked.

"We'll all go," she replied. "Maybe make her a gooseberry pie if they are ripe yet."

"Oh, I know just where to go get some," Millie told her. "There is a bunch of bushes by the oak tree in the back field. I'll get them in a couple of days."

"Think of me when you are all eating a piece of pie," Father said. "By the way, why haven't you picked them by now?"

"I have been," Millie told Father. "I just kinda eat them before I get home." She leaned against her mother and said, "I'll leave 'em for a couple days so they'll be enough for a pie."

"Why don't you two take the pistol out and see if you both remember what I taught you about shooting? Make sure it works and everything," Father said.

"It works just fine," Mother said with a tone that said "I don't like guns."

"For someone who doesn't like guns, you sure are a good shot," Millie told her mother. "You must be a natural shooter."

"Well, you both need a little practice," Father told them. "Besides, it tells everyone within earshot that you mean to protect what's yours. Just remember to clean it when you are done and reload it before you put it away."

Mother put her arm through her husband's arm, lay her head on his shoulder, and said, "We'll be fine. You worry about yourself, and take care of the things around you."

"I know." After a deep breath, he said, "I will." Father promised to write as often as possible.

Arriving at the north end of the courthouse, there was a large crowd of people gathered there to see the new soldiers off. A few troops from the Fredericktown and Ironton area came in the evening before. They would all leave together and meet with the recruits from

Cape Girardeau and Ste. Genevieve in the town of Festus. From there, the men would go on to St. Louis to receive their uniforms, arms, and supplies. After two weeks of training, they would be assigned to the front lines or other places of defense.

At the sound of the trumpet call, men and their families were saying their goodbyes. Through the crowd of people, Millie heard someone calling her name and then spotted Cecil. Cecil made his way through the crowd, waving his raised arm, leaving his parents and siblings behind. Feeling a hand on her shoulder, Millie turned to see her father, and he said, "Gotta go, give me a hug, and I'll leave you two be and always know that I love you."

In Father's ear, Millie whispered, "I'm so confused."

Holding her tight, Father replied, "I know you are. You're very lucky you'll have your mother and plenty of time on your side to sort this out." Father pulled away, said goodbye, and gave her a wink.

Tears flowed from her eyes, and she heard a soft whisper behind her, "Millie." She turned to see Cecil standing there. "I want you to have this," he said as he handed her a box that had been wrapped with beautiful wrapping paper. "Don't open it now—wait till you get home. I have to leave." He reached down and gave her a kiss on the cheek. Millie returned his kiss with a hug and said, "I made something for you. Here, close your eyes and hold out your hand."

Cecil held out his hand, with eyes shut tight as Millie placed an object and a letter in his hand. She closed his fingers over the object and letter, gave his hand a kiss, and whispered, "I love you too."

Cecil opened his eyes to see Millie running away and looked down at his hand. In it, along with the letter, was a small wooden cross with a brown string attached. When he looked back up, Millie was gone. As hard as he tried, he couldn't spot her anywhere. He began to open the letter when he heard one of the men in a blue uniform say, "Okay, everyone, fall in line. It's time to move out!"

Cecil moved to get in line while tucking the letter in his pants pocket. The soldier yelled again, "Forward march!" Everyone moved forward to follow another soldier riding a horse. Trying to place the cross over his head, Cecil dropped his bedroll and got knocked over when he tried to pick it up. Grabbing hold of his bedroll, he ran to get back in place, hearing the snickering of some of the other men. Cecil tucked his cross under his shirt and smiled to himself when he felt the cool wooden cross next to his heart.

As the rising sun was fully exposed, the small town of Farmington waved and cheered to their finest and bravest men as they marched out of town toward the north and to a war everyone was praying for to end.

Millie saw her mother and ran to catch up. She told her, "Let's hurry home. We might be able to see them going north on the St. Louis Road." Millie and Mother hurried to get in the wagon when Mother said, "Young lady, I'll drive."

"But, Mother!" said Millie.

"No buts, you'll go too fast. We have plenty of time," Mother told her daughter. "We'll even get the girls and bring them up so they can watch too."

"By the way," Mother said as she flicked the reins to get Ole Smokey on the move, "what's that you got there?"

Millie looked at her hand holding the gift and said, "It's from Cecil. It's too pretty to open, don't you think? I'm afraid I might tear the paper."

Mother flicked the reins once more to bring Ole Smokey to a trot, which threw Millie back as she squealed with a smile, "Mother! I didn't think we were in a hurry!"

"Just to be on the safe side," she replied and clicked her tongue against her teeth to make Ole Smokey step up the gait a bit quicker. "Better to be early than to be late!"

In no time at all, the pair rounded the bend of Maple Road to see the small cabin with a hillside full of sheep behind it. As Mother brought the horse to a stop at the gate, Millie had already jumped off and was running to open it. "Stay here," Mother told her. "I'll get the girls and be right back."

In just a few minutes, Mother returned with Mrs. Bell sitting next to her, and Evelyn Rose and Mattie hanging on in the back, making their way back up the hill with Rusty following close behind. Millie yelled out, "Don't stop. I'll jump on the back!"

As the wagon passed the gate, Millie quickly shut and secured it closed with a wire. She ran to catch up and just like always, jumped and, in midair, turned to land just right on the back of the wagon. In the blink of an eye, Rusty jumped and landed squarely in her lap. Millie yelled to Mother, "We're all on now!"

Mother took the outer road that passed by the Link farm to a good vantage point to see the troops heading north to their destination. Mrs. Link came out to watch them and invited them all for a cool drink afterward. It didn't take long until the troops came passing by, and the girls began waving. The whole company of soldiers waved back. "Where's Father?" cried Evelyn Rose. Mother pointed him out.

Millie pointed out Cecil and said, "I didn't think they would all wave. Hope Father is not upset with us."

"No, he isn't. He was proud. I could tell," said Mother.

"I saw one of Cecil's friends give him a shove while he was waving," Millie said. "I sure hope he'll be all right."

The troops passed by and then there was silence. It was a sad silence that was almost deafening until Mrs. Link said, "How about that cold drink?"

Everyone, even Millie, said, "Oh yes," just to break the clutch of the quietness.

Chapter 11

Later that afternoon, Millie decided to open her wrapped gift from Cecil. With all the anticipation of a young girl opening her first gift from a boy, she did the best she could to save the paper. Once the paper was removed, she sat there with a box on her lap. Millie noticed Evelyn Rose and Mattie bent over with their elbows on the table and their chins resting on their hands with eyes as big as saucers. "Why don't you two go out and play?" she said to the pair. "Surely you have something else to do," she said, placing her hands over the box

"Millie," Mother said, "that wasn't nice, and you know it. Besides, I want to see too."

"I know. I'm sorry," she told her sisters. "Just let me see first."

"That's fine," Mother said with a smile and told the girls to come help her finish drying the breakfast dishes and put them away.

Millie took the box and placed it on the table. Slowly lifting the lid and setting it exactly next to the box, she took a deep breath and lay half the tissue paper covering the contents to the left. Raising the other half while bending her head sideways to see under it, she said, "Oh, isn't that the prettiest thing you've ever seen!"

"What is it?" Evelyn Rose asked as they rushed to the table to examine the gift.

"It's handkerchiefs with embroidery on it," Mother told them. "They're all hand stitched."

"Look," said Millie excitedly, "there are three of them. This one has a sheep on the corner, and this one is me, I suppose." She held it up to show her mother. "This one is…oh, what is this?" Millie lifted the last handkerchief with a dog stitched in the corner, and underneath was a silver hair barrette in the shape of a shepherd's staff.

Mattie squinted and said, "That's so pretty. What is it?"

Millie handed it to her mother, who told them it's a hair barrette. "See, you have a clasp on the back of the staff. When you slide it open, you place it in your hair and then you lock it back." Mother placed the barrette in Millie's hair and said, "There, that's how it works."

Evelyn Rose grabbed a piece of mirror from the shelf and handed it to Millie, saying, "Take a look. It's so beautiful!"

"Is this Rusty?" Mattie said as she held up the third handkerchief.

"I believe so," said Millie, "and don't be getting it dirty!"

"But I didn't get them dirty!" Mattie said as she put her arms together on the table and thumped her head down on her forearms to hide her eyes.

"Don't cry, Mattie. Just wash your hands, and I'll let you hold the handkerchief," Millie told her.

Mattie kept her head down and said, "I'm not crying. I'm just darning!"

Mother walked over and sat next to her. Patting her back, Mother asked, "You're doing what?"

Mattie raised her red face with eyes full of tears, looked at her Mother, and said, "You know, darning. Darn it, I got dirty hands and can't touch nothing. I'm not crying, just darning!"

Millie and Evelyn Rose cracked up laughing, and Mother put her arm around Mattie's head, pulling her to her bosom. Hugging and rocking her in a sideways motion, Mother said, "It's okay, nothing is hurt. You just 'darn' all you want, but remember to keep your hands washed."

Mattie turned her head sideways just enough for one eye to see Millie and Evelyn Rose laughing and stomped one foot. Then she started laughing too.

Chapter 12

Cecil settled in on his bedroll a few feet away from his two friends who enlisted the same time he did. He was far enough away so they couldn't watch him read Millie's letter, but close enough to see by the firelight. After the long march of about twelve miles, the new recruits and their officers were camped by the Big River a few miles north of the town Bonne Terre. Millie's father had come by to eat with the boys and talk about the long day's walk. Finally, after everyone settled in from being so worn out, Cecil tore open the end of the envelope to reveal the written words that he had been carrying next to his heart all day long.

Millie started the letter with wishing there was no war going on and how he was too young to be leaving. How everything happened so fast, and so much was going on that it was too hard to think, especially with her father leaving too. She told Cecil that as young as they both were, that she would wait for him if he promised to be patient with her. The two-page letter didn't take long to read, and as fatigue came over him and he began to drift off to sleep, he held on to the words "Someday we'll be together forever, and I'll love you always."

* * *

Mother put Evelyn Rose and Mattie to bed while Millie sat on the big rock porch with Rusty. Mother opened the door and asked, "You mind if I come out and sit with you?"

"I wish you would," Millie told her mother.

They both sat in their own silence listening to the sounds of the late spring night. The peepers and frogs were singing to one another over by the spring. Katydids and June bugs were having a competition for the loudest sounds. Off to the west past the pond and on into the valley between the two hills, a whip-poor-will was singing to the world about his search for a love he's yet to find.

"The stars sure are bright tonight," Mother said to Millie.

"Yes," Millie replied. "I guess 'cause there's no moon shining tonight. You can really see the Big Dipper."

"You know," Mother told her, "if you follow the last two stars in the cup of the Dipper in a straight line to the next star, you can find the North Star."

"Yeah," she answered her mother with a bump of the shoulders. "We learned that in school."

"But did you know," she said with a shoulder bump back, "that your father is looking at the same star right now?"

Millie looked at her mother with tears in her eyes. "Yep, he told me as soon as the girls go to bed, to look at the North Star, and he would too. That would keep us connected."

Chapter 13

Cecil's eyes shot open, and he jerked his head up to see what he heard. Not seeing anyone else looking around, he was not quite sure what to make of it. Thinking someone must have gone to relieve himself, he rose higher to see who was missing. Feeling that something was just not right, Cecil crawled out from under his blanket and made his way over to Millie's father.

Lying awake looking at the stars, Millie's father jerked with a startle when Cecil touched him on the shoulder. "What's the matter, Cecil?"

Cecil put a finger to his lips and whispered that he had heard someone walking in the woods but didn't see anyone go out.

Millie's father, believing him, got up, and at the same time, one of the officers saw the two men up and yelled, "What's going on there?" Everyone in camp was awakened, and the men jumped to their feet.

Getting ready to explain, Millie's father opened his mouth, and at that instance, a shot rang out and high-pitched yelling from the woods could be heard. The Union soldiers grabbed their guns and began firing at the yelling men on the outer edge of the camp. Some of those men made it into the camp and were fighting hand-to-hand. It was an ambush, but to the surprise of the attackers, the Union soldiers had returned fire, and enough of the recruits were awake due to Cecil and Millie's father trusting their instincts that someone was in the woods. The attackers fled, but a couple of them were caught and held.

Cecil looked around and saw Millie's father lying on the ground. He ran over and rolled the man over onto his back. Millie's father said, "I've been shot."

The officer that first inquired what was going on came over and said, "I saw you go down on the first shot. Are you hurt bad?"

"I've been hit just below the knee," Millie's father said. "I think it shattered the bone."

The officer had one of the other Union soldiers and another man get a tourniquet above the knee and stabilize the leg. He told the soldier to prepare the injured man to be transported back to Bonne Terre at first light.

The officer looked at Cecil and said, "Son, if you hadn't been wary of what was going on, I'm afraid those Southern sympathizers would have snuck on in here and had their way with us. You saved a lot of people here tonight, and I won't forget that." Standing face-to-face with Cecil, the officer held out his hand, and the two men shook hands.

"Now bring me those captives," the officer barked out the order. "I want to question them now while they are good and scared!"

A couple of boys in blue brought the two youngsters, who were probably no older than Cecil and looked like they had been worked over pretty well, to the officer. "Now you fellas aren't Confederate soldiers," said the officer in charge, "so that pretty well gives us the right to just go ahead and shoot you as troublemakers or instigators. I do believe your bunch is the one burning farmhouses and killing cattle and such."

The two boys looked so scared that they just might pass out either from fear or the beating they just took.

"Tell you what I am going to do," said the officer in charge. "If you cooperate and answer just a few questions, we'll take you to St. Louis with us and treat you as any Confederate captive. Three meals a day, place to lay your head, and at the end of the war, you go home. But if you don't," the officer said through gritted teeth, standing nose to nose with the men, "I'll kill you, him, and every one of you right here, right now, and leave your bodies to feed the worms." He pulled his pistol out, pulled the hammer back, and placed the barrel against his temple. "It's up to you."

Taking the captives one at a time, the officer interrogated the men. Less than an hour later, the commanding officer gathered his men and most of the new recruits and said, "Can't tell you everything, but I do think you need to know that the ring leader is a man named Hildebrand, and he lives in these parts. Seems he had a spy hid out in the hills just west of Farmington. He's been staying with miners and such just past a sheep farm."

Millie's father let out a loud groan as he tried to stand, and it took Cecil and his friends to keep him down. "That's our farm!" he yelled. "Did they tell you anything else?"

The commanding officer said, "Yes, he did."

Cecil let go of Millie's father to the care of his friends and stood in front of the officer, saying, "You gotta tell me what these men told you."

The officer nodded and told him how the spy could see from the hill all the way into town with a telescope, and when they started their march this morning, he left ahead of them. He rode out as hard as he could to alert Hildebrand so he could have time for this ambush. "Thanks to you, it wasn't a success," he told Cecil.

The officer raised his hand to Cecil's shoulder and gripped it real tight and leaned in and said, "The boys said he'd told them he had done his job and started bragging about going back for some little shepherd girl."

Cecil tried to tear away, but the officer anticipated his attempt to leave and held him tight. He yelled out, "You've got to let me go! That's Millie!"

Another soldier helped the officer to keep him from leaving as the officer explained, "I'll let you go, but not like this. You'll never make it in time." The officer barked out orders for a fresh horse with a saddle. He looked toward a guard and told him to break out one of the new carbine rifles and a handful of ammunition. After some quick explaining and instruction on the rifle, he said to Cecil, "Remember, you are in the Army. You, this gun, and this horse belongs to the government. If you can, bring him back alive."

Cecil turned to leave and saw Millie's father standing behind him, held up by his friends. Without any words, the two men embraced. No words could have said any more than the look in Millie's father's eyes. Cecil nodded, mounted the horse, and rode off into the night toward the south.

Chapter 14

Early the next morning just after daylight, Millie crept out of bed so not to wake her sisters. She tiptoed into the room where her mother was already making the daily bread. "Need any help?" Millie asked.

"No, not really," Mother replied. "But if you really want to help, you could go and milk the cow."

Millie looked straight down, put her chin on her chest, and whined, "Do I have to milk the cow?"

"No, you don't," Mother calmly told her. "What else were you going to do since you asked to help?"

"Well, I was going to go get the gooseberries for Mrs. Link's pie," said Millie.

"That's why I wanted you to milk the cow," Mother said as she pulled Millie's chin up with her fingers and gave her a wide-eyed smile. "You can take her some fresh milk to go with her pie."

Walking toward the bucket that was sitting by the door, Millie said, "I'll get some berries from Mrs. Bell's place. They are just on the other side of the fence. We can have a pie too." She grabbed the bucket and headed out the door. Shutting the door behind her, Millie took a deep breath of fresh air and thought out loud, "I just love it out here. Come on, Rusty," she yelled, looking around for the dog. "What have you been up to all night?" Millie whistled for Rusty and said to herself again, "I think I could live under a tree if it wouldn't rain on me."

As she walked toward the lean-to barn that housed their milk cow and horse, Millie told herself, "Might as well let Ole Smokey out so he can eat some fresh grass."

"Hey, Smokey," Millie said, "have you seen your little buddy, or is he out running a rabbit?" Millie looked under the horse and then got the halter and slipped it on the horse's head. She hooked a short rope under his chin to lead him out to the pasture. Millie rubbed the horse's front legs and placed a cast-iron ring around each front hoof that connected to the short rope. "There you go, now eat all you want," she said. "Just don't you wander off too far. I wonder where Rusty is?"

Millie walked back to the pole barn to where Bessie waited patiently to be milked. Getting a bit of feed to keep her calm during the milking, Millie grabbed the milk stool and then enticed the calf outside to give her room to sit down and begin the milking.

* * *

Cecil gingerly got down off the lathered horse and led him to the Flat River to give the poor horse a break and some fresh water. "Don't know how you did it," Cecil said to the horse, "but you've held a good steady pace all night. I'm so sore I can't make my legs stand straight." A couple more gulps, and Cecil lifted his head and said, "I'd like to let you drink more, but we've got a bit of a ways to go yet. Tell ya what,"—Cecil took off in a jog, pulling on the reins to make the horse follow—"I'll jog for about a mile if you get me there in a couple of hours. I need to get some life in my legs."

"I'm guessing it's been a mile," Cecil said and mounted the horse. "Do your best, fella. It's not that far now." A flick of the reins commanded the horse into a canter, leaving dust and dirt clots in their wake. Cecil only hoped they got there in time. He knew he couldn't run the horse to death, but he did little to slow him down.

* * *

"Here you go, Mother," Millie said as she made her way to the table with the bucket of fresh milk. "That calf Mrs. Bell gave us isn't leaving much milk for us. By the way, have you seen Rusty?"

"Yes, I did," Mother told her and explained, "Just at daylight, I heard him barking at something and looked out the window to see him run straight across the field towards the woods. Didn't see what he was after, but when he got to the woods, Tennessee's hounds started barking too."

"Oh boy!" said Millie. "I sure hope it wasn't a skunk!"

"No." Mother nodded as she sprinkled the fresh milk on the pie dough. "That dog is smart enough to not make that kind of mistake again. Maybe he saw that hen turkey you saw here a while back."

Millie got a tin cup down off the shelf and asked her mother, "Can I have just a little?"

Mother leaned over and looked in the bucket. "Just a little," she said. "Cut off some of that fresh bread if you want. Then go get those berries. I'd like to go to Mrs. Link's 'bout the time the sun is straight up."

* * *

Off in the woods after making a sharp turn away from the barking hounds, a young man sat on a downed tree with a club in his hands. "Stupid dog!" he said to the brown-and-white dog lying dead on the ground. "I tried to shake you in the woods, but you wouldn't give up. What did you think? I was just gonna let you bite my leg off!"

The young man looked down at the torn pant leg and could see blood filling his shoe. He tore off a piece of his shirt and tied it around the wound and hoped for the bleeding to stop. Looking through the woods past the giant oak and into the pasture where the sheep were grazing, he thought to himself, *She'll be back here to check on the sheep soon. Damn dog! Now how do I tie her up and carry her out to the horse with a bum leg?*

* * *

Great globs of lathered sweat flew off the horse as Cecil wondered how in the world the horse had made it this far. *Maybe these warhorses are a lot tougher and trained better than the ones I'm used to in town.* He reached down and petted his neck while in full gallop and said, "I don't know who's going to last the longest. My inner thighs and rear are so sore and blistered. I just don't know if I can walk or sit."

Cresting the hill, Cecil brought the warhorse to a halt. Blowing snot and slobber, the horse tried to catch his breath and pranced around in circles. "This is where we leave the road," he said while trying to calm the horse down. Finally relaxing a bit, Cecil pointed to a bluff and told the horse, "That's where Millie and her family were waving when last I saw them." He patted the horse's neck again and asked, "You got another mile in you, fella?"

The horse reared his head and shook his long mane back and forth as though he understood every single word that was said. Setting his heels into the horse's flanks, the pair took off to the open range, hoping beyond all hope to make it in time or die trying.

Chapter 15

Just as Millie was getting ready to leave the small cabin, she heard a voice in the back room say, "Wait for me, Millie! I want to go with you."

"Okay," said Millie, "just hurry up! I'll be out here waiting." She went out the door, left it open, and sat on the big, flat rock porch.

Evelyn Rose came to the door and told Millie she was ready. "Wait just a minute," Mother told the pair. "Here, Evelyn Rose," and she handed her a slice of buttered bread and a tin cup with a small amount of milk in it.

"I'll take it with me," Evelyn Rose said. "Thanks, Mom."

"Wait, I want to go too!" came a cry from the doorway to the bedroom.

Millie rolled her eyes and sat back down on the porch and said, "Get your bread and milk. We will all just go out for a picnic!"

"Now, Millie!" Mother said, standing in the doorway with her hands on her hips. "Why you in such a hurry?"

"Well, you said you wanted my help with the milking so we'd be at the Links' home around noontime," Millie explained. "Besides, I'm wanting to go see where Rusty might be. This ain't like him."

"No, it really isn't like him," Mother said as she got Mattie something to eat and drink before they all ran off. "Now, young lady, try to stay clean, and mind your big sister. Keep your shoes tied, okay?"

Mattie smiled at her mother and bounded out the door as the other girls stood up to leave.

"Grab the bucket," Millie told Evelyn Rose.

"No! You get it!" came Evelyn Rose's reply.

"Evelyn Rose! What did I just say," Mother sternly said. "I meant that for the two of you. She'll carry it back."

Evelyn Rose got the bucket and mumbled something about too young to be the oldest and too old to be youngest, then walked off saying, "Ain't fair!"

Following their big sister across the open field toward the woods and Mrs. Bell's house, Evelyn Rose and Mattie just looked at each other and shrugged their shoulders, wondering, *Why this way?*

Once the three girls got to the fence, Millie told them, "Mother said she saw Rusty come this way barking at something. Then she heard the hounds start barking at something. I'm gonna go in the woods and walk toward that way." She pointed toward the southwest hill that lay just beyond the big oak tree. "You two stay together and just walk next to the fence. Once you get past the pond, go through the gap, and I'll meet you back by the big oak tree. Okay?"

"Okay," said Evelyn Rose, "but I just don't know why you don't whistle or call for him."

"I have been, knucklehead," Millie said as she climbed through the fence. "Now watch for snakes. They like laying on the flat rocks over here and warm themselves in the sun. See you at the oak!"

* * *

Standing at the corner of the fence, the young lying Southern instigator sees the three girls leave the small cabin and walk to the woods that he came through. Saying out loud and to himself, "Bet she's looking for her stupid dog. I just hope she doesn't go toward the road where I've got my horse hid in the brush." Limping back through the woods toward the oak, he made a plan in his mind to kidnap Millie.

"Whoa!" he said in shock and surprise. "Where did that damn dog go? I know I beat him to death." The young killer looked all around by the downed tree where he left Rusty for dead. "Dang, the stupid dog wasn't dead after all, or else he crawled off to die somewhere else."

He heard a loud whistle followed by the holler of a young girl calling her dog, "Rusty!"

"I've got to hide," he said to himself with an evil grin.

Chapter 16

Passing the Link farm and getting to the lane that went from there to Maple Road, the horse faltered in the front legs and almost went down. "Oh, please don't!" Cecil said as he somehow righted the horse back into his gallop. "You're okay," he said and reached down to pet his neck. "Just around the bend, and we'll be there." Soon the pair made their way into the gate to the sheep farm. Coming off the horse before he stopped, Cecil's feet hit the ground and finds out there's not much feeling in his legs. Trying to keep his balance, he quickly found himself flying forward and about to stick his chin in the dirt road. He tucked his chin down, turned his shoulder, and the next thing he knew, he had done a complete roll and was right back on his feet. Trying to stand as straight as he could, Cecil finally got the wire off the gate and led the soaking wet horse through.

As he got the saddle off and let it fall where they're standing, Cecil surveyed the cabin and then scanned the whole farm as best he could. Through the smoke from the chimney, Cecil noticed Millie's two sisters playing on the dam. Taking a deep breath, Cecil rubbed the horse's nose and noticed blood flowing from it. "It seems we made it in time," he said to the horse and led him to the spring for some fresh water.

"Cecil!" came a voice from the front of the cabin. "What are you doing here?" asked Millie's mother.

Cecil gave a quick explanation as not to scare her until he knew all of them were safe. He asked, "Where's Millie?"

"Gathering gooseberries and looking for Rusty" was her reply.

"Where's Rusty?" Cecil asked, looking back up the hill where the two girls were still playing.

"Not sure," she told him and asked for more information about last night.

"I'll tell you what," he said, "I'll go get Millie and tell you the whole story. By the way, have you seen anyone else here about?"

"No," Millie's mother said, "but we did see that fire yesterday morning as we were going into town. Thought it might be miners. It was just over there." She pointed to the northwest hill.

Cecil thought back to what the officer in charge told him about someone watching from the hills to know when the march left the town of Farmington. Getting the feeling back in his legs, Cecil ran back to where he took the saddle off and pulled the carbine rifle out of a scabbard. He told Millie's mother he would send Evelyn Rose and Mattie back and then go back to help Millie find Rusty.

* * *

"Rusty! Here, Rusty! Where you at, boy?" Millie hollered as she walked through the woods, getting closer to the fence by the oak.

The young renegade held stark-still behind the hickory tree between Millie and the big oak. Holding his musket rifle between himself and the hickory with an evil sneer on his face, he prided himself for knowing Millie would be coming to the big oak. Just getting ready to step out, a movement off to the side caught his attention.

"Rusty!" came the yell again as the girl got closer.

The sneer widened with evil as the young man thought, *This is just what I need to keep her from running.*

Just before Millie got to the hickory, she heard a whine coming from the left. As she veered off toward the sound, Millie spotted Rusty crawling on the ground. "Rusty!" she yelled, "What hap—"

"Stay where you are!" came a voice from behind.

Millie turned in an instant to see the young man she had been sheltering all spring. "What-what are you doing?" Millie asked in stark surprise. "What's wrong with my dog?"

"Shut up!" the young man said through gritted teeth and lowered his rifle directly at the dog. "Or I'll blow the damn beast in half! See what that mutt did to my leg!"

"He never did like you," Millie told him, holding her head high and looking him straight in the eyes. "I don't think I do either. What are you doing here anyway?"

"Well, sister—" he started to say.

Millie cut him off. "I'm *not* your sister!"

Looking back to meet Millie's stare, he said, "I will shoot that dog!"

"No! Please don't," she said and looked away while lowering her head.

"That's better," he told her with the evil grin returning on his face. "I'm here because I'm the one who warned the Confederates when these farming soldiers were coming."

Millie gave a quizzical look and, with eyebrows knitted together, said, "You're not making any sense. There's no Confederate soldiers around these parts."

"Well, maybe not!" he yelled back, causing spit to fly toward Millie's face. "Let me explain. I've been spying on your father and these soldier boys here in town. We may not be Confederate soldiers, but we're paid to cause trouble for you blue bellies. So when I knew they were leaving town, I rode north to my Uncle Sam's place." The young man did a little jig around Millie and with a snake-eating grin, continued, "He got his boys together and set up a little surprise for your precious soldier boys."

Millie's eyes widened, and a look of fear came to her face.

"Yeah, that's right!" he said, sticking his nose right in Millie's face. "We ambushed 'em just after they went to sleep. Probably killed them all."

With tears coming down toward Millie's trembling lips, a glaze formed over her eyes. Visions form of her father and Cecil in the parade of soldiers with smiles and waves coming her way. On the verge of passing out, she heard someone say in the distance, "Tell your dog to back off or I'll kill him!"

Trying to see, Millie made out through a black tunnel that Rusty had regained consciousness and was fiercely growling at the young man, who was aiming his rifle straight at the dog. Out of stark frozen fear, Millie found the strength to say, "No, Rusty, stay!"

This time, the dog didn't listen. With teeth bared and his hackles all raised down his back, Rusty ran full force to the man aiming the gun.

The tunnel lengthened. Millie felt her legs collapsing, and the last thing she heard was the loud report of a rifle just before everything went black.

Chapter 17

Hearing the voices of people talking, Millie refused to come out of her darkness and forced herself to hear nothing but the sound of her own voice. "Stay here," she said. "This is the safe place. Stay here."

Again, she heard a voice, and Millie's mind told her Cecil was calling her. *He's calling me from heaven,* she thought. *If I can find him, I'll find Father too, and maybe Rusty will be there. No, stay here, stay in the dark! Out there, they're all dead.* Sinking again into her darkness, Millie said in a very soft voice, "This is the safe place."

"Okay, everyone, I think it's time we just let her rest," said the town doctor. He looked at Millie's mother and said, "We've done all we can. I need to go back into town and tend to the young man Cecil shot."

Cecil looked up from the table in the gathering room where Mrs. Bell, Evelyn Rose, Mattie, and Cecil's parents were all watching the doctor and Millie's mother tend to Millie. Getting up and walking over to the makeshift cot that Millie was lying on, Cecil told the doctor, "The sheriff said he'd be lucky to make the ride into town. Said he'd be surprised if he was even still alive at all."

"Well, I still need to tend to him regardless," said the doctor. "It's my job." Looking over at Cecil's parents, Doc asked, "Mind if I ride back with you two? Cecil needs to stay here and try to get some rest. That must have been one hell of a ride." Then he said to the ladies, "Sorry, ma'am. I'd like to hear the whole story, but for now, I want you to drink some of this." Doc gave Cecil some white powder to mix with water and told him, "If you're taking Millie's mother to Bonne Terre tomorrow, you'll need to rest. So take it, okay?"

"Yeah, sure," said Cecil with hesitation.

Doc led Cecil to the door and whispered, "That medicine will give you the rest you need, and I'll tell you what, son." Doc put an arm around him and leaned nearer to his ear. "This family needs you real bad, and if you are not rested up, well, let's just say, it won't be good. Listen to me. I know what I am talking about."

Cecil nodded.

Doc gave him a wink and said as he and Cecil's parents were heading out the door, "The sooner, the better!"

As soon as Doc and the others left, Cecil drank down the powdered stuff and told Mrs. Bell, "Think I'll go check on the horse and see how—" Cecil reached for the door, but instead started falling sideways. Tennessee jumped up from the table to catch him from falling to the ground.

"Oh my!" said Millie's mother as she got up from Millie's side. "Let me help you."

Each woman placed a shoulder under his arm, and Millie's mother told Evelyn Rose to pull the covers down on the bed in the back bedroom. "Mattie," she said, "move this out of our way," with a stern "please!"

Looking over at Tennessee, the girls' mother said, "That must have been some powerful medicine!"

"I think the poor boy was on his last leg anyway. What a day he has had," remarked Tennessee.

Walking Cecil through the small hall, the pair finally got him to the bed. Letting him down as gently as they could, the girls' mother said, "From what I understand, it's been quite a couple of days."

Returning to Millie's side, Mother got a rag out of the bucket to wipe Millie's face, neck, and arms with some cool water. "I think you girls probably need to get some rest too," Mother said to Evelyn Rose and Mattie.

Before the two girls could say anything, Mrs. Bell told them, "Listen to your mother. She'd like some peace and quiet too. Give your mother and Millie a kiss good night, and I'll tuck you in bed."

After tucking the girls in, Tennessee came back to the room and gently laid a hand on Mother's shoulder, saying, "I'm going to run home and feed the hounds and make a quick check on things."

Mother patted the hand on her shoulder and told Tennessee, "You are a true friend. I just don't know what I'd do without you." Getting up to give Tennessee a hug, she whispered in her ear, "You're a friend we will always treat like family."

Tennessee stepped back, wiped her nose, and headed toward the door. Before going, Tennessee looked back and said, "You are my family. I will always treat you as my best friend."

Opening the front door, Tennessee said, "Well, would you look who's up and feeling better." Sitting there on his haunches on the big, flat rock porch was Rusty with his tongue hanging out and a big doggie grin on his face. Mother said, "Okay, just for a bit. Let him in."

Tennessee returned to the small cabin and helped make provisions for the night's stay. She made Mother a pallet on the floor so she could sleep next to Millie. "Rusty," she said, "I'm glad you are feeling better, but you can't stay in here."

As though he understood every single word, the poor dog walked with his head almost dragging against the floor toward the door. Gone was the tongue hanging out and that all too familiar doggie grin. Mrs. Bell opened the door and said quietly, "See you at daybreak, and enjoy your midnight snack." Lying there on the rock porch was a big chunk of cooked roast beef. Almost two pounds of pure heaven for a dog that's had an awful day. Giving the meat a sniff, Rusty looked up, and Tennessee said, "Yep, there it is. There's that silly grin of yours." She shut the door, and Rusty carried his treat off to his spot to enjoy.

Millie's mother got very little sleep, and the night passed oh so slowly. At every simple sound, she would look to see if there was a hint of movement out of Millie.

Mrs. Bell slept in Millie's bed, which gave the girls quite a treat. She told new stories from a land far away and a life completely different from what they knew. Though it didn't take very long for the girls to fall asleep, she thought the stories would take their minds off the awful happening of the day.

Just before daybreak, Mr. Highley, Cecil's Pa, and the reverend from their church came to check on the family, bringing with them some medicine for Millie along with instructions from the doctor. They also gave news that the young man that Cecil shot had survived the night and stood a chance to recover. The pastor of the church let Mother and Mrs. Bell know that Cecil's mother and some women from the church would soon be there with food and to help with chores.

Mother got an embarrassed look and protested about ladies coming because of the meager living conditions they had.

Mrs. Bell told Cecil's father where Cecil was and asked the reverend and Mr. Highley to step out for just a bit. Alone with Mother, Mrs. Bell told the worried woman that people were coming out of compassion and love. Tennessee said, "These people care about you and your family. Let them help."

"I know," said Mother, "but look at this shack we live in."

"Now shush!" said Tennessee and threw her arm around her. "This is the most beautiful and well-kept shack I've ever seen. They'll have more to say about you and your family's character than anything else. I do so admire you."

"Okay, let them come," said Mother, "but I'd like to move Millie into her bedroom where it would be a bit quieter."

CHAPTER 18

Just as the new day dawned and the first rays of daylight from the east brought its warmth through the window, a weak voice from the corner said, "If it would be all right, I would like to stay in here."

With a gasp, Mother threw both hands over her mouth and turned around to see Millie lying there with both eyes open and a faint smile. Mother ran to the bedside of her daughter. Her emotions got the best of her and she could barely speak. Sitting on the edge of the bed, Millie was raised into her mother's arms. With all the love they had for each other, they hugged, ever so gently rocking back and forth.

Mrs. Bell walked out onto the front porch where the three men were waiting and watching the sheep in the pasture as the night shadows disappeared with the new day. "Good news!" she said. "This morning has brought us good news! Millie is awake!" she exclaimed as she tried to calm herself.

The three men rushed to the door and stuck their heads in to see mother and daughter sitting on the makeshift bed hugging, crying, and rocking with joy.

Finally regaining enough composure, Mother told them all to come in and asked Mrs. Bell to wake the girls. She then told Cecil's father where Cecil had been sleeping so he could bring him in too.

After everyone was gathered around Millie and rejoicing as quietly as they could, the family's pastor asked to say a prayer. Millie and her mother both agreed as Millie reached out her hands to hold her mother's and Evelyn Rose's hand. Mother held Mrs. Bell's, and Evelyn

Rose held Mattie's. Everyone in the small cabin gathering room was holding hands, including a very drowsy Cecil, as the prayer was said.

A most wonderful prayer was said for Millie's return to the family and for the family's safety. Reality was brought back to them when the pastor prayed for their father and his safekeeping until he returned. Hands were gripped a little tighter at the closing of the prayer, and everyone said "Amen" in echo to the pastor.

The girls sat with Millie as Cecil's father and Mr. Highley talked to Mother and Cecil about leaving to go north to Bonne Terre and check on the girls' father.

"I have some business there," said Mr. Highley, "and Cecil's father is wanting to ride with him to see him off for a second time. Rumor in town is that Cecil might be some kind of a hero. We heard he saved a lot of lives."

"Well, it seems the family owes you a great deal of gratitude," Mother said to Cecil.

"Not me, ma'am," Cecil said. "It was only by the grace of God that got me back here when I did. Never knew I could ride a horse like that." With prideful pats on his back, he jokingly said, "I just hope I can walk right again someday."

Millie whispered something to Evelyn Rose, who jumped up and ran to their bedroom. Cecil walked to Millie's bedside and sat in the chair next to her. Taking a deep breath, he said, "I'm glad you're okay now."

Evelyn Rose returned with the box that had Cecil's gift in it. Millie opened the box and took out the shepherd's hair barrette. She handed the barrette to Cecil and asked, "I know my hair looks a mess, but would you mind?"

Feeling his face turn red, he placed the barrette in Millie's hair just when Mrs. Bell said, "Sounds like we got company."

Everyone went out to meet the ladies from the church, which gave Millie and Cecil a few seconds of private time. As everyone went out, Rusty rushed in. "Oh, I'm so glad to see you," Millie said as Cecil moved his chair over so the dog could be closer to Millie. Hugging the dog with one arm, Millie reached out with her other hand and took hold of Cecil's. "My two heroes!" she said. "I love you both!"

Goodbyes were said all over again as the ladies began bringing in their vittles for breakfast. Mrs. Bell tried to leave once, but Mother said, "No, not now." So she stayed awhile.

The pastor offered up a parting prayer and for the safe return of Millie's father. Millie found the strength to get up and go outside to see the menfolk off and to have a look at the horse that made the impossible trip. Under protest of everyone there, she found strength in the fresh air and sunshine.

Cecil brought the mighty warhorse to the back of the buckboard where he tied him off. As Millie approached, she asked, "Aren't you going to saddle him and ride him back?"

"If he's anywhere near as sore as I am," Cecil replied, "I'll just give him a break on this return trip. I'm only going to ride him to the mining town up north."

Millie let the horse smell her hand before she stroked his neck and said, "You're some fine horse. I can tell." Reaching under his neck with her other hand, Millie stroked both sides and lay her head against his thick muscular neck. "I have to thank you too," she told the mighty horse. "You're just like Rusty. I believe you understand things. I can see it in your eyes." Millie backed up just a bit and rubbed his soft pink nose with hers. "Hope you two get to stay together," she told Cecil. "I do believe there is a bond formed here."

"If that is to be, I'd love to go to a cavalry school," Cecil told her.

Mr. Highley told them both, "At least you've got a good start. We need to go. Daylight is burning."

The ladies and girls all waved 'bye to the three men as they headed out through the gate.

"Well, ladies," said Mother as she smiled and gave Mrs. Bell a wink, "welcome to my home. Let's all go in and get Millie back down so she can rest, and we can have ourselves a visit."

"Mom," came a voice from behind, and Evelyn Rose said, "Can me and Millie go get the gooseberries?"

"Not today," she said. "They'll have to wait a little longer."

Chapter 19

The following day around noon, Cecil's Pa and Mr. Highley returned with news of Millie's father, first telling the family about Cecil's departure first thing this morning and how he complained with every jolt the horse made. "Thought I heard him say to the horse," said Cecil's father, "'So you're going to get even with me.'"

Everyone laughed, but Mr. Highley could tell Mother wanted to know about her husband, and he hated to give her his news.

"Why don't we go inside," said Mr. Highley. "If you have some of that sweet spring water, we'll sit, and I'll explain."

Mother nervously started wiping her hands on her apron, and with a quiver in her voice, expecting the worst, she said, "Yes, let's go inside. Millie, would you please get the glasses down for our guests?"

Once inside, Mother could see that Cecil's Pa and Mr. Highley were very nervous and wouldn't say anything while the two younger girls were there. So, under the girls' protest, Mother sent Evelyn Rose and Mattie out to do their daily chores in the garden. "No fussing!" she said. "You need to get it done before the day gets too hot. Now go, and I better not hear any fighting!"

"Thank you," said Mr. Highley and then looked at Cecil's Pa with a look that said, "Do you want to tell them the news?"

"There's no way of really sugarcoating this," Cecil's Pa told them, "but"—he looked at Mother—"your husband's been shot just below the knee. The bone was somewhat shattered, and he has lost a lot of blood—"

Mr. Highley cut in to say, "He's in a place that the Mining Company built that's sorta like a hospital."

"Is my father going to lose his leg?" Millie burst in, trying to get the two men to hurry up.

"What about doctors?" Mother asked.

"There are two doctors there," Mr. Highley said. "As a matter of fact, the company pays them to take care of the miners and their families." Mr. Highley looked at Millie and told her, "They are not sure if he will lose his leg or not."

"The doctors cleaned his leg and took out bone slivers as best they could," said Cecil's Pa. "These doctors are young, and they really seem to know what they are doing."

Millie got up for some more water and asked if anyone else wanted any. "Yes, sure," said Mr. Highley as he held his glass up. Then he continued, "Both doctors agreed if infection didn't set in, he would more likely keep his leg."

By the look on his face, Mother knew there was more. "Go on," she said. "Tell me the rest."

"Well, all right," said Cecil's Pa. "If your husband doesn't lose his leg, he will always need some kind of a crutch. He will always have a limp."

"Does he know this?" inquired Mother as she got out of her chair and walked over to look out the window.

"I'm afraid so," Mr. Highley said.

"Not much of a life for a man who cuts timber and farms all day," she said, still staring out the window.

"No, ma'am, it's not," came a voice from behind her.

"He needs me, doesn't he?" she said, bowing her head and looking at her folded hands.

Cecil's Pa walked over to her and said, "He's mighty depressed. Yes, he needs you really bad."

"Millie," Mother said, "call the girls in. We'll all go see your father."

"Well, wait a minute," said Mr. Highley. "I've got a man going back tomorrow for supplies I ordered. Why don't you go with him?"

"Yeah," said Cecil's Pa, "and we can load your wagon up, and the girls can stay with our family. Cecil is gone, and my kids would love the company."

Seeming to be about the only way, the plans for Mother to leave and the three girls were all placed in order. Mrs. Bell would keep close watch on the small farm while Mr. Highley and Cecil's Pa would take turns bringing Millie out to check on things. With a bit of help from some other friends and neighbors, Mother almost felt comfortable about leaving.

Mother gave the girls strict instructions about what to do and what not to do. "I might not be back for two weeks," she told them. "So you mind Millie, okay? And, Millie, do be patient with your sisters."

The rest of the day after Mr. Highley and Cecil's Pa left, Mother, Millie, Evelyn Rose, and Mattie gathered their things to stay in town. Millie led the milk cow and the calf up the road to Mrs. Bell's home. Millie explained everything to Mrs. Bell and told her that she and Rusty would be by to check on the sheep and their home. "I'm just glad this is the first of May. There is plenty of grass from the spring rains, and it is not yet too hot."

"Yep," replied Mrs. Bell. "This is the one time, though it be short, that the outdoors pretty well takes care of itself. Hay season is movin' in fast, and it will get hot."

Getting ready to leave, Millie unexpectedly threw her arms around Mrs. Bell and said, "I love you. Thanks," as she bounded off the big front porch with Rusty in tow.

Mrs. Bell watched the pair go past the tied-up hounds and watched Millie turn her head and wave. Mrs. Bell waved back and softly said, "I love you too, you little whippersnapper."

Mother and her daughters leave the small sheep ranch early the next morning. They met Cecil's family at Mr. Highley's livery stable so Ole Smokey would have a place to be kept and taken care of. Mr. Highley introduced Mother to his employee who would be taking her to the Bonne Terre area. The three girls got reacquainted with Cecil's brother and sisters, and everything seemed fine until the driver said, "We need to go, ma'am!" Through the tears, they all said their goodbyes, and the girls remind their mother to give father the gifts and letters they made for him. Cecil's Pa, at the last second, handed Mother an envelope and whispered to her, "A gift from the church. You're going to need it."

Mother looked to the side as if embarrassed. She said with thankfulness, "You didn't need to—"

He cut her off, tipping his hat to her, saying, "But we want to." He took off his big hat and slapped one of the two horses on the rump and said, "Get up there, horse." As the wagon jerked, Mother grabbed the armrest with one hand and her bonnet with the other then waved 'bye to her family.

Standing there in the middle of the street with a sister hugging her on each side, Millie put an arm around them and said, "We'll be fine. I just hope they are."

For Millie, Evelyn Rose, and Mattie, the days went by fast, but the nights dragged by ever so long. Thoughts of their parents' absence and being away from their three-room cabin, playing and working with the farm animals, and being kept busy with their daily chores brought on a nighttime melancholy that made it difficult to sleep.

Chapter 20

To the north lay a different kind of melancholy, one full of fear and of loss. Fear of not being able to do the things he knew how and not being the man he once was. A melancholy that brought on contempt and rejection as Mother found out on her first visit to see her husband.

Being warned by the two doctors before her initial visit but still shocked by the angry and remorseful attitude, Mother did her best to keep her husband calm and to find the peace he needed to bring their family together once more.

After a few days, the doctors had a talk with Mother and informed her there was no more fear of infection setting in her husband's leg. That being the good news, they then explained the mending process. Changing bandages was not the difficult part but keeping him calm and at the same time having him do certain things to strengthen his body. In about two months, he would have to go through a rehabilitation process and learn to walk with a crutch or, if lucky, a cane. The most important thing was for him to find his will to live. With that all being said and more, the two doctors told Mother they thought the best thing for him would be to go home. The love of his family may be about the only thing that could help, and perhaps friends would give him encouragement. It would just take time for both ailments to heal.

After more instructions on the care of his leg, the doctors explained that perhaps after some healing, he could go to St. Louis to have surgery to correct the damage and help him to walk better. The two doctors left Mother to her thoughts so she could decide to move her husband or wait a while.

Feeling the effects of depression herself, Mother decided to leave the next day. *This family has been apart too long,* she thought to herself. She let the doctors know her plans, and they helped her prepare for the journey south. Mother paid the doctors and hired a man to make a slow two-day journey home with the money she received from her church.

Evening storms brought cooler temperatures the first day. Though the road was pretty soggy and rutted out, the three made it to an inn just south of the St. Joe mining town of Flat River. Per the doctors' recommendations, they made an overnight stay in the town of Flat River before continuing to Farmington so Father could rest. Being the middle of the week, very few people were at the inn, and all went well until Mother and Father were ready to leave before daylight. It seemed the hired driver had quite a night and left them with a large bar bill. Mother paid the bar bill and had the hired driver thrown into the baggage area of the small coach. She drove the rest of the way home herself.

Father took notice of how well his wife was able to handle the situation. Feeling less a man, he told her, "I always admired Mrs. Bell and her ability to run a farm by herself."

"She does a great job," she replied to her husband. "I think Tennessee has an inner strength that drives her to keep going. But I'm not sure where it comes from."

"I do," he said, "and I can see it in you too."

Mother stopped the coach dead in the center of the road. She hopped off and went around to the back and grabbed the hungover man by the collar and dragged him to the ground. She then got a dead limb from under a nearby tree and threatened to waylay the tire out of him. She said, "You can pick your horse and coach up at the Highley Livery Stable in town. You'll pay the keep on your horse and can only have him back when you pay your liquor bill from last night. You cost me an extra twenty dollars, which I didn't really have. If you don't..." She raised the club as to strike him in the head.

"No, please don't!" he begged.

Mother got back in the coach and turned back to look at the man. "Enjoy your walk to town," she said and threw the club down.

The husband and wife rode in silence until they were just in sight of their home. Mother brought the horse to a stop on the hill where Maple Road made a left to go into town. Off to the right and a bit to the north was the Links' place. On ahead and to the south was the Bell cattle farm. In the holler in between the two farms lay the small sheep farm with a small log cabin at its forefront. The two looked upon the hills in the west and northwest and saw the valley that sat to the back of their large field dotted with grazing snow-white sheep.

Mother took a deep breath and said, "Yes, I am a bit like Tennessee Bell. I've had a year to prepare for this journey. I'm not like her as in one day her husband was killed, but I have learned to harden myself so I could run the farm with the help of the girls while you were away. Look out there! Look really close and see how beautiful this place is. Everything you see out there is made by your hands and your will. I'll tell you right now, right here that this place and this family will not survive if you don't have the will to make it happen. Don't let this"—she pointed to his leg—"affect what is in here." She pointed to his heart. "Now you tell me, do I take you home and we hold tight to each other all night, or do I turn here and go get the girls?" She firmly placed her hands with the reins in her lap and stared straight ahead.

With tears streaming down the sides of his face, Father stared for a long minute. While staring at her firm beauty, he finally said in a soft voice, "Take me home."

Sitting a little taller and still staring straight ahead, she smiled back at her husband. "Get up, horse!" she said as she shook her hands and slapped the reins on the horse's back. "Take us home!"

Having a bite to eat after some of the most wonderful intimate time locked in each other's embrace, Father asked, "Where'd all the food come from?"

"We have friends," Mother told him. "Good friends because they all know you're a good man. So when there's an offer of help, how about you swallow a little bit of pride and thank the Good Lord for the friends we have."

Father reached out and took his wife's hand and enfolded it into both of his. "Friends are really nice," he said, "but I thank the Good Lord for you."

For fear of a setback, Mother chose her words carefully and pulled his hand toward her lips and said, "There's some news I need to tell you."

"Yes," he said, "good news, I hope."

"The Lord above," she continued, "has truly blessed this family if we look back from where we began."

He smiled then laughed a tender laugh and said, "I never would have dreamed in these short years, we'd be where we are now. You do know I always did say a man's wealth didn't lie in how much money he had, but in the family he raised and their character."

Mother took her other hand and placed a finger over her husband's lips and in her small voice said, "Yes, and it is so true for those beliefs we both hold so dear. I believe God is going to bless this family a little more and make us richer for it." She brought her finger down and tenderly smiled as their hands were entwined together.

Father stared and then blinked once, then twice. He started to speak but left his mouth slightly open as if searching for a word.

What word? she wondered as she tried to read his face. *Say it or at least give me an expression.* It's as if time stood still, and Mother wondered if all creation had come to a halt. She began to say something, but in an instance, he lightly squeezed her hands as if to say, "Don't, not yet." He gently caressed her face and then held on to her to stand. They gently embraced, and at that moment, she knew he understood, and all would be well.

Early the next morning, Mother rose from bed to get breakfast going. She decided to stop outside first and take in the sights and sounds and smells of an early morning just before daylight. Looking to the east, she could see the morning stars in the dark night sky, just above the hint of blue sky that was right above the rising red morning sun. She prayed out loud, "Lord, give him a son." To herself, she said, "I sure miss my girls."

After breakfast, Mother changed the bandages on Father's leg. Not sure how it's supposed to look, she noticed a bad smell. She made a mental note to ask the town doctor to come and have a look to make sure the healing process was going right. After boiling the bandages, she sprinkled a little sulfur on the wound and then wrapped the leg with the sterilized bandages. "How's that?" she asked Father.

"That's good!" he replied. "It's every bit as good as a doctor." Pulling the covers up around his shoulders, he told her, "That trip home really took it out of me. I'm feeling a little chilly."

Taking a cloth, she soaked it in a bowl of cool water and placed it on his forehead. She explained that she's going to take the horse and coach to the livery stable and get Ole Smokey and their wagon. Knowing how he felt, she asked, "Should I bring the girls home today?"

"Oh, yes, do bring them home," he said. "But I really don't want any company. Is that bad of me to say?"

Looking down on her husband, she smiled and told him, "I'm sure they will understand. I will hurry. Don't be surprised if Mrs. Bell stops by though. She'll probably see the smoke coming out of the chimney." Going out the doorway, she turned back and saw that her husband had fallen asleep. Creeping back to his bedside, she bent down and kissed his forehead. With a concerned frown, she whispered, "I'll hurry."

As Mother got the horse and coach ready to leave, she noticed the eerie silence of a missing family. She got the horse and coach through the gate. As she stopped to close the gate, she surveyed the homeland and said to herself, "It may be a beautiful place, but it's not home without the family."

Chapter 21

Arriving at the livery stable, Mother saw the driver pacing back and forth and talking very fast. Mr. Highley was holding his hat in one hand and scratching his head with the other while the sheriff just watched them both.

Seeing Mother, the driver from Bonne Terre yelled, "That's her, and that's my horse and coach!"

She got down off the coach before Mr. Highley could lend a hand and said to the out-of-towner, "Did you pay Mr. Highley?"

"Sheriff!" he yelled. "That's the woman who stole my horse and coach. Are you gonna arrest her?"

Before the sheriff could say anything, Mother walked directly into the livery stable and to a barrel of handles. Picking out an ax handle, she turned and started walking straight to the man that owed her money.

Mr. Highley told the man cowering behind the sheriff, "Mister, after what this lady has been through, you better think twice before you say anything else."

The four of them stood in shame. Mother with her ax handle beside Mr. Highley and the hired driver cowering behind the sheriff. Finally, the hired driver reached into his pocket and stuck his hand out from behind the sheriff and said, "This is all I have." He places what money he had left in her hand.

Mother didn't count the money. She took a couple of the bills, gave them back, and said, "I'm not a woman without compassion. Take it and go!"

The driver placed the bills in his pocket and walked away thinking about what just transpired. He walked to his horse and pets him on the nose, acting like he was checking him for injury. Finally, he stood up and nodded his head a couple of times. He saw the sheriff walking across the street to the jailhouse and Mr. Highley carrying the ax handle back to the livery stable. He looked toward the woman with a look of concern and compassion on her face. "I'm sorry," he said. "I'm truly sorry, and I'll never forget this." He tipped his hat, and she smiled back as he left town.

Watching the young man leave and hoping he learned a lesson, Mother straightened her dress and made sure her hair was in place. She entered the livery stable and saw Ole Smokey in the stall. Mother walked over to Mr. Highley and said, "We're home, and I've come to settle with you on Ole Smokey's keep."

"I'm glad you folks made it back," he told her. "As far as a bill, you just paid it."

"Well, I'm not sure what you mean," she said.

"Seeing the way you handled that fella was worth the price of admission," he said with a big smile and shoved the ax handle into the barrel. "I just got to ask though. Would you have—?"

Smiling back at Mr. Highley, she said, "He has no idea how close he came to getting hit. I was just hoping I wasn't going to hit the sheriff with a bad swing."

They both laughed. Mother then told him all about her husband and asked how the girls were doing. An employee got Ole Smokey hitched up to the wagon, and she tipped the young man for his help. As she left to get the girls, she said to Mr. Highley, "Don't be a stranger, come visit sometime!"

As she approached Cecil's parents' home, Mother spotted the girls in the back by the barn. Feeling the excitement of seeing the girls, she decided to first talk to Cecil's mother, figuring Cecil's father was working at the store. Mother accepted the invite to enter the home, and the two ladies briefly talked about the situation with her husband. Mother inquired about how the girls have been.

Feeling the need to return home, the three girls were called in along with Cecil's brother and sisters. The girls were elated to see their mother and asked many questions. Mother explained that they needed to hurry home, and in no time, the girls and Mother were on their way home.

Mother decided to make a stop at the doctor's office and asked him to come out as soon as possible to check on her husband. The doctor advised Mother that he had several patients in town to tend to and it might be tomorrow evening before he could come out.

He told her about a retired doctor who lived just on the edge of town going out the Columbia Road. He recommended that she go to his house and see if he could tend to Father. "It's the big house on the left," he said. "You can't miss it."

Mother, Millie, Evelyn Rose, and Mattie sat close together as Ole Smokey's nose headed west and out of town. They passed the county jail. Millie told her mother how the place gave her the creeps knowing her attempted kidnapper was in there.

Mother placed her right arm through Millie's left arm and said, "It's been a bad couple of weeks for everyone. I just hope things make a turn for the better. Lord only knows we need it." Millie lay her head on her mother's shoulder, and Evelyn Rose and Mattie put their arms around the two of them from behind the wagon seat.

With a happy sigh, Mother smiled and said to herself, "It's good to be home." She looked to the sky and said a silent "Thank you."

The wagon full of girls pulled up to the big two-story house. "Hey! I know this place!" Millie told her mother. "This is where Father brought me to help with the slaves from the South."

Mother leaned over and quietly said in Millie's ear, "Yes, it is, but you don't want everyone else to know it." She nodded her head toward the back of the wagon and said, "Young ears are listening, and you just never know if there is company here."

As the horse stopped and they prepared to get down, Millie hunkered her head between her shoulders and said, "Sorry, Mother."

"That's okay," Mother told Millie, "but you need to stay here with the girls. I won't be long."

A few minutes later, Mother stuck her head out the door and yelled, "Would you girls like something to drink?"

Evelyn Rose and Mattie bounded off the wagon and ran past Millie to the front porch to join their mother. Their eyes were as big as saucers and about to burst with excitement. Mother calmed them down and explained, "You say hello and sit in your chairs. Don't get up. Don't touch anything, and only speak when you're spoken to."

Trying to worm her way past the others just to look inside, Mattie said, "Okay, Mother."

"Mattie, please," Mother said, "have some patience too."

A man and woman came to greet the girls. When they saw the girls, the old man said, "Well, I'll be."

The heavyset woman jerked her hands up and slapped them on her cheeks and said, "If it isn't Millie. It is good to see you again." She walked over and gave Millie a hug. She reached out and pulled her sisters in for a group hug. "My, my, my," she said, "you have the most beautiful girls I've ever seen."

"Why, thank you," Mother replied.

"You girls are the spittin' image of your mother," she said while placing them in height order. "Now, Millie—I know, and your mother—I know, but you two must tell me your names. Here, let's go in and sit at the table so I can get to know you." Bending over and looking at Mattie, she whispered in her ear just loud enough for Evelyn Rose to hear, "We'll have some sweet bread too."

Walking into a parlor room, the girls all had a seat at the table, and the old man said to Mother, "While you all get acquainted, I'll go get my things and get the horse ready to go."

Millie turned to look at the man and said, "Are you a doctor?"

"Yes, I am, or let me say, I used to be," he told her. "But now I'm kinda retired."

His wife laughed and said, "He's a doctor, and doctors never retire. Maybe slow down some but not retire. It's kinda like asking a dog not to bark at a stranger. It's what they do."

Mother said with concern, "I am very grateful."

He smiled at all the ladies and told them, "Don't be long. If possible, I'd like to be home before dark." Then he went out the back door.

Millie said with an embarrassed look on her face, "I thought he was the butler."

The lady of the house laughed again, and with a wink at Millie, she said, "That was quite a night, wasn't it?"

After a cool drink and some sweet bread, Mother apologized for the rush. The doctor's wife understood Mother's wish to get back to her husband and told the girls they had an open invitation to come visit anytime. Looking at Evelyn Rose, she said, "I know your older sister has a lot of farm chores to take care of, but if you'd like and your mother wouldn't mind, I could use someone like you to help keep this big old house clean for me."

Evelyn Rose, in shock, tried to find some words to say, but nothing came out of her mouth.

"I'd pay you, of course," the lady said and smiled at her.

Without looking, Evelyn Rose reached back for her mother and said, "Mother?"

Mother reached and took hold of her hand and patted it, saying, "We'll discuss it later with your father, okay?" Then she said to the doctor's wife, "Thank you, ma'am" and backed out the front door with her girls in tow.

They waved 'bye to the kind lady of the house while her husband, the doctor, followed them out the path and onto Columbia Road.

With the girls anxious to get home, Mother settled Ole Smokey into a smooth trot while the doctor galloped along on his horse behind them. Soon they passed by Mrs. Tennessee Bell's farm and waved to the redbone hounds as they passed. "Next stop," Mother yelled, "will be home!" Rusty greeted them all at the gate, and Millie flew off the wagon to let Ole Smokey through followed by the good doctor.

"Go on!" she told Mother and the doctor. "I'll shut the gate and be right there." With a wave, they headed to the cabin.

Missing her father something fierce but knowing he needed to see the doctor first, Millie decided to give each horse a fresh bucket of water. Finishing up, Millie raced to the cabin just as Evelyn Rose and

Mattie were made to come outside. Mother told them, "Why don't you all take Rusty and check on the sheep?"

The three girls stood on the flat rock porch staring at their mother with concern on their faces.

"Father's fine," she said. "The doctor just wants to maybe clean some infection out of the wound."

"Then why can't we come in to see Father!" cried Evelyn Rose.

"Well," Mother said, "your father has this thing about him called pride." She bent down to be eye level with the girls and whispered, "He doesn't want you to hear him if it hurts."

Mattie huffed up and said, "That man better not hurt my father!"

"No, no!" Mother replied. "It's like when you have a splinter in your finger and it hurts something terrible and even hurts worse when I pick it out. Just like that, only maybe a little bigger."

"Oh, poor Father," said Mattie. "I guess you're right. I don't like nobody to see me cry either."

The girls left, and Rusty went with them to the upper field. Mother got fresh water for the doctor.

After a little more than an hour, the old doctor told the injured man's wife that it wasn't near as bad as he thought it might have been. "You did the right thing though," he explained. "There was a small piece of bone that was left in his leg when the other doctors cleaned it out, and it was festering around it. Easy to do when a bone is shattered like that."

Mother thought of the splinter and then thanked the doctor for checking on her husband.

"This healing is going to take time," the old doctor told her. "You have to keep him down, but if he gets up, have him sit with his leg elevated. Give him this for pain." He gave her some white powder to mix with water and said, "Make sure he gets plenty of fresh water. If he can sit in the sun, that will make him feel better. I'll be by every so often to check on him." Looking over his glasses, he gave her a kind smile, took her hand, and said, "He'll be fine. What about you? How are you doing?"

She tried to pull her hand back, but the doctor wouldn't let go. "Tell me," he said.

Mother sat down, and the kind old doctor sat across from her at the table. She told the doctor all that had been going on. He already knew most of it, but he listened to her with concern. She then let him know about her expecting another child. "I'm trying to be happy, but every time I do, something goes wrong," she told him and began to cry. Sobbing and heaving, Mother apologized to the doctor.

"It's okay. Let it all out, my dear," he said consoling her.

The doctor got her a fresh drink of water, sat back down, and said, "Your husband is going to be fine. He'll have bouts of depression, but that will go away." He leaned back in his chair and folded his arms and continued, "Now your oldest daughter may take a little longer. She hides it so well, I can tell. Right now, she is occupied with you, her father, and the farm, but she's at that age that feels the burden will all be on her."

Mother wiped the tears with a clean dishrag, took a deep breath and a drink, and said, "It's been a tough row to hoe for her."

"Do you feel a little better, now?" he asked.

"As a matter of fact," she replied, "I do some."

"Don't be afraid to cry, and don't hold it back. What Millie needs is to learn to laugh again. You and her need to be close friends and find a way to laugh together. Best medicine for the both of you."

Mother nodded her head while biting her bottom lip and told the doctor, "I do understand, and we'll do our best."

"Okay then," he said and stood. "Anything else before I leave?"

She thought about it, shook her head no, and said, "Not really, I guess not," as she thought about it again.

"Fine," he replied in his authoritative voice. "Everyone is going to be fine. Gather your strength from one another. I admire your family's love and devotion to each other. It's a great asset. Now I must be on my way if I want to be home before dark."

Mother got to her feet and walked the doctor to the door. "How much do I owe you?" she asked.

"You know what I'd like more than anything?" he said while looking up the hill where the girls were.

"What might that be?" Mother questioned.

"I noticed you've got a churn and I'm guessing a milk cow," he said.

"Why, yes, we do," she said with a puzzled look.

"When your Evelyn Rose comes to help madam with the house, how about she brings some fresh butter with her?" the good doctor said with a look of "The sooner, the better."

"I'll even pay you for it!"

"No, you won't pay for the butter," she said with finality. "Do you like honey churned in the butter?"

The doctor's eyes grew big as he said, "Oh, you bet I do. I'd love that!"

"Fine," she said. "Consider it done."

Saying their farewells, the fine old doctor reassured Mother of the well-being of her family. He waved 'bye to the girls as they came running. Millie met him at the gate to let him out. As he passed her, the doctor tipped his hat and told Millie, "You've got the best-looking sheep in the whole county. Good luck with them!"

Closing the gate, it dawned on Millie, and she hollered back, "Hey! I got the only sheep in the county!"

Millie heard the doctor let out a laugh, and without looking back at her, he took off his hat and waved it high in the air. The girls watched him disappear around the bend going toward Mrs. Bell's place.

Turning back toward the cabin first, Mattie let her sisters know she wanted to see her father but was passed by as the other girls raced in front of her. "Not fair!" she yelled but was soon in line with the others as Mother explained all about Father's situation. Today they could only see him for a few minutes, then they must let him rest.

"Tomorrow will be better," Mother told them. "When you are done, I need you girls to go get the milk cow from Mrs. Bell. Think you can do that for me?"

They all agreed, but Mother said, "Not you, Millie, I need your help here. Do you two think you can go by yourselves?"

Feeling big and grown-up, Evelyn Rose and Mattie told their mother yes and that they would be very careful.

"Good!" said Mother. "Now you can go see your father." With a finger pointing straight up, she added, "Go very, very quietly."

Very quietly, the three girls left the gathering room, tiptoed past their room, and noticed it was just as they left it. They entered the room where Father was in bed, sleeping. Standing in silence, Mattie finally reached out and patted her father's arm. She was startled when Father reached up and weakly took her hand and held it in his.

With his speech a little slurred, Father said, "My girls, I've been wondering where you've been." All the girls reached out to touch their father's hand. He smiled as each took turns to kiss him on the cheek. Mother made them leave the room so that he could rest.

"What's wrong?" Evelyn Rose asked with tears streaming down her cheeks.

"It's the medicine," Mother explained. "The medicine lets your father rest and not be in so much pain."

Drying her tears with her hand, Evelyn Rose said, "Will he get better?"

"Yes, sure he will," Mother told the girls, being strong for them. "Now come on. Let's all go to the table, and we will talk there."

Mother explained to the girls what the doctor had done and how it would take time for the wound to heal. "Now how about that milk cow," Mother said. "You two think you can lead her back home?"

"Yes, we can do it," Evelyn Rose said.

"We both can," Mattie said as she went to stand next to her sister.

"Millie," Mother said, "would you go with them to make sure they have the right halter and lead rope?"

"Okay," she told her mother. The three girls went out to the open-ended barn where the animals were kept.

Mother yelled from the door, "But, Millie, I need you to come back in as soon as possible."

Millie waved her hand to indicate she heard her and turned while walking backward, saying, "I'll be right there!"

Getting the girls what they needed and explaining how to lead the cow home, Millie walked her sisters to the gate and said, "One word of advice, if something scares Bessie and she tried to run, don't hold on. Just let her go. She'll be okay, and we'll get her when she calms down. Oh, and be sure not to wrap the rope around your hand." She gave the girls a stern look to make sure they understood, and they indicated they did. Off they ran to Mrs. Bell's farm.

Before going back to her mother, Millie took care of Ole Smokey since he had had a chance to cool down. She led him to his stall, and he enjoyed the hay and grain that Millie gave him. She used the currycomb to remove some of the debris from the horse's coat. As she brought in a bucket of fresh water, she said to the horse, "You deserve a good rest for the rest of the day. That was quite a run Mother put you through to get home." Millie lay her head into the neck of Ole Smokey and softly said to herself, "I'm just so glad we are all home. Thank You, Lord." Walking out of the shed, she looked to the sky, smiled, and headed back to the cabin and her mother.

Millie and Mother chatted a little and agreed that they both need to work as one and not let just one person carry the burden for the family. Agreeing how most things will get better once Father could let them know what needed to be done, Mother poured Millie another cup of hot tea with honey in it. "There's one more thing we need to talk about," Mother said.

Millie furled her eyebrows and said, "Can I guess what?"

"Well, if you want," Mother replied. "Go ahead."

Millie unfurls her eyebrows, and a soft smile covered her face as she said, "You're going to have a baby!"

"How did you know that?" Mother probed.

"I wasn't for sure, but when you had one more thing to talk about," Millie said, "I put two and two together with what Father was mumbling about when he mentioned something about a boy."

"So what do you think?" Mother asked.

"I think it's great!" she replied. "I am surprised though. You know, a happy surprise. Can't wait for the girls to know, especially Mattie."

"It'll be like a baby doll to her," Mother said. "You know how she's always playing house with rag dolls and acting like their mommy."

"Yeah, she's funny sometimes." Millie then asked as she measured the table with her arms, "So when is all this going to happen?"

"Midwinter, first of the year," she replied. "Doctor says maybe around Christmas, and don't you worry about the space. If we have another good year, we'll have a larger place up north like we planned."

Millie laughed a lighthearted laugh and said, "I'm not worrying. We can always add on here if we have to."

"I suppose," Mother said. "If Mr. Highley would allow it. But I don't want to worry about that. It's down the road a piece. Let's just take care of what's at hand, all right?" Mother got up and wiped the table off with one hand and reached out with the other to give Millie's arm a loving shake.

Millie agreed and got up to help clean but instead told her mother the girls should be back soon, and she should probably watch for them.

Mother agreed, but to Millie's surprise, she said, "Let me check on your father, then we will both go watch while we do a little work in the garden." Knowing how Millie felt about garden work, she gave her a big grin and told her, "We don't want the weeds getting ahead of us, do we?"

Their garden consisted of corn, pole beans, squash, pumpkins, turnips, potatoes, and tomatoes. Millie got the hoe and rake out of the lean-to shed while she grumbled to Rusty all the way to garden. Like anything on a farm, you hate to get started, but once you are doing the work, it doesn't seem near as bad and always has a rewarding feeling.

As Millie and Mother got into a good rhythm of work, Rusty started barking, and they could see the girls leading Bessie down the road while Mrs. Bell was following behind. The girls begin waving, which caused Bessie to jerk her head and pull the lead rope out of Mattie's hand. Evelyn Rose didn't let go, so Bessie settled back into her lazy walk as if nothing had happened. Mrs. Bell wiped her hand across her forehead as if to say, "Whoa! That was close!"

After Bessie was let loose to graze, Mrs. Bell greeted the girls' mother with a hug. Millie got fresh water from the spring so they all could have a cool drink.

Taking advantage of Millie's help in the garden, Mother had Evelyn Rose get Mrs. Bell one of the logs by the lean-to so she could sit in the shade and visit while they worked. About an hour later, Mother told Mrs. Bell, "I do wish you could come by more—just look at all the weed-pulling and hoeing we get done."

"That's 'cause Millie helped today!" Evelyn Rose exclaimed.

"No, no, I don't think so," said Mother. "I think it's 'cause you girls don't stand and complain when we have a guest."

Calling it a day, and what a day it had been, Mother and the younger girls gathered around Mrs. Bell with a log of their own to sit in the evening shade by the cool spring. Millie decided it's time for her and Rusty to check on the sheep since they moved off to the back pasture.

Chapter 22

Making it past the pond, Millie started through the gap but stopped to gaze out across the small back field. She thought to herself how this was one of her most favorite times of the year. The oak and hickory trees were in full leaf, and the pollen had quit floating in the air. The cool breeze came from the valley and was funneled through the gap because of the two hills from the west and Mrs. Bell's woods to the east. The Missouri summer humidity hadn't hit just yet and made it feel even better. She could tell the lambs were enjoying this time of year by the way they danced and pranced all over the place, never wandering too far from their mother.

Making her way down the fence row toward the big oak tree that's on this side of the fence, Millie stopped and took a look at what also made this time of the year special. On the west side of the woods where there were dead oak trees and ash trees grew the most wonderful, best-tasting morsels ever to be had. Going through the fence to where she spotted the Missouri treasure, she first looked for snakes. She bent down and started pinching off the famed morel mushrooms. "Oh, Rusty!" she said out loud. "Would you look at all these mushrooms. You watch for snakes while I pick." She picked until she filled her shirt full. "I bet I've got close to thirty here," she told the dog. "Father's gonna be so happy." Not spotting any more mushrooms, she told Rusty, "I'd like to stay and watch the sun set, but maybe we can get home in time to give Mrs. Bell a mess for her supper."

She walked as fast as she could back the same way she came without dropping any mushrooms. Some people called them Missouri gold. The sheep watched as Millie worked her way past the pond and down the hill toward the small cabin. Halfway down, she spotted her mother letting Mrs. Bell out the gate, so she began to yell for them to wait. Not getting any response, Millie knelt and placed her treasure on the ground. She then placed her two index fingers on the tip of her tongue and pushed back into her mouth. She pressed her lips over her teeth and lightly bit down just past her fingernail, took a deep breath, and let out a whistle that could be heard halfway to town.

Evelyn Rose and Mattie raced outside from the cabin. Bessie let out a bawl, and Mother and Mrs. Bell turned to look up the hill. Millie waved her arms, and when she saw that Mrs. Bell was not going through the gate, she gathered her treasured morsels and quickly made her way to the garden area. Mother, Mrs. Bell, and her sisters met her there to see what Millie was so excited about.

"Oh my!" said Mrs. Bell. "These and some spring onions fried with steak! Well, it doesn't get much better!"

Millie divvied up the tasty treats. Mrs. Bell took enough for her supper and headed home trying to beat the setting sun.

"You think these mushrooms will make Father feel better?" Millie asked.

"I don't know," Mother replied. "But I do know it won't make him feel worse. It's just a shame we don't have a couple of squirrels to go with them."

"Hey, I know," Millie said. "It's too late now, but if I find some more, we'll catch a couple of catfish from the pond for a real treat."

"Can I go fishing with you?" Mattie cried out.

"You bet," Millie answered. "Just don't get burned like you did the last time."

Mattie made a big frown, shook her head, and said, "Oh no! I don't ever want to do that, never again."

Mother laughed and asked the two younger girls, "Would you two bring in some fresh water, and, Millie, behind the holding pen is some wild poke greens. How about picking a mess for supper?"

"Oh boy!" she said and rolled her eyes.

"What! What's that all about?" Mother asked as she turned her back to keep Millie from seeing her laugh.

"You know what that is all about." Millie laughed as she left the flat rock porch. "Fresh mushrooms, fresh poke greens, and we'll all be loose as a goose!"

"Millie, I'll swear," Mother said. "Now go while I check on your father. Oh, and tell your sisters to bring that jar of butter out of the spring please."

Millie did as her mother asked. Mother went to check on how Father might be doing. Softly saying out loud and to herself, "I hope he's awake and feeling like sitting up."

With enough light coming through the window, Mother could see he was still asleep. She felt his forehead for fever. His eyes remained shut, but he said, "Wow, don't know what that medicine was the doctor gave me, but I feel like a new man."

"You might, but you just lay still while I clean you up a bit," his wife told him. "Then we will get you to the table for a fresh mess of morel mushrooms."

"Oh!" he said. "I'd crawl on my belly to get some of those. Where'd they come from?"

His wife told him all about the afternoon they had after the old doctor left and how Millie helped in the garden and then went to check on the sheep and returned with the tasty delights. She cleaned him up with a wet cloth and shaved him with his straight razor, making him very handsome and presentable to the girls.

The girls were very excited to have their father at the table for the first time since he had left. They all held hands, and Father gave the supper blessing.

Chapter 23

For the next couple of weeks, the girls did their chores just like they would have if the man of the house was still gone. Only they did so with the enthusiasm and cheer of having him home. Father continued to heal rather quickly. Mrs. Bell used some neighborly craftsmanship to fashion a crutch made out of dogwood so that Father could get to the outhouse and back.

On the night of June 22 while they were all eating, Father said, "Well, does everyone know what tomorrow is?"

Millie ducked her head down and didn't say a word. Mother smiled as the two younger girls looked surprised, having no idea what tomorrow might be.

"Well," Father said as Millie rolled her eyes. "It's your sister's sixteenth birthday! Yep, June 23. I remember it like it was yesterday, sixteen years ago. It was probably one of the hottest days I have ever remembered."

Millie squinted her eyes at Father and then looked at her mother and said, "Do we have to listen to this again?"

Mattie came out of her chair to get next to her father.

"Here, little one," he said. "Stand on this side. I don't want you accidently bumping into my leg."

"Sorry," she said as she made her way to the other side. "Don't listen to Millie. I really want to hear the story."

"Me too!" said Evelyn Rose with a little jealous tone to her voice.

Catching Evelyn Rose's tone, Father said, "Well, I'll tell it under one condition."

"What?" said Mattie.

"Only if Evelyn Rose comes and stands next to me on the other side," he told her.

Evelyn Rose's eyes brightened up as Mattie said, "But you just told me I couldn't stand on that side."

"That's 'cause Evelyn Rose isn't nearly as squirmy as you are," Father explained. "Now I got one of you on each side for this exciting story."

Millie dropped her head with a thud on the table and said, "Just hurry!"

Seeing his wife by the cookstove with a cup in her hand, Father said, "Well, not so fast. A good story can't be told unless the storyteller has a good, fresh, hot cup of coffee!"

The two girls gritted their teeth and wrinkled their noses as Millie said, "Mother! Please get this man his cup of coffee!"

Not saying a word, Mother handed her husband his hot cup of coffee with a big smile on her face. She then pulled her chair next to Millie and wrapped her arms around Millie's shoulders. Millie raised her head off the table and looked at her mother.

"Okay, Father, you win!" she said as she scooted closer to her mother and lay her head on her shoulders. Mother brought her other arm around in front to give her daughter a comforting hug. With a sigh, Millie said, "I'm ready now."

Evelyn Rose and Mattie leaned in front of Father to look at each other when Father said, "It's okay, you two are sitting next to the storyteller. It doesn't get any better than this."

Taking a sip of his coffee, Father cleared his throat and began. "Sixteen years ago, your mother and I lived in a small one-room apartment on the back of the house we showed you on Washington Street. You know, it's the street that goes beside the courthouse." The girls nodded their heads to indicate yes, they knew the street.

"Anyway, when we first got married," Father continued, "that's where we lived. We didn't have a plug nickel to our names, but it didn't matter. Your mother did a little house cleaning for a couple folks, and I worked at the livery stable for Mr. Highley. I had been working for him for quite some time. I cleaned stalls, fed the livestock, and ran errands."

Mother gave a soft cough and said, "Sorry, got a little tickle in my throat. Go on about the birth of Millie."

"Oh, yeah!" Father said as he took another sip of coffee and winked at his wife while looking over his cup. "Back to the story," he said. "It was on this very night sixteen years ago, and I'll never forget it was so hot that most people in town would lay out in their backyards at night so they could get some fresh air. There had been an early drought that year, and most everyone's wells were starting to go dry. So the busiest place was where the cool springs were, and one of the best was right down the road from us. I here tell that spring is why this town was settled. Anyway, your mother asked me to get her some water because she felt a little sick to her stomach. So off I went, and I don't mind telling you one bit that I was scared. I knew time was close for the baby to be born, so I didn't waste any time at all getting there and back. The only problem was that when I got back, your mother wasn't there. I was running all around the house hollering her name, but there was no answer.

"I ran into the house, and she wasn't there either. Finally, I ran back out into the street just a-crying and hollering your mother's name when out of nowhere, our landlord put his hand on my shoulder. I have no idea where he came from, but anyway, he said, 'Son, are you okay?' I wanted to tell him I couldn't find my wife, but all I could get out was, I-I-I, and he said, 'Are you looking for your wife?' And again, all I could say was 'Ye-ye-ye.' He said, 'Calm down, it's okay! She's in there laying on the bed. We sent the neighbor to fetch the doctor.' Then I tried to say why, but all I could get out was 'Wha-wha-wha.' He put a kind arm around my shoulder and said, 'Well, son, I think you might be a father tonight.'"

Looking at the girls staring at him, Father said, "That's why I always wanted to be called Father instead of Pa or Daddy or something else. When he said *father*, it was like a whole new world for me.

"Anyway, the landlord says, 'I think you might be a father tonight, so why don't we go in and take her some of that fresh spring water she said you went after.' I looked at the bucket, held it up, and finally said, 'I think I spilled it all out.' The man laughed and said he had plenty in the house. He told me I could go into the bedroom and sit by my wife and that he would get some fresh water while we waited for the midwife to get to the house. His wife left us alone for a few minutes to check the water boiling on the stove. I was so nervous trying to make your mother comfortable, but all she wanted was for me to sit next to her. She would take my hand and place it on her belly. I could feel Millie move some, then your mother would say in a painful voice, 'Can you feel that?' I wasn't sure what she wanted me to feel, but her muscles would move and tighten up. I didn't like that your mother was in pain, but there was nothing I could do about it.

"Like I said," Father continued while his daughters listened intensely, and Mother made sure the story didn't get blown out of proportion, "it was so hot that a lot of people stayed outside at night to keep cool. Those that were close by would wander over to see what all the commotion was about. Just before the midwife got there, I bet there was twenty people standing and sitting on those poor people's front yard. This went on all night, and the longer your mother held on, the larger the crowd got. The folks would bring coffee and sweet bread to eat. I drank so much coffee and was so jittery I didn't know if I was coming or going. If I wasn't going to the outhouse, I was looking for someplace to throw up. Your mother took it all in stride. She'd stay calm and do her best to calm me down. Believe it or not, your mother would even fall asleep between contractions."

Father continued his story while Millie fell asleep on her mother's shoulder, and Evelyn Rose infected Mattie with her yawning. Mother cleared her throat and indicated that her husband needed to speed the story up. Father clapped his hands, and everyone jumped, and he said, "Just before daylight, the town doctor got there followed by one of the town's law officers. He wanted everyone to leave, but no one did, so he didn't try anymore. As daylight crept in on us, the crowd swelled to twice the size, and I was so in awe of the crowd and that anyone would be interested in a couple of poor neighbors. I started that speech problem again. My eyes were full of water or maybe it was coffee coming out, and at that very instance, a baby started crying. The crowd began cheering, and the next thing I know, the midwife hollered out the window, 'It's a girl!' I started crying, and the cheering got louder. A man pulled up a chair and told me to sit down. I sat in the chair, and the doctor came out and laid the baby girl in my arms. Your mother said she was the most beautiful baby she had ever seen, but when I saw her, it was this red, screaming, slimy little thing."

The girls laughed, and Millie squinted her eyes at her father as he continued, "I was as proud as I could be sitting there holding my first child. I got up to take her back to her mother when I saw her smiling and watching the two of us from the window. Someone from the crowd shouted, 'What are you going to name her?' I had no idea, and your mother never said anything about a name. Someone yelled, 'How about Summer since it's so hot!' Then someone said, 'June is a good name!' Then your mother whispered to me that she would like it to be a family name. I never knew my folks, and your mother's mother died while having her. Your mother's Aunt Mildred was like a mother to her. Mother whispered that she wanted to name our baby girl after her. Your mother always called her Millie. I looked at the baby and told Mother, 'Yes, she looks like a Millie.' I turned to the crowd, stood up, and held the swaddled baby up and shouted, 'Her name is Millie!' The womenfolk oohed and aahed at the name, and several clapped. Then they all went home, and that's the story of your big sister's birth. Tomorrow, it will be sixteen years since that time! And that's the end!"

"Oh, no!" exclaimed Evelyn Rose. "You have to finish the story!"

"Yeah, you have to," Mattie said, squirming up under her father's arm.

Millie smiled and nodded.

"All right then," he told them, "but the short version. I don't want to stay up much longer." Father continued, "The following Monday, I went to the livery stable and did my usual work of cleaning up manure, feeding the animals, and making sure the tack was all where it should be, when one of the owners' boss men told me to load the wagon and take his feed out to the farm just west of town out the Maple Road and drop it off at the end of the road. He said there was a farm where two big hills rose up behind it to the southwest and one to the northwest, and at the front was a small cabin. 'Can't miss it!' he said. 'You'll see Highley's wagon there.'

"I told him I would take the wagon there and be back as soon as possible. When I got there, I saw Mr. Highley's wagon by a lean-to shed that he had built. I went through the open gate and left my rig next to his. Just as I was getting ready to holler for Mr. Highley, I heard this funny sound coming from a makeshift pen off to my left. Well, I go over and check on it, and there they were, two ewes, and each with a little one. I got to playing with the sheep and talking to 'em when from the cabin, Mr. Highley shouts, 'So what do you think of them?' I jump up because he kinda scared me, and I said, 'Well, guess this feed is for them.'

"'Nope,' he said, 'it's for you, if you want it.' I scratched my head some trying to figure out what he meant. Mr. Highley invited me into the cabin. He showed me around and told me that when he had moved here from Kentucky, he and his brothers built the place before they moved into town. I told him it looked built really well. It was tight, walls were chinked well, and the foundation seemed to be sound. He said, 'The door and windows are good too. There is a nice spring just over by the holding pen. How would you and your family like to move into it?' It really threw me off guard, and I didn't know what to say. 'Tell you what,' he says, 'I like your hard work and I believe you to be an honest man."

Looking at his girls and knowing they really liked this part of the story, Father said, "Well, it's bedtime, don't you think?"

That brought them to full attention, and Mattie said, "Aww, no," clinging to her father's arm.

Evelyn Rose chimed in right behind her and said, "Not yet, you're just about done!"

"Okay, okay!" Father said, laughing.

Millie looked at her mother and said, "He does this every time he tells a story."

"Okay, like I said," Father continued, to the girls' delight, "Mr. Highley called me an honest man, and I thought, wow, I've become a father and an honest man in just a couple of days. But anyway, Mr. Highley says, 'How'd you and your new family like to live here? I need a hard worker out here. See all that timber out there? It needs cut for the new plank road the State is talking about building. We cut on shares, and I'll lease you the farm. I'll even give you a couple of sheep to start with. You can make this farm into what you want. Be a great place to start. I'll even let you keep the horse and wagon to haul the timber. Oh, and the feed is for the sheep.'

"I didn't know what to say, but I finally got out a word and said, 'Why?' Mr. Highley walks over to me and holds out his hand for me to shake and said, 'I was there the morning your daughter, Millie, was born. You and your Mrs. really touched me. The farm is yours if you want, and if you do, the sheep is for Millie.'"

Finishing his story, Father said, "Mr. Highley told me to drop the feed off in the shed and take the wagon home. 'If you want, take tomorrow off, and bring the family out and look the place over. Think about it. If you stay, it will be good. If you don't, I'll see you back at the livery stable.' We shook hands, and we've been here ever since.

"Now for sure, that's the end of the story," Father said, giving the girls a tight squeeze. "Big day tomorrow, so I think you girls need to head off to bed."

They all took their time getting drinks and trips to the outhouse, but finally, the girls were settled into their beds. They said their prayers, and then Mother took the oil lamp and went back to the kitchen.

"I'm not tired myself in the sleepy sense, but I do feel worn out," Father said.

"It's been a long day for me," Mother let him know. "I believe I'll step out back and then head to bed." She grabbed the crutch Mrs. Bell made and said, "Come on. I'll help you outside, and we'll both go."

As they left, they had to run Rusty back so no one tripped, and the pair struggled to the outhouse. "You go on first," Father said, "I want to just sit on the wait'n stump and watch the stars some."

She smiled and pointed to the east, saying, "Big ole moon be coming up soon. If you want, we'll sit out a while longer on the flat rock porch and watch it come up."

"That'd be nice," Father replied. "Air might be a little fresher over there."

Mother laughed and agreed with him. They soon made their way back, and with a little situating, Father got comfortable, and the two watched the big orange nearly full moon rise over the town of Farmington.

Chapter 24

The next morning, Father woke first, letting his wife know that the medicine really made him sleep and kind of drowsy. "I don't think I want to use it today and see how much pain I'm really in."

"That would be fine," Mother said. "Just don't try to endure too much. Stay off it as much as you can, okay?"

"That might be hard to do," he said with a chuckle. "But I definitely don't want another setback. It will be good for a while."

"What say we go get the girls up and get an early start on the day," Mother said with eagerness. "Maybe I can get Millie's surprise cake made before the heat sets in."

"I'll do my best to get her out of the house," he said, straining to get up off his back. "Shoo wee, getting up is always the worst part."

"Well, if you had a little patience," Mother said, scorning him, "I would help, and it wouldn't be near as bad."

"I know, and I will," he said in that depressed tone as before. "Just let me try."

Mother smiled and tried to build his confidence with encouraging words, letting him know that he's well ahead of the healing process.

"Well, I'll be," he said as the two of them hobbled past the girls' room. "Millie must have gotten up early and already gone out to check on the flock."

Halfway up the hill but not quite to the pond, Millie stopped to look back to where she just came from. Leaning on her new walking stick she made from a hickory sapling, she looked down at her dog, Rusty, and asked, "So what do you think?"

Sitting on his haunches, Rusty looked up at his master and blew out his upper lip and let out a light "woof!" He looked back to the east where the sun was just rising over the small cabin.

"Yeah, I know," she said, talking back to the dog. Millie sat down to watch the sun rise, and Rusty took his nose and nuzzled it between her elbow and side to get a hug. "Been quite busy around the little cabin," she said, scratching the dog under his neck. "Seems like it's a new adventure every day. Looky there," she said as she took the hand she was scratching under the dog's chin and pointed his nose to the cabin. "Mother's up. See the smoke coming out the chimney?" The dog gave another one of his puffed-out lip woofs, and Millie shook the top of his head between his ears. "I swear, sometimes I think you can understand every word I'm saying!" Rusty looked her in the face and gave a quick lick and doggy grin.

"Come on." Millie laughed as she pulled herself up with the walking stick. "Let's go check on them sheep."

Rusty took off past the pond and headed to the gap in the fence. Once there, he sat on his rump to look back at Millie and barked for her to come on. Arriving at the gap, the pair moseyed on down to the big oak so they could get a better view of the southwest hill. Hoping to spot the flock back in the woods where the temperature was probably ten degrees cooler than out in the pasture, Millie heard the rustle of leaves on the other side of the fence. She jumped and was about half scared out of her wits until she spotted a squirrel feeding on the ground about thirty yards into the woods. "Oh, Good Lord," she said, trying to catch her breath. "Finding mushrooms didn't scare me, but a squirrel does!" Rusty paid no attention to the squirrel but stared to find the sheep.

"I don't know about you," she told her dog, "but I still get weak-kneed thinking about that crazy man trying to hurt us." Millie crossed the fence and had to make Rusty follow her. "Well, which way is it?" she asked. "Do you get weak-kneed too or are you just wanting to find sheep?" She walked to the spot where she thought the man held her but couldn't quite seem to find the tree they were near. Pointing to a dead tree that had fallen, she asked her dog, "Is that where you were?"

Rusty went to where Millie was pointing. He sniffed around the downed tree then looked back at Mille. With her hand, she slapped her thigh, and the dog leaped and then ran to her side. Once there, Rusty raised his head to look through the woods past the big oak and over to the other side of the field. "There, there," Millie said, giving the dog a light shove with her knees. He leaned into her leg enjoying the affection but watched her hand for the command to go. Millie giggled and said, "You silly dog." With that, she took a deep breath, looked around a bit more, then said out loud to herself, "Funny how I can only remember bits and pieces of what happened. It's probably for the better." Laying her hand on Rusty's head, she noticed his hind legs quivering. She said, "Okay, boy, go get 'em!" as she threw her hand out, pointing to the other side of the field.

Tearing up the leaves better than the squirrel, Rusty barreled headstrong through the fence, past the giant oak, and out over the field after his prize. Millie took a couple of steps to follow but suddenly stopped in her tracks. Thinking out loud, she said, "I suppose I could remember this as a bad place. A place where he tried to take me away, but I won't. This is a good place. A place where I was saved." She looked up past the treetops to a single cloud in the sky, smiled, and said, "It's a good place!"

In no time at all, Millie followed the trail Rusty left behind and was across the small field to see the flock herded down the hill to the creek. She took a head count while Rusty proudly pranced back and forth, making sure none of the sheep broke away until Millie was done with her count. Satisfied with the count, she took a second look, but this time, she evaluated the flock's physical condition. She observed each sheep's movement and looked for any signs of illness. She looked at Rusty and calmly said, "If they look good to you, they look good to me. Let 'em go." She slapped her thigh. Rusty relaxed and calmly walked through the flock to return to Millie's side. She gave him a good head rub and quick scratch behind both ears. Rusty closed his eyes and gave a big grin with his tongue hanging out, knowing he had pleased his master.

The sheep moved to the pasture to graze, and Millie went up the southwest hill toward the back side to check on the fence. "Haven't been back here in a while," Millie murmured. "Since we are this close, we might as well walk the whole farm and see what needs fixing."

Making her way to the southwest corner, Millie made a right and started walking north, back down the hill to the valley where the creek had its beginnings. She continued north to the northwest hill. Halfway up the hill, Millie stopped and said, "Hey, fella. You look like you might need to rest a minute."

She found a large rock to sit on and wished she had brought some water. Rusty came to her side. Looking around, she said, "Look at the size of those trees. Some of these are about as big as our large oak. Guess Father doesn't do any cutting up here. Either he's saving them or it's too steep and rocky to get Mr. Highley's mules up here to haul them out." She leaned back against the large rock, lay her arms behind her head, and told Rusty, "We'll rest a little longer." Rusty came to her side and lay down next to her, resting his head on her stomach. No sooner did the pair get good and relaxed when a rustling next to the rock brought them to their feet. "Okay, stay back!" Millie ordered the dog. "It's either a snake or a lizard, and I don't care for either one." Picking up her walking stick, Millie walked back to the rock and flipped a few leaves aside but didn't see a thing. "Don't mind so much as long as I can see them, but if I can't spot them, I get the heebie-jeebies. Come on, Rusty, let's go! I hear the spring water calling us."

They walked up the northwest hill. Once on top, she stepped out of the timber onto a small rock glade. From there, she could view all the way down to the cabin. She got a chill when she realized that this could have been the place the young man was watching them from with the telescope. If the trees weren't fully leafed out, you could probably see all the way to town. Deciding to cross the fence on the back side toward the Link farm, Millie thought she might find the place where they saw the lights the morning the troops marched out of town. Before stepping back into the woods, Millie spotted movement at the cabin. She could see the wagon being brought to the cabin. Holding on to her walking stick, Millie waved it back and forth trying to get somebody's attention but failed as she saw her family loading up. Millie could see Father in the back between a couple of sacks of food, and Mattie was glued right next to him. She watched Evelyn Rose run ahead of the rig and open the gate to let them out.

"What the heck!" Millie said loudly. "They've turned south. Must be taking Evelyn Rose to clean that house on Columbia Road and go on into town. That's not supposed to be until the Fourth of July! Come on, Rusty!" She tapped the dog on the head with her walking stick. "That wasn't nice not to wait for me." She ran down the hill trying not to turn her ankle on the loose rocks and made her way down to the spring. Fresh cold spring water was all she thought about as she ran past the cabin and knelt next to the cool, sweet water. Millie and Rusty had their heads together as they lapped up the water. Realizing this, Millie stopped to watch the dog. Rusty raised his head and gave Millie a quick kiss across the face then went back to drinking.

"All right! I should have known better," she said, grabbing the ladle out of the bucket. She took a drink from the ladle and then dumped the rest on Rusty's head. The dog jumped, and Millie said, "That's for the wet kiss."

Having had enough water and feeling better, Millie looked in every direction to see where the family went. She checked on Bessie and her calf and saw they had been turned loose to graze some more. "Well, everybody's gone," she said to Rusty. "What say we go in and see if they left a note?" Stepping up on the rock porch, Millie snapped her fingers to coax the dog to follow her. Millie immediately noticed a note on the table. She sat down and said to Rusty, "It says here they waited as long as they could and had to leave without me. Yeah, right!" She looked down at Rusty, who was waiting patiently for a bite to eat. "Let's see, they also say Mrs. Bell could use my help with some barn repairs 'since your father is unable to work for a while. Please hurry. Mother.'"

Millie cut a piece of bread and a slice of cured ham and told Rusty, "We gotta go again." Starting toward the door, Millie heard a high-pitched whine coming from the dog. She laughed and said, "I love it when you beg like that. Don't worry, I got some right here." She opened her other hand and showed the dog some meat she had for him. Rusty came up off his haunches and followed Millie out the door trying to snatch the meat out of her hand, and to his delight, he succeeded. They grabbed another drink, and off they went to their favorite neighbors.

Chapter 25

Just a hop, skip, and a jump down the way, and Millie turned into Tennessee Bell's Hereford cattle farm. Staying in the lane herself, Rusty dove under the wood-plank fence to get a better look at the red-bodied, white-faced cattle with short legs. In order to get a better look, Millie put her feet on the lowest plank and leaned her elbows over the top, admiring the beautiful herd of cattle.

This must be where she keeps the cows with new babies, Millie thought. Out in the pasture were eight cows, all with new babies. "You better be careful!" she yelled to Rusty. "A head butt by one of them, and you won't forget it!" Rusty ran the cattle and soon had them huddled together while keeping their babies toward the center for their protection. Then just like a true Hereford cow with a baby, one of the mothers charged Rusty. "See, I told you," Millie yelled out. Rusty loved a challenge and soon had the mad mom back with her baby and the herd.

"That's enough!" Millie yelled as she slapped the plank with her hand. Rusty bounded her way and was soon back on this side of the fence feeling proud of himself. "Yeah, I know," Millie said, giving him a good head rub. "Well, would you look at that." She pointed toward the fence. One of the babies had followed Rusty and was looking through the fence. "I think you've made a new friend."

"Stay with me," Millie told the dog. "Let's go see what Mrs. Bell wants before we get into trouble." Walking down the lane, the two had to pass the redbone hounds Mrs. Bell kept tied in the front of her house. Rusty made sure Millie stayed between him and them. She had to laugh but wondered why Mrs. Bell hadn't come out to greet them or to just see what the barking was about. She reached the porch and knocked on an unlocked door. "Ummm," she said and opened the door. She yelled for Mrs. Bell. There was still no answer as she looked into the house. "Well, what you think?" she asked the panting dog. "Should we go around back or go into the house?" She turned to go down the steps and answered herself, "Let's go around back first."

Hearing some noise to the back of the house as she rounded the corner, Millie strained her ears to make out what the sound might be. Rusty ran ahead to see first with Millie close behind. As she rounded the corner, Millie jumped in sheer surprise and shock when everyone yelled "Surprise!" and broke into song, singing "Happy Birthday." Millie turned red as a beet as her sisters grabbed her hands and led her to the table with a birthday cake sitting right in the middle. There to wish her a happy birthday were her mother and father, Mrs. Bell, Mr. Highley and his wife, Cecil's parents and his brother and sister, and the old doctor and his wife. The pastor from church and his family and a few of her school friends were also in attendance.

"How did you do all this!" Millie asked in a bashful voice. "I had absolutely no idea. What a surprise!"

"As soon as you left the house, we got busy with the cake and just prayed you wouldn't turn around and come back," Mother replied.

Father also explained, "But if you did, we had the girls ready to have you take one of them to try to catch a fish."

"Yeah," Evelyn Rose chimed in, "you gave us that idea when you brought the mushrooms in."

"But the real planning started when Doc here suggested you might need something to get your mind off recent past events," Mother said. "Doc and his wife helped get the word out, and everyone came," she explained, spreading her arms out, indicating the large crowd.

One of Millie's friends from school started clapping and in cadence yelled, "Speech, speech, speech!" Everyone joined in the chant.

"Okay, you guys!" Millie said, holding her hands up to make them be quiet. "It's a birthday, not a graduation."

"We still want a speech," said the old doctor while laughing and enjoying himself that Millie was embarrassed.

Mother placed an arm around Millie's waist and whispered, "Just say something. I'll stand here with you."

"Okay," Millie said. "I'm not good at this, so I'll just say thank you for being here. I am surprised, but more importantly, I am very glad you are here to make this a very special day."

Mrs. Bell clapped and said, "Well said." Everyone applauded.

"Well, now for the surprise," said Mr. Highley. "Just so you know, Miss Millie, this party actually started last night." He pointed over toward the garden area. "See that stake on the ground. Believe it or not, there is a hog buried under the ground, and he's been slow cooking all night." Some of the adults gasped at the thought of cooking in the ground. "One of the boys that works for me is from Arkansas, and he says this is the way to cook a hog. So I just had to try."

The day was filled with plenty of food and lots of fun. It was just what the old doctor had prescribed. Millie knew in her heart it was the best medicine ever. The ham turned out delicious, and everyone wanted to know how to cook a ham in the ground.

"Now for dessert!" Mother announced as Mrs. Bell sticks sixteen candles in the cake, and Mr. Highley lit them. "Okay," she said, "everyone ready to sing one more time." The crowd began singing "Happy Birthday" to Millie.

Handing Millie the knife after the song, Mother said, "You get to cut your first piece. Then I'll cut for everyone else."

"My, that's a big cake!" Millie proclaimed. "And it's chocolate, my favorite!"

"Mine too!" said Evelyn Rose as she, Mattie, and Millie's friends from school all rushed over to watch.

Admiring the cake, several ladies told Mother what a beautiful cake it was and asked for the recipe. Mrs. Highley and the doctor's wife asked if she ever considered making cakes to sell. "I'd pay you well for one for the Fourth of July," said Mrs. Highley.

"Oh, I don't know," Mother replied and whispered, "we'll see how well we're getting around," referring to the speed of Father's recovery. Mrs. Highley understood and changed the subject quickly.

Afternoon soon became evening, and most were eager to head home before dusk turned to night. Most prepared to leave in groups so someone could follow in case of an emergency. The old doctor asked Mr. Highley if he could wait for them as they would probably be the last to leave. Mr. Highley agreed to wait.

The church pastor invited everyone to the next day's services as they prepared to leave with Cecil's parents and their children.

Millie, Evelyn Rose, and Mattie were busy looking at the gifts that Millie received for her birthday. Mother and Mrs. Bell cleaned up and carried things into the house while Rusty followed to snatch up any fallen scraps.

Mr. Highley and the doctor saw Father trying to clean the table while holding on to his crutches. They walked over to help him. The old doctor said, "I took the liberty of doing some measurements during the last examination. I made you something and hope you will give it a try and use it."

"Well, my goodness, Doc. What is it?" Father asked.

"It's a prosthesis," he explained.

Mr. Highley said, "It's a what?"

Doc rolled his eyes and said, "You know, a special shoe."

"Oh yeah," Mr. Highley said.

"Will you go get it?" Doc asked Mr. Highley.

"Now?" replied Mr. Highley.

"What is going on here?" Father said in agitation while sitting down in a chair and then trying to get up again.

"No, no, no, don't get up," Doc said to Father and looked at Mr. Highley and said, "Go, go get it!"

Mr. Highley returned with a box. Doc told Father while taking it from Mr. Highley, "A few years back, I was in Chicago visiting a doctor friend who showed me a new idea he had learned from back East." Doc pulled out of the box a shoe. He looked at it really closely as did the other two men, and Doc told Father, "Try it on!"

For a moment, Father looked at the odd shoe. He held it upright, then upside down. He bent the toe of the shoe on the table. Finally, he held it in one hand and bounced it up and down as though figuring out the weight of it. Looking at the old doctor, who had a smile on his face, Father said to him in a straightforward voice, "Is this going to fix me?"

"No," Doc said as he sat next to Father, and the smile was gone from his face. "You're never gonna be all fixed," he continued, "but this will help."

Both men looked at Mr. Highley as if to say, "Be on my side and say something."

"What have you got to lose?" Mr. Highley finally said.

"My dignity!" Father said a little testy.

Mr. Highley took a step back as if shocked by his statement and then said, "You're a sheep farmer in cattle country! Since when did you go and let pride cloud that noggin of yours?"

Father got a little red, and Doc told him, "Just try it out with us, and no one has to know. If you don't like it, we won't say another word."

"And you can hobble around with that fancy crutch," Mr. Highley said, taking another step backward.

"Yeah, you better back up," Father told Mr. Highley. "Okay, I'll try it just so you two will shut your yaps."

Doc bent down to help change shoes, and Mr. Highley said, "I'd help, but I didn't bring my anvil with me."

"Yeah, right, and I just might drop one on your foot," Father said. "Then we can make you a special shoe!"

"Well, now that you got your sense of humor back," Doc said, "see if you can get up."

"So we can all have a good laugh?" Father said.

"No!" Doc yelled. "So you can walk!"

Putting his good leg under him, letting the bad leg hang, Father leaned to the left on the fancy crutch. Straining with both arms and being very careful not to fall and make a fool of himself, he slowly and gingerly rose to his full height.

Doc stood almost nose to nose with him and said, "How does that feel?"

"I, I don't know," he told Doc. "My crutch is too short. Now what do I do?"

"Well, for starters," Doc said, "hand me your crutch and try to walk."

Mr. Highley scooted in next to his side, ready just in case he falls. Doc threw the crutch to the side and held both arms out.

Looking straight into Doc's face and with determination, Father started to take a step, but stopped. Looking past the good doctor's face, he spotted Evelyn Rose standing in the doorway of Mrs. Bell's barn. Both of her hands were drawn up against her cheeks, and the expression in her eyes of compassion compelled her father to take another step. She took one too. Sweat began to roll down his face, and he heard from under the tiny fist, "You can do it, Father." He took another step while Doc and Mr. Highley walked next to him. Evelyn Rose took two steps and repeated to her father, "You can do it!" Father took two steps. Evelyn Rose dropped her hands and slowly walked to her father as he strained to take more steps.

A dozen small steps later, and Father and the two men met Evelyn Rose. Reaching up to touch his hand, she smiled and said, "I like your new shoe. Will it make you well now?"

Wiping the sweat from his brow, Father told Evelyn Rose, "I'm not sure if it will make me well." He reached out for a little help from his friends and said as he returned to his seat, "It does help me keep my balance."

"That's it!" Doc said excitedly. "That's exactly what the shoe is supposed to do. All you need to do now is get some strength back in your leg. It looks like you just might have the right nurse to help you."

Evelyn Rose's head perked up at the sound of *nurse,* and she said, "You bet I will. I like to help."

"When you come next Friday to help the missus," Doc told her, "I'll teach you some exercises that will help strengthen the leg. But for now,"—he looked at Father—"continue to let it heal and do what you can."

"Young lady," he said to Evelyn Rose, "don't let your father do too much."

"How will I know?" she asked.

"Today was almost too much," he explained.

After the friends talked some more over a last cup of coffee, they decided it was time to leave and try to get home before dark.

The doctor's wife explained to Evelyn Rose and Mother that next Friday when they come to town, she would like for Evelyn Rose to help clean and, if possible, stay until they bring her to church on Sunday morning.

Mother said, "I don't know." After some pleading by Evelyn Rose and some convincing from the older lady, Father made the decision and said, "Yes." He explained that he didn't want Evelyn Rose around if there was any underground movement. Doc agreed, and both Evelyn Rose and Doc's wife gave hugs to each other over the decision.

Later that evening, making their way to the small cabin, Father asked Millie what she thought of the surprise party. "It sure was a surprise. I can tell you that!" she said. "But I didn't like it when everyone was gone."

Father laughed and said, "We didn't think you would ever get there, and when you did, we thought you and Rusty would never leave those cows alone."

Mattie turned around in the wagon seat and, looking down at Millie and her father in the back, said, "We were watching you from inside Mrs. Bell's house."

"I thought I saw someone, but I knocked on the door, and no one was there," Millie told her.

Mattie snickered and told her, "We were right behind the door!"

"Yeah," Evelyn Rose said, giving her an elbow. "You almost gave us away."

Giving Evelyn Rose a taste of her own medicine, she elbowed her, saying, "But I didn't, so there!"

"Okay, girls. Settle down before you both get it!" Mother said, giving them both that furled eyebrow look. "Now, Evelyn Rose, you get ready to open the gate."

"Why me?" she whined.

"Because you started it, and I said so. That's why!" Mother replied.

Evelyn Rose growled softly in her throat, and Mother turned her head back toward Ole Smokey, saying, "Careful there, young lady."

Just before jumping off the wagon seat, Evelyn Rose made sure her mother wasn't watching and in the blink of an eye, stuck her tongue out at Mattie.

"Mother!" Mattie yelled. "She—"

"I don't want to hear it," Mother told her. "As soon as we get home, you girls get cleaned up and go to bed. Make sure your Sunday dresses are hung up."

"Aw!" the two girls said. Evelyn Rose tried to explain, "But it's too early!"

"I don't care. I'm tired, your father is tired, and we are all just ready for some peace and quiet."

Evelyn Rose stuck her bottom lip out while opening the gate, and Mattie dropped her chin to her chest. Nothing but quiet for the rest of the night.

Millie took care of Ole Smokey with a quick brushing and a little feed. She then gave Bessie a little hay and had to push the calf back so she could finish out the milking. Settling into a good rhythm, Millie got a little more than a half-gallon and said to Bessie, "Thank you, girl. I love fresh milk in the mornings." Hanging the stool up out of the way, she petted the milk cow's neck and said, "Especially when it has cooled in the spring all night." Millie made her way to the cabin where her mother and father were sitting on the rock porch. She showed them the bucket of milk and let them know she's going to put it in a couple of bottles and cool them in the spring. Mother told her to tie cheesecloth on top to keep the bugs out.

Chapter 26

For the next few days, Evelyn Rose worked hard with her father and his new shoe. Mattie, for some reason, had taken the role of doing garden work with her mother and was always at her side while cooking and cleaning. Millie continued being the shepherd of the field and spent most of her time with the sheep, Ole Smokey, Bessie, and her adopted calf. Every other day, she went to Mrs. Bell's to help with the Hereford cows and check on the fences. The other days, she went to Mrs. Link's farm to help with her chickens and gathers eggs.

Friday finally arrived, and Evelyn Rose was so excited to go to town and start her job for the old doctor's wife. She did her best to get everyone up early so the chores could get done. Heading to the garden before breakfast, she called to Rusty for company. They headed straight for the potatoes. Evelyn Rose took the hoe in her hand while Rusty watched her as she began hilling some of the potato plants. She spotted the cucumber on the ground just past the rows of corn. "Oh my! Would you look at that!" she said, pointing them out to Rusty. "Finally, something is paying off in this garden."

The pair walked around the rows of corn, and Evelyn Rose searched with her hoe for the young tender cucumbers. Lifting up a vine, she spotted a couple of cucumbers on the ground. Without any warning, Rusty began barking just as Evelyn Rose reached down to pick them. "What is wrong with you? You nutty dog," she said. She reached again, and the dog growled deep within his throat and snapped at her hand. Evelyn Rose drew back then quickly picked up a clod of dirt at her feet and threatened Rusty if he didn't behave, "I'll put a knot on your head if you do that one more time." Reaching with her left hand and holding Rusty back with the right hand, she reached for the third time for the cucumbers.

This time, just as her hand was about to touch the cucumber, Rusty lunged and grabbed her hand in his mouth. Before she could get a word out of her mouth, she saw the lightning strike of a copperhead snake sink his fangs into the side of Rusty's nose. The dog let out a yelp, and Evelyn Rose screamed. Barking furiously, Rusty kept the snake coiled for another strike while Evelyn Rose reached for the garden hoe. Frantically grabbing the hoe, she yelled at Rusty to get back. Rusty obeyed, and Evelyn Rose struck the copperhead, killing it. She struck it several times, cutting it into pieces. Satisfied the snake was dead, Evelyn Rose yelled for Millie as she rushed over to Rusty. Trying to ease the pain, Rusty pushed his head along the ground in a circular motion. Evelyn Rose took the dog in her arms, cuddling him as she rushed toward the cabin. The closer Evelyn Rose got, the harder she cried until Millie came flying out of the house and helped her to the porch. They lay Rusty on the flat rock porch. Mattie and Mother come to the doorway to see what all the commotion was about.

Catching her breath between sobs, Evelyn Rose finally got the words out, "He's been bit by a copperhead."

"Where?" Millie yelled.

Evelyn Rose pointed to the puncture marks on Rusty's snout. About halfway between his eyes and the tip of his nose were two small holes about an inch apart with yellow venom leaking out.

"That must have been a big snake," came a voice from behind Mattie and her mother.

Evelyn Rose looked up at her father and said, "He tried to warn me, but I wouldn't listen. Just as I was reaching for a cucumber, he covered my hand with his mouth. I thought he was biting me when the snake struck from under the vines."

"Will he live?" asked Millie.

"The snake didn't sink his fangs deep into the muscle tissue," Father explained. "But there is a lot of venom there. I just don't know. Did you see where the snake went?" he asked Evelyn Rose.

"He's dead," she answered. "All chopped up."

"What can we do?" Millie asked as she started crying along with her sister.

In a tender voice, Father said, "Girls, crying won't help him right now. If we had some turpentine to put on the wound, it might draw some of the poison out, but I don't have any."

"Where can I get some?" Millie pleaded through her tears.

"Closest place I'd know of," Father told her, "is the livery stable. Mr. Highley keeps a jug of it in his office for just this kind of thing. Mostly—" Before he could finish speaking, Millie took off running to the gate.

Mother yelled to saddle the horse, but Father said, "Let her go. She might be able to outrun the horse. Besides, by the time she got the saddle on Ole Smokey and through the gate, she'll be halfway to the town. This will give her something to do."

"Is there anything we can do?" asked Evelyn Rose.

"Let's get him in and make him as comfortable as possible," he told Evelyn Rose and Mother. "Mattie, if you'll help me, we'll go to the spring and get some fresh cold water. Maybe walk over and see this copperhead your sister killed."

"Oh, I don't know!" she told her father. "You always told us, if you see a snake, there is always a mate somewhere nearby."

"I also told you two people can always guard each other," he instructed his youngest child. "Four eyes are better than two."

"All right, but I'm taking Evelyn Rose's hoe just in case," Mattie said all wide-eyed and with a shaky voice.

"And I'll take my crutch. How about that?" he told her.

Mattie and Father left to get water and to have a good look at the copperhead. Evelyn Rose and Mother made a place for Rusty and tried to make him as comfortable as possible.

Meanwhile, Millie made it to the edge of town and decided to run through the schoolyard and had to jump a couple of fences in order to save time. She raced as fast as she could through the alley and around the livery stable. She almost knocked down a young employee, who had been cleaning stalls, and caused him to dump a bucket of manure. She yelled "Sorry!" without looking and burst into Mr. Highley's office.

"Not here!" she said.

"Millie! What are you doing?" came a voice within the barn.

"I need your help," she explained as fast as she could.

"Millie! Slow down and take a deep breath," Mr. Highley said as he held both her arms. "I can't understand a thing you are saying."

Millie explained without going into great detail but couldn't control her emotions and started crying.

"Let's have a seat in the office so you can catch your breath," he said while trying to lead her to the office.

Millie spotted the young employee peeking around the corner, which caused her to regain her composure. "I don't have time," she said while wiping the dirt-streaked tears from her face. "Rusty was bit by a copperhead, and Father said I needed turpentine."

"I have some," Mr. Highley told Millie. "So have a seat in the office while I get it." Hollering at his employee to get some turpentine in a small jar, Mr. Highley turned to go back and talk to Millie. He poured her a glass of water that's kept in a pitcher and then started explaining. "Most copperhead bites aren't that dangerous, and the turpentine will draw out some of the poison. *But*,"—and he lingered for a couple of seconds to make sure Millie was listening—"but if it was a bad bite, he'll be gone before you get home."

"No!" Millie shouted. "He'll be fine once we put that medicine on him."

"That's true to a—" Mr. Highley tried to explain, but Millie cut him off.

"Where'd that kid go anyway?" she said as she got up out of her chair.

"He's coming," he said, trying to calm her down. "Listen for just a second. The turpentine will help draw out some venom, but if he was bit in a vital spot, it won't help. The venom will go to his heart and stop it," he explained.

Millie lowered her chin and squinted her eyes. "I don't believe you!" she said in a scornful tone.

"Fine!" he said. "Believe what you want. Fact is, I don't ever recall a person or animal dying from a copperhead bite."

As the young man returned with the bottle of turpentine, Millie grabbed it from his hands before he could hand it to his boss. The employee backed out of the office and quickly disappeared.

"So what do I need this for?" she asked, still in an angered voice.

"To help with pain and swelling," Mr. Highley replied in a compassionate voice. He placed his hand on her shoulders and asked, "Do you want me to take you home?"

Speaking just above a whisper, Millie answered, "No, thanks anyway." She started to leave but stopped short of the doorway and turned to face the livery stable owner, and from her dirt-streaked face came the words, "I'm sorry."

"Don't be. I'm sorry this has happened. Go home, and I'll be praying for both of you," replied Mr. Highley.

Going home the same way she came, Millie climbed the rail fence. Almost over the fence, Millie saw the young livery stable worker coming back from dumping another bucket of manure and yelled, "Thanks for the jar of turpentine." To her surprise, when he looked up and saw her on the fence, he froze for just a second. He dropped the bucket then turned and ran the opposite direction. Millie hopped off the fence, furled her eyebrows, shook her head in wonderment of the kid's odd behavior, and took off running. She ran back through the yards, past the school, and out to the hard-packed ground of Maple Road. Heading out of town toward the west as fast as she could run, Millie's mind started remembering. Remembering when the grumpiest old man she ever met got down on his hands and knees and pulled the last remaining pup from under the porch. The runt of the litter that no one wanted. How he told her that if their lives connected, he would be the hardest working and best friend she'd ever have. Millie stumbled. Her eyes so welled up with tears that she couldn't see where she was going.

Having a hard time breathing because of her emotions, she stopped, dropped to her knees, and just waited. After a minute or two, Millie regained enough composure to start walking again. In her deep thoughts, she laughed, picturing that silly grin Rusty would give her when he acted like he understood what she was talking about. She recalled how he learned so fast the hand signals and voice commands she taught him. Millie began to pray. She pleaded and begged God for Rusty to recover. She made bargains and promises with God. Tears fell as she asked, "Please, Lord, save his life." Millie's mind was on nothing but her prayers for her dog, her friend. Each step was a plea, and each stride was for his life.

Being consumed in her thoughts and prayers, Millie blinked and realized she had stopped and was standing at the gate. Looking at the cabin for some kind of sign, she lifted the cord to open the gate. The cord was heavy and, for some reason, was difficult to undo. Struggling with her hands and breathing heavily, Millie finally got through the gate and started her walk to the cabin and what lay inside. The closer she got, the harder it was to move her legs. Wanting to go but not wanting to know, her steps became slow, and her feet seemed to be so heavy. She looked down to see what was causing the heaviness. "Nothing," she thoughts. "I feel as if I'm dreaming."

Looking around just before she got to the flat rock porch, Millie's eyes grew larger when she spotted her father across the field at the edge of the fence, digging with a shovel. Mattie was standing next to him, and Millie noticed she was holding the edge of a tow sack in her hand. Millie threw her hand up, clutched her face, and then dropped to her knees for the third time. She tried to scream, but nothing came out. No breath and no sound, and her face was scarlet red as the blood vessels in her temples felt as if they were about to burst. The next thing Millie saw was her mother's face right in front of her, and the scream "No!" echoed from the small cabin.

Father and Mattie came running as Mother helped her distraught daughter through the door. Millie threw her head back in sheer surprise when she saw Rusty lying in the corner of the gathering room with Evelyn Rose at his side. Father rushed through the door as best he could with Mattie behind him, still holding the tow sack.

Knowing what Millie had seen, Father explained, "We were digging sassafras roots to make a tea for Rusty's pain and swelling."

Holding out her still trembling hands, everyone looked at the jar of turpentine. Mother gently lay her hand on Millie's and said, "You can let go now, I'll take care of this."

Millie let go of the jar and slowly walked to the corner to join Rusty and Evelyn Rose. Speaking in a whisper to no one in particular, but yet to everyone, Millie said, "He's not dead? I thought you were digging a—"

I know," Father said, cutting her off. "I'm sorry, I didn't think you'd be back that quick."

Millie sat on her hip next to Rusty and reached out to touch his head that was swollen twice its normal size. The lightest touch caused him to whine and cry without moving. He opened his eyes when he heard Millie say, "Mr. Highley said if you was alive when I got home, that you'd probably make it." A soft whine came from Rusty's throat. Rusty looked up and slightly moved his mouth. Millie smiled and said, "I see that silly grin of yours."

Father brought over a rag with some of the turpentine on it and laid it across Rusty's snout where the fang holes were. He whined some, but Millie pet his flank, and Rusty knew he was being helped. Mother boiled water and placed the sassafras roots in the water to make a sweet-smelling dark red tea.

After cooling the tea, Mother soaked a rag in the pot of tea and handed it to Millie. "Here," she said, "let the tea drip in the corner of his mouth. Go slow so it will go down his throat."

"How will I know he's getting any?" Millie asked.

"You'll see him swallow," Mother replied. "Seven or eight swallows will be good."

The evening dragged on. Millie stayed with Rusty while Mother prepared a squirrel stew. Mattie helped Evelyn Rose pack a few things while Father hitched up the horse to the wagon for a quick evening trip to town to take Evelyn Rose to her job at the doctor's house.

Before their evening meal, the family gathered around Millie and Rusty. Instead of prayers at the table, they held hands and prayed in the corner of the room where Rusty lay. Father said his usual prayer for the meal about family and safekeeping, but tonight, he added a prayer for their pet and his healing.

After the quick meal, everyone said "See you later" to Millie, and they headed out the door, except for Evelyn Rose, who hung back to have a quick talk with her sister.

Kneeling next to Millie at the dog's head, Evelyn Rose said, "That could be me, but he saved me. He warned me, but I was in too big of a hurry."

Millie reached up and took Evelyn Rose's hand in hers and told her, "It's okay, it's what he does."

Looking at their hands holding together, Evelyn Rose said, "Just like that, then he takes the strike."

Mother yelled, "Time to go!" Millie squeezed her hand, and Evelyn Rose squeezed back. Their eyes shared a bond that can only be shared by sisters, and nothing else had to be said.

Chapter 27

Heading south in order to get to Columbia Road that connected Farmington and the mining area of Doe Run seemed to take forever for Mattie and Evelyn Rose. "Always seems long on the journey there," explained Father.

Mother smiled and told the girls, "That's because of the excitement. Just like it seems no time at all coming home. The excitement is gone."

"But we should have been there hours ago," Evelyn Rose told her parents.

"It'll be okay," Father explained. "They'll understand. Then you can work twice as hard tomorrow."

They all laughed except Evelyn Rose.

Arriving at the large two-story house late in the evening, the family apologized for not being able to visit longer as there were only a couple of hours of daylight left. Apology accepted and being understanding, the doctor and his wife waved goodbye to Evelyn Rose's family. They invited her in to make herself at home. The three of them sat together in what the doctor's wife called the greeting room. Another man and woman quickly entered the room with a silver pot of tea, a glass pitcher of milk, and some sweet cakes.

"I didn't know you had servants," Evelyn Rose said.

To which the doctor's wife stared wide-eyed and then let out a belly laugh that embarrassed Evelyn Rose. "No! My dear!" she explained, then introduced the pair.

"This is my husband's brother and his wife. Actually, the house belongs to them."

"I am so sorry," Evelyn Rose apologized. "I thought—"

"I understand," she said to Evelyn Rose. "As a matter of fact, I think your sister, Millie, thought all of us were servants when she was here before."

Evelyn Rose took her sweet cake and dunked it in the milk. The old doctor laughed and told her, "I think you are a girl after my own heart."

Evelyn Rose didn't understand. The doctor's wife leaned over and whispered to Evelyn Rose, "He likes to dunk too."

A little confused, Evelyn Rose looked at the old doctor. With a kind smile, he demonstrated a dunk of his own.

"Oh!" Evelyn Rose said.

The doctor's wife looked at him with a distaste. Then she smiled and said, "Don't encourage him." She proceeded to explain, "When the mine incorporated in Doe Run, the company had homes built here on Columbia Road. The doctor's brother, who worked for the company, lives here. Then when we retired, we were invited to move here with them, and this is where we have been ever since. We were originally from New York and, unfortunately and sadly, neither of our families had any children."

Evelyn Rose was introduced to the doctor's brother and wife and was given a quick walk-through of the home. Evelyn Rose was shown what was expected of her and her job duties and then shown to her room.

Evelyn Rose was at a loss for words when she opened the door and stepped into her room. The upstairs room alone, she guessed, was bigger than the whole cabin she lived in. Feeling a little guilty and overwhelmed, Evelyn Rose softly spoke, "This bed is bigger than my bedroom."

The doctor's wife sat on the bed and patted the blanket to invite Evelyn Rose to sit next to her. Holding Evelyn Rose's hand, she said, "I hope you don't judge us until the weekend is over. Yes, we've been blessed with a beautiful home and nice things. We travel and go to different places, but"—she paused to makes sure Evelyn Rose looked at her instead of the room—"my husband and I would trade it all for just one child."

Evelyn Rose saw the sincerity in the old lady's tear-filled eyes and said, "It will take some time getting used to it."

Chapter 28

"Hey, you!" the scruffy man with a half-filled bottle of liquor in his hands yelled as he veered sideways to keep from walking into the mining wagon.

"What is wrong with that man?" Mattie asked.

"It's Friday evening," Father explained. "Lots of miners and mill workers get paid. They come to town, cash their paychecks, and some buy liquor before they go home."

"I guess that's not a good thing to do," she said. "Especially the way he is acting."

With a bit of a bitter tone, Father told Mattie, "Some have a social drink and just go home to their families. Others don't know when to quit and never know where home is or what it's like to have a family."

Mattie bit her bottom lip at the strange mood Father developed and decided not to say any more. No one said another thing until they arrived at the General Store.

Arriving late and just before dark, the family caught Cecil's Pa before he locked the door. Father apologized for coming so late and explained the predicament.

"Never a problem among friends," Cecil's Pa told them. "Come on in, and I'll get you a lantern."

Mattie stayed on the wooden sidewalk while her mother and father got what supplies they needed. In no time, the wagon was loaded, and Cecil's Pa yelled out, "Don't worry about the bill. I know you need to go!"

Thank yous and goodbyes were said, and Cecil's father gave Mattie three hard candy sticks and told her, "If you don't eat all three before you get home, share with your sister, okay?"

Mattie agreed and later asked her parents, "Why'd he wink kinda funny at me?"

Mother laughed, but she could tell Father was still in that strange stupor.

They rode through town, past the livery stable, past the church, and to the schoolhouse when Father told Ole Smokey to hold up. Knowing the routine, Mother reached under the seat for the lantern. Father lit it and hooked it on a long rod that hung toward the horse. The oil lantern had a reflector on the back side of it, so it wouldn't shine in their eyes but reflect out past the horse. As they traveled down Maple Road a little slower, Father asked Mattie for a piece of her candy.

"Before this stupid leg accident, I'd probably stew in my own self-pity," Father said to his youngest daughter.

Sitting between her parents, Mattie looked up at her father while Mother slipped her arm through Mattie's just for comfort. For what she knew would soon be said.

Father looked down at the young girl and said, "Your mother tells me confession is good for the soul." Then with a hint of a smile, he told her, "So is this hard candy? How about another small piece?"

Placing the hard piece of candy between his cheek and gum, he began his confession. "A long time ago when I was about your age, I lived with a family that had taken me in when I was just a baby. I never knew my mother and suspect she had died when I was born or maybe soon after, according to what some folks say. I kinda moved around from family to family never knowing if I had any kin. I sometimes stayed with whoever had a meal to share but mostly with one certain family. Went to school some when I was young. Learned to read and write. Was pretty good at it too. I knew my numbers. You know the basics. I do have to say this family does well in the learning part of life. You know, your Mother was raised by a teacher."

"Yes, we know," Mattie said. "Especially when we get home from school. Mother's always making sure we've done our work right." Feeling a slight tug from her Mother's hooked arm, she looked up at her mother. Seeing her lips pursed together, Mattie knew she was to shush.

Father continued, "Didn't take long to fall out of school, especially since there was no one to push me in the right direction. So I spent a lot of time just running the streets, doing odd jobs here and there, and just getting by. Then one day when I was thirteen or fourteen years old, my friend that I was staying with and I were walking down an alley behind the town hotel, and we saw this man getting up from behind a pile of trash. We didn't see him at first but heard him holler at a dog to leave him alone. Seeing this man stagger and then eat out of the trash and take a bottle out from inside his coat for a drink, we thought we'd have a little fun. So we started hollering and throwing things at him. The more we did, the more he staggered and fell down, breaking his bottle. We were just a-laughing when old man Brightwell comes up behind us and grabs me by the ear. My buddy took off and left me all alone with the hotel owner.

"He drags me inside the back door. He told me to look at that man. I did. He was down on all fours crying and trying to drink what liquor he could lick up off the ground. Old man Brightwell didn't say it right then, but I knew something wasn't quite right when I looked at that drunk.

"'Have you ever been starving for food or about half froze to death?' the hotel owner asks me as he makes me sit in a chair in the kitchen area. I just kinda slouched in the chair 'cause I didn't really care anything at all about the situation." Father continued the story. "Nope, didn't care. I had my chin down while looking at Mr. Brightwell out of the top of my eyes and rubbing my ear when the next thing I knew, he kneels right in front of me, staring eye to eye.

"'A lot of people have watched over you,' he says to me, 'just to make sure you didn't go hungry and at least have a warm place to lay your head.'

"'I never asked anybody,' I said to him. Then I turned sideways to avoid the man. That's when he gets up and backs away toward the door and, in a voice that chilled me to the bone, says, 'The next time you ever wonder about your daddy, just take a good look at that man's face.' Then he leaves through the door and leaves me all alone."

Mattie was just a-staring at her father, understanding most of it but was afraid to ask anything.

"Okay, well, anyway, that's why I don't like being around drunks," Father stammered and continued, "I went back outside, and the man was gone. I think I even heard myself holler 'Dad!' Don't know what happened, but he was never seen again. I even asked Mr. Brightwell once, and he just hugged me and says, 'Best you never know. Such is the way of life.' So I never asked again. I've always wondered if something happened to cause that kind of pain or was that the cause of an unforgettable pain. But anyway," Father said, "now you know, and so it goes."

Mattie leaned her head against her mother and said, "Just think, none of this would be if you'd known."

"Look out that way," Father said, nodding to the northwest. "See the heat lightning in the sky?" He pulled a little on the reins to slow Ole Smokey down a bit. He and his wife smiled at each other as they headed toward home. "Yep, nighttime ride with my girls watching the lightning in the sky, the fireflies coming off the ground, and listening to peepers and katydids singing their songs." About that time, a whip-poor-will cried off in the distance, and Father thought to himself, *Life is, after all, what you make of it.*

The three rode in silence for about a quarter of an hour when they came around Maple Road and could see their homeplace in the distance. No one said another word. Father sighed and took a deep breath. Mother said a silent prayer. Mattie's grip became a little tighter on her mother's arm. They all thought of Millie and the snake-bitten dog, Rusty.

Bringing Ole Smokey to a halt at the gate, they got down from the wagon. Still no words were said. Father opened the gate, and Mattie and Mother walked toward the house, leaving Father to put Ole Smokey away for the night. Still nary a word, Father did his best to hurry but still had some trouble adjusting to the new shoe. After giving Ole Smokey a little feed, he petted the horse and thought to himself, *I'll brush you good in the morning.* Hobbling along to get some fresh water, he saw his wife, and Mattie came back outside and just sat down on the big flat rock porch. Trying to read their mannerisms, he came to the decision that things were just as they were. He finished in the shed and made a deliberate slow walk to the cabin.

Finally, standing at the rock porch, his wife looked up and said, "They're both sound asleep, and I think this one is too," looking down at Mattie with her head in her mother's lap.

"I guess he's going to make it," Father said as he sat down on the porch next to his wife and sleeping daughter.

"Yeah, he will," Mother replied. "But his head is as big as a late summer watermelon."

"I'm sure it hurts something fierce," he said.

Father tried to pick up Mattie, but his wife told him, "I got her, but the way she is growing, it won't be long before I can't."

Father helped Mother to her feet. She smiled and said, "Or I'll be too big," looking at her belly.

Chapter 29

Millie heard a scratching sound along with a soft whine and realized someone put a pillow under her head and a blanket over her shoulders. She was still half asleep but awake enough to tell it's morning because of the light behind her eyelids. *There's that sound again*—a light scratching and soft whining. Millie bolted straight up in a sitting position with both hands still on the floor. "Rusty!" she cried. "You're up! What is wrong with your neck?" Rusty let loose with a good bark then looked back at the door and started scratching again. "Okay, okay," Millie said as she got up. "I'll let you out." She walked to the door just staring at the giant waddle about the size of the dog's head hanging from his neck. They both went out. Rusty went to the tree, and Millie went to the outhouse. Millie watched Rusty move about with the big waddle swinging back and forth.

"Well, it looks like someone is feeling better," Father said from the doorway.

Millie looked his way and saw Father and Mother standing together in the doorway of the cabin. "I'd say so," Millie said, "but what is going on with his neck?"

"I suspect all that poison from the snakebite has settled in his neck," Father told her. "Looks like it doesn't bother him though. You might try to keep him calm as much as can, at least for a little while."

Millie called the dog and took him to the shaded side of the house and tied him to the lean-to. Rusty struggled some but was too sore to try very hard. She left him with some fresh water and a few scraps from last evening's mess of squirrel. The dog was content for a while.

As Father went to let Bessie and Ole Smokey out to graze for the day, Millie got his attention and indicated she was going to check on the sheep and pointed to the southwest hill. Father looked at Rusty to make sure he wasn't noticing and gave Millie a thumbs-up.

Millie started toward the pond being sure to keep the house between herself and her dog. Every so often, she took a quick glance back and half hoped to see Rusty running toward her. Knowing better and not seeing him, she told herself he needed to stay home. She quickly made it through the gap that led to the back field next to Mrs. Bell's woods. Not seeing any sheep, Millie headed to the valley between the two hills. Walking along the creek, Millie saw the sheep not too far in the direction she was going. A quick glance from front to back, Millie knew the general health of the sheep was good. Then a count from the farthest to the nearest, and all twenty-seven sheep were accounted for. This time, Millie walked toward the southwest hill for her fence inspection when at the edge of the valley, just at the north base of the hill, she found what she had been expecting.

"Oh, yes, perfect timing," she said out loud, talking to the sweet, black juicy dewberries. Millie bent down and picked a few for now and decided she would need two buckets for dewberry cobbler for the Fourth of July picnic. Thinking she should pick enough for canning and jelly and jam this year, or maybe pick enough to sell, she then decided, no, they would want to keep them all. It's too much work to let others have them.

After gobbling down a dozen of the black tasty treats, Millie traveled up the hill to the fence line. She stopped once to go around the spot where she first met the young man that was now in jail for his evil deeds. For a few seconds Millie got heavy legged, and cold chills started to climb up her back. "No!" she shouted and then shook off the weak feeling of uneasiness. She took long strides on up the hill to the top and, without hesitation, made a left to follow the fence to the Bell farm. The more she went, the faster Millie got and was soon jogging and then running until she walked around the tree with her left arm stretched out. With her hand against the oak, Millie walked counterclockwise until she caught her breath and sat down.

Missing Rusty and hoping he's all right, Millie decided not to linger. As she left, she thought about how the old oak always seemed to put her in a better mood. A few steps down the fence, she turned to see the outstretched arms of the giant oak and returned to it a pleasant smile then headed home.

"I need some buckets," Millie said, coming through the front door.

"What for?" asked Mattie, who was sitting with her mother and father at the table.

"Dewberries" was all Millie had to say.

"Are there very many this year?" Father asked.

"More than I've seen before," Millie answered him. "And they're as big as the end of my thumb!"

Mattie and Father started to get up, but Mother made everyone sit until breakfast was done. Eggs, bacon, and skillet bread were placed on the table along with cold milk Father had brought in from the spring. "Dewberry jam," Mother said as she spread butter on her hot bread. "There ain't nothing any better on hot bread."

The whole family dug in and hurriedly ate breakfast so they could go get the newly found dewberries. Father asked Millie, "Do you think I should hook the wagon up so we all can ride back to the spot?"

"You can," Millie answered, "but I am going now. A flock of turkeys could clean that patch out in no time!"

"I'm going with you," Mattie mumbled, stuffing the last of her breakfast in her mouth.

"Good! You can help carry a bucket," Millie said to Mattie. "And if you guys bring the wagon, could Rusty ride along?"

"If he's doing well," Father told Millie. "You know how he is. If he sees you leaving, he'll bark his head off. But if he just sees me in the wagon, he'll think you're still here and not get so excited."

Millie scrambled to her feet, grabbed a couple of buckets, and said, "Let's go, runt."

Liking the attention but not the name-calling, Mattie grabbed another chunk of skillet bread and left the cabin following close behind her sister.

Taking the same route as she did earlier, Millie explained to Mattie about staying close and directly behind so the cabin was between them and Rusty. Father did what he could, drawing the attention of the dog as he got Ole Smokey hitched up to the wagon.

Before reaching the pond, Mattie yelled out with what little breath she had left, "Please, Millie, slow down some! I can't keep up!"

"We'll rest on the other side of the dam," Millie informed her little sister. "Come on, we're almost there, and keep up."

Not more than thirty yards, and the pair ascended the dam to the lower side of the pond. Halfway up, Millie heard Mattie's bucket hit the ground. She stopped to give Mattie a hand and pulled her up and over.

"I'm sorry, sis," Millie told Mattie. "I just don't want Rusty to see us." Sitting down under a shade tree, they both took a breather by the water's edge before going any farther. "You did good keeping up," she said, giving her little sister words of encouragement.

"This water makes me thirsty," Mattie said. "I hope Mother and Father bring us something to drink."

"Yeah, me too," Millie replied. "I'm sure they will. Climbing this hill right after breakfast sure will make a person want something to drink. Hey, this reminds me of when we were going to come up here and catch some fish."

Mattie's eyes lit up as she excitedly answered, "Oh, Millie! I thought you forgot all about taking me fishing!"

"We will soon, very soon," Millie told her. "I just didn't know how busy we'd be ever since Father left and then came back wounded. Now listen," Millie said, explaining how they were going to leave, "we'll have to hunker down from here to the gap in the fence. Once there, we'll be okay and just walk down to the giant oak. Then we will cut across the field, follow the creek a little way, and we'll be there."

"All right," Mattie said, "you lead the way, and I'll follow."

"No, not from here," Millie explained again. "From here to the gap, we'll go side by side. Make sure you stay bent over."

Mattie grinned, and Millie patted her on the head. "Let's go," Millie said.

They continue on and soon were through the route Millie had laid out for them. Once they were through the gap, it was a nice leisurely walk to the valley creek. All the sheep had moved off and were making their way around the base of the northwest hill in order to stay out of the warm summer sun.

"See, look over here," Millie yelled. "Look at all the dewberries. I've never seen this many before."

Mattie rushed over to Millie and asked, "I wonder why there are so many, and they look big too?"

"Well, I think it's because of the cool start to the summer and not having any drought time so far," Millie guessed. "I'm sure we've beat all the other animals in the woods to them. The deer and turkey can almost clean them out in one day, not to mention the squirrels and quail."

"Could have been that fella that was staying out here in the woods that kept all the animals run off," Mattie said.

"Could have," Millie said, turning to Mattie, "but that's enough talk about that. This is a good thing, so let's not talk about bad things. Here's your bucket. Let's see how many we can pick before Father and Mother get here. Come on!"

"Yeah, I bet I can pick more than you," Mattie challenged her big sister.

"What makes you say that?" Millie asked.

"'Cause I'm closer to the ground, and it don't make my back hurt," Mattie said with a giggle.

Millie placed both fists on her hips with the bucket still in one hand being held by the bail. "You know, you just might be right," she said. "Of all the berries here, dewberries are the hardest to pick. The thorns aren't near as bad as the blackberries', but this bending over does hurt my back. If it wasn't for being the best-tasting berry ever made, I doubt I'd go to the trouble of picking them. Besides, the people in town will give top dollar for dewberries, especially right before the Fourth of July."

"You think Mother will let us sell some?" Mattie asked.

"She will, if we don't have enough jars to can all of them," Millie replied. Then she noticed Mattie had the whole bottom of her bucket covered with the black sparkling jewels. "I guess I better quit talking and get to picking!"

"You know what Mother always says," Mattie remarked.

"Yeah, yeah, yeah! I know," Millie answered. "'It's okay to talk, just not with your hands when there is work to be done.' I heard it before."

Millie bent over and started picking, and it didn't take long before the picking became a heated race. Millie had to straighten up to move to the next spot while Mattie just stayed close to the ground. Mattie couldn't hold as many in her small hands, and Millie had no trouble picking them with both hands. But it was a close race.

"Hello," came a nearby greeting.

Shocked and surprised, both girls lifted straight up to see their father standing just a few yards away.

"You scared us half to death!" Millie said and gave her little sister a shoulder bump that almost knocked her over.

Mattie regained her balance and asked, "Did Mother come with you?"

Laughing at the girls' competitiveness and holding up a big jug, Father said, "Yes, she's back at the wagon with Rusty. Thought I'd bring you two some drinking water before we all come down. Are you ready for a drink?"

The two girls looked at each other and made a race of it to get to the water jug. "You bet we are!" Millie said, getting there first. "I beat!" she said to Mattie, then wrinkled her nose but quickly changed to a smile as she handed Mattie the jug to have the first drink.

Mattie took three large gulps of water and said "Thanks" and handed Millie the jug.

Millie took a big mouthful and gargled out "You're welcome," and the three started laughing.

Father left, still laughing, to go back to the wagon and yelled, "Be right back!"

Millie and Mattie resumed picking the dewberries until Mother and Father got there along with Rusty on a rope. With his big neck swinging back and forth like a turkey waddle, Rusty pulled Mother to get to the girls. "I'd hoped you would come!" Millie yelled out.

"I think he is fine," Father said. "If he stays close, I believe you can let him go. Can you make him stay close by?"

"Yes, I think if he was loose, he would calm down," she replied.

Before Mother could slip the rope off his neck, Rusty lunged toward Millie and pulled the rope right out of her hands. "Fine," Mother said, "I didn't want to untie you anyway. Just let Millie do it."

Rusty did his bunny hop all the way to Millie. "Now calm down," she scolded, "so I can untie you! What was it that made you feel so much better, the turpentine or the sassafras root? Or was it what Mr. Highley said about bites not being that bad?"

"I do believe he would have been all right if left alone," Father replied. Father placed a piece of leather on the ground to kneel on. Then slowly got on his knees with the use of his walking cane. Noticing Millie watching, Father squinted his eyes at her and said, "What? You think maybe I should try some?"

Mother interrupted with her theory and said, "It was love and prayers that got him well. Sassafras just tastes and smells good, and that turpentine just stinks. Anything that stinks that bad will either kill you or cure you. This time, the Good Lord heard your cries and answered your prayers. Now let's get to picking. I'd like to make the preacher and his family a nice pie!"

"What about us?" Mattie questioned.

Mother smiled then with a wink said, "If there are enough berries, we'll see."

It was a good season for the dewberries. In all, the family had picked almost seven gallons. There was more than enough for a couple of pies and several jars of dewberry jam. There was even enough left to give their neighbors.

Millie took a gallon to Mrs. Link when she went to gather the eggs. Mattie and Mother took a gallon to Mrs. Bell. Father started a fire so Mother could begin baking pies.

Chapter 30

Millie arrived at Mrs. Link's to find several people at her house. Before Millie's knuckles hit the door, a man about her father's age yelled out, "Look, it's the neighbor girl! Come on in!"

Familiar with most of the people but introduced anyway, Millie greeted each of Mrs. Link's children. Millie handed the gallon of dewberries to Mrs. Link and politely excused herself and said, "We picked these this morning, and I can come back later to gather the eggs."

"Millie," came a voice from the man who invited her in, "if you don't mind, we'd like to talk to you for a minute."

Taken aback by the invite, Millie looked at Mrs. Link still holding the berries with a very sad expression on her face. She walked over and took the berries out of her trembling hands and asked, "Is something wrong?"

Before she could reply, one of the children, a daughter, spoke up, "Please, Millie, if you'll have a seat, we'll tell you why the long faces."

"All right," she said, holding on to her neighbor's hand as they walked to the sofa to sit and listen.

"Ever since our father died, we've been terribly worried about Mother—" the daughter explained.

"It really started before that," the brother said, cutting off his sister.

Mrs. Link bowed her head, and Millie held her hand tighter when the shaking became worse. Then a teardrop hit her hand.

The son folded his arms and raised one to put his chin between his thumb and index finger as he turned back to his mother. The daughter knelt down in front and placed her hands on theirs. "We worry," she said. "We've worried for a long time. None of us live nearby, and now we've got families of our own. So we'd like to sell the place and have Mother live close to us."

Millie patted Mrs. Link's hand after the daughter removed her hand. She bent down to look into her moist pale-blue eyes and said, "That's not so bad. Don't you want to live with one of your family?"

Millie was surprised when her neighbor turned her head and heard the son say with his back turned, "I'm afraid you've misunderstood. Mother won't be coming to live with us. We're putting her in a place where she will be with other elderly folks."

Millie stood and blinked a couple of times. She took a deep breath, trying to remain calm, and asked, "What do you mean a *place?*"

Saying to his sister as he walked away, "Why are we even telling this girl?"

Sitting next to her mother, the daughter apologized to Millie and then explained, "A man from St. Louis by the name of Jennings wants to buy the farm. Mother won't sell, so the best thing we can do is move her closer to us. She is getting forgetful, and we're afraid she'll wander off, and no one will be around."

Millie took a couple of steps backward and with a free hand, she covered her wide-open mouth. Through her hand, she said, "You're having your mother committed?"

"No, it's not like that," the daughter said, reaching her hand out to Millie.

Millie took another couple of steps backward while saying, "Just to sell the house?"

"Listen, please," the daughter pleaded as she stood. "We want you to have the chickens."

"Please don't!" Millie said as she backed out the front door. Not knowing what else to say, she left the berries on the porch and ran down the road. Not understanding and trying to figure things out in her mind, Millie remembered what her mother said earlier, and she began praying for Mrs. Link.

Chapter 31

Walking through the door, Millie saw Father kneading dough to help Mother with the pies. "Where's the eggs?" he asked.

"There won't be any," Millie explained. "I just talked to Mrs. Link's family and—"

"I know," Father said, looking down at the dough as his strong hands continued to knead.

"Why didn't you say anything?" Millie asked as she sat at the table. Rusty got up from his spot and came to lie down at Millie's feet under the table.

"The plan was to tell you when we all go into town for the Fourth of July celebration," Father explained as he picked back up the kneading of the pie dough. "Mrs. Link's children weren't supposed to be here until after the Fourth."

"Did you know about them selling the farm?" she asked.

"Yeah," he said, "they asked Mr. Highley to buy it first. Then they asked me. Your mother liked the idea of the big house, but we both love the farm east of Bonne Terre better. Then we can build the house the way we want."

"It's not right!" Mille said in a bitter tone.

"No, it's not," Father agreed. "But she can't stay by herself, and they don't want her to interfere in their lives."

"She'll die," she said.

"She's old, and we all die," Father replied.

"Not alone and without your family!" Millie cried.

"No, you're right," he said.

"I'm going for a walk," Millie told Father. "Will you keep Rusty in?"

"Sure," he said, "I'm sorry."

Chapter 32

Looking up the field toward the gap in the fence next to the Bell place, Millie decided to take the shady route on the north side of the farm. Her walking staff in hand, she walked the hillside knowing the sheep would be somewhere next to the wood line. From here, she could view the Link farm and the homestead.

Almost to the tree line, Millie noticed the sheep just above the pond, hugging the edge of the woods. She thought about how many sheep they had while looking how close they ate the grass to the ground. "Twenty-seven is too many for this farm," she said out loud. In her mind, she heard the words of some cattle farmers saying sheep eat the grass so close that nothing else can feed where they have been. "Too many sheep," she said again. "Just a bit of a drought would ruin us." Finally making the walk up to the tree line, Millie found a nice rock under one of the hickory trees and sat down with a long, slow sigh. "I love this place," she spoke aloud.

Seeing people go in and out of the Link home and loading some of the furniture out the back door, Millie whispered, "I love my family." She sat in silence and stared out across the overgrown fields of the Link farm where no single animal roamed. She took a deep breath and sighed again and said, "I love our animals." Thinking of all the events the past few months, Millie closed her eyes and prays, "I love you, Father in heaven. Please watch over Mrs. Link." She thought of others who were gone and asked for Cecil's protection and that Evelyn Rose made it home okay. She thanked God for her father's speedy recovery and asked that Mother stayed strong and the baby was well. She also thanked God for her home and the love and happiness there even though it was small. Millie looked out across the field and let her mind just wander. A breeze awakened her senses, and she closed her prayer.

Leaving the rock behind, Millie walked to the edge of the woods toward the south and sound of the sheep on the hill. Staying in the shade and from the high vantage point, Millie spotted her mother and Mattie on the road almost to the cabin. "Oh, Mrs. Bell is with them and pulling a cart," she said. Letting her curiosity get the better of her, Millie left and headed down the hill to see what was going on.

As Millie made a beeline to her home, she had to laugh as all the sheep made steps to follow her, and each giving out a baa. She slapped her staff on the ground and laughed even harder when some of the lambs jumped and bucked in small attempts to challenge the slapping staff. Finally, they all just watched as Millie traveled toward home.

Rushing to the cabin door, Millie caught a glimpse of the cart filled with several dirty canning jars and lids with wire bells on them. "Somebody's got their work cut out for them," Millie mumbled to herself. Opening the door, Millie said, "Wow, it sure is hot in here."

"Glad you are home," Mother said. "Do me a favor and prop that door open."

Placing a stick made just for that occasion, Millie propped the door open to let out the heat from the boiling dewberries. She looked at her father slaving away and keeping an eye on the two cobblers. Millie greeted Mrs. Bell and told her, "I'm so glad to see you."

"Good to see you too, Millie," Tennessee returned the greeting.

Millie held her hand as to block her view from her parents and said in a whisper, "We never fuss when you come to help."

"I heard that, young lady!" Mother exclaimed. "Now why don't you take that cart of jars to the spring and give them a good scrubbing."

"Okay, I can do that," Millie replied.

Mattie looked up from cleaning and picking out bad berries and said, "What no fuss?" Everyone chuckled as Millie left to do her part in the canning process.

After several hours of hard and tedious work, everyone stood back to admire the several dozen jars of dewberry preserves. Taking a good dozen, Father set them aside for Mrs. Bell, who instantly said, "No, that is too many." Mother and Father gave her a stern look, and she gladly conceded, "Well, if I must."

"Now then," Father said as he prepared to lift one end of the kitchen table, "will someone help with the table?" Millie and Mattie helped Father carefully lift the table with all the jars of preserves on it out of the way. Mother pulled the handwoven rug from under the table to reveal the bare floor. Father got four T-pegs from the shelf and placed them in four holes in the floor. Millie and Mother got on one end, and Father got on the other end. On the count of three, they all lifted the floor up to reveal a four-foot by six-foot root cellar that was about five feet deep. The cellar was very carefully lined with cut stones on the four walls all the way up to support the center of the cabin floor. The floor of the cellar was made of red clay dirt. Providing coolness in the summer as well as warmth in the winter, the hole was a great place to store most of the food for long periods of time.

"Mr. Highley knew what he was doing when he and his brother built this place," Father said as he admired the goods he had stored. Father got down in the cellar, and they all began handing him the jars of dewberry preserves.

"Wait a minute!" Mother said. "You have to hand them back."

Looking puzzled, Father asked, "Why?" He then realized before she could answer that they forgot to put the date on the jars.

Everything was soon in order and back in place. "Perfect timing," Millie said. After a hard day's work like that, I'd say it's time to all go out in the cool evening and have some fresh dewberry cobbler."

"I agree," Mattie said as she clapped her hands.

Father looked at Mrs. Bell and said, "How about you, Tennessee? Will you join us for some fresh cobbler?"

"Don't mind if I do," she answered. "Thank you very much!"

A soft breeze drifted out of the valley from between the two hills. "It's always cooler here than at my place," Mrs. Bell told the young family. Enjoying the freshly made cobbler, they watched the large setting sun that sat directly between the two hills of the far end of the valley.

Chapter 33

Early the next morning, Millie and Mattie washed up after a quick breakfast and started getting ready for church. They were all excited to see Evelyn Rose and find out how she did at her cleaning job at the doctor's house in town.

The ride to town was filled with chatter about Evelyn Rose and her stay away from home. Millie and Mattie sat with their parents on the bench seat of the buckboard wagon to keep their clothes clean. "You girls act like she's been gone all summer," Mother told them.

Mattie replied to her mother, "She's been gone long enough to become snooty like most town folks."

"Cecil's not snooty," Millie sternly informed her little sister. "And neither is his family or the Highley family or the doctor and his wife, for that matter."

"They are some," Mattie said, folding her arms and sticking her bottom lip out. "Just look how they dress in their fancy clothes."

"Hey, you two!" Father interrupted. "We're on our way to church." He gave Ole Smokey a flick of the reins to step it up a bit. He then said, "Just remember who lived in our cabin before we did."

"Yes," Mother said. "Cecil's pa was just a floor sweeper and worked very hard to become part owner in that store."

"I think you're just jealous," Millie told Mattie.

Mattie began to cry, "She's calling me names."

"That's enough," Mother said. "Your sister will not be snooty."

The rest of the ride to church was in silence, but Millie and Mattie rode with their arms crossed, trying to hold themselves still and prevent them from uttering another word.

Arriving a little early, they got one of the best spots under a shade tree to hitch Ole Smokey. Mattie took off at a dead run to see if her sister had made it. "Young lady!" Mother yelled. Mattie made an abrupt stop. "You'll not run like a heathen, and you'll wait and walk like a lady with the rest of us."

"Aww," Mattie whined.

"Don't aww me," Mother said. "We've already had this talk." Taking her by the hand to the back of the wagon and lifting her up to sit on it, Mother said, "Now please try to stay clean." Mother took a rag and wiped the dust off Mattie's shoes.

"Sorry, Mother," Mattie replied.

As the four of them walked through the double front doors, they could see all the way to the front. Evelyn Rose jumped up and almost flew past the rows of wooden benches to greet her family. Soon she was followed by the pastor, who greeted them with a warm smile and told them, "This young lady was here waiting at the front door early this morning before I arrived."

Looking up at the reverend then to her parents, Evelyn Rose said, "I couldn't wait another minute to see everyone."

"We missed you too!" said Mattie. Stepping back to get a better view, Mattie remarked, "That's some fancy dress!"

"Okay, girls," Mother said before anything else could be said. "We'll talk about the dress after church. Here, Reverend," Mother said, handing him the cloth-covered cobbler. Millie let him know that the pie was made of dewberries.

"That makes it even better!" the reverend said, covering the cobbler back up. "Dewberries are sweeter, and the seeds aren't as bad as blackberries. They are the best of the best."

"We hoped you would like it," Mother said, keeping an eye on Mattie fingering Evelyn Rose's new dress.

"I'll set it in the back with the others," he said.

"Oh," Mother said. "I'll take it back. You go ahead and greet the people."

"Thank you. It must have been a good spring for dewberries. A couple more, and we can have a cobbler social after church," Reverend remarked.

Father looked at Mother, and they began to laugh. "It's the thought that counts. Besides, I know mine will be tastier than the others. Now go find us a seat while I take this to the back."

The service ran a little longer than usual because of all the talk about Wednesday's Fourth of July holiday. Plans were for an outdoor afternoon meal right after the parade. A potluck meal pleased everyone.

Millie asked her mother, "Can we bring chicken?"

"Why would we bring chicken when we don't have any chickens?" Mother replied with a quizzical look on her face.

Millie whispered back, "When I was at Mrs. Link's house yesterday, one of the children kinda said that I might have her chickens."

Father leaned over to look past his wife and told Millie, "We'll go by after church to check on Mrs. Link. I'll offer to buy the chickens."

Mattie leaned over to look past her father and mother and bit her bottom lip when Millie saw her. Millie wrinkled her nose back at her when Father gently took his hand and pushed Mattie back to sit up straight.

After church services were over, Evelyn Rose told her parents that the old doctor wanted all of them to stop by his house.

Father looked at Evelyn Rose with a straight face then at her new dress. He then looked at his wife and with a bit of a frown, looked back at Evelyn Rose. "Is it important?" he asked.

"I'm not supposed to say," she said. "But he's been working really hard on something." She then took her hanky that was made to match her new dress and wiped the dust off his shoe that was made for his bad leg.

Mother took his arm and with a light pat, whispered, "It's not charity."

"I know, but—" he started to say.

"But nothing," she said, stopping her husband in mid-sentence. "Swallow a little bit of that thick pride of yours, and we'll put the canopy up and take the long way home."

With a short ride through town and west on Columbia Road, Father guided Ole Smokey into the lane of the large home where the old doctor and his wife were sitting and waiting at their gazebo. "I was hoping you would stop by," the doctor said as he and his wife came to greet them. "I've made something for you and hope like the dickens it works."

With a friendly handshake and warm hello, they were all invited to the back porch where glasses were set up for some cool drinks. Father whispered to his wife, "I wish we had saved the cobbler for here."

Mother whispered back, "Patience was never my strongest virtue."

"You have a seat and go ahead with the drinks," the doctor said. "I'll be right back."

Millie and Evelyn Rose walked around looking at the different potted plants on the patio while Mattie chased after a couple of cats. Mother scorned Mattie for getting dirty.

"Here we go," the doctor said as he came out of the back door. In his hand was a new pair of boots that were the lace-up kind and came high over the ankles.

"Listen," Father said. "I really appreciate you doing this and all, but these have to cost, and I—"

"Don't worry about that," said the doctor.

"But I just can't take them," he explained.

"You're not," the doctor said seriously. "There are a lot of people just like you. Some with injuries and some with disease. You, my good man, may be helping a lot of people. This might be the answer for some people." Taking the left shoe and unlacing it, he said, "You're helping me help them by being the first to try it out. See if you can tell a difference."

Evelyn Rose came next to her father and said, "I'll hold this while you take yours off."

Father sat down and took off his left shoe and held it up next to the one Evelyn Rose was holding. "Well, it's quite simple," he said. "The new one is taller and has laces." Squinting his eyes, he took the old shoe from Evelyn Rose and held them next to the new one. Looking up at the doctor, he said, "The heel and sole aren't as thick."

"That's right," said Evelyn Rose.

"But I was getting used to this one," Father told the doctor, holding out his old shoe. "I don't need crutches or really even a walking stick."

"Go ahead try the new one on," the doctor said, pointing to the new shoe.

"Here," Evelyn Rose said, taking the new shoe from her father. "I'll help you with it." Evelyn Rose laced the boot nice and tight and told her father, "The doctor said you'll be able to use your leg muscles and not just your ankle."

"That's right," the doctor said smiling and nodding his head. "Now stand up and give it a try."

Walking around the back patio and getting a good feel for the boot, the doctor suggested that the two of them try out the stairs in the house. Going up was a breeze, but coming down was where the real challenge was. "Wow!" said the doctor. "If I didn't know any better, a person would just think you had a little hitch in your giddyap. How did it feel?"

Looking down at the boot and taking a deep breath, he asked the doctor, "Will I be able to walk like this if I quit taking the pain medicine?"

Watching him rub the bad spot in his leg, the doctor told him, "We'll soon start cutting back on the medicine. But to answer your question, I do believe in a month or so, you'll be back to chopping down trees again. You're doing great. But now, there is something else I want to talk to you about."

"Oh, what might that be?" Father questioned.

"It's about your daughter, Evelyn Rose," the doctor said, pulling out a chair so they could have a seat at the table. "I'll be brief, and it's just something to think about."

Sitting down together, Father said, "This sounds serious. Is something wrong?"

"No, no, nothing is wrong," the smiling old doctor said placing both of his hands flat on the table. "Your daughter has been here only a few days. She is a smart girl and a hard worker as have been most of the people who have worked for us, but Evelyn Rose is different."

Father's head snapped back as he asked, "Is there something wrong with Evelyn Rose?"

Taking a deep breath and a hint of impatience, the doctor said, "There is nothing wrong. Bear with me, if you will, please? Evelyn Rose was cleaning in my study that is also somewhat like a lab. No one has ever done that without getting disgusted with the bones and jars of human parts that I have in various places. She cleaned, arranged papers, and put specimens in their places. What I am trying to say is that Evelyn Rose is smart, and she seems to have an interest in medicine."

With somewhat of a concerned look, Father leaned across the table and said, "We know that, so why don't you tell me what is really on your mind?"

The doctor said "Okay" and looked down at his hands, then without moving his head, looked up and over his glasses at Father. "We've never had children, and when the time is right, we'd like to send your daughter back east to a private school and hopefully to medical school."

"You may like to," Father said in shock, "but you are forgetting some very important things." Getting up out of his chair, he continued, "Evelynn Rose is too young, and she wouldn't want to leave. Besides, we wouldn't let her go." Shaking his head as he walked out of the study, he then stopped at the doorway. Without turning around, he made a quick laugh and says to the doctor, "Girls don't do that. She would be the laughing stock." Father stormed out the door.

Before Father could make it to the outer door, the old doctor yelled out, "Girls aren't shepherds either!" This stopped Father in his tracks. Again, he shook his head and left.

Looking at his wife as he walked to the chair, he said to her, "Get everyone in the wagon. We're leaving."

By Father's tone and mannerisms, no one argued. The doctor's wife watched as he struggled to change his shoes. "Thank you and good day," he said to her. He grabbed his walking stick and exited the house.

This time, the three girls sat in the back leaving their mother to listen to the rants coming from their father. When he was done, there was nothing but silence the rest of the way home.

Bringing Ole Smokey to the edge of the homeplace, Evelyn Rose spotted Rusty watching the horse and wagon from the front porch. One yell from Evelyn Rose, and the dog recognized the family and came at a full run. "He's all well!" Evelyn Rose yelled, looking at her big sister.

"Well, yeah," Millie responded. "Do you think a little ole copperhead could ever keep that dog down."

"But he was in a real bad way when we left," Evelyn Rose said.

"Yes, he was," Millie told her.

Mattie wormed her way in between her sisters and told Evelyn Rose, "Should've seen him yesterday. He had this great big ole neck that hung way down to here." She held her hand below her neck to about the center of her belly, showing Evelyn Rose. "When he ran, his neck would go back and forth like this."

"Father said that's where the snake's poison settled," Millie said while pushing her little sister's hand down to stop swaying.

Mattie put her hand back and told Evelyn Rose, "It was kinda funny to watch him run."

"It wasn't funny, Mattie," Millie said, grabbing her head. "Now stop, or I'll throw you off the back of this wagon."

"No you won't," she said. "'Cause I'll tell."

"It's so good to be home," Evelyn Rose laughed out.

The wagon stopped at the gate. Millie gave Mattie just enough push on the backside to cause her to jump off the end of the wagon. "Hey!" Mattie yelled.

Father turned and saw Mattie already on the ground and told her, "Go ahead and open the gate, will you, honey?"

If looks could kill, Millie would be breathing her last. "Yes, Father," Mattie sulkily said. By the time she got to the gate, Rusty greeted her with dirty paws all over the front of her dress. She unhooked the chain and hopped on the second rail to ride the gate all the way open to the stop post. After Ole Smokey passed, she saw her mother and father with their hands over their eyes, and Father grinning ear to ear. After they passed through the gate, there stood Millie and Evelyn Rose.

"Here, we'll help close the gate," Evelyn Rose said.

Millie yelled to her parents, "We're gonna walk the rest of the way!" Father waved, and the three girls walked to the cabin as Rusty bounded in front of each of them with that silly little grin when he was happy.

Chapter 34

The Sunday clothes were all changed and put away except for Mattie's. Mother took the dress and socks to wash the paw prints off and have them clean for the upcoming holiday.

"When are we going to Mrs. Link's and see about the chickens?" Millie asked Father.

"Not now," Father replied. "Let's wait until after dinner. I'd like to take a nap." He turned to walk to the back room.

Helping her mother with dinner preparations, Evelyn Rose remarked, "That's not like Father. He never takes a nap."

Mother looked at Evelyn Rose and asked, "You have no idea why he is in such a mood?"

"No, I don't," she said. "I do know the doctor asked Father to sit at the table because there was something he wanted to discuss."

"You don't know what they were discussing?" Mother inquired.

"They asked me to leave," Evelyn Rose told her mother. "Then I came out with the rest of you."

"Guess we'll talk when he is ready," Mother mumbled. "I can't imagine him getting that upset about a new shoe that works." Then Mother asked Millie to let Ole Smokey graze before he was put up.

"Yes, I will!" Millie excitedly said, eager to get out of the hot cooking area.

"Can I go too?" cried Mattie.

"Yes, you may, if you take your good shoes to the spring and clean all the dirt off."

Frowning, but deciding it was better than kitchen work, Mattie agreed.

"And here," Mother said, handing Mattie the water bucket, "I need some fresh water, and could you girls bring back some bell peppers, tomatoes, and cucumbers?"

"And watch out for snakes!" Evelyn Rose warned her sisters.

"Come on," Millie said, grabbing the bucket from Mattie. "Let's go before we're told to plow the back field."

Evelyn Rose laughed, but Mother gave Millie a stern look and stuck out a long wooden spoon. "Want to trade?" she said, pointing the wooden stick in her direction.

"No, ma'am," came the reply. "Let's go, Mattie, while the gettin' is good!"

Evelyn Rose and Mother did the cooking while Millie and Mattie got some outside chores done before dinner was ready. "Girls! Let's eat!" came the call from the front door of the cabin.

"About time," Millie told her little sister. "I'm about starved to death."

"Me too!" Mattie replied as she grabbed the bucket to bring in more water.

Millie helped Mattie carry the bucket and was met by their father about halfway. "I'll carry that if you would like," he said as he reached for the rope handle.

"It's okay," Millie told him. "I know you're not feeling well—"

"I'm not feeling bad," Father said, cutting her off. "Just have a lot to think about. Some stuff in my mind is bothering me."

"I go to that big tree up there on the hill," Millie said pointing toward the gap in the fence. "It gets me away from it all, and once you make it there, you are generally too tuckered out to worry about what's bothering you."

Father laughed and took the bucket of water from the girls. "That's the way I am when I pray," he said. "I'm all worried or mad about something, but when I bring it before the Lord, He shows me what I couldn't see on my own. As a matter of fact, that's what I have been doing in my room. We'll talk later. Right now, your mother wants us at the dinner table."

"I don't know how you do it," Father said. "That was the best Sunday dinner ever."

"Oh, you say that every time we have a big meal," Mother replied.

"No, really!" he said, reaching for a second helping.

After dinner, Millie asked Father if they could walk up the road and talk to Mrs. Link about the chickens.

"I think that's a good idea, but only if Mother comes with us," Father said.

"I'd like to go if I could get some help cleaning the kitchen and doing the dishes," Mother said.

Evelyn Rose and Mattie said in unison, "I want to go too!" Then they looked at each other and laughed because they said it at the same time.

"Tell you what, girls, if you will stay here and clean up for Mother, I'll pay you. You can spend it however you want at the Fourth of July picnic."

"We'll do it!" the two girls replied in unison again.

"Evelyn Rose is in charge while we are gone. Mattie, you listen and no fighting!" Father explained. "We won't be gone long."

As soon as Millie and her parents went through the gate, Father told them what was upsetting him and how he wanted to talk about it before making any rash decisions. He explained everything the doctor would do for Evelyn Rose. He told how the doctor and his wife never had children and would like to do for Evelyn Rose as if she were theirs.

Millie never spoke, waiting to hear what Mother had to say. Finally, the silence ended when they got to the Link home. Mother said, "She's a smart girl. We'll discuss this with Evelyn Rose and see what she thinks about it. Personally, I'm flattered someone recognizes her talents. Now let's go check on those chickens."

Millie knew it would be a shame to keep someone like Evelyn Rose from an opportunity like that. Without thinking, she remarked out loud, "A woman doctor!"

Walking down the lane, they could see some horses and carriages at the front of the house. "I thought they were coming for Mrs. Link the week after the Fourth, not the weekend before," Millie pondered aloud.

"That's the sheriff's horse. Something is not right. Why don't you stay here? I'll see what's going on," Father said.

Mother reached out and touched her husband's forearm and said, "I don't like the looks of this. Be careful."

"Sure glad we didn't bring your sisters," Mother said to Millie as Millie stepped in close to her Mother.

Watching Father talk to some men on the front porch, Mother said, "I'm almost sure the man on the right is the sheriff, but I don't know who the other man is."

Father walked to the steps and motioned for the two of them to come on. As they started walking, he came down the wooden steps and walked to meet them. "What's wrong?" Mother asked.

"Seems her daughter stayed in town last night while the brother went back to St. Louis," Father explained. "When she came back around noon, she found her mother lying in bed all dressed up, dead."

Millie placed both of her hands over her mouth in shock and surprise.

"Millie, since you were one of the last to see Mrs. Link, the Sheriff would like to speak with you," Father said.

"Why? Does he think I had something to do with this? I didn't do anything," she said defensively.

"Just answer him truthfully, and everything will be okay," Mother assured her.

Millie walked to the porch to meet the sheriff. The undertaker and Mrs. Link's daughter were there too. From the red swollen face of Mrs. Link's daughter, Millie knew this wasn't going to be an easy matter.

The sheriff asked them what brought them to Mrs. Link's today. Millie explained that she would come to the farm and gather eggs and feed the chickens for Mrs. Link. She told him she came yesterday but did not gather the eggs because Mrs. Link's children were there. She told him the daughter told her that they were selling the farm and Mrs. Link was going to live in a home. The daughter told her she could have the chickens, so she brought her mother and father to make sure it was okay to take them.

The sheriff assured her that he knows she had nothing to do with Mrs. Link's death. "Could you tell me what it was like when you were here yesterday?"

"Well, Mrs. Link looked very afraid. Her son kept pacing. I don't think he liked me being there. I think his sister was upset because of him. After she told me I could have the chickens, I backed out the door and left."

"Did you feel threatened?" the sheriff asked.

"I was watching Mrs. Link. She seemed afraid, so I was afraid. They told me they had a buyer for the farm," she answered.

"Okay," said the Sheriff. "You know, Mrs. Link was old, and it hasn't been that long ago that her husband passed. I'm sure it was difficult for her to be alone. I'm not suspecting anything. I need to get the suspicion out of the way."

"Do you think someone killed Mrs. Link?" Millie asked.

"I can't answer that," he said.

Millie and the sheriff walked into the house. Mother greeted Millie and gave her a hug.

"It's like she willed herself to die," Mrs. Link's daughter said. "She was all dressed up like she was going to church. She was all dressed up, shoes on, hair brushed, and makeup on. Her Sunday bonnet was lying beside her, and her handbag was in her hands."

"Your mother was a good Christian woman," Millie said to the daughter. "We will all miss her."

Millie watched the young woman's hands shake so hard she knew what the Sheriff suspected. Something wasn't quite right. With a half hug and a soft pat on the back, Millie told the daughter "I'm sorry" and walked out of the room.

On the walk home, Millie and her parents talked about the unfortunate situation. "Just seems odd that Mrs. Link would be like that," Millie pondered out loud.

"Yeah," Father agreed, "but she always dressed like that for church. It's not unusual for her to go to Sunday services."

"I don't mean that," Millie explained. "She never wore makeup."

"Well, maybe her daughter put it on her," Mother told her.

"Or maybe someone made her do it," Millie replied.

"She was old and frail," said Father. "She didn't want to move, so she dressed up and gave up the will to live and went to meet her Maker."

"I suppose you're right," Millie said as they continued walking down the dirt road toward home. "There's just one more thing."

"What one more thing?" Father asked.

"It looked like she had just eaten pokeberries. You know how they can make you sick, and you can tell when someone has eaten them. That's how she looked," Millie said.

Millie's parents stopped in the middle of the dirt road and stared at her. "The skin under her fingernails was even black," Millie exclaimed. "You think I'm crazy, don't you?"

Mother grabbed Millie's hand and said, "Let's go, and no, I don't think you are crazy."

"I don't either," Father said. "Which do you think it was?"

"What?" Millie asked, frustrated.

"Did she take the pokeberries herself, or did someone give them to her?" Father asked.

"Did she take them herself so she didn't have to move?" Millie wondered.

"Or her children could have given them to her for the same reason," Father cut in.

"Ooh, this can't be happening," Mother chimed in. "All I know is that Mrs. Link wasn't sick and wasn't that sad and was a good Christian woman."

"I agree," Millie said.

"So do I," Father said. "We'll go back in a couple of hours to check on the chickens and then go look where you said the pokeberries were. We can check if any had been taken."

Chapter 35

On the return trip to Mrs. Link's farm, Evelyn Rose and Mattie went along to help. Nothing was said to the two younger children about their suspicions about the cause of death. The first thing Millie noticed and brought to her parents' attention was where the pokeberries were and how somebody had completely cut them and all the brush away from the chicken coop.

"Looks like somebody has been clearing brush," Millie told her parents as she walked to the brush pile.

"Guess maybe to make the place look better for the sale," Father said. "Let's get the chickens loaded. I'll talk to the sheriff tomorrow."

Moving the chickens turned out to be harder than any of them thought. They were almost impossible to catch and left them dirty with chicken poop on their shoes.

"I hope they like their new home," Mattie said as she helped load the flopping burlap bags filled with chickens.

Evelyn Rose asked Millie, "You think Rusty will try to herd the chickens?"

"He never did here," she replied. "I just hope Ole Smokey and Bessie get along with them."

"Bring out the nesting boxes," Father explained. "We'll keep them cooped up for a day or two and just let four or five out at a time. I would like to finish the outside pen before we let them out in the yard."

"That might be best," Mother said.

Father had Ole Smokey move at a slow pace as Mother sat in the back of the wagon keeping check on the chickens. The ride home went without a hitch. The laying hens were placed in the coop, and the two roosters ran free in the small pen. Coming out of the coop, Father said, "So far, so good. We never lost a single one."

"How long before you think they'll start laying again?" Millie asked Father.

"If they take to their new home, it might be just a few days. You never know," Father replied.

"I'm starved," Millie said. "Is there any more of that pie left, or did Mattie eat it all?"

Looking up at her mother, Mattie cried out, "I didn't eat all that pie!"

Mother smiled. Father gave Millie a firm look. Evelyn Rose said as she took off running to the cabin, "There might be one piece left!"

Millie and Mattie raced after Evelyn Rose.

Mother and Father walked toward the house. Mother asked Father, "How are you doing?"

Giving her a smile, he replied, "I'm plumb wore out. My leg is killing me. The neighbor lady is dead, and we have chickens."

Holding on to his arm, Mother said, "Let's go put that leg in the deep part of the spring. Cool water will do it some good."

"Might do my whole body some good," he said as he patted her hands. "Maybe even clear my head some."

Knowing exactly what he was talking about, she gripped his arm a little tighter and asked, "Got problems going on in your head?"

As the two of them got to the spring, she held him steady as he pulled his shoes off and then stepped out of his trousers. He sat in the deep end of the spring and said, "Wow! This is really cold. Take your shoes off and stick your toes in here."

Mother dipped her feet in the spring, and the two sat in silence. Breaking the silence, Mother said, "So what's been messing around in your head?"

"Shoo wee! That's got to be the coldest water," he said as he lifted himself out of the water.

"Probably cold because it comes right out of the center of the St. Francois Mountain Range," she said. "Are we gonna talk or not?" Mother asked, getting to the point.

"Evelyn Rose, there!" he blurted out as he slipped his pants back on over his shivering legs.

Wanting to get her opinion out, she said, "Do you want to know what I think?"

"I know what you think," he said. "So convince me."

Lifting her feet out of the spring, she said, "I will." She stood up and then paused. "I was like you at first. I was upset like you were. But then while I was cooking, things became clearer."

"So you had to—" her husband started to say but was cut short.

"Just hear me out," she said, looking at him. He sat down on the log and began to listen. "I grew up in a schoolhouse and was raised by an aunt who was the teacher. I loved learning and couldn't get enough of it. Then there was nothing left to learn." Shifting to a different direction, she continued, "The old doctor and you have the same kind of heart. You both care for others, and it's been proven by what you both do for the underground railroad."

He smiled but kept his mouth shut as he propped his elbow on his knee and rested his chin in his hands.

"They couldn't help not having children," she said. "I'm thinking the old doctor saw something in Evelyn Rose, and he and his wife would like to help her so they could leave some kind of legacy." Mother stopped talking, and the two just looked at each other. He waited for her to finish, and she waited for a response.

Finally, she asked, "Does this make sense?"

"Sure, it does," he replied. "If your thinking and his are the same."

Mother leaned toward him with her hand on the ground and said, "She's smart enough!"

"But she's a girl," he replied.

"I think she has the will to overcome that" came Mother's answer.

Taking a deep breath, he said, "It's so far from home."

"She's not afraid," she said.

"I am," he said, dropping his chin and looking away so she couldn't see any tears building.

Watching him break, she told him, "I am too! But it's her life. It's her future."

"I agree with you," Father relented. "But hear me out on this."

"You listened to me, so I'll hear you out, and then we will talk to her," Mother replied.

Taking a deep breath and then letting it out slowly, Father said, "We need to wait one year." Talking faster so he wouldn't get in an argument, he continued, "With the war heading toward an end and soldiers traveling home, it might be too dangerous. It wouldn't hurt to wait another year. If we buy a new place, I want her to be part of it. She's young. One year won't matter."

Looking into her eyes, he became silent. With a smile on her face, she replied, "You're a good father and so wise. I agree with you wholeheartedly." Placing a log on end to sit as high as her husband, they both put their feet back in the cool spring and sat in silence.

Chapter 36

The next morning while everyone was eating breakfast, Millie noticed Rusty perking up. "Someone's at the gate!" she informed the rest of the family.

Father gave Millie a sleepy-eyed look and said, "No, he's just thinking the same thing I'm thinking."

"What, Father?" Mattie asked.

Rubbing his red bloodshot eyes, he looked at Mattie and told her, "If that rooster crows one more time, I'll either wring his neck, or Rusty will beat me to him and bite his head off."

Rusty stood up and lowered his head with his hackles raised. A deep growl came from down in his throat, and they all knew it's something other than an early risen rooster.

"Yo! In the house!" came a distant man's voice.

Rusty barked, and the girls all scramble to the door as Millie shouted, "Someone is at the gate!"

"It's the doctor!" Mother shouted to her husband. "Guess he figured we had enough time to think."

"That, or he figured your wisdom would prevail over my thick skull," Father replied.

As the two younger girls ran to open the gate, their parents came outside and stood on the rock porch to welcome the doctor.

"I hope I'm welcome," shouted the old doctor.

"More than welcome!" Father shouted a reply.

Mother asked Millie to take her sisters to check on the sheep. "I'll explain later," she told her. "We need to talk about a personal matter."

Millie gave a disappointed frown and said, "I'll do my best, but they won't be happy." Millie convinced her sisters that Mother and Father needed to spend some time alone with the doctor, and this was a good time for them to help her with some fence work.

Evelyn Rose and Mattie did their best to convince everyone they should stay and visit with the doctor. Mother gave them a stern look and told them to go with Millie.

"Let's go!" Millie said, holding a small wood saw, a hatchet, and a jug of water. "If we hurry, maybe we can get back before he leaves."

"Before you go," the doctor said, "you might want this." Taking his black doctor bag from the saddle horn, he opened it up. He pulled out some wrapped peppermint sticks. He pulled his hand back before Mattie could grab them and said, "If it's fine with your parents."

Eyes as big as buckeyes, Mattie said, "Please, Mother!"

"It's fine," Mother replied. "Now what do you say?"

All three of the girls thanked the doctor as they started the long walk up the hill toward the pond and through the gap to the back field. At the pond, Mattie cried out that she needed to stop and wash the peppermint stick off because she had dropped it.

"Are you sure you didn't try to lick the dirt off?" a laughing Evelyn Rose asked.

"No, I didn't," Mattie told her. "Why?"

"'Cause it's all over your face with dirt," she told her.

Millie pulled her shirt tail out and told Mattie, "Come here, Mattie. Let me wipe your face off."

"I'll do it in the pond," Mattie said.

"No, you won't!" Millie demanded. "Now come here, and I'll use this clean drinking water."

Handing her peppermint stick out to her big sister, she asked, "Will you wash the dirt off this too?"

"There," Millie said, "good as new. Be more careful, okay?"

Crunching the last of her candy, Evelyn Rose said, "See, I'm done, and I didn't get any on me at all."

"That's 'cause you ate it so fast," Mattie told her. "I still have mine."

Evelyn Rose rolled her eyes and said, "Yeah, dirt and all."

"That's okay, Mattie," Millie said as she wrapped up half her candy stick and placed it in her shirt pocket.

"Aren't you going to eat yours?" Mattie asked.

Making sure that it wouldn't fall out of her shirt pocket, Millie then told them, "I did eat half of it. I'll just save the other half for when we take a water break."

Mattie looked at her sticky candy stick that she had licked to a sharp point, then looked over at Evelyn Rose. Evelyn Rose was wishing she had some more and then said, "Save it if you want. We don't care, do we, Mattie?"

Hearing Rusty barking took their attention off one another. "Let's go," Millie said. "Hope Rusty hasn't found a skunk."

"Oh boy!" Mattie said as she and Evelyn Rose followed their big sister down the fence toward the giant lone oak.

"There he is," Evelyn Rose pointed out.

"I see him," Millie said as she pointed toward him so Mattie could see too.

Rusty was snapping with his head going side to side then he would bark and turn a complete circle. He appeared to jump straight up and snap at nothing but air. He would yelp and then gnaw at his own hide and roll on the ground.

"What's wrong with your dog?" Evelyn Rose said pointing and laughing. "He's gone crazy!"

"Looks like he's found some bees or a nest of ground hornets. Let's walk over and see. Mattie, you stay here."

"Why?" she asked.

Millie turned to look and explained, "'Cause your too little and too sticky!"

"Aww," Mattie whined.

"For your own good, stay by the big tree," Millie warned.

Millie and Evelyn Rose lightly walked toward Rusty. Occasionally, he would look back at the girls then go back to snapping.

"Must be honeybees," Millie told her sister. "He knows better than to hang around those yellow ground hornets. Rusty!" she yelled and then pointed out a big mass of bees in the tree above Rusty.

"That, my dear, is what you call a swarm. Rusty!" she yelled. "Come here!"

"Oh no!" Evelyn Rose said in a panic. "He'll bring them over here."

She started to back away, but Millie grabbed her arm and told her, "No, they won't. Not a single one."

Trying to pull away, Evelyn Rose asked, "How do you know?"

Millie explained as she walked closer, pulling her sister, "When a beehive becomes too big, a single queen bee will leave the hive. Then a whole bunch of the other bees will follow her and stay with her until she finds a new place to make a hive. They all gather around her to protect her. That's what that is. It's called a swarm."

"A swarm?" Evelyn Rose curiously asked.

"Yeah, see how they all swarm together," Millie showed her. "Come on, I'll show you the queen, if I can find her."

As they walked closer, Millie told Rusty to stay back and informed Mattie that they would be right back. The two girls quietly and cautiously walked right up to the swarm that was about four feet off the ground. "See," Millie said, "they won't hurt us if we don't hurt them. Now let's see if we can find the queen. Just make sure you move really slow."

Helping Millie look among the swarming bees, Evelyn Rose asked, "How can you tell which one is the queen?"

"You'll know when you see her," Millie explained. "She'll be about twice the size of the others, maybe bigger."

"Like this one?" Evelyn Rose asked as she pointed to a bee.

Millie bent her neck to look toward the swarm then grinned at Evelyn Rose, saying, "Yep, that's her. Look how big she is."

The two girls watched the queen work in and out of the swarm, disappearing and then reappearing. "You want to see something really amazing?" Millie asked. "Wait till you see this!" Millie reached out to pick up the queen.

Shock came over Evelyn Rose's face as she silently yelled, "No!"

Millie froze and puts her finger to her mouth, signaling her sister to be quiet. "It's okay," she said. "I've done this before." She reached back up to the queen and said, "Just watch."

In an instant, the buzzing became so loud that nothing else could be heard. Then all the other bees start letting go of one another and flying toward Millie as she walked away. Evelyn Rose was frozen like a statue, holding her breath. Bees flew all around Millie and Evelyn Rose in all directions. Millie placed the queen on a branch in a different tree about twenty yards away. Inhaling deeply and walking away from the queen and Evelyn Rose, she stopped at a safe distance. Evelyn Rose ran to her side.

With terror still on her face, Evelyn Rose asked Millie, "Are you all right?"

"Yes," Millie replied.

"Are you crazy?" she said, grabbing Millie by both arms and giving her a quick shake.

Millie nodded her head toward the queen bee and told her sister, "Turn around and watch."

Looking toward the tree where Millie placed the queen bee, a dark cloud moved from the tree the bees were in to where the queen was now. One by one, the bees came to the queen until once again, there was a swarm of honeybees hanging from the limb to protect their queen.

"Close your mouth before a bee flies in it," Millie said. "Let's go get the fence fixed."

Rusty intercepted the two girls as they met Mattie by the big oak. "I saw that!" Mattie told them.

"You saw it!" Evelyn Rose said excitedly. "I won't sleep for a week. I can even still feel the buzzing in my body."

"Weren't you scared?" Mattie asked Millie.

Kneeling down on one knee to check on Rusty, she told her sisters, "Kinda, sorta. To tell the truth, yes, I was scared."

"How did you know to do that, or *why* would you do that?" Evelyn Rose asked.

"When I was little, about your age, Mattie, I was with Father, and we came upon a swarm just like that one. I watched Father move the swarm to an old hollow tree. That way, he knew where to go to get the honey."

Rusty's ears perked up, and Millie looked in the direction he was looking. "Here they come," she said. "You can see some white right up there. The sheep are making their way to the creek for water. They'll all be out here in the field grazing soon. We'll get a head count and then head back home."

"Aren't we gonna do some fence work?" Mattie asked.

"There's not much wrong, so it won't take too long," Millie replied as she reached into her pocket and pulled out the rest of her candy stick. "After I finish this, we'll fix the fence."

Evelyn Rose and Mattie stared at the candy stick as Millie watched them with a smile on her face. Bringing the candy to her lips and pretending to put it in her mouth, she quickly broke it into pieces and shared with her sisters.

"Oh, thank you, Millie," Mattie told her.

Evelyn Rose nodded her head as if to say yes after placing the whole piece in her mouth and crunching it to bits. "You're the best," she mumbled.

Mattie dropped hers but in a flash without wiping it off, picked it up and put it in her mouth hoping no one saw.

Millie laughed and put her arm around Mattie's neck and rubbed her knuckles across the top of her head telling her sister, "You two are a couple of squirrels. You know that? Now let's check the fence out."

After a quick drink from the jug, Millie showed her sisters how fence work was done. The fence that ran along the Bell farm was made of split oak trees. Millie told the girls how Father made the fence when he started logging years ago. The fence was constructed in a continuous *W* shape from one end of the field to the other and stacked in alternating fashion so there was support from both directions. "We'll check if any parts of the fence are rotten. Main thing is, we don't want any cows over here, and Mrs. Bell doesn't want any sheep over there."

The sisters didn't seem to care about learning how to mend a fence. Mattie was busy feeling her sticky, dirty fingers, and Evelyn Rose appeared to be overwhelmed with boredom.

In the shade of the old oak tree, Millie leaned back and stared out across the valley that lies between the two hills. She felt Mattie lean her head against her shoulder, then Evelyn Rose did the same on the other side. Listening to the bleating of the sheep, she took a deep breath, and a sigh of contentment passed through her lips.

A few minutes went by, and Millie clapped her hands, causing the two girls to jump. "Time to go back to work!" she told her sisters. "We're burning up daylight, and we haven't done a thing yet."

The girls began checking out sections of fence for sturdiness and put the rails back up that had been knocked down. Millie made mental notes of any rotten rails or posts that will need to be replaced. They finally made it to the corner of the field by the road. Relieved to be done and making sure the doctor hasn't left yet, the girls hightailed it for home.

Mattie began running, trying to beat her sisters, but to her dismay, she ran through the downstream of the spring. "I'm stuck!" she yelled. "Come help! My foot's stuck, and I can't find my shoe!"

Millie groaned. There was no way Evelyn Rose would wade in and pull her out. "You go on," she told Evelyn Rose. "I'll get Mattie out and try to find her shoe."

"Thanks, Millie," Evelyn Rose said. "I'll try to keep our guest from leaving."

Evelyn Rose found a narrow place in the stream and jumped it quite easily and raced home.

Millie took her shoes off and waded in to help Mattie get unstuck. "Here's your shoe," Millie said. "You lost it on your very first step in."

"Oh, thank you, Millie," Mattie joyfully told her. "I was afraid I lost it and was in big trouble."

Millie reached out to grip her hand and said, "You won't be in trouble. We'll wash this off, and it'll be good as new." Wanting to teach Mattie a lesson, she said, "I just hope some old snappin' turtle doesn't bite your toes off."

Mattie's head snapped up, and a high-pitched squeal yelled out in desperation, "Please don't let go, Millie!" Hanging on to Millie, she quickly pulled herself out of the mud. "I didn't think about that," she said, looking at all the mud covering her all the way up to her knees.

Millie did everything she could to keep Mattie from seeing her laughing and said, "Well, Mattie, if I was to guess, I'd say you pretty much didn't think of anything." Finding a dry bank, they sat down and washed the mud off. Millie continued telling Mattie, "Maybe you should think before you do something. You might not get so dirty."

Mattie said "okay" as Millie washed the sticky mud off her fingers.

By the time Millie and Mattie got to the cabin, Millie overheard the old doctor tell her parents that he'd be by early tomorrow morning. "So there you two are," he said as he turns to leave. "I was hoping I'd get to tell you girls goodbye before I left."

"After messing with some honeybees, we hurried as fast as we could," Millie explained. "At least until we got stuck in the mud."

"Do you have to go now?" Mattie begged.

"Tell you what, girls," the doctor suggested, "how about we go sit for a few minutes at the spring. I love the taste of that sweet cool spring water. We can visit there, then I must be on my way."

The visit was great, but Mattie was so excited hardly anyone else could say a word. Millie would scold her, but Doc laughed and said it was quite all right.

After a while, the doctor informed, "It was a nice visit with you young ladies, but it is time for me to be on my way."

"Aww," Mattie said, and Millie blushed at being called a lady.

Father, wearing his new boots, and the rest of the family walked to the gate to let the old gentleman out the gate. He told the girls' mother to take it easy and again apologized to Father for the misunderstanding.

"Likewise," Father said, and they all waved goodbye.

Turning to his daughters, he put an arm around his wife, and Father said, "I guess right now would be as good as any to let you girls in on why our friend was paying us a visit."

Mother did the same and placed her arm around her husband and told him, "I'll fix us something to eat. That way, we can talk at the table."

More talking than eating was done especially when Father brought up why the old doctor had come for the visit. The girls thought it was about a new shoe for Father and his hardheadedness that Mother always talked about. Now they know that Evelyn Rose might have a chance to go to a private school if the country was in a better and more peaceful state. Everyone seemed to be happy for Evelyn Rose although Millie's mind was set on the sheep and Cecil.

"By the way," Mother said as she carved some more ham, "the doctor and his wife would like to pick up Evelyn Rose in the morning to help prepare for the Fourth and stay with them until after the fireworks."

Everyone got quiet. Father reached for a slice of ham and a chunk of bread and headed for the door.

Before he reached the door, he stopped dead in his tracks, hearing the words from Evelyn Rose, "No, I don't think so. I was really hoping we could do something about those bees."

"What bees?" Father said as he pulled his hand back from opening the door and turned back around.

Millie looked up from the table and told her father, "Yeah, we found a swarm of bees just across the fence on Mrs. Bell's place."

All excited, Mattie told how Millie captured the queen and how she and Evelyn Rose moved them to a different tree while she watched.

"Millie!" Mother scorned as she placed her fists on her hips. "What did you do?"

Not missing a beat, Father joined in, saying, "You could have been hurt—bad!" With a change in his tone, he then said, "Are they still in a swarm?"

With her knuckles getting whiter, Mother asked, "And what are you planning to do?"

All eyes were on Father, and Millie was glad some of the pressure was off her. "Guess we'll talk to our neighbor and see if we can find a good tree for them." Millie smiled at her father as he told her to grab the hatchet and a small saw.

Explaining all that must be done to his wife, he gave orders for the girls to milk Bessie and let her out, feed the chickens in the pen, and gather the eggs. He told them to leave Ole Smokey in his stall. "I might need him after a while," he said.

"Can we come?" Mattie asked.

"Sorry girls," he answered. "It's not the safest thing to do."

"But Millie and I moved—" Evelyn Rose started to say.

Father cut her off, telling her, "Don't tell me what you girls did, and don't do it again," giving her a smile that indicated, "I know you are brave, but don't be stupid." Father nodded to his wife and said, "Be back soon."

Dropping her hands from her hips and folding her arms in front of her, she told her husband, "Just be careful! Don't do anything foolish!" He nodded then gave the girls a sheepish grin and left.

Chapter 37

Meeting Millie at the spring, they both got a big drink of fresh cool water. They crossed the fence and traveled down the road to Mrs. Bell's home. "So far, so good," he told Millie.

"What's good?" she asked.

He slapped his leg as they walked and said, "No walking cane! Felt so good I didn't even think to bring it. Now back to you."

Millie cocked her head and furrowed her eyebrows and asked, "Me?"

"Yes, you!" Father said. "I'll say this, and we'll not talk about it anymore." Slowing down, he said, "You shouldn't have done what you did. Just like I shouldn't have shown you how to do it. You were lucky. You never know about those bees."

A few steps in silence, and Father and daughter looked at each other with understanding smiles.

After getting permission from their neighbor, Millie and Father cut through Mrs. Bell's back pasture and on into the woods where the bees were located. Father scouted for a good tree to relocate the bees. He found a good sturdy oak with a large hole about eight feet off the ground. A perfect spot for the bees. This time, instead of handling the queen, Father cut the limb and carried the whole hive. Reaching the hollow oak, Father took some wire and tied the bees to a dogwood tree next to the oak. They both stood back and watched the bees swarm around the queen.

"Now what do we do?" he asked.

Millie looked surprised at her father and said, "We need to do more."

"Yep," he said. "Something else I've learned since last time. I got this from Mrs. Bell when I was in her house." He pulled out of his bag a wrapped piece of paper. As he unwrapped, his secret was revealed, a chunk of honeycomb with sweet honey dripping from it. "Now all we have to do is get this honeycomb up there."

Millie looked up at the hole in the hollow tree and said, "Put your hands together, and it'll be as good as done."

Father placed his shoulder against the tree to steady himself then squatted a little. He intertwined his fingers and told Millie, "When you're up there, smear the honeycomb all around the hole so it sticks to it. "Ready?" he asked.

Millie put a corner of the paper between her teeth. After getting a grip on the tree, she placed her outer foot in her father's hands. "Ready," she answered. She pushed up with her inside leg, and Father lifted at the same time. Lifting her as far as he could, Millie stretched and started smearing honeycomb all around the hole. "That's it," she told her father.

He lowered her down to his knee, and Millie then stepped down. Backing away and looking up, Father said, "Perfect. Couldn't have done better myself." He gave Millie a hug and told her, "We'll come back in a couple days and check on 'em."

"Think we'll have honey this fall?" Millie asked her father.

"If I'm a betting man, I'd bet on it," he answered. "Let's go and let the bees do their thing. With a little luck and a lot of prayers, I'll be collecting on that bet this fall."

Returning home by the sheep trail that led to the creek, Father and daughter crossed over the back field to the fence under the giant oak and toward the gap. Millie made a sudden stop and looked back at the old oak tree. "Something wrong?" Father asked.

Millie shook her head and said, "Not really." She stared at the lone tree a couple of seconds then asked, "Why did you save this one?"

Father smiled and said, "Come here, and I'll show you." They walked the short distance back to the lone old giant and stopped just about where the girls were sitting earlier.

"Well," she said.

Father leaned with his back against the tree, "Well, what?" he said.

Millie did the same and asked again in a soothing content tone in her voice, "Why this one tree?"

"For the reason right here," he began to tell her the story. "When you were born, and we moved out here, I had the job of cutting and hauling trees down to the road. Your mother said you had the colic. You cried all the time. Anyway, I started cutting back here first." Father spread his arms out to show the field and said, "This is where the best oak trees were. Don't know for sure why, but they were big and solid. But this one here"—he pat the tree—"was the biggest and most solid. The branches were spread out, and the leaves so thick you couldn't see the sun."

"That probably should have been the first one that was gone," Millie said as she looked up at the mighty limbs and thick growth of leaves.

"As a matter of fact, it was going to be the very first," Father said as he continued his story. "We drove Ole Smokey back here. Your mother and I brought you along, carrying you in a basket. I grabbed my ax and saw and stood just about right here." Father maneuvered himself with his back to the field facing the tree, arms stretched out as if holding his ax. "I then spit in my hand, smiled at your mother, reared back, and just before I came forward to strike the tree, you cooed."

"I cooed?" Millie inquired with a puzzled look.

Father nodded his head, yes, and said, "I thought you did, but anyway, your voice made me stop. You seemed to like it here. Anytime you were colicky, Mother would bring you up here and sit under the tree. It seemed to calm you down."

"Well, I still like sitting here," Millie told him. "With all that's going on, a war, Cecil gone, and just plain hard times, like seeing those slaves, I like being here. Especially since that man tried to hurt

Rusty and me." She let her hand drag along the side of the tree then curled her arm through her father's as they walked away, and she told him, "This is the place I like to come to and pray."

Father shook his head as they walked toward the gap and whispered, "Pray for some honey this fall."

Chapter 38

Back at home, the talk and excitement were about Evelyn Rose having a chance to go away to a private school. Mattie's excited right along with her but has some mixed emotions. "I'll miss you. Why can't I go too?" she asked. "Hey, wait a minute," Mattie shouted. With tears in her eyes, Mattie said, "If Evelyn Rose goes away to school next year, and Millie gets married in a year or two, what will I do? I'll be all by myself!"

Evelyn Rose gave Mattie a bit of a snide look, which Mother caught and told Mattie, "Nothing is for sure. A year is a long time, and so many things can happen. Just remember when they are gone, if they go, that will make you the big sister to your baby brother or sister."

Mattie's eyes got as big as the *O* she made with her mouth. She folded her arms and gave her sister a curt nod and stiffened her bottom lip.

"You two girls need to straighten up. It's time you get your chores done before Father gets back," Mother instructed.

Making their decisions who would do what while standing on the flat rock porch, Evelyn Rose pointed out to Mattie that Father and Millie were standing by the pond. "Oh boy!" Evelyn Rose said, "They are coming. If you hoe weeds, I'll milk Bessie and try to get her out before Father gets here."

"Okay," Mattie agreed. "We'll meet at the new chickens. Just holler when you're finished milking."

"I will," Evelyn Rose said as they took off to do their chores. "Mattie!" she yelled, stopping her in her tracks.

"Rusty! Go with Mattie," she commanded as she snapped her fingers and motioned toward Mattie.

"Take Rusty with you and watch out for snakes!" Evelyn Rose told Mattie.

"Come on, boy!" Mattie called to Rusty, slapping her thigh.

"Pond looks really good this year," Father told Millie.

"We've had good spring rains," she replied. "The sheep would rather drink out of the creek than this pond any day."

Father looked off toward the sheep at the upper end of the pasture and informed his daughter, "Just a short drought could ruin this farm for the whole year. We need to start thinking about thinning the flock some."

"I was hoping we wouldn't have to," she suggested.

"But, Millie, look at the ground now," he said. "The grass is so short. I know it's still green, but if we have a couple of days of ninety-degree weather, you know it's coming. There won't be grass for even a few sheep."

"I understand what you're saying, but I was hoping just maybe if I get the chance, I could talk to whomever buys the Link farm," Millie explained. "There is so much green grass over there going to waste."

Father gazed off in that direction and told her, "Ever since the death of her husband, I've thought the same thing. Hasn't been a thing on it since." He rubbed his hand over the stubbles on his chin then looked back at Millie. "Tell you what," he said. "I have to go into town in the morning since the stores will be closed on Wednesday, and I'll talk with the sheriff. I'll see what's going on with the death of Mrs. Link. Then I'll find out what I can about the new owner. If there is one."

Millie threw her arms around her father's neck and with a big hug said, "Thanks so much." She stepped back, telling him, "I really hope everything is on the up and up."

"You and me both," he said.

"You know, it might not be a bad idea to let whoever the owner is to let them know the sheep will keep the place cleaned up," she said. "Keep the critters and varmints away too. And it'd be only till next June, maybe."

Father smiled at Millie and said, "Are you starting to like the idea?"

Millie smiled back with a tight lip, nodded, and then told him, "I won't fight you on it."

As father started walking toward the small cabin, Millie heard him say, "Just wait till you see it."

She headed in the direction of the flock, pondering the thoughts of selling sheep, the death of her neighbor, moving to a new farm, and her kidnapping by a stranger. As she reached the shade of the trees on the northwest hill, she reminisced about the proposal made by a boy she's known all her life. Now he's a man who has gone to war and has become a stranger. She struggles at the thought of Cecil saving her and is now her hero.

"So what do you think?" she asked one of the sheep. "That's what I thought," she said as the sheep raised its head, looked her way, then walked to stay close to the flock. Millie made a head count just to clear her mind of the prior thoughts. At this high vantage point, she looked out over the farm. She saw Father just about to reach their house, and Evelyn Rose and Mattie running to find out about the bees. Rusty was with Mattie, and then Mother came to the doorway. They said a few words, and Mother held her hands over her eyes and looked up the hill toward her. Another discussion, and they all walked toward the garden.

The pond looked beautiful and bigger from this angle. The back field is still green as it was back in April. Thanks to well-placed spring rains. Then she spotted it, her giant, peaceful oak tree. She laughed at the thought of saving the tree when she was just a baby. She smiled and felt peace just looking at it and admiring the majesty of the mighty tree.

A slight breeze seemed to turn the leaves upside down, and in unison, the branches swayed from one side then back. Millie shook as a chill ran up her spine, and the short hairs on her neck seem to stand out. She crossed her arms and placed her hands on her shoulders, squeezed herself, and shook again. Watching the lone sentinel at the edge of the field settle down as its leaves softly came back to rest, Millie felt a connection and for a moment felt content. Nothing felt important or real. The feeling scared her, but she had no thought of what to do. The sun put a glare on the pond as Millie got another chill. The pond looked as though it was covered. She squinted her eyes and leaned her head forward while still holding her shoulder.

Millie thought out loud in a whisper and said, "It looks like it's covered with ice." A gentle breeze brought a light ripple across the pond, and her feelings returned to normal. She jerked at the sound of sheep bleating. "Shoo wee," she said. "I must be daydreaming on my feet." She laughed at herself and began walking down the steep side of the hill next to the fence by the Link farm.

Once back home, Millie went straight to where her family was working in the garden. "How's the chickens doing!" she shouted out.

"No eggs today," Mother replied. She leaned on her hoe and placed her hand flat across her eyes just under the bill of her bonnet to shade her eyes from the sun. "Two of the old hens didn't make it," Mother whispered.

"I'm surprised more didn't," Millie said, walking to her mother between the pole beans and the newly sprouted corn.

Mother dropped her hand as Millie got closer and proudly said, "Me too! The rest of them are in the fenced area and seem happy as can be."

Father popped up over by the tomato plants and shouted out, "Guess what I got!"

Shouting, "What! What!" Evelyn Rose and Mattie came running from where the squash was vining. "What have you got?"

He held up the red vegetable and shouted to everyone, "The first tomato, and it's before the Fourth!"

It's always been a big thing to get a ripe tomato before the Fourth of July. Seemed to be the first thing the farmers do was to compare their first tomatoes at the Fourth of July picnic.

Father gave a grin as they all gather around and looked at it when Mattie said, "Still looks kind of green to me. Don't you think?"

Millie and Mother smiled at each other when Father said, "Well, yeah, but I'll put it on the windowsill. That way, it will finish ripening. Don't worry, it will be ready."

Chapter 39

It was the Fourth of July. The day started early. Mother rose early to start making pie dough so the pies could be baked when the air was cooler. Father took the wagon to town to get some supplies. Mrs. Bell was preparing the ingredients for the dumplings. Everything would be ready when the neighbors gathered to make the drop dumplings for the chicken and dumplings to be served at the Fourth of July picnic. Mrs. Bell's dumplings and fresh chickens would make for some good eating.

Mattie spent most of the morning complaining because she wanted fried chicken. Mother explained there will be plenty of fried chicken brought by others to the picnic.

The morning was busy as everyone worked hard to get all the daily chores done.

Father returned home. Evelyn Rose and Mattie accompanied Mother to Mrs. Bell's, taking the fresh chickens for the chicken and dumplings.

Father called to Millie who was out in the garden. "I'll finish this if you get me some water from the spring."

"I sure will," Millie happily obliged. "By the way, did you find anything out?"

"Yeah, water first," he said, "then we'll discuss it."

Returning with a bucket of water, she then ran to the house for a tin cup and had to jump over Rusty on her way back out. Patiently waiting, but before the first cup of water was down, Millie asked, "What did you find out?"

Father looked over the rim of the tin cup and with his other hand held up one finger. Finally, taking the cup away from his lips and dipping it back into the bucket, he took a deep breath, and said, "Let's go sit by the sycamore by the spring. The humidity is terrible today."

"Did you notice the thunderheads building to the west?" Millie commented.

Father sat on his usual log with his cup of water in his hand. Millie did the same. Rusty sat on the ground next to her as water dripped off his tongue and looked at Millie with his silly grin.

"I got some good news and some bad news," he finally said.

Millie gave her father a bit of a smile and asked, "How 'bout you tell me the good news first?"

Placing his cup on the ground and pushing Rusty's head away with the toe of his boot to keep him from getting near the cup, Father said, "Good news is, Mrs. Link's family was in town for her burial."

Millie looked at Father and told him in a dry tone, "Suppose Mother will take them some chicken and dumplings and maybe a pie. We'll need to go to the funeral." She paused for a moment then asked, "This is the good news?"

Father swallowed, then with a frown, looked up into the big leaves of the sycamore. Without taking his eyes off the leaves, he told Millie, "Mrs. Link was buried yesterday. No funeral, just buried next to her husband. Talked to the sheriff, and he told me the children were at the hotel and would be leaving this afternoon. Told him I wanted to pay for the chickens and asked if he would go with me to the hotel. On the way over, he explained Mrs. Link had been crying over the bickering of her children and moving her. He said the old woman didn't want to leave, so she just dressed up, laid down, and gave up." Father paused then looked into Millie's eyes and said, "I guess she got a little help from Mother Nature. That's speculation, nothing else. Same story told by all of them."

Millie looked down, and when she did, her tears fell straight to the ground. She watched the drops hit the dirt between her feet, and the dust clouds that floated up each time. She felt her father's hand on her shoulder and looked up to see the tears in her father's eyes.

They leaned toward each other and gave each other a comforting hug. She whispered in Father's ear and said, "I'll never let you or Mother be alone."

Father pat her back and said, "I know." He then told Millie, "There is other news."

Millie's eyes widened as she leaned back and exclaimed, "I don't want any bad news if that was the good news!"

"Well, now, just let me finish," Father said. "We get there at the hotel, and I extend my condolences, and we talk some. We were all polite, and before I left, I asked about leasing some pasture land. I asked the sister, the one that was nice to you."

Millie nodded her head and said "Yes" while wiping her nose on the sleeve of her shirt.

"Well, she wants us to lease the whole place," he told Millie as he pulled out his red hanky and handed it her. "But the rest of them said no 'cause cattle farmers didn't like sheep farmers. They say the sheep eat the grass."

Millie cocked her mouth to one side and thought out loud, "Some truth to that."

"What?" Father stopped and asked.

"Nothing," she said. "Just thinking they're right in a way. But that's only if they are pasturing together. Cows can't eat as close to the ground as the sheep. They don't have any teeth."

"Yes, that's right," Father said, agreeing with her. "So they said we could pasture them on the thirty acres around the house and barn. They think it will keep the place looking cleaned up and the critters away."

A broad smile came across Millie's face. "That would be great," she said. "How much?"

Father looked down with a bit of a snicker and told Millie, "I was just getting ready to ask that very question when the sheriff told the family that it sounded like a fair trade to him. They let us pasture the sheep in exchange for watching the place and keeping the place cleaned up for them. Thing is, we have no idea how long."

"Don't need long," Millie told him. "Anything just to take a little pressure off this place."

"Good," he said as he stood up. "We'll open the fence and herd them in tomorrow since we'll be gone the rest of today." He held his hand out to take the hanky back. As he walked away to unsaddle Ole Smokey, Father turned back and told Millie, "Best part is, they agree to let us use that big barn if we'd paint it."

Millie inhaled and excitedly said, "Ooh boy! That would be great!"

Mattie and Mother made it back from Mrs. Bell's. Closing the gate and not paying attention to anything else, Father did his usual prank when he's not spotted. Creeping out from behind the tack shed and slipping in beside them, he said, "Good afternoon, ladies."

Both of them jumped, and with a pointed finger, Mother sternly said, "One of these days, you'll do that, and I'll have this baby right here on the dry sod."

Mattie hugged her mother, enjoying every bit of the fun of being scared. "Yeah, Father, you shouldn't do that!"

"Oh, you know you liked that," he said. "Just look at that grin and twinkle in your eyes." He grabbed Mattie and did a little roughhousing before picking her up to carry the rest of the way to the cabin. "Where's your sister?" he asked.

Mother rolled her eyes and said, "She's gone. She stayed to help Mrs. Bell."

Father got Ole Smokey ready and made sure the buckboard wagon was cleaned up. Mother made sure he packed the canvas covering just in case it rains. "We need to hurry so we don't miss the parade," Father yelled as Millie and her Mother came out the cabin door with pies balanced in each hand. "Not too hurried!" he said, running over to help. "I'd rather miss the parade than drop one of those pies."

The plan was to pick up Evelyn Rose and Mrs. Bell, who was bringing her famous southern style chicken and dumplings, and take the trail south to the Doe Run Road then east to Columbia Street. Then proceed to the church through the back way next to the cemetery where the slaves were buried and unpack the vittles and unhitch Ole Smokey. From there, it was a short walk to Highley's

Livery Stable and across to the courthouse to find a spot to watch the parade.

As usual, the politicians were out on their wooden crates, giving speeches and asking for your votes. Farmington was like most towns in Missouri, but Missouri wasn't like most states. While there was a civil war going on in the nation, most of the state's battles was to defend itself against other states trying to pull it one way or the other. There were very few slaves in Missouri, and most people didn't believe in slavery. The one thing everyone did believe in was state's rights and didn't like Yankees or the Confederates to interfere with their way of life. Although the nation was divided in this war, this Fourth of July celebration was about the freedom of all men whether independence from someone else or a man's individual freedom. It was a celebration of a nation just seventy-five years old and a state itself in infancy.

Many people that came to Missouri were like Mrs. Bell. They came to escape the bitterness of a savage war. Others profited from the war, and yet there were spies and instigators that you had to be wary of. The citizens of the town knew one another and kept close ties on each other.

Cecil's parents found Millie and asked her and her parents if it would be okay if their two youngest children stayed with them during the parade. "First things first," Cecil's mother said to Millie. "I received this yesterday, and it's for you." She pulled a letter out of her handbag and handed it to Millie. "I trust if anything is wrong, you will let me know," she asked, holding Millie's hand and the letter together.

Millie smiled and replied, "But of course." She showed her mother and father, and to everyone's disappointment, Millie folded the letter and placed it in her pocket. "I'll read it at home," she said.

"What if there is something that you should tell his mother?" Mother asked.

Millie gave a panicked expression to both women. Cecil's mother apologized, "It's fine. If anything was wrong, I'm sure he would have written me." She gave Millie a hug to ease the tension and asked, "Just let me know how he is, okay?"

"Just great!" Mattie said. "All we will hear for the rest of the day is, 'we need to go' just so Millie can be alone to read that letter."

Father put a light headlock on Mattie with a little Dutch rub and told her, "Don't you worry one little bit, little one. We're not going anywhere till after the fireworks."

Mattie laughed then checked her apron pocket to make sure her bullfrog is okay for the hopping contest.

Millie looked down toward the city hall, and without looking at anyone but making sure everyone heard, said, "That's fine. I can wait." She then told Mattie, "You need to keep your bullfrog wet, or he won't go in the contest. Should have gotten a leap frog. They're the best."

Mattie frowned and looked at her father. He nodded and said, "She's right, but if you get him in some water, you just never know."

Mattie looked around for something to put some horse trough water in but couldn't find anything.

"Tell you what," Father said, "run over to Highley's place and ask for a can or a jar. Just tell them what it's for. They'll give you something."

Mattie took the frog out of her apron and handed it to her father. "Save my place," she yelled as she hurried off.

Millie and Mother laughed as Father tried to hold the bullfrog with his thumb and finger. He yelled out, "Get a clean rag too!" Looking at the two of them, he explained, "That way, I can clean my hands, get it wet, and cover the frog." With a prideful grin, he said, "Ain't I smart."

Just before the parade started, Mattie made it back with a small quart-size can with a wire run through a couple of nail holes for a handle and some torn cloth for rags. "Hurry," Father said, "Run over to the horse trough for some water."

Mattie returned with the water, and in no time, the bullfrog had a nice wet, dark place to hunker down in and be happy, at least until the contest.

"Here they come!" yelled a boy sitting in a tree, signaling the start of the parade.

The parade seemed better than those of previous years. The only soldiers parading were in the very beginning. Leading the way was the typical drum and fife on each side of the American flag. There were lots of politicians handing out papers to voters. Wagons were decorated advertising banks, the mercantile, and other stores. All were handing out hard candy to the kids. One of the best wagons was the fire department's new pumper. It could be moved by four men while the rest fought the fire. All kinds of horses from Clydesdales to Shetlands strutted down the street. The local Osage Indian tribe and the Cherokees also participated in the parade. The Indians in the area had broken off the Trail of Tears March when President Andrew Jackson moved a whole nation of Indians out of the southeast United States. Both groups had pride in their heritage and always showed it individually during parades or special events.

"Millie!" someone yelled from across the street.

Father pointed out a couple of boys from her class at school, waving. Millie spotted them, held a hand up in a wave, and yelled back, "What?"

One of them put his hands to the sides of his face and yelled back, "Are you in the race?"

Millie shook her head and mouthed the word *no*. Both boys started jumping and slapping each other's back in celebration.

"Looks like you made somebody's day," Father said. "So why aren't you racing?"

"No competition there," she said. "Besides, I really only like beating Cecil. It used to make him so mad." Millie looked down at her dog, sitting between the two of them and told Father, "Thought I'd enter Rusty in the dog show." At the sound of his name, Rusty looked up at Millie, pulled his lips back, and gave her that grin. "He's got talent when he wants to," she said to Father. "Don't you, Rusty?" she questioned as she pet her dog.

"He definitely does in the field," Father commented. "The arena might be different. Look at him. He knows we are talking about him."

Millie scratched between Rusty's eyes, and they all laughed when his grin gets bigger.

As the parade winded down, Mattie and Cecil's little brother and sister headed to the watering trough for fresh frog water. "Mattie!" Mother yelled. "Just look at yourself. You're soaked!" Then Mother noticed her shoes. "Come here," she said.

Mattie walked back over to her mother with her chin hanging down to her chest. "I'm sorry," she quietly mumbled.

"It's okay," Mother told her. "Just listen to me." She dabbed her hanky around Mattie's neck to get the tater ring off and told her so no one could hear, "I don't care if you get wet, but please try not to step in horse manure. Okay? There now, let's go find where the frog contest is, and when we get in the grass, try to get that off your shoes."

Father gave them a wink, looked down toward Long Hall, and said, "I think we need to go that way."

They walked east toward Long Hall joining in like everyone else heading toward the picnic area. Past the hall and toward the gazebo looked like the best place to find out where the events were taking place.

"Over here!" Mother let the rest know, pointing out the board that showed the events and times.

"Mother, look," Mattie said. "The frog hopping contest is the first to start after the parade."

Father leaned down next to Mattie's head and pointed where several kids are lined up and told her, "Bet that's the place we need to be."

Millie yelled, "Wait! Look at this!" She pointed out another posting that read, "Essay Contest 2:00 p.m. Gazebo."

"Yeah, so?" Mother asked.

"No, down here," Millie pointed out.

Looking under the heading was a list of names. Surprised and a little bewildered at not knowing, Mother pointed out Evelyn Rose's name on the list. "Did you know?" she asked Millie.

Millie shook her head and said, "No, not even a hint, and I know Mattie didn't 'cause she can't keep a secret."

"She's just like her father," Mother said. "They keep it to themselves unless they're mad or upset, then the whole world knows.

Guess we'll be here after dinner." The two of them made their way to catch up with Father and Mattie to watch the frog contest.

"Let me explain the rules!" barked out the man in charge. "Hold your hopper in the center of the ring. At the word 'go' you let your hopper go. Your hopper will hop hopefully three times. After each hop, we will take a measure. If you touch your hopper anytime during the three hops, your hopper will be disqualified. This year will be different than years past. We will have four categories. The first category will be bullfrogs. You need to line up over here!"

Mattie raced over to the area for bullfrogs and so did the biggest portion of the kids with frogs.

"The next category is leopard frogs, then the small but long leaper tree frog, and last category is the…" He paused for a few seconds of anticipation then said, "The toad frog."

The whole crowd started laughing, and someone yelled out, "You better set a time limit!"

"Anyone here with a toad," yelled the man in charge. "Well, that's a shame," he said when no one came forward. "Guess we'll use these prizes somewhere else. Speaking of time limits, from the time you start, you will have one minute to get your three hops in. Don't forget, when you start any contact with your hopper, you will both be disqualified. Okay! Let's get started."

The contest began with the two tree frogs of which both were disqualified. The thing about tree frogs is they may be long leapers, but they like to leap to trees or the nearest standing object, which they did—their handlers.

Next up were the leopard frogs. Long great leapers although they have problems too. They usually don't leap in the direction their nose is aiming. So if their first leap is seven feet, their second might be seven feet but in a different direction. The total distance might still only be seven feet. The whole crowd roared with laughter when one of the leopard frogs on its third hop, landed just inches from his starting point.

Last up was the great green pond-dwelling bullfrogs. Over a dozen kids were standing in line, waiting for their turn. Mattie noticed most of the kids have been standing around all morning either holding their frogs or keeping them in some kind of dry container. She hoped keeping hers wet would give her an advantage.

Millie cupped her hands to her mouth, and when Mattie looked her way, she yelled, "Keep him wet till its's your turn!"

Mattie was seventh in line, and so far, the first few hadn't done very well. One was so dehydrated he would only jump about two feet at a time. Another one looked like it was kept in the kid's pocket and was probably just about to die. Some man in the crowd yelled out, "Maybe we ought to cut their legs off and just eat them!" The men laughed, but the womenfolk didn't see the humor in it.

The next girl up, leaned over too far on the frog's second leap, and he jumped right into her chin. A big "Aww" went over the crowd when she started crying. The boy in front of Mattie told her she was stupid for keeping her frog under a wet rag. Just as he was getting ready to enter the ring for his turn, Mattie heard Millie whistle, and she jerked to look her way. Standing next to her was Father with his hands cupped at the side of his mouth, leaning forward and saying something that Mattie couldn't quite make out.

"What?" Mattie mouthed back.

"When you slam your hands down," Father tried to yell as he moved his hands downward in a slamming motion.

Mattie nodded her head to indicate she understood what he was saying, and Father started blowing really hard.

Mattie furled her eyebrows and reared her head back just a tad trying to figure out what he was doing. Then she heard, "Young lady, it's your turn." She stepped up to the circle and waited for the final tally of the boy's frog's three hops.

"Eighteen feet, six inches," yelled the man who was measuring.

Oh my! thought Mattie. *That's the best so far.*

"Okay, young lady," the man said. "You're number seven, and your name is?"

Mattie told him her name, and he yelled out for her introduction. She walked to the center of the circle and squatted, gently putting her frog on the ground. He sat there soaking wet. Mattie slowly raised her hand and saw her father still bringing his hands down hard like he was in the circle. She slammed her hands down on the ground just to the side and a little toward the bullfrog's rump. Mattie stayed down like she was told earlier so he would stay calm and not do a little hop. Slowly coming in behind the frog, she carefully raised her arm and noticed Father doing the same thing. She crinkled her forehead in bewilderment when in a flash, she thought, *Blow on the frog.* As her hands slammed in the right spot, she blew hard on the frog's back, and he hopped. His hop was like a practice for the next hop, and what an incredible hop it was. The crowd went crazy, and everyone cheered for her.

Mattie stayed in the circle while the measurement was going on. "Wow, young lady!" the announcer said. "I don't know what you fed that frog, but he really made a great final jump."

One of the men doing the measuring brought Mattie's frog back and handed it to her and gave her a smile and a wink. Holding up his left hand high in the air to signal quiet to the crowd, he announced, "Bullfrog number seven belonging to Mattie has a total three hops of…" He paused and looked down at Mattie with a broad smile on his face. The crowd was so quiet Mattie thought she could hear her heart beating. He then looked at the paper in his right hand and yelled, "Twenty-one feet, three and one-quarter inches!"

Mattie thanked the man and waved the bullfrog to the crowd before putting him back in his tin and placing the wet cloth over him. Running back to her parents, she asked, "How many more to go?"

"Just six more," Father answered. Then he told her, "But that will be a hard one to beat. Did you get what I was trying to tell you?"

"To blow on him?" she asked.

"Yep, that was it," he said. "And it looks like it worked."

Mattie appeared puzzled and asked, "But why?"

"Not real sure," he explained, "but I think it might be when a bird tries to catch a frog, they feel the breeze from their wings and hop away."

Millie and Mother watched and laughed while Father mimicked a bird trying to catch a frog.

Mattie gave them both a hard look and told them. "I think it all worked. The water and the blowing." Then she yelled at Rusty, "Hey! Get your nose out of the tin. That's my bullfrog!"

Rusty jumped back and got behind Millie's legs. Millie scratched his ears and told him in baby talk, "It's okay. We'll get you something to eat soon."

None of the other contestants came close to Mattie's score though a couple had one good leap but nothing else. The winner of each group was given their prizes, and Mattie's was a kite from the hardware store, a free dinner for two at the local eatery, and a cane fishing pole from the general store. To Mattie's surprise, the announcer said, "For the overall grand prize winner, five dollars has been donated by the City of Farmington and the Mercantile Exchange." He paused and then called out Mattie's name and bullfrog number seven. "Come on back up here," he said.

Mattie set her tin with the frog on the ground and bashfully goes forward to accept her prize. "Well, young lady," he said, "what did you do to make that frog leap so far?"

Mattie shrugged her shoulders, put her head down, and mumbled, "I did what my father told me to do." She raised her head, pointed, and yelled, "Millie! Rusty! No!"

Everyone looked to where Mattie was pointing at Rusty. Frog legs were dangling from his mouth.

Mattie ran to save the frog. Millie reached for Rusty, but he jumped out of the way as the girls tried to catch him. Rusty kept jumping as though he was playing tag. Everyone was laughing at the girls' expense. Mother remarked, "I think someone is jealous and not getting enough attention."

The girls finally trapped him, and Father grabbed his collar and sternly commanded, "No!" Rusty dropped the bullfrog. The frog was unharmed as he made a couple of leaps before Millie snatched him up.

Embarrassed and upset, Mattie ran back up to the announcer, got her five dollars, and said, "Thanks." Without looking at anyone, she ran back to her parents, grabbed her tin from Millie, and hid behind her father. The crowd awwed and clapped for her. It didn't make her feel any less embarrassed.

"Now for the turtle race," announced the same man. "Need to register and receive your racing number over by the gazebo."

Millie, Mattie, and their parents waited for the crowd to leave. Mattie gave Rusty a squinted eye stare, and he turned his head trying not to look at her.

"Let's go check out the dog show," Millie said, trying to cheer everyone up. "It's on the back side of Long Hall, just over there," she said.

Placing a hand on Mattie's shoulder, Father said, "Cheer up, little one. You won!" He knelt in front of her and gave her a smile. "This will make some of the best memories ever of the picnic."

Mattie thought for a second, then she started to smile and said, "I did win, didn't I?"

Back in a good mood, Mattie and Father hurried to catch up with Millie and Mother. Just as they turned the corner of Long Hall, Millie gasped, "Oh no! Where did all these dogs come from?"

"Hey, Millie!" came a yell off to their right.

Looking into the crowd, Mother said, "There, there's Mrs. Bell waving at us."

Making their way and trying to keep together, they finally got to Mrs. Bell. "Thought this is where I would find you. How'd the frog jumping go?" she asked.

Father held up the fishing pole and kite and said, "First place."

Mattie then held up her five dollars and blue ribbon telling her, "Grand Champion!"

Mrs. Bell threw her arms out wide and yelled, "Grand Champion! I'm so happy!" She gave Mattie a hug.

Mattie cringed a little but remembered what her father said so she smiled and happily said, "Thank you."

"Well now," Mrs. Bell told Millie, "we need to get that dog of yours registered. Come on over here. I know right where you need to go." Millie followed Mrs. Bell and soon found the line to get registered. Most people were already done, so it didn't take long to get her number to put on Rusty and go over the rules. When asked what breed Rusty was, Millie was unsure. She wanted to say heeler, but he looked more like a spaniel. Although she knew the judges would frown on a mixed breed, she decided to tell them "Mixed." She returned to where her parents and Mrs. Bell were standing.

They huddled together to go over the rules before the event started. "Here," Mother said, "let me read them while you all listen and watch the course to figure it out."

They figured out that at each station was a judge that gave a command for the dog to obey. The commands were basic, heal, stay, sit, but the course looked a little difficult. The dogs must jump fences, walk a log, crawl under a bunch of braided ropes, jump a water ditch, and retrieve a piece of rope. They had to take it to their handler and lay it at their feet. Best time wins.

Looking at the different groups of dogs, Millie asked, "Which group should I enter?"

"That group," Mattie yelled, pointing to a large collie. "That's the pretty group."

Millie stared at Mattie and said, "Mother, Rusty's a mix. He is half hunting and half herd dog."

Mother got between the two girls and told Millie, "Nearest I can tell, there's three different categories. Herding, hunting, and open or house dog. He qualified for all three. So why don't you let him choose?"

Millie looked down at Rusty, scratched her head, and asked, "How'll I do that?"

Father and Mrs. Bell stepped up, and Father suggested, "Why don't you just walk around out there and see where he's the happiest?"

"Dog show starts in ten minutes!" shouted a man with a megaphone. "Pick your places now. Show starts in ten minutes!"

"Okay," Millie said. "You watch and let me know where he has the biggest grin!"

They looked at each other and started laughing. "I guess that is as good a way as any," Father said, still laughing. "Better hurry!"

Millie slapped her leg and told Rusty to follow. Millie took Rusty around the course like the others were doing while trying to decide where he would fit in. After a complete round, Father yelled out, "Do it again, only a little slower!"

Millie made another round but a little bigger this time to get a closer look at the three groups. Rusty made a stop right at the working dogs. Millie looked back toward her parents. Father gave a thumbs-up. Mother was nodding yes, and the rest were softly clapping. *Good,* she thought and turned back to her dog—and he was gone. Looking frantically for Rusty, she eyed him next to the well-groomed collie. The other handlers were trying to keep their dogs away from the well-groomed collie. "Come here, Rusty!" Millie commanded, slapping at her leg. He didn't respond. Instead he began smelling the collie. "Rusty, heel!" she commanded again. He started her way but quickly turned back for another smell and raised his paw to the collie's wagging tail. "No!" Millie yelled.

"Hey!" the collie's handler yelled. "Get that dog on a leash!"

"I'm sorry," Millie replied. "I don't have a leash."

"This is a purebred collie," the handler shouted back to Millie. "So keep your two-bit mongrel away from her!"

Millie's neck stiffened, her eyes got about the size of a twenty-dollar gold piece, and her face got as red as a beet. In the blink of an eye, Rusty placed his other front paw over the collie's wagging tail.

"No!' yelled the handler.

Millie jumped in the handler's face and hollered, "What did you call my dog?"

Father stepped in front of her just in time. Someone else yelled, "Don't look!" as the handler tried to pull the collie away. She wasn't going anywhere, and Rusty would not leave.

"Get a bucket of water!" a man yelled.

Millie and Father grabbed Rusty by the collar and pulled him away.

While the collie's handler was demanding Rusty be put on a leash, everyone else was demanding the dog in heat be taken home. The judges ruled that the dog in heat had to leave the contest. It was too distracting for the male dogs.

"What a day!" Father said at the end of the show.

"I'll say," Mother agreed and then asked Mrs. Bell, "Are we all ready to go back to the church for dinner?"

"I guess so," Mrs. Bell replied. "But I do have to say, this has been the most fun I've had since I don't know when. What do you think, fella?" She asked, directing her question to Rusty. "Between bullfrogs and the ladies, I think you've been having a good time." She put her hand under his chin and gave his head a friendly shake.

Mattie pointed her finger at the dog and sternly said, "I'd like to put a knot on your head!"

Father placed an arm around Mattie as the dog got behind Millie and said, "Let's get some dumplings, and maybe we'll find a piece of fried chicken for you."

"Or maybe some frog legs," Millie laughed and took off running to avoid Mattie's wrath.

Father hung on and told her, "It's okay. We're just having fun." True to her nature, Mattie sulked a bit and then started laughing.

Walking back on the Columbia Road, they crossed over to Liberty by the courthouse, passed Highley's Livery Stable, and walked down the alley to the schoolyard where many people had gathered. Greetings and friendly hellos were spoken to schoolmates and their parents. A short distance further was the church. The churchyard was dotted with open fires with large black kettles over them full of cooked food. Long rows of tables were set up that would accommodate the whole church congregation.

"Where's your mother's pies" Father asked the girls.

"Inside," Mattie told him, "where the flies aren't so bad. Why are they so bad?"

"'Cause we are having a picnic," Millie said.

"That's one reason," Father said. "Could be all the animals around too. Storm clouds are building. Flies usually get worse before a rain."

The girls looked down Maple Road toward their home and noticed the tall white billowing clouds that seemed to come right out of the southwest hill.

One of the ladies was putting tablecloths over the picnic tables and overheard their conversation and commented, "That's usually where we get the worst storms. Weren't too long ago, we had a dandy come from that way."

Millie helped the lady straighten the tablecloth and told her, "I remember it. The rain was coming down so hard I couldn't see to get home."

"And that lightning was just awful," the lady said. "It's a wonder you weren't struck."

"Yes," Millie said. "I was pretty lucky that day."

As Millie smoothed out a wrinkle, the lady reached over and patted her hand and told her, "Weren't lucky, honey. The Good Lord was watching over you."

Millie looked at her, smiled, and said, "Yes, I believe you're right."

Father sat at the table, and Rusty moved to lay at his feet, knowing that's the best place to pick up table scraps. "You know girls," he said, "before I met your mother and we had you girls, it seemed I was always alone. I just watched from the outside. Being somewhat bitter and a bit of a troublemaker, there was no fun when I was supposed to be having fun. So I guess you could say I am making up for lost time. I just love it with you all."

The lady came back out of the church house and started clanging on an iron triangle yelling, "Time to eat!"

"All right!" Father said jumping up. "Now don't be telling your mother what I said. Okay?"

Both girls laughed and gave Father a wink.

People came from all directions as the ladies came out of the church house with bowls and buckets of food to set on the tables. This was a great time as it always was. Church social seemed to bring out the best cooking, and holidays were twice as good.

"Here comes Mother and Mrs. Bell with a big pot of chicken and dumplings," Father told the girls as he got up to help carry the pot. "I'll get that, ladies," he said, trying to help.

"We got it," they replied. Then Mrs. Bell said, "Just clear a place for us there in the middle."

No sooner do they set the big pot of chicken and dumplings down when Evelyn Rose along with the doctor and his wife came walking up with some fresh warm bread. "Did you see the parade?" Evelyn Rose excitedly said.

Everyone told her about Mattie winning the frog hopping contest and the disastrous dog show. Father remarked about how good the bread smelled, and Mother wanted to know about Evelyn Rose's essay.

"May I have your attention please!" yelled the preacher.

For the most part, everyone turned their attention to the church pastor. Those that didn't hear soon got the message to be quiet.

"All yours, pastor," someone up front yelled out.

"Thank you," he said. "Just like to give a blessing before we eat. First, let me just say a word about this day and why we are here." With some shuffled feet and throat clearing, the preacher raised his hand and said, "I know, I'm hungry too, but there is a seriousness here, and it is this freedom and our independence that we must always hold dear to us. People have died, and several of you here today had relatives give their lives for this day we celebrate. I just want to remind you all here today, it's not done yet. So in honor of this day, let's remember we still have loved ones fighting for a man's freedom."

Several moans and amens came from the crowd, and the pastor said, "Let's pray and give thanks."

Millie holds Cecil's letter and got misty-eyed as she felt Mother's arm come around her. As the prayer ended, Father gave Evelyn Rose a big hug, looked around, and then said, "Well, Mattie, you go find a piece of fried chicken, and we'll all fill our plates."

On Mattie's quest for fried chicken, she saw Cecil's sister and decided to stay and eat with her. Mother gave the okay and returned to the rest of the family.

"Hope she isn't intruding," Father remarked.

"Not at all," Mother replied. "They begged her to stay as long as the frog wasn't with her, and they had plenty of fried chicken."

Mother ladled the chicken and dumplings made by Mrs. Bell on everyone's plate. Mrs. Bell assured everyone there was plenty to go around, pointing to the big black kettle over the fire.

Clearing his throat to speak while wiping his mouth with a napkin, the old doctor asked, "Did anyone notice that Evelyn Rose had entered the essay contest?"

"We sure did," Millie answered.

"Father and I noticed while reading the day's activities," Mother said and then asked, "So what is the essay about?"

"Or is it a surprise?" Father inquired, giving Evelyn Rose an option to tell or not.

"Nope," she said without a glance up from her plate. Then told everyone without missing a bite, "It was really quite simple once it was pointed out to me." She gave the doctor and his wife a quick glance.

With a stern look on her face, Mother said, "How about we point out some manners to you!"

"Oh, the poor girl, I'm sure she is starving," the doctor's wife explained. "She just about starved herself with my cooking. I'm afraid I'm not a great cook, and our cook was away visiting her family."

Softening her stare, Mother said, "Starving or not, you can still have manners."

With everyone watching, Evelyn Rose dramatically dabbed the corner of her mouth with her napkin.

Trying to avert a public scolding, Father said, "So your essay, what's it about?"

Evelyn Rose swallowed her mouthful of dumplings and said, "Well, like I said, once I thought about writing an essay, the subject was quite easy. So I thought I'd write about a family member that almost lost his life."

Father's smile began to disappear as his face started to get red.

"And with the love and help from family and friends, everything turned out good," she said.

Father's fist began to tighten to where his knuckles turned white.

"How a family member will sacrifice his self in order to save another," Evelyn Rose continued.

"That's it," Father said as he stood up and leaned over Evelyn Rose speaking to the doctor. "You're not going to read about me so everyone will feel sorry for me and stare at me!"

"I should say not!" the doctor's wife said. "You should have spoken to your father first. That way, he'd understand."

Evelyn Rose took another bit of dumplings while father stood over her and glared at the old doctor. "Oh my!" said the doctor's wife. "The essay isn't about you. It's about Rusty and his snakebite. How he saved poor Evelyn Rose. I even helped her outline it."

Father's temper cooled as the doctor explained, "It was Evelyn Rose's idea. Though I must let you know, I have written a journal about the events we've done with your leg. It's just a medical journal, you understand."

"I'm sorry," he said to Evelyn Rose as they all continued their dinner in silence except for a little snicker from Millie.

"What now?" Mother asked.

"Oh, nothing," Millie said. "I was just thinking."

"Thinking what?" Father asked.

"Just how Mother knows you like the back of her hand and if I'd be that way with Cecil when we are married," Millie responded.

Father looked around and quickly changed the subject and told Evelyn Rose, "You should have seen Rusty at the dog show."

"Not now," Mother quickly said.

"No, I'm just saying," Father added. "It'd make for a good chapter in your essay."

Covering her mouth, Mrs. Bell started laughing and said, "Don't know if I've ever seen a dog lose a dog show like that before." Everyone laughed as the humor returned to the table again.

After the meal, the women cleaned and put things away. The men played horseshoes, talked about the weather, and several pulled out their pipes for a smoke. The girls found friends they hadn't seen in a while. Mattie ran everywhere with Rusty, and in no time at all, she was dirtier than most of the animals. Millie and her friends talked about boys and who they planned to marry. Evelyn Rose was going over and fine-tuning her essay.

In the distance, a low rumble could be heard coming from the southwest. Heads raised and conversations paused for a look in that direction. White billowing towers were starting to turn dark. "Well, what?" Father said. "Looks like we might get a dandy." Finding his wife, he told her, "I'm going down to Highley's Livery to see if he's ready for a crowd in his stable."

"Listen up, everyone!" yelled the preacher from the porch of the church. "It might not be a bad idea to bring the desserts into the sanctuary."

A few laughs were heard in the crowd, and the pastor raised both hands and said with a bit of a laugh, "Just don't want the hard work to get soaked!"

Walking with the girls, the doctor said to Father, "Overheard you say you're going to Highley's place. Mind if I go with you?"

"No, not at all," he told the doctor. "Your wife can stay here with the girls."

"Not me," Millie informed. "I'm going with you."

"Me too!" yelled Mattie.

"No, you're not," Father said and then explained, "Your mother will need your help if that storm gets as bad as I think it might. I need you to keep Rusty from following us."

"Oh, yeah," Mattie said, giving Rusty a hard look. "I better stay to make sure you don't eat my champion frog."

Another low rumble rolled in from the southwest just a bit louder than before. "Just never know," Father told Millie and the doctor. "It might clear off like it did yesterday."

The doctor followed up and said, "Or it might be a gully washer, and no one will be able to get home if the creeks wash out. We best be on our way, and while we are walking, I need to talk to you about something."

"Well, go ahead," Father said.

"Hang on, let's get down the road a bit farther," the old doctor said.

Just past the schoolhouse and coming to the livery stable, the old doctor explained to Millie and Father, "I got a young colored family hiding under the horse stable." Father stopped in the middle of the alley, and the old doctor reached out to hold the younger man's arm and said, "I'm truly sorry Evelyn Rose had to be there. I would never intend to place her in any kind of danger." Looking at Millie, he explained, "With our family and servants out of town, it put a strain on the situation when their guide just shows up in the middle of the night."

Father assured the doctor, "It's all right, it's over, and she's safe. What are the plans now? Same as usual?"

"That's another problem," Doc said as the three continued toward the livery stable. "It's a young family. He's brash, and they have a child not old enough to walk."

"What do you mean by brash?" Millie asked the doctor.

"It's hard to keep him hidden," Doc explained. "He wants to go, and I mean now, in the daylight."

"In the daylight?" Father repeated. "That could ruin this whole operation. If they are caught, we are all caught. The law says if they're caught, they have to go back to their owners, and we could be tried like horse thieves."

They all stopped in their tracks right behind Highley's livery stable. Father put his hand on Millie's shoulder and told her, "It could be a hanging offense. So I need you to go and try to talk some sense to them. Show the young mother the danger that if they get caught, they all could be separated. She would lose her baby. He would lose his whole family."

The doctor shook his head, saying, "I was always afraid this might happen someday."

"Millie, you need to hurry," Father told her. "We'll find Highley and maybe the sheriff. We're all in this together, now go!"

As Millie left in the direction of Columbia Road, Father noticed the towering dark clouds building ever higher. The rumble of thunder growing seemed a tad closer and a bit louder.

"It should be close to two o'clock," the old doctor said. "Evelyn Rose will probably be heading to the gazebo area for the essay contest."

Father stopped just short of going through the doorway of the livery stable and asked, "Why, I thought it was this evening, just before the fireworks. Why did I think that?"

"The essays are read at two this afternoon, and the winners will be announced just before the fireworks. With everything going on, I can understand the confusion," the doctor said.

Walking through the door, Father mumbled, "I don't know what I'll do if the next one is a girl too."

"Well, what are you two doing in here," came a voice from inside the livery stable.

"Is that you, Highley?" yelled Father.

Doc asked, "Where are you anyway?"

"Down at the end stall," the stable owner explained. "Just preparing for a storm. Doubling up on the horses just in case."

"In case you need the room for people?" Father asked.

"Yes, sir," Highley said. "So what do you fellows think?"

"As humid as it is, I say it's a dandy. Especially since there's high clouds coming in out of the northwest," the girls' father informed the two men.

They quickly walked to the front of the livery stable then went out in the middle of Liberty Street. They looked at each other, then Highley turned to the girls' father and said, "That could be a cold front rolling in. This humidity, that storm, and a cool front could be cause for maybe a tornado."

"That's why we're here," Father said. "To help, but we got other problems too." He explained about the young slave family and their anxiety. A bolt of lightning streaked from the sky in the distance as the rumble could be felt in the ground. "Now we got this coming!" he told the two men whose eyes were glued to the sky.

"There's Millie," Father said. "Maybe she's convinced them to sit tight. I sure hope so."

"They're gone!" she yelled from a short distance. Everyone turned to see if anyone noticed her. "Sorry," she said coming up to the three men, "but I'm guessing from what sign they left behind, they might be in the old cemetery across from your house," nodding to the doctor.

Another streak of lightning, and the thunder roared a little louder. Mr. Highley quickly said, "Why don't we send Millie down to the gazebo and warn everyone to go to the shelters. Doc, you go across the street and tell the sheriff, in private, to have the deputies stand guard. Tell him I need him over here to help with crowd control. Give him the handshake so he'll know there is trouble." He looked at Millie's father and told the whole group so everyone understood. "I've got some pieces of canvas the runaways can use to cover themselves. Now here is the way I hope it goes. I'm taking the nag with us to find the family. Once we find them, you take the horse north of town," he said to Millie's father. "I'll use the canvas to cover ourselves, and when the storm hits, we'll hightail it out of town on the southside. We'll meet you on the other side of Cecil's parents' farm. They can take the horse a few miles and let it go. She'll find her way back, but they need to stay off the road till they get to Ste. Genevieve. We'll draw a map on a piece of canvas so they'll know where to go once they're there. What do you all think?" Highley asked.

"It just might work," Millie said, looking at her father. 'We'll be scattered in a perfect north, south, east, and west formation. If the Lord above gives us a storm that's not too bad, but bad enough to help us, we could do this." She smiled and said, "Lord, give us a perfect storm."

Closer still, the lightning streaked from the heavens, and the earth sounded as if it's being torn apart. Highley came out of the livery stable with his old horse and yelled, "This old nag's been through many a storm. She won't be so skittish!"

Millie left for the gazebo as the old doctor headed to the county jail for the sheriff. Father and Mr. Highley tied on pieces of canvas to a wooden pack saddle that contained food and water and proceeded west on the Columbia Road toward Doc's place and the old cemetery.

"Let's hope everyone is watching the clouds instead of any strange going on," Highley told his partner.

Making their way out of the town, Father told his landlord, "Might be better if we split up here. I'll go to the cemetery, and you take this canvas and check out Doc's place. If you find them, send them to me. Then we'll go as planned."

As each went a different direction in search of the runaway family, a clap of lightning hit just west, startling both men.

Standing on the stage waiting her turn to read her essay, Evelyn Rose saw Millie running toward them in the middle of the street. Getting her mother's attention, Evelyn Rose pointed toward Millie.

Mother and Mattie stood to see what Evelyn Rose was pointing at. They saw Millie, and at the same instance, a streak of lightning bolted straight down behind Millie, hitting at the far end of Columbia Road. Running past the stunned crowd, Millie jumped on the stage area of the gazebo. She raised both hands high in the air. She told herself, *Whatever you say, make it believable,* and she shouted…

The old doctor stopped dead, still looking directly at three prisoners in shackles, alone, and in the hall. "Come on!" demanded a voice from the hallway. "Keep moving down toward the basement. What's the holdup anyway?"

The prisoners shuffled toward the basement door as one of the deputies followed up behind them. At the hall opening, he saw the visitor and with a bit of a shock said, "Whoa there! I never heard you come in. Dad gum, if you didn't give me a bit of a scare!"

Doc, still in a bit of a fright, stuttered a bit, and then said, "I'm sorry."

"That's okay. What can I do for you?" the deputy asked.

"Who's out there?" came another voice from the hall.

The deputy stepped back as the sheriff stuck his head around the corner and said, "Thought I recognized that voice. What are you doing here, Doc?"

"We need your help over at the Highley Livery Stable," Doc explained.

"Fine, just let me get the men chained," the sheriff started to say then noticed the doctor's hand out for a handshake. The men shook hands, and the sheriff told the deputy, "You lock these fellows up against the wall. Tell one guard to stay with them, and the other guard needs to stay here at the top of the steps. You stay in the front office."

"Yes, sir," replied the deputy.

On the way out, Doc explained the situation and the plan. Stopping in the middle of the street, both men looked east toward where Millie was on the stage at the end of Columbia Road. Lightning struck again, causing the sheriff to look west from down the opposite end of Columbia Road. "Let's hope your plan works," the sheriff told

Doc. "Why don't we stand where the crowd can see us? It will keep their eyes on us when they come…"

Dark rolling clouds moved ever closer from the southwest. Some looked so heavy that they could fall and collapse right on the earth. A lighter bank of clouds slowly moved toward the darker clouds from the northwest. The two clouds met like great armies pushing against each other with the clashing of thunder and lightning. The wind picked up and swirled a gust of cool wind and gust of hot air. Then silence, a dead calm fell over the graveyard. The sky looked green, and the leaves hung still on the trees. From nowhere came a baby's cry. "It must be them," Father said. "I'm a friend!" he shouted softly as he moved toward a headstone. "I'm here to help."

Father heard another cry. A dark hand gripped the top of the headstone. The runaway slave slowly raised his head from the side. His eyes widened, unsure whether he was caught or was going to be freed. From behind the stone grave marker, a young woman popped straight up, trusting the word *friend*. She was dressed in two large flour sacks. The top was plain with three holes for the young woman's head and arms. The bottom had both ends open, held on her waist by a piece of twine. Both of her arms held a small naked child with a grip that indicated she would die before letting go. The young man wore nothing but threadbare wool trousers. Neither wore any shoes.

Father told them to go back where they were, and soon they would be directed out of town. He would meet them as soon as possible. He gave the family one piece of canvas to protect them from the elements and the sight of others. "Now go!" he said. He gripped the man's hand, and a slight smile came upon both of their faces.

"There are tornado clouds," Millie yelled from the stage area. "The sheriff wanted everyone to either get in their homes or the shelter at the livery stable, school, or churches. They're waiting for us." Grabbing Evelyn Rose's hand, the two jumped off the stage and hurried to their mother and Mattie. As another crack of lightning streaked across the sky, it became a foot race to make it to a shelter. Some went to the schoolhouse, and a few went to the church, but most of the crowd stopped at the nearest place, which was the livery stable. Women and children huddled in the empty stalls. Doc and the sheriff tried their best to move the men back though without much luck.

Watching the young family come his way, Mr. Highley placed his two fingers in the tip of his tongue to whistle. "Over here!" he yelled.

With the same kind of fear and trust, the young family hurried toward Mr. Highley just as the winds started to pick up. Lightning cracked the sky so hard everyone froze in fear. Looking to the west, the young runaway father pointed at the white wall that has caused trees, hills, and everything behind it to disappear. "Hoodoo!" he yelled. "The hoodoo of the world is gonna swallow me up!"

"Not just yet!" Highley yelled back as he grabbed the canvas and wrapped over the couple and their baby. "Keep your heads under and follow me. Hurry!" he yelled.

He thought to himself, *If the hail is not too bad, this might be our break.* "Hailstorm!" he shouted as they all headed east staying south of the Columbia Road and town.

As the wind picked up, the sheriff told the men at the barn doors, "Let's shut these doors before the wind blows them off the hinges."

"Sure thing, Sheriff," one of the two men said. He pulled the left side of the double doors shut as the other fellows ran outside to grab the right side. The wind picked up and hail started to fall causing difficulty bringing the doors completely shut.

"Look! Look over there!" the first man shouted and pointed at someone or something running east at the far edge of town.

The old doctor and the sheriff stepped to the doorway, and the sheriff said, "Not sure, but we don't need any more out in this. Get in here, now!"

Coming from the back side of the livery stable, Millie overheard what was said. Showing concern and fear, she said, "We need to gather together and pray for the poor souls that are out there." While everyone huddled together, Millie noticed Mother and her sisters were not in the barn. She tried to ask, "Have you seen my mother?" The hail was beating so hard on the sheet iron roof, no one could understand a single word she said. At the beginning, Millie was a little scared, but now fear covered her like a blanket, and her mind flashed back to the kidnapping. "Please not again," she said, speaking against the roaring wind and the hammering hail. She knelt with the others and prayed for her family, for the runaway slaves, her dog, and Ole Smokey.

Millie squinted her eyes tight and covered her ears with her hands, trying to pray and trying to concentrate, but the noise was so loud. Tears were squeezed out of her eyes. She reached down and felt Cecil's letter in her pocket. Millie pulled the letter out and held it close to her heart with both hands and said, "Please, dear Lord, make it stop." She felt a hand on her shoulder, and thinking it's the old doctor, Millie reached up with one hand and patted the top of the steady, firm hand on her shoulder. Feeling the comfort of the strong hand, she noticed the wind and hail were letting up. Without stopping her prayer, Millie brought her hand down and placed her letter back in her pocket. The hail and the wind stopped, and she thanked God and turned to thank Doc, but no one was there. Millie looked the other way and then behind her. No one was there. The kind old doctor and the sheriff were standing by the barn's double door, and she yelled out to Doc, "Was you just here with me?"

The old doctor gave her a quizzical look and took a couple of steps toward Millie. "I'm sorry, Millie," he said. "Did you ask if I was over by you?"

"Yes!" she answered with a bit of demand in her tone. Then she asked again, "Were you here praying with me?"

"Wasn't me," Doc answered. "I've been helping the sheriff with the doors and trying to watch the jailhouse. Sorry."

"No, no, it's okay," she said. "I'm sorry. I just, I, oh, never mind. That hail was really loud." Millie turned around a little embarrassed. She lowered her head just a bit and rubbed her shoulder where the hand was. "Somebody was," she whispered to herself.

"Are you all right?" Highley asked the young family coming out from under the canvas.

The young father looked up and told Highley, "Yes, sir, we's fine."

Taking his hat off and breathing a deep breath, the stable owner told them, "That was some hailstorm. We were lucky."

"Don't know how you folks kept up so well, but it felt like I was running all by myself under the canvas," Highley remarked. "Wrap the canvas around the woman and child."

The young family shivered and then responded to Highley with a friendly, trusting smile.

"That's the way we do it," the young man said.

"Do what?" Highley asked.

"When we come in from the fields at night, we all have chains on and has to run close together," he explained to Highley.

Highley blinked a couple of times and imagined how it must have been, night after night in the dark, running out of the cotton fields, hoping not to trip or fall with chains on your feet. "We need to go," he tried to say, having trouble swallowing. "We are almost where we need to be."

"Come on old girl," Father said to Highley's old horse. "Good thing we found this old footbridge to get under." Horse and rider walked about a hundred yards before they got to a place where the bank was not so steep and flat enough to be able to get out of the creek. "Well, girl," he said, patting her neck, "I sure hope everyone else has been as lucky as we've been." As he looked back to where he came from, he told the old mare, "Creeks filling up. We better go." A light tap with his heels to the flanks. and they carefully crossed the ice-covered field.

Millie ran out the big double stable door as soon as the sheriff and the doctor opened it. Trying to make a left to go around the building, Millie almost fell because of the hail on the ground but caught herself with one hand.

"Careful there," the old doctor said.

Without looking back or slowing down, Millie yelled back, "Gotta find Mother." She disappeared around the corner.

"I better go too," Doc told the sheriff. "Hope my missus is with Millie's mother."

"Yeah, I think we're good here," the sheriff replied. "I need to check in the jailhouse, and I'll ride down east of town and check on those folks we saw in the storm." He gave Doc a wink and headed across the street kicking up balls of ice as he went.

The ice balls melted against the warm earth as the early evening air became almost cold. "Mother, look!" yelled Millie. "Here comes Father."

Passing by the schoolhouse and walking toward the church, Father raised his hand and waved his hat high in the air. A broad smile across his face caused everyone at the outdoor table to breathe a sigh of relief. Evelyn Rose and Mattie ran to greet their father while Mother followed close behind. "Well, I bet you've got some stories to tell," his wife said as they greeted one another.

"Yes, I do," he said, bending down to hug the girls. "How about we not talk about me till we're going home tonight. I want to hear what went on here, okay?"

"Girls," Mother said, "it's very important not to say or ask anything about your father not being with us during the storm."

"Okay, Mother," Evelyn Rose said with just a bit of agitation.

Mattie climbed up her father's neck to be carried and asked, "Did you hear about the essay contest?"

Placing Mattie back to the ground, Father said, "No! I haven't! Why don't you tell me?"

While walking back to the muddy picnic area, Evelyn Rose and Mattie argued over who gets to tell Father about the evening plans. "Tell you what, girls," Father said, which stopped the girls from arguing, "why doesn't Evelyn Rose tell me about her essay contest, and you"—he rubbed the top of Mattie's head—"tell me about the rest."

Mattie told Father about the events of the day. The horseshoe contest was canceled because of the mud. The essay contest would take its place at the gazebo stage. A band with singers was going to sing while the judges judged the essays. Evelyn Rose explained that the winner of the essay contest would be awarded just before the fireworks display.

"Sounds like a lot of fun," Father said as they all got to the table. "But now what say we have some desserts. I'm starved." He noticed Doc looking his way with some concern on his face so he gave him a reassuring wink and a thumbs-up with a smile.

Doc let out a sigh of relief and gave a slight nod to let Father know that he understood.

The rest of the early evening was spent trying to dry out what needed dried around the bonfires. Gathering wood kept the youngsters busy while most adults visited or listened to a banjo or fiddle playing.

"What a way to cool a hot day," Millie told her parents.

Father puckered his lips to one side of his face and clicked his tongue against his teeth. He leaned forward on the log he was sitting on and softly said to his family and Mrs. Bell, "I just can't help but believe that the Lord above was listening to some prayers during that storm. It was a bad one, but it didn't ruin the picnic. Not a soul was hurt. The hand of God was with us this day."

Millie took her eyes off the fire and looked at her father, remembering the touch of someone's hand on her shoulder while praying during the storm. She started to tell her mother about it just as the bell started ringing for folks to make their way to the gazebo. "I guess it's time to hear your essay," she said to Evelyn Rose. "Good luck. I can't wait to hear what it's about."

"Thanks, Millie," Evelyn Rose replied. "To tell the truth, I wish it was over. I'm so nervous."

Millie smiled and reassured Evelyn Rose that she had a gift for writing, and she had nothing to be nervous about.

The folks that didn't go home after the storm started making their way back to the gazebo where they were before the storm hit. A small band made up of townsfolk was playing while people made their way around mud puddles and wiped down benches so they could sit. The same announcer that did the frog hopping contest oversaw the essay contest. As he stepped to the front of the stage, he asked for quiet by raising both hands up to shush the crowd. Millie and her mother found a good spot and waved to the rest of the family to join them. Mattie sat in her father's lap, and Mrs. Bell sat next to Millie. The old doctor and his wife had a seat just in front of them while Rusty curled up between Millie and Mother's feet.

"This essay contest will be about," the man in charge said then paused for their attention. "Since this is a farming community, and this is the town of Farmington, the essay is about"—he paused again for suspense—"the importance of farm animals."

"Just what we wanted to hear since we work with them every day," someone in the crowd yelled.

Some chuckles from the crowd and a red face on the announcer's as he held his hands up to quiet the crowd. "Now then," he announced, "we have two essays about cows, two about horses, one about pigs, one about chickens, and one about a dog."

The crowd chuckled again, and the heckler yelled back, "We gonna eat a dog?"

Quieting the crowd for the third time with raised hands, he then introduced the three-judge panel and gave a brief rundown of the rules.

Horses and their strengths were the first essay by a lady who raised giant Belgian horses. She told of how they work the land and haul the timber. She reported how these horses pull wagons filled with lead ore and wagons across this great nation. When she told about pulling cannons that freed us from England and a ruthless king that gave us our independence, she received a standing ovation.

"Wow," Millie said, looking again at her father. "That was really good."

He agreed with a straight face, fearing for Evelyn Rose.

Out of the seven contestants, Evelyn Rose was second behind what was possibly the crowd favorite.

"My name is Evelyn Rose," she told the crowd. "My essay is about my sister's dog, Rusty, a farm dog, and no, you can't eat him." The crowd laughed, and this eased her tension, just the way Doc's wife taught her.

"Farm dogs and dogs in general have played an important part in the life of a farm and the lives of the farmer," Evelyn Rose began. She talked about how dogs are taught to herd, hunt, protect, and be a constant companion. She's brief and to the point in all the ways of the farm dog. Then her essay changed to Rusty, her sister's dog, and gave a brief story how Rusty saved Millie's life from a kidnapper. Then Evelyn Rose told how Rusty took the bite of a snake that was meant for her. Finishing her essay, she talked about how dogs love their master unconditionally even when mistreated and will stay at the graveside of their master. "God gave us farm dogs to herd the cattle and sheep, to steer and move great horses, hunt for our food, and to stand guard and protect against all odds. This is true of our farm dog, our dog, Rusty."

Evelyn Rose walked back to her seat as the crowd remained silent. The only sounds that could be heard were a few sniffles and wiping of tears while trying to clear the lump out of their throats. Millie stood and clapped followed by her father and family. The old doctor and his wife stood, and soon the whole audience was on their feet applauding Evelyn Rose's essay.

Chapter 40

Later that evening, after the fireworks and everyone was packed for their trip home, Evelyn Rose settled between her parents with a long face. Mrs. Bell rode in the back wrapped up in a blanket with Mattie, who was sound asleep. Millie sat on the end with her feet dangling off the back of the wagon with an arm around Rusty, watching all the other wagons leave with their wagon lamps hanging near the front of their horses lighting the way home. "Biggest crowd of people I believe I ever saw," Millie told everyone up in the front.

"Yep," Father agreed then told Evelyn Rose, "Best one I've ever seen. Especially the fireworks in this cool night air. Don't you think?"

"It wasn't fair," Evelyn Rose grumbled to her father. "Mattie got first place for her stupid frog, and I didn't get anything."

Mother pulled the blanket up over both their shoulders and told her, "Shouldn't look at it like that. You know your essay was the best, especially when everyone booed the judges."

Father chuckled and gave Evelyn Rose a slight elbow bump, then told her, "I know the one judge didn't care for sheep one little bit, and the other judge had bought a team of them big horses a while back—"

"Okay now," Mother said, cutting him off. "Let's not get all worked up again! It's over, and they'll just have to live with themselves and the decision they made. Besides, everyone knows who won."

"I'm not getting worked up," Father said, flicking the reins and causing Ole Smokey to step up a pace.

Mother reached over and lightly pulled back on the reins to slow Ole Smokey down. "Just look at that big ole crescent moon," she said. "I just love seeing a new moon like that. Especially after a storm like we had."

Father took a deep breath then tightened his lips and gave his smiling wife a quick glance. He returned her smile and said, "Especially with that big bright star right next to it."

"That's not a star," Evelyn Rose commented.

"What! You sure?" Father asked.

"I'm sure," she told him. "It's a planet. Not sure which, but I think Venus 'cause Mercury is now the morning star we see in the mornings at the eastern horizon. We learned that in school."

"If you look straight up," Millie yelled from the back, "you can see the Big Dipper!"

Everyone but Mattie, who was sound asleep, looked straight up. Sure enough, when the passing limbs part enough, you could see the crystal clear night sky. There it was—the Big Dipper.

"Can I go back there?" Evelyn Rose asked.

Husband and wife both acted disappointed, but with a smirk on his face, Father told Evelyn Rose, "Well, I guess, if you don't want to ride up here with us."

"I don't have to," Evelyn Rose said, knowing her parents.

Millie gave her a squinted-eyed stare, and Evelyn Rose said, "Okay, okay, I'm going."

"Don't wake Mattie," Mother told her.

Mrs. Bell raised her hand and held Evelyn Rose's arm telling her, "Here, let me help."

"Thanks," Evelyn Rose replied.

Mother and Father scooted close together and wrapped up tight in their blanket. Evelyn Rose laid next to Millie and let her feet dangle off the back of the wagon too. Rusty laid his head on Millie's stomach as she scratched behind his ears. Mrs. Bell pointed out the North Star just off the cup of the Big Dipper. "It's nights like this that remind me of home back in Tennessee," she told them. "I always loved lying out in the cool grass just staring up at the night sky and all them stars. When my husband was young, he worked on a whaling ship and knew all about the stars and planets. Guess you could say that's how he stole my heart. I loved the stars, and he loved talking about them."

Melancholy set in until Mrs. Bell said, "See those milky streaks among the stars?"

"Yeah," Millie and Evelyn Rose replied.

"That would be the Milky Way," she explained. "I'm sure you two already knew that."

"It's our galaxy," Evelyn Rose said.

"That's right," Mrs. Bell agreed. "My husband told me that it can only be seen on a crystal clear night like tonight. He used to say that when our loved ones who have gone before us take their walks, they walk on those paths and watch down over us."

Millie raised her head to look at Mrs. Bell and said, "I like that, it's such a nice and romantic thing to say."

"He was romantic," Mrs. Bell replied with a chuckle.

Almost everyone jumped when the sound of "We're home!" shocked everyone. Hounds started barking, and Millie, a little confused, said, "We're not home."

Mrs. Bell laid Mattie down, looked at Millie, and said, "No, but I am." She gave Mattie a little kiss on the forehead and patted the girls as she slipped off the back of the wagon. "Had a wonderful time," she told the girls' parents. "I'll be down in the morning to get my things. They'll be all right just where they are."

Everyone but Mattie told Mrs. Bell good night, even though Evelyn Rose's was more of a sleepy mumble.

Home was the next stop. Mother and the two youngest were first to go in while Millie and Father made quick work tending to the livestock. "Cows and calf fine," Millie said. "I'll close the chicken coop while you put Ole Smokey to bed."

"Sounds good to me," Father told her. He wondered what he would ever do without her. Hearing a couple of young sheep baa up the hill, he told Millie, "Sounds like they're doing fine."

Millie glanced at Rusty and told her father, "I believe he agrees with you. He doesn't seem concerned either."

Walking back toward the house, Father asked, "You read your letter yet?"

"Not yet," she replied.

"Tonight?" he asked.

"Nope, I'll read it up there," she said, nodding toward the back field.

Father bobbed his head and said, "Kinda figured." He then said, "I'm done here. How about you?"

"I'm just done, period!" she said. "It's been a long day, and I'm tired."

The two walked together in silence to the small cabin. Millie slipped her muddy shoes off at the door and went in. Father sat on the big rock porch to pull his boots off. Looking up at the stars, he asked God in a prayer to watch over and give safe passage to the young runaway family.

Millie crawled in her bed. While holding on to her letter, she turned over and stared at the stars through the slightly opened window. Thinking of the adventures of the past day, Millie noticed there weren't as many stars as there were when she came into the house. She noticed the sky had a hint of light blue starting to push through the dark toward the west. Beams of golden rays began to streak in with the blue. It seemed she never even closed her eyes to sleep and yet the morning was on its way. Feeling the letter in her hand, she pulled it out and sat up in bed. Still dark in the house, Millie slipped out of bed and felt around for some clean clothes. Quietly, she slipped to the front door and picked up her shoes. After placing the letter in her pocket, she gently opened the front door. Still very dark on the side of the house, Millie stepped onto the big rock porch, leaned back in to get her walking staff, and almost screamed when the feel of a cold wet nose brushed against her bare foot. "One of these days," Millie said as she sat down to put her shoes on, "I'm gonna put a knot right on your head." She grinned then rubbed Rusty's ears.

Heading off toward the spring, Millie told Rusty, "How 'bout a drink and a quick stop at the outhouse before we head out?" Rusty made a yawning noise, and Millie said, "Yep, I know how you feel."

The two stops were quick, and the pair headed off up the hillside toward the pond. Walking in silence in the short, wet grass, Millie listened to and enjoyed the sound of an early summer morning. Almost to the pond, she saw a young doe getting a drink. Next to her were a pair of spotted fawns. The twins showed absolutely no fear of the girl and her dog until their mother caught a whiff of their scent. Millie laughed at the three bouncing white rear ends. She then told Rusty to stay. At the gap, the mother and her babies stopped and turned to see what the two intruders were doing. The doe blew out a warning then stomped her front hooves. Rusty barked. The three deer threw up their white tails and bounded over the fence to disappear in the woods.

"Wow!" Millie said. "I just love to see baby deer. Come on. Let's go."

They headed past the pond then stopped at the gap. Rusty smelled the ground while Millie looked in Mrs. Bell's woods trying to spot the deer. "It's so thick in there. We'd never spot them," she said to Rusty. Millie bent down next to Rusty, pointed to a deer track, and told him, "See the difference. This is a deer track, and this one is a sheep. Hey! Looky here! It's a piece of flint!" She dug at the edge of the flint sticking out of the mud and pulled out a complete, perfectly made arrowhead. "Oh, wow!" she said in excitement. "A perfect arrowhead!" She showed it to Rusty then spat on it to get the mud off. Rusty watched and then turned his attention to the woods when he heard a dead limb crack.

"This is my lucky day," Millie said, holding the arrowhead out in front of her. "Come on, fella. Let's go." She turned to look toward her home and mumbled "Sleepyheads," as there is no one out yet or smoke coming from the chimney.

The pair went through the gap and walked in the shade of the woods next to the fence and headed down to the lone giant oak tree. The closer Millie got, the quicker and lighter her pace became. Reaching in her pocket, the letter was pulled out as she sat in the comfortable spot made by the oak tree's roots. "You go have fun," she told Rusty as he smelled everything he passed by. "I'm ready for some words of love."

As with everything else, Millie took her time to open the letter. Being careful not to tear the envelope, she slowly pulled the glued paper apart. Carefully and gently, she removed the word-filled pages from the envelope. The first line was read. Then she took a deep breath and held the letter under her chin and sighed. Closing her eyes while embracing the written words, Millie said out loud, "I love you too." For the next hour, Millie read and reread the letter. She laughed, and at times, tears fell down her cheeks. She even talked to the letter as though she was talking with Cecil and scolded him to be careful. She held the letter to her chest and hugged it as though he was there. Closing her eyes tight and looking upward, she said, "I miss you too, so much."

Opening her eyes at the sounds of panting, Millie looked straight into the face of Rusty. He pulled his tongue in his mouth, licked his lips, then grinned his funny-looking grin. "Okay," she said. "Let's go find those sheep."

Millie jumped up, feeling the love and happiness in her step as she kissed her letter and placed it back in her pocket. To find the sheep, they went across the field to the shadows of the southwest hill and the dense foliage covering it.

Again, as always, Millie and her dog found the sheep making their way to the creek. Anxious to get back home, she made a quick head count, inspected for cuts, limps, watering eyes, scours, and even tussles with coyotes.

"What do you think?" she asked, looking at the dog, waiting for an answer. "Okay then," she said. "Let's go home for something to eat." Rusty led the way back. Reaching the pond, Millie could see smoke coming out of the chimney and knew that fresh eggs would be waiting for her on the table.

"Wow!" Millie shouted as she entered the door. "I could smell the food halfway up the hill. This is quite a spread. What's the occasion?" Millie looked at a table filled with ham, fried potatoes, skillet bread, butter, and blackberry jam.

"Nothing special," Father said, holding up a fresh egg. "We got almost a dozen fresh eggs today. Thought we'd just celebrate with these and all the trimmings."

Millie clapped her hands in joy and told her parents, "Our very own eggs. I'm glad those chickens are laying."

"Look at this one," Mother said. She tilted the frying pan in her direction and showed Millie and Father a double-yolk egg.

"Hey, what's everyone so noisy about in here?" Evelyn Rose said, walking in the room with Mattie close behind.

Father picked Mattie up and told her, "We got fresh eggs," and he walked over and showed her the double-yolk egg.

"Girls, wash your hands and faces," Mother told them. "Breakfast is ready."

After a short prayer, the family tied into the hearty breakfast. Breakfast time during the summer was always fun as there was no hurrying off to school. The family talked about what didn't get done the day before and what needed to be done that day. Mother and the two youngest had plans for the garden and chores close to home. Father asked Millie to help lay out a new logging road through the woods to Mrs. Bell's place. "What?" she said, coming out of a daze.

Mother got up for more warm gravy and asked, "Cecil doing good?"

"Yeah, what's in the letter?" Mattie blurted out.

"So you all want to know what Cecil wrote to me?" Millie said with a smirk on her face.

Walking back with the gravy, Mother told her, "Oh, if it's private and you don't want us to know, you don't have to tell us."

Father looked at Evelyn Rose and acted as though he's going to get her ham but said to her, "We'd just like to know if he's all right. Wouldn't we?"

"Yeah," Evelyn Rose replied with a giggle.

"If you really must know," Millie said while giving Rusty a piece of ham, "Cecil is doing really good." She took her bread and sopped it through the gravy and onto the egg yolk. "Mmm, this is so good," she said.

Mattie furrowed her brow and said, "Hey!"

"Hey what?" Millie replied. "Oh, you want to know more?"

Everyone at the table leaned a tad closer to Mille as she said, "I'm just joshing you. I want to tell you all about what Cecil has been doing. He's doing very well, and he misses me a lot." Millie told them about his training, schooling, and how the incident that happened here moved him up in the ranks. "He wants to know how your leg is doing," she told Father. "He asked how everyone here is doing too. He told me his education here at home has sent him to officer's training school. Oh, the one thing he talks about the most," she told them, "is the horse that he rode on to get back. He said the officer gave him the horse and got him into cavalry training for all he did."

Then Millie frowned a bit and told the family, "He also said he wouldn't be able to come home until almost Christmastime. Seems he might go out west after training to patrol the Indian Territory.

"Oh, that reminds me, I found this," she said slowly, taking the arrowhead out of her pocket. "I hope it's not a bad sign."

Mattie suddenly became more interested in the arrowhead that was in Cecil's letter and asked to hold it. "Wonder if this ever been stuck in a person?" she asked.

Changing the subject, Mother asked Millie if she wanted any more fried bread before cleaning off the table.

Father quickly told Millie, "Mrs. Bell is coming by this morning, and we're going to walk around in her woods between our two places."

"Why would you do that?" Evelyn Rose asked.

"Mr. Highley told her I was gonna start cutting again. He offered her a good price on those big oaks and said he'd pay me to cut them and haul them to the road. She even offered her big young mare to help haul the logs out."

"You mean Goldie Girl?" Mattie squealed.

"Yep, she's the one," Father replied.

Picking the plates up off the table, Mother said, "That's very gracious of her to do that, but I don't know if Goldie Girl can do that kind of work."

"Mrs. Bell lets me ride on Goldie Girl every time I go up there," Mattie told her mother.

"I know that horse is young and doesn't like to work," Father explained. "But if we team her up with Ole Smokey, I'd bet she'd do just fine."

"I know she would!" Mattie shouted.

"Besides that," Father continued, "it'd save a lot of wear and tear on Ole Smokey." Father watched Millie holding the arrowhead in one hand and rereading the letter with the other. He told her, "Millie, I could sure use your help this morning."

"Huh, what, I'm sorry," she said, placing the arrowhead in the envelope along with the letter. "What did you say?"

"Said I could use your help, if you've got the time?" he asked again.

"Sure, but why?" Millie asked, a bit puzzled.

"I'll go with you," Mattie said and jumped up to get her shoes.

"Not so fast, little one," Mother said. "After yesterday, we've got a lot of work that needs getting done."

Father explained, "We need to clear a path from the field behind Tennessee's house through the woods and come out somewhere on the north side of the woods."

"You mean to make a logging road over on the other side of the field?" Millie asked.

"There's lots of brush on this side," he said. "But it is all downhill."

"Be close to home like that," Millie said. "Even though we'd have to put up a gate by the road before you get to the stream. Or else go all the way around the house and shed to use our gate. But then you'd have to skid the logs uphill."

"I'd rather put up a gate," he agreed. "Save a lot of time. Highley can haul from there just as easy."

"Okay," she said. "Just holler at me when you are ready."

Millie went to her room and lay on her bed to read Cecil's letter again. Only this time, she's a little more worried as she read and held the flint arrowhead in her hand.

Chapter 41

"**H**ey!" came a sound in the dark distance.

"Hey, Millie," came the voice again; this time, the voice sounded like her father. He gave her a light shake and softly asked, "You gonna go with us?"

"Yes, yes, I am," she said, sitting straight up in bed. "I must have really dozed off."

Father laughed and patted her shoulder and told her, "Tennessee is here. I've been hollering for you."

Millie yawned and stretched and told her father, "Whew, let me get my bearings. I'll be right there."

"Okay," he said with a bit of a laugh. "We'll save you a cup of Mother's coffee."

"Guess I should have drunk it after that big breakfast," she said while folding Cecil's letter and placing it with the arrowhead into the envelope.

After coffee and some talk with Mrs. Bell about plans for a logging road, everyone in the room moved toward the door to go outside. As soon as the door was opened, Mother threw her fist on her hips and shouted, "Mattie! You get down from there right now!"

Millie and Evelyn Rose laughed. Father hurried to her side saying, "I was wondering where you were."

"She's fine," said Mrs. Bell. "Goldie Girl is as gentle as a lamb."

"How in the world did you get up there?" Mother asked.

Millie walked over to stroke the big mare's neck and said, "I hope you're gentler than my lambs. They'll head butt you every chance they get."

"I just stood on the wagon, and she held real still for me to get on," Mattie explained. "I told you, Mrs. Bell lets me get on her."

"Yeah, but let's not do that anymore unless someone is with you," Tennessee said and patted Mattie on the head. "Okay?"

Dropping her head and sticking out her bottom lip, Mattie agreed to stay off the horse.

"That is one big horse," Evelyn Rose said. "Bigger than Ole Smokey."

Tennessee stroked the horse's white blazed nose and gave the muzzle a little kiss and told her neighbors, "Miss Goldie Girl is big enough and gentle enough, but I've got my doubts that she's the worker Ole Smokey is."

Anxious to find out, Father asked Tennessee to bring Goldie Girl to the shed area. "Let's just see how she'll handle the pulling equipment."

With the halter left on Goldie Girl's head, he placed a harness over the horse's head and attached the harness. Goldie Girl gave some resistance to having the bit pushed into her mouth, but after a little getting used to and a lot of slobbering, she settled her head down and allowed the reins to be attached.

"I think that is good for now," Father said. "So, Millie, if you would saddle Ole Smokey for me, I'll walk Goldie Girl around and let her get a drink. She needs to get used to the bits in her mouth."

In no time, Millie brought Ole Smokey out all saddled up and ready to go. "Here's what we'll do today," Father explained. "Millie, you ride Ole Smokey next to Goldie Girl and Tennessee, if you would, just walk next to Goldie Girl's head and hold the lead rope on the opposite side but don't stand too close. I'll walk behind holding the reins to get her used to stopping and going."

"So you really want Goldie Girl to follow Ole Smokey's lead?" Millie asked.

"Yeah," Father explained, "and let's all pray the two of them will get along."

For little more than an hour, Millie, Father, and Tennessee worked Ole Smokey and Goldie Girl nice and slow just so they could get the team pulling.

"Okay," Father said, "Let's take them to the back field and mark us a road in the woods."

Mattie and Rusty took off to follow, but Mother called her back, and Father yelled to keep Rusty there too.

"When we get our chores done, maybe we'll walk up and see how they are doing," Mother explained to a pouting Mattie.

Millie rode Ole Smokey next to Goldie Girl while her father controlled the reins. Ole Smokey reacted to Father's commands while Goldie Girl reacted to Ole Smokey and the voice of the commands. Up the hill and past the pond the three of them took the two horses nice and slow, on through the gap, down by the fence to Millie's big oak. "We'll leave them here while we lay out a road through the woods," Father said, pulling the bits out of Goldie Girl's mouth. "I don't want her mouth getting sore. We might be in there awhile," Father explained.

Millie, Father, and Tennessee crossed the fence and went toward the center of the woods. From there, they laid out the best path for a road from Tennessee's back field through the woods to the new gate. Father pointed out that the woods were mostly flat but about thirty acres were on a natural knoll. "If you notice," he pointed out, "right through the center is the ridge." Kicking the leaves aside and some of the dirt, he said, "See how there's no trees growing on the natural ridge." He scraped what little dirt was under the leaves and said, "That's why. There's nothing but rocks all the way from one end of the crown to the other. If you look closely, it goes from your house all the way to the gap in the fence."

Millie stood where her father scraped the dirt back and looked toward the field between the woods and her neighbor's house. Then she looked the other way and noticed she could see all the way to the corner of the woods and the other side of the gap in the fence. "How come I never noticed that before?" she asked.

"Probably 'cause you weren't hauling logs," Father said laughingly.

Somewhat offended, Millie looked at him with lowered eyebrows and asked, "Well, is this where we'll make the road?"

"Are you two always like this?" Tennessee asked.

"Should have seen us when we moved the bees," he told Tennessee. "The thing is, when I got shot, I lost a daughter and gained a mother. In fact, several mothers, it seems. Back to the road, I think we should stay on the crown as far as we can and then veer off just about where that tree is." He pointed to a medium-size tree about seventy yards from the wooded corner near the gap in the fence. "From there," he continued, "we'll veer to the right and go downhill to the field then go straight to the road."

"Why don't we just go on out the ridge and use the gap?" Mrs. Bell asked.

Quick to answer as they got to the tree, Father told them, "See how the ridge starts an incline at the point."

Tennessee and Millie both nodded their heads as Father told them, "With one old horse and one inexperienced, I'd be afraid it would be too much for them. We'll have a nice skid to pull the logs on. So if we don't get too much rain, I think we'll be fine."

"Yeah, you're right," Tennessee agreed. "Besides, it is a whole lot closer to the road."

"So it's up to you," he told Tennessee. "It's your trees and your land."

Tennessee laughed a little as she told Millie, "Your father's been down this road before, so to speak. I'd say he knows best."

"Well," Father said, "lets lay the road out, and tomorrow I'll start clearing it."

"I'll help," said Millie.

"I've got some free time until we have to cut hay again," Tennessee told him.

Father stood in the middle of the ridge and looked toward the back field of the Bell farm. "Going back that way will be easy," he said. "But from this tree then down about one hundred yards will be a little more difficult. If you two clear the saplings out, I'll start at the fence. I'll make a gate then work my way back to here."

"That's what we'll do tomorrow?" Millie asked.

"Yep," Father agreed. He pulled out a big wad of string and started cutting six-inch pieces to tie on limbs to mark the new logging road.

Patting the tree she was standing next to, Millie asked, "What about this tree? Will it need to be cut too?"

Father walked around the oak and looked it up and down. He then looked from one end of the logging road to the other. He measured the circumference then said, "It's really just a tad small, but it's right here where we'll make the bend in the road." He looked again up and down the road and looked up to the top of the tree. "It's got great height, so it will have a lot of lumber in it."

"Since it's not that big, can I cut it down?" Millie asked.

His eyes got big as he said, "Your mother will skin me alive if I make a lumberjack out of you."

Millie leaned against the tree with one arm around it and said, "Please!"

With a long drawn-out yes, her father finally agreed to let her cut the tree down. "But since that's the smallest, it'll be the only one you cut down," he explained. "What we'll do is leave the stump about this high," pointing to a spot on the tree. "We'll use this stump as the woods focal point."

"Why a focal point in the woods?" Tennessee asked.

"So we know where everything is," he said, explaining how things work. "The tools will be kept here, the team and riggings and the food too. We can use this spot as a place to rest."

Millie smiled at her father and Mrs. Bell and said, "Okay then, let's go to work."

The rest of the morning was spent tying pieces of twine on limbs to mark the logging road. About twenty yards to the north end of the fence, thick brush of poison ivy, grape vines, and sweet-smelling honeysuckle had to be cut and pulled in order to finish the road.

The rest of the day was filled with preparation for logging. Axes and two-man saws were sharpened and had rust sanded off. Ropes and rigging were made ready and even Mr. Highley brought out the log skid and said he hired a couple of boys to help if needed.

"We need logs as fast as we can get them," Mr. Highley told Millie's parents. "Demand is high for the plank road, and the price is high for good logs."

"These St. Francois Mountains have some of the best white and red oak found anywhere," Father said. "I'll take the equipment tomorrow but give me a couple of days before you send the boys out. Millie and Tennessee want to help. So I'll give them a couple of days before they want to go back to herding livestock."

Highley chuckled a little and said with his head looking down, "Wouldn't surprise me if Millie outworks you."

He slapped Highley on the back and placed his hand on his neck and said, "You're probably right. Just don't forget she loves shepherding her sheep. She also has to make a way for the sheep to get to the Link farm."

"You all ready for some hot sassafras tea?" Mother asked.

"Ooh, yes, I am," Mr. Highley replied. "Do you have any honey?"

"Already in it," she answered.

Millie came in wanting to know if the sassafras tea was ready and then told Mr. Highley about all the ticks they got into while clearing the logging road.

"I had a hunch that's what the tea was for," Highley remarked. "Sassafras works really well for ticks, but I'd check anyway."

"Going to cut my first tree tomorrow," Millie told Mr. Highley as Mother listened in.

"I beg your pardon," she said.

Father leaned over his hot cup of tea and told his wife, "It's not what you think. It's just this one tree, a small one that's next to the bend in the road. She wants to, and Tennessee said she'd help."

"And you'll be right there with her, right?" Mother said, standing with her hands on her hips.

Mr. Highley and Millie drank their hot tea, watching the exchange about safety and being a girl until finally Millie got up and asked Mr. Highley to come out and see how big the lambs were getting.

Chapter 42

The next morning, Millie and Father grabbed a light breakfast of some meat and vegetables left from the night before and fresh water from the spring. They left just before daylight.

"Your mother said she'd bring up some food and coffee later," Father said.

"Good thing," Millie replied. "I don't think this is gonna last very long."

The pair left the farm through the gate and traveled the road to Mrs. Bell's. From there they hitched Ole Smokey and Goldie Girl together for more training and maybe a little work on Millie's tree.

Goldie Girl was fairly docile being hitched to Ole Smokey but flinched some when the bit was put into her mouth. Father lowered his voice and cooed to the big mare with a promise of being very gentle with her for the next few days. "Our muscles will probably be sorer than your mouth," he told the horse.

Walking behind the team, Millie and her father passed by Tennessee as she held the gate open. "Not too bad in the cool shade," Father said as they entered the woods.

Millie rolled her eyes a little in agreement and then said, "But the humidity is just awful."

"That's Missouri weather for you," Tennessee told them as she joined the pair. "Between the pollen and the humidity, I believe Missouri is the worst place I've ever been."

"Wouldn't know about that," Father told her. "I've never been to anywhere else."

"It's not that bad," Millie said. "But I wouldn't trade these Ozark Hills and streams for any other place in the world. There ain't nothing like 'em."

"I do have to agree with you for the most part," Tennessee said. "But for lookin' at there just nothing like the Blue Ridge Mountains especially after a cool summer rain, and the smoke comes off the peaks." Her voice trailed off, and she stared off in the distance, remembering family, love, and happy memories in a place far away.

A light misstep and the sound of throat clearing caused Tennessee to blink and said, "Guess that's why they call them the Smokey Mountains.

"I've heard of them big hills," Father said.

"Yea, we studied about them in school," Millie told her neighbor. "Lots of coal comes from them mountains, but they're not a good place to live 'cause they're so big, and it takes a long time to travel around them."

Trying to change the subject and to get away from Mrs. Bell's past, Father said, "There's your tree, Millie. You want to chop, saw, or both?"

"Okay, how about both?" Millie questioned.

Father showed her and Tennessee how to chop for the guide notch. He then showed them how and where to saw on the back side of the notch to drop the tree right where they want it to land. "Nothing to it," he said. "Main thing to remember is let your tools do the work. Don't fight it. If you do, you'll be so worn out and sore, you won't be no good for tomorrow. You got what you need," he said, pointing out a single-bit ax and a small one-man saw with a second handle for two people. "There's wedges and hammers to help guide the felled tree. I'm going on down the slope to clear brush and build a simple gate. Just yell if you need me or come on down." Father told Ole Smokey to get up, while Goldie Girl follows Ole Smokey's lead.

Millie mumbled a "See you later" while giving Mrs. Bell and the ax a determined look. She reared back and gave a mighty swing into the trunk of the tree. A loud thud came from the tree as the ax bit the tree. Millie felt proud of her ability to swing the ax until the second swing. "Shoot!" she said, "This ax is stuck in the tree!" She looked at Mrs. Bell for help then heard her father.

"Like I said, let the tools do the work. Now you have to use more energy just trying to get it out."

The two of them finally pried the ax out, and Millie tried again. This time, she let the weight of the ax head float into the tree next to the first strike. Sure enough, a big chip flew out, and Father yelled out, "That's better!"

Mrs. Bell grinned and said, "Guess he could tell just from the sound."

In no time, Millie had a nice bird's beak notch in the side of the tree. Then the two leveled the saw on the back side and started the sawing. After a few pushes and pulls, they got the knack of it as the saw glided, and the saw dust flew out. About halfway through, they thought it best to rest a minute and have a water break.

Both of them were dripping wet from the heat and humidity. Millie took a big swig of water then told Mrs. Bell, "This tree is bigger than I thought."

"It's not bad," Mrs. Bell replied. "But I'd rather tend to cattle. Leave some of that water for me."

Millie passed the water while agreeing with Mrs. Bell. "Yeah, shepherding is a whole lot easier, and you get to yell at 'em when you mess up."

"You ready?" Mrs. Bell asked.

"I guess," Millie answered. "This tree won't fall all by itself."

Both women laughed then jumped when Rusty ran up next to them. "Where did you come from?" Millie said while giving him a good scratching behind both ears.

"Hey! Where you all at?" came a voice in the direction of the big lone oak.

"Mother!" Millie yelled. "We're straight down this way."

In just a few seconds, Millie saw her mother waving and Mattie's head sticking out from behind her.

"Looks like you've got a good start," Mother said as she walked up to greet them. "Where's your father?"

Millie pointed in the direction, and Mrs. Bell said, "He's cleaning out brush next to the fences. Don't believe I'd go down there. It's pretty wooly."

Mother set a basket down and told them she had brought some food. "I just don't know where you'll be able to sit down and eat."

Walking back to the saw, Millie told her mother, "As soon as we get this tree down, there'll be plenty of places to sit."

Mrs. Bell joined Millie and told her, "Okay then, let's get that tree down."

"Can I help?" Mattie yelled as she tried to get in the middle of felling the tree.

Hot and agitated, Millie sternly yelled, "No! Get back!" Millie caught her mother's eye and stopped sawing. "Yes, you can. Take Mother over by that tree over there and make sure she stays there."

Taking her hands off her hip, Mother picked up the basket as she and Mattie moved back.

Again, the sawdust flew in the air as the saw bit deeper into the tree. Pushing and pulling, the saw bit a good inch every stroke. The closer the saw got to the bird's beak notch, the more determined Millie and Mrs. Bell were to fell the oak tree. Suddenly there's a pop then a crack. Knowing they're close, the two women saw faster and prepared their footing to run out of the way. Then a ripping sound at the base, and the oak tree started to lean. Millie looked up at Mrs. Bell as she nodded her head and looked in the direction to run.

A loud crack came from the widening cut as if the tree itself was yelling, "Get back!" Millie and Tennessee ran in the opposite direction from where the tree was falling, straight to Millie's mother and sister. All four watched with wide eyes and amazement as the tree thundered to the ground. Small trees snapped and popped as big limbs smashed them flat to the earth. Dead limbs bounced high to meet the falling leaves left by the wake of a giant. The limb shaking and the death throes of a giant were over. Silence filled the woods. Birds, squirrels, and all animals were frozen from fear. The air hung heavy as if sorrow filled the woods. The leaves from other trees hung heavy like tears.

Millie, Mother, and Mattie, along with Mrs. Bell watched as though a funeral procession was passing by. "Good job!" Father sharply said, causing the women to jump in shock.

"Where did you come from?" his wife asked.

"Guess you were all amazed to see that tree fall that you didn't see me walk up here," he said.

Regaining her composure, Millie asked, "Did you see that?"

"Yes, I did," he said. "And I always react the same way."

"Oh?" Mother responded.

"Yeah, it's the stillness that really gets to me," he said. "You never get used to that dead stillness," he continued. "But then slowly life begins again. A bird chirps, and then a squirrel jumps. Air and sunshine rush in from the hole in the canopy left by the felled tree. Life has begun anew on the forest floor."

He saw the smile on his wife's face and smiled back, saying, "What?"

"Oh, you're such a romantic," she told him.

A little embarrassed, Father's cheeks began to turn red. Looking down, he said, "Did you bring us something to eat? I'm starved."

She picked up the basket and walked next to her husband. She slipped her arm through his and said, "Shall we find a limb for two, and I'll show you what I have here."

Tennessee laughed as Millie rolled her eyes and told Mattie, "Now I see why Father enjoys chopping trees so much."

"Why?" Mattie asked.

"Never mind," Millie said. "Let's just get something to eat."

They sat together on the felled tree as Mother handed out meat and bread along with some jam. She poured out fresh milk from a quart jar to wash the food down.

After a few moments of rest, Father looked at Millie and said, "Now the work starts."

"What do you mean *now*?" she asked.

"Yep, now you have to cut the limbs off, pull them out of the way, and then cut the crown away from the main trunk. After that, you cut the trunk into hauling sections. In your spare time, cut the limbs and crown up into firewood and hopefully split some sections for fence posts and rails," he explained.

Millie looked at Mrs. Bell with a grim expression and said, "That's wearing me out just hearing about it. Maybe a few more minutes of rest, then we'll all get started," she told her father as she got comfortable leaning back against a limb. "By the way," she told everyone, "have you noticed what a pretty site this is? Wouldn't this be a great place to build a home?"

"Too many trees and brush for me," Mattie said.

"No, just imagine a house right here," Millie explained. "Clear the front that way"—she pointed to the east—"with a path going all the way down the hill to the road. Then all of this"—she waved her hand back and forth—"would be the back. Clear out to the corners, leave a few trees for shade, and you'd have that big giant oak right square in the middle of your backyard." Then in a whisper, she said, "This is where I'd like to live."

Mrs. Bell turned to look at Millie with a very somber expression and said to her, "I'm not fond of selling off my property. I love it too. But if you'd like, I'd give this section to you and Cecil as a wedding present."

Millie leaned her head forward toward Mrs. Bell and tried to say something but couldn't find the right words. Her eyes glazed over, and a tear fell.

"That's thanks enough," Tennessee said. "Besides, if your parents move up north, who'd be my neighbor?"

Millie wiped the tears from her face while trying to find the right words of thanks for the gracious gift, but instead of words, Millie took a couple of steps toward Mrs. Bell and threw her arms around her neck. "We all love you," she whispered in Mrs. Bell's ear.

"I know," Mrs. Bell said as she returned the hug along with several pats on Millie's back. "But I do think it wise to check with Cecil first before you start planning your house."

"Okay," Father interrupted. "It's time to clear this tree out of the way. Rest time is over."

Mattie jumped off the tree and asked her father, "Can I stay and help? Please."

"Ask your mother first," he told her. "I don't know what she has for you to do."

"That's up to Tennessee and Millie," Mother said. "You might be in their way."

"No, it's fine," both agreed.

"Tell you what," Father said to Mattie. "Why don't you come with me and help pull out the honeysuckle in the fence. Then you can watch for Mr. Highley to bring his log skidder. That be okay?"

Mattie agreed to help her father. Mother left the basket and leftover food on the new stump and returned to the cabin. Millie and Mrs. Bell each got a small handsaw and started cutting branches off the crown of the tree.

Time flew by as Millie and Mrs. Bell soon had the tree stripped of all its branches. They decided to take a break and walked down to watch Father, and Mr. Highley hooked the skid to Ole Smokey and Goldie Girl. With Father at the reins, Millie rode the skidder back to her felled tree while Mrs. Bell and Mr. Highley chose to walk with Mattie.

Father unhooked Ole Smokey and Goldie Girl. He marked the sections for the tree to be cut. "It's your tree," he said. "You've got four nice logs here. We're going to go measure and mark other trees to be cut. We'll be back before you are done."

With tight lips and a bewildered look, Millie simply shook her head yes and grudgingly picked up the saw.

"No, don't use that one," Father said. "This one here is the one you want. Remember, let the saw do the work."

"Okay," Millie said.

"Can I help?" Mattie yelled from the other side of the tree.

"Let us get through the meat of the tree," Millie told her. "Then we'll let you try. Okay?"

Mattie jumped on the felled tree, excited that she finally gets to help.

"This is good," Mr. Highley said. "If she lets us have half of these trees, we'll all make a nice sum of money."

"Yeah, I know," said Father. "Kind of a timber man's dream, if he had two good legs."

"Just don't push it," Highley told him. "You'll do fine. Now let's go check on the girls."

Showing the girls how to use the hooked log roller, Father and Highley had the tree in four sections within minutes and ready to load on the skid.

"This tree was bigger than I thought," Father commented. He then showed them how to load the logs with a block and tackle. "Now we will just hook the team up and be on our way."

Mattie asked if she can ride down on the log. "That's one place I better never, ever catch you," Father said, making sure she never forgets. "It's too dangerous. Too many things can happen or go wrong. So you don't ride on a log, okay?"

Sorry she even asked, Mattie agreed to never ride on the logs.

Father gave the command for Ole Smokey and Goldie Girl to start their pull. Father slapped the reins, and the horses dug in with their hooves. With a slight jerk, the skid was freed from its resting place. Ole Smokey relaxed, and the team pulled together with little effort.

After two trips, the four logs were in place to be hauled to the sawmill just a couple of miles south. Highley was well impressed with logs ready, and Tennessee was more than happy with the pulling done by Goldie Girl.

"Looks like we're in business," Highley told the others.

"Send your boys out after tomorrow, and I'll have some trees on the ground," Father informed Highley.

Mr. Highley agreed and headed back to town.

"I'm glad Goldie Girl worked out, but between the cattle farming and an old body, don't count on me for much help," Tennessee told Father.

"I understand," he agreed. "Now that we're getting started it's better that none of you ladies are around," he said, looking at Millie.

"Won't get an argument out of me," Millie told her father.

The horses were unharnessed. Mrs. Bell took Goldie Girl back to the barn while Millie and Mattie got Ole Smokey to head back to the house by their father.

After a nice meal along with a little rest, Millie and her father made a new gate to Link farm.

With a little help from Rusty, all twenty-seven sheep reluctantly greeted their new grazing grounds. "Best we leave them here for a couple days, that way they'll stay close to our fence and away from the other side. I'll have to water them twice a day since there's no pond or spring," Millie told her father.

"There's the watering trough," Father pointed out. "Ready to go right behind the house. And look, there's a gate where you can let the sheep into the yard for some quick yard work. Come on, let's check out the well pump."

Applying some oil to the rusted joints and a little priming, Millie and Father soon had fresh, cool, clean water coming out of the spigot into the trough. "If I remember correctly this pump goes into a pretty good size cistern," he explained to Millie.

"Let's get the sheep over here for a drink so they know where the water is. Oh! Don't leave the sheep in the yard unless you stay with them," Father told Millie.

"Okay," she said and then told Rusty, "let's bring the sheep to water."

Rusty gave a confused look but obeyed the simple command. Soon the curious sheep were head-butting until the pecking order of who drinks first was fulfilled.

Millie and Father made a quick trip around the barn and made sure all was in order. They closed the gate and headed for home.

"It's funny how things work out," Millie told her father.

"You mean the use of the Link farm and barn just when we needed it most?" Father questioned.

"Yeah, you know, we've always done well and never been hungry, though we live in a small log cabin," Millie said.

"Hey!" Father said. "It's sound, in a perfect location, and a good lease price."

"I know it's good," Millie said. "You know how I love it here. What I mean is… Well, there's a war going on, and it's been tough on people especially families. I know you and Mother have struggled.

You had so many logs hauled out of here. Then wool prices were high, and our sheep had an abundance of wool."

Father chuckled a little and then said, "But then I got shot!"

"That's exactly what I'm talking about!" Millie halfway shouted. "Who has half their leg blown off and then ends up like this. I know people walking away from their farms just so they could dig lead."

"Now, Millie, there is nothing wrong with digging for lead," he said with a bit of chastising. "But I do understand what you're talking about. With our faith in God and your mother's smarts and determination we've never given up. Each one in the family has rolled up their sleeves and tended to business. Yes, we've truly been blessed. The Lord was with us when you were kidnapped, when I got shot, and when Rusty was bitten by a snake. How many times did we drop to our knees during these times?"

Millie cut Father off and said, "Someone touched me."

Father looked puzzled, and then she told him of the touch she felt on her shoulder during the storm.

"Yep, it hasn't all been honey and clover has it?" Father asked. "Then again, when you walk in the way of His Word, He walks with you."

Before Millie and her father rounded the corner, Mattie greeted them with cane pole in hand. Excitedly, she asked Millie, "Will you take me fishing?" She held out her new fishing pole and said, "Mother said if I worked really hard and finish the chores that you would take me."

"Hey! What about me?" Father asked.

Trying not to hurt her father's feelings, Mattie explained, "Mother said you would want to rest before going into town."

With a surprised look, Father told Mattie, "I would like something to eat and a little nap, but I don't know about going into town."

The front door swung open, and Evelyn Rose shouted out, "It's about time! Mother said you'd take us fishing."

"I didn't think you liked fishing," Millie said.

"Yes, I do!" she said. "Please!"

But you told me," Millie started to say.

Evelyn Rose corrected Millie, saying, "I told you I like to catch fish. It's just when they weren't biting that I didn't like it. It gets boring, and I don't like touching them and putting the worms on."

At the sound of worms, Mattie said, "We got a bunch of these little red worms from the garden. I don't mind touching them at all."

"I can tell," Father said, looking at Mattie from head to toe. "Did you leave any dirt in the garden?"

Millie laughed, but Mattie didn't. Evelyn Rose shouted to her mother over the laughter, "Millie's going to take us fishing!"

Father gave Millie a wink as she told her sisters, "I don't think it is a good time to go fishing. Let's check the almanac."

Finding the treasured book on the shelf behind the cookstove, Millie flipped through the pages and said, "Here it is," looking at the fishing calendar. Not a sound was made as Millie's fingers traveled down the days of the month of July. "Today is," she began to read. She looked up as all eyes were on her. "Fair," she said.

"It doesn't matter," Evelyn Rose said in doubt. "I don't believe in those moon signs anyway."

Clearing his throat, Father said, "I wouldn't plant crops without checking."

"Preacher says we shouldn't believe in those zodiac signs," Evelyn Rose told him.

Father scratched his head, and after a moment of hard thinking, he said, "I'm no preacher, but the way I reckon on it is, the Bible says somewhere that there are seasons and times to plant, sow, and harvest. You know, to be born or to die. I don't believe he put them stars out there just so we'd say how pretty they are. Besides, I planted potatoes in the wrong sign once, and we had the most beautiful plants you'd ever seen but very few spuds."

"That might be," Evelyn Rose argued, "but—"

Father continued stopping her from completing her sentence saying, "Now to use signs for fortune-telling and things like that isn't good. No, not good at all."

Before anymore discussions could be made, Millie said, "Okay, I'll take you both fishing. We've got poles and worms. So let's go."

"Thank you," Mother said, slipping her arm into the crook of her husband's arm. "Are we still going to town?"

With a smile on, he said, "You bet, I'll get cleaned up while you fix dinner."

"Pardon me!" she said, placing both hands on her hips. "I'll fix the children their dinner, but you're taking me to town."

"Yes, I am," he told his wife. "That's what I meant."

The girls laughed as their father hurried out of the room. Whispering to Evelyn Rose, Millie said, "Mother is starting to show, so she'll have Father out as often as she can."

"Why?" Evelyn Rose whispered back.

"I think it's so Father will tell her how pretty she is," Millie explained. "It's weird. I remember how mother would look at herself then cry when she was going to have Mattie. She'd ask Father if she was ugly and then they'd hug a while, and everything would be fine."

Evelyn Rose whispered back, "That is strange."

Millie turned to see what her mother was doing and jerked back in her seat when she saw her standing by the cookstove staring at her with squinted eyes. One hand was on her hip, and the other hand was holding a big wooden spoon pointing straight at Millie. Mother raised one eyebrow and asked, "Who wants soup?"

Chapter 43

After dinner, the girls told their parents that they'd clean up so they could leave for town sooner. They waved goodbye at the gate, and Millie then told Mattie to go to the cabin and get her new fishing pole. Mattie rode the gate as Evelyn Rose pushed it shut. She jumped down and ran toward the cabin. "Get the worms and a tin too," she instructed.

Running as fast as she could, Mattie ran right out of her left shoe and stopped to put it back on. Evelyn Rose laughed and asked Millie, "If we are going to the pond, why don't we just get them as we walk by?"

"We're not going to the pond," Millie informed her. "We are going to catch a bunch of grasshoppers then go over to the Link farm."

Evelyn Rose furled her eyebrows and gave Millie a tight-lipped frown and said, "Why, that little old mudhole behind their barn wouldn't have nothing but a frog or two and maybe one of those snapping mud turtles in it. I'm betting there is no fish in it."

"I'm not talking about that mudhole," she said. "I'm talking about a place at the back end of their farm. They have a valley just like ours. There is a spring like ours that feeds a pond. It's like a small natural lake."

"How big is it?" Evelyn Rose asked.

Millie thought for a few seconds imagining the comparison and said, "Probably about three times as big as ours."

"Mattie!" Evelyn Rose yelled. "Would you hurry up! Come on, let's get some grasshoppers. I want to see this place."

After a quick gathering of grasshoppers all placed in the tin, Millie tied a cloth over the top with some string found in the horse stall. She then cut a couple of limbs out of the big willow tree next to the spring area. She looked over Mattie's fishing supplies and told her sisters there's plenty of hooks and line for the three of them. As they walked the fence that separated the two farms, Millie explained it would be best to stay on their place all the way to the top of the hill and then go through the woods on the back side to the small lake. "That way," she said, "we won't have to go through the grown-up field and fight all those ticks."

"Is this an adventure?" Mattie asked.

"A little one," Millie told her.

"I'd say the adventure is that we are going without Mother or Father," Evelyn Rose said to her sister. Then asked, "Do you think they'll care or be mad?"

"I don't think so," Millie said with a bit of a worried look on her face. "I only wish we had told them or left a note."

"What could happen?" Mattie asked just as Rusty started barking about fifty yards up ahead of them.

Evelyn Rose looked at Millie and said, "I hope it's not a snake."

Mattie stopped and reluctantly said, "Ooh, I hope not!"

"Come here, Rusty!" Millie yelled. She pointed a finger and commanded Rusty to stay close.

The rest of the walk to the small lake was a little slower and a little more careful. They traveled up and over the northwest hill then descended after crossing the split rail fence on the Link's side of the hill. About halfway down, Millie pointed through a break in the trees. The glistening blue water of a spring-fed lake lay a couple of hundred yards away. The three girls stepped up the pace but not so fast as to outpace Rusty and his sharp senses for snakes and his curiosity for any ground critters. At the base of the hill, Millie made a left to swing around the overgrown edge of the woods and came to the small lake from the valley side. As soon as the girls made their appearance, a mother duck and her young came out of the brush and quickly swam to a safer place. Off to the left side, they heard a sudden crash just a little ways from the bank.

"That was probably a deer," Evelyn Rose whispered.

Millie squatted down next to Mattie and softly told both girls, "That or a bear."

Mattie gave Millie a very sober look, asking her, "Are you sure, or are you trying to scare me?"

"No, look right here," she told Mattie, pointing at the ground at a set of deer tracks.

"This place is really something," Evelyn Rose said. "Did someone make it?"

"No, no one made it," Millie explained. "It's one of those places that formed since the birth of the earth. See how these two hills make a horseshoe shape? They curve into each other. Our two hills go out opposite directions." Millie pointed across the end of the lake and explained, "There's a constant flow of fresh water coming from those rocks and at the far end." Pointing to the far end, Millie said, "There's a beaver dam. This is one of those places that is just natural."

"Did God make it?" Mattie asked.

Still squatting at the deer tracks, Millie smiled and rubbed Mattie's arm with the back of her hand and said, "Guess you could say that."

"No, he didn't," Evelyn Rose quipped. "It formed over the years with rain and wind."

"What?" Mattie shouted and looked back at Millie.

Quick to reply, Millie explained as she wrapped her arm around Mattie's shoulder, "Yes, God did make the lake. He just used the wind and rain as his tools. You don't need to talk like that to her," she scolded Evelyn Rose.

"That's not nice!" Mattie said.

"You're a baby," Evelyn Rose spouted back.

"All right, you two, let's see if we can catch some fish before we have to go back," Millie said to avert another argument.

Sitting on some rocks by the shore, Millie and Evelyn Rose started tying line to the poles. Using Mattie's small tin tackle box, she found hooks to tie to the line. First Millie fixed Mattie's new cane pole then her own willow pole. "That's some pole," Millie said as she attaches the two pieces of cane together to make a pole long enough to reach out about ten feet. "Just be careful you don't get the hook caught in a tree, okay?"

"I will," Mattie said and thanked her sister.

"You will what?" Evelyn Rose asked. "Get your hook caught in a limb?"

"No!" Mattie angrily said. "I will be careful!"

Millie pointed a finger at Evelyn Rose and told her, "You need to stop that."

When Millie wasn't looking, Mattie stuck her tongue out at Evelyn Rose.

"I saw that, Mattie!" Millie said. "Your reflection is right here in the water."

Mattie looked down and noticed the reflection was just like a mirror. "Ooh," she groaned.

"So you stop it too!" Millie demanded. "Or we'll go home right now!"

For the next hour, the girls did their best to catch a fish. Letting their bait settle to the bottom but no luck. They tried tying a piece of wood in for a bobber and still no luck. They switched back and forth from worms to grasshoppers but not even a nibble.

"Think we was too noisy?" Evelyn Rose asked.

"No," Millie responded. "I think this close to the spring makes the water too clear. Besides the sun is to our back casting our shadows and our movements."

"Maybe it's the almanac," Mattie said while drawing pictures in the mud.

"Could be," Millie answered her.

They sat a little longer until the sun went behind the trees and the hill behind them. "See that big rock over there?" Millie pointed to a big boulder a few yards off the shoreline. "I think I'll try to wade over to it and try to catch something on the other side."

"That might be over your head," Evelyn Rose pointed out.

"Yeah, I don't like that," Mattie fretted.

"Then I'll swim," Millie told them. "The water is really clear. Can I use your cane pole, Mattie?"

"If you promise to be careful," Mattie told her.

"Don't worry, it's not that far out," she assured her little sister as she took her shoes off and rolled her pant legs up. "What could happen?"

Millie carefully put a red wiggle worm on the hook and followed up behind it with a grasshopper. She pulled the line nice and tight while wrapping it around the pole itself till the hook and the handle of the cane pole were the same length. Stretching the line tight, Millie took the baited hook and hooked it into the bottom of the pole. "Okay," she said from the bank and stepped into the clear water. "Wow! This is cold!" Gritting her teeth, Millie looked back, and said, "Sure hope it gets warmer once I get past the spring water."

Evelyn Rose and Mattie stood in anticipation, watching Millie quickly waded to her waist then up to her armpits till she has to swim to the rock.

"It's deep here!" Millie told her sisters. "And a bit warmer." She reached the bolder and sat on another rock a couple of feet under the water near the boulder. Carefully undoing the fishing line before getting out, she let the bait drop to the base of the boulder and stuck the handle end of the cane pole in a crevice where the boulder and the underwater rock met. "There," she said, "now I'll just," Millie started to say as she climbed to sit on top of the big boulder but froze in place. Not saying a word, she stared past the boulder at the water's edge.

"Millie!" Evelyn Rose yelled out. Millie quickly raised her hand and pointed up.

Evelyn Rose and Mattie looked at each other. Mattie loudly whispered, "Are you all right?"

Millie slowly turned her head to look at her sisters and told them in a slow whisper, "Get Rusty, and don't let him go."

Before Millie could turn her head back to what she was seeing, and before the girls could latch onto the dog, an ear-shattering sound came from the lake's edge. Rusty rushed out after the sound, and Millie fell backward into the water. In a flash, Millie swam back to her sisters while Rusty chased the critter back into the woods.

As Millie got out of the water, both Evelyn Rose and Mattie, who were scared to death, asked Millie, "What was that noise?"

"Is it going to get us?" Mattie asked, almost crying.

Evelyn Rose said while backing away, "Let's get out of here!"

"It's okay, you two," Millie told them. "Now calm down. It's nothing that will hurt us."

"Well, what was it?" Evelyn Rose demanded to know, wanting to leave.

Mattie stood between her two sisters not knowing which one to run to. Millie replied, "It's a donkey!"

At the same time, Mattie and Evelyn Rose responded with the same question, "A what?"

"Yeah," Millie explained, "it's a little donkey. We need to try to catch it. You two stay here, and I'll see if I can get Rusty to quit chasing it."

"Don't get lost," Mattie told her as she regained some courage.

Ducking under the thick brush at the lake's edge, the woods opened to where Millie could see her dog. A few steps into the forest, she made out the well-camouflaged small donkey. The donkey and the dog were facing each other. Millie studied the pair so she would know what she was in for. The donkey's giant ears were pitched forward. His ropelike tail with frayed ends was casually flicking flies off his rump. Rusty was yelping as if telling the donkey he just wanted to play. Millie walked slowly toward the animals, fearing the donkey might run off with a barking dog chasing it even farther away. Nearing the donkey and the dog, they both turned their attention to Millie. As she was readying to calmly call Rusty to her, the donkey let out another ear-shattering "Eeyore!" The donkey started walking toward Millie, with Rusty keeping pace next to it as if the donkey was Ole Smokey.

Taking a deep breath, Millie blinked her eyes a couple of times as she said out loud, "A tree, find a tree to get behind." Before she could move, the donkey was standing right in front of her, sniffing and blowing until he was satisfied Millie was of no danger. He lowered his head and sniffed Rusty. Rusty returned a couple of sniffs and looked up at Millie and the donkey. "Okay, now what?" Millie asked as she slowly raised her hand to pet the beast. She scratched the donkey behind his gigantic ears, and he seemed to like it. He leaned closer to Millie and almost knocked her down. "You sure are a friendly fellow," she told him, still a bit wary of him. "And you are full of ticks." Millie picked a few ticks off and laughed when she saw how he trusted her enough to close his eyes as the ticks came off.

The girl and the beast relaxed to the new friendship, and Millie soon coaxed him to follow her using some leaves from a maple tree.

Breaking out into the opening of the lake's shore, Evelyn Rose and Mattie backed away with eyes wide open and jaws dropped. "That's a, that's a, a…" Evelyn Rose stuttered.

"A donkey," Millie said, finishing the sentence.

Trying to get behind Evelyn Rose, Mattie asked, "Is it wild?"

As if to answer, the donkey brayed another loud "Eeyore!" causing Evelyn Rose to scream, which caused the donkey to bray again. Evelyn Rose and Mattie both began screaming, and the donkey "Eeyored" again, and Rusty started yelping.

Millie held up both hands to the girls and yelled, "Don't scream again!"

When they remained still for a minute, the donkey slowly walked straight to Evelyn Rose. Mattie came out from behind Evelyn Rose and said, "I think he was just saying hello to us."

"Maybe so," Evelyn Rose said as she stiffened her body at the greeting. "But that sound he makes is enough to wake the dead."

Soon all three sisters were petting and picking the ticks off. They asked each other where he had come from, whom he belonged to, and should they take him home.

Mattie looked over and excitedly said to Millie, "Look at my fishing pole!"

Millie rushed to the lake and waded back into the water. Shivering, she swam over to the rock and quickly grabbed the handle of the cane pole and headed back to shore. Holding the pole high in the air, the girls on the bank could tell it was a big fish by the way it was jerking her arm. Swimming with one arm was wearing Millie out. Mattie even noticed and yelled, "Be careful, Millie! Let it go if you have to! It's okay!"

No sooner did the words come out of Mattie's mouth, Millie's feet touched bottom. Nothing but her head and hands were above water. Millie played the fish, giving a slight pull then letting the fish pull back. She was careful to guide the fish in different directions and not straight back where it could break the line. After what felt like a long time, Millie was finally in waist-deep water. "He's weakening!" she yelled to her sisters. Turning to look how far she needed to go to get back to the water's edge, Millie started laughing at the sight of Mattie, Rusty, the donkey, and Evelyn Rose standing at the bank's edge. "Get back!" Millie said. "I'm going to drag this thing out." With renewed strength, she walked out of the water. Millie reached for the line to pull the fish onto the bank. "It's a catfish!" she yelled at the first sight. Letting go of the cane pole and grabbing the line with both hands, she pulled hand over hand until the catfish was pulled on the lake's bank.

Once the fish was out of the water, Millie gave one last hard pull, and the fish made a big flop. As Millie pulled, the hook came flying out of the catfish's mouth, almost causing Millie to fall into her audience. The fish flopped back into the water. Millie lunged forward to scoop the fish and brought it closer to the bank when she slipped on the wet mud and landed her rump right on top of the fish. "Ow!" she yelled and jumped up to finish the job of getting the catfish out of the water.

"You're bleeding down your leg," Mattie said, pointing at Millie's backside.

Trying to twist her head to see, Millie said, "I don't doubt it. I sat right on that horn." She pointed to the fish's dorsal fin.

"A horn, a fish has horns?" Mattie questioned while looking the fish over.

Still rubbing her rear end and doing a little high-stepping, Millie said, "Yeah, just reach down and touch it. Catfish have three horns, one on the back, and one on each side. Go ahead and touch it. You'll see."

"Don't do it, Mattie!" Evelyn Rose yelled. "You might get stuck like Millie did."

"Oh, you silly goose," Millie told them both, wincing in pain. She reached down and pulled the laid-back fin just behind the catfish's huge head straight up, showing the girls the spiny, sharp dorsal fin. "See," she said, "and they have one on each side," pointing them out.

"Then why aren't they called cowfish since they have horns?" Mattie asked.

Millie rolled her eyes, and Evelyn Rose turned her head to snicker. "Because of the whiskers," Millie pointed out, showing Mattie the fish's whiskers.

Mattie blinked a couple of times and told her big sister, "Don't look like cat whiskers to me."

A little perturbed and in pain, Millie said, "Well, they are. Grab your stuff and let's go home. My seat hurts, and you're asking too many questions."

As Mattie and Evelyn Rose gathered up their fishing poles, Millie ran a piece of rope through the fish's gills and out its mouth. She tied it to a tree limb to carry it home.

Mattie carried the tin of red wiggle worms and grasshoppers while Evelyn Rose got Mattie's cane pole and tackle box. Glancing back at Rusty and the donkey, Evelyn Rose and Mattie both asked Millie, "What about the donkey, mule?"

Millie snapped her head up, saying, "Who called that donkey a mule?"

Neither girl said anything, but after a couple of seconds, Evelyn Rose looked down at Mattie. "I, I guess I did," Mattie told her big sister then gave Evelyn Rose a mad stare.

"That's a donkey," Millie explained. "A mule is a cross between a horse and a donkey. They can't have babies. They are big and hard-working animals. We have them in our state here. People call them Missouri mules. Now a donkey is a beast of burden. They're little and sure-footed. Usually, they just carry heavy loads for miners around these parts."

"But in the Bible," Evelyn Rose cut in saying, "Mary rode one when Joseph took her to Bethlehem. Then Jesus rode one when people laid palm leaves down on his way into Jerusalem."

"That's why they have a cross on their backs," Millie said, walking over to the little donkey. "See, come here and look."

Mattie walked over next to Millie and tiptoed as high as she could. Millie laid the catfish down and lifted Mattie high enough so she could see the cross. Looking down on the gray animal was a brown line of hair going from the donkey's neck down the back. Right at the shoulders was another line crossing over from one shoulder to the other. Mattie's eyes were big with amazement of seeing the cross on the donkey's back when Millie let her down. Mattie looked up at her big sister and asked, "Is he going home with us?"

"I can't make him," Millie replied. "But if he wants to come home with us, I'd be happy to have him."

Watching her two sisters, Evelyn Rose said, "Me too."

As the girls left, Millie yelled for Rusty. He barked at them and the donkey. The donkey replied with an ear-shattering bray and followed Rusty and the girls.

"Think I'll call him Bray," said Millie.

Just before dark, the girls made it down from the northwest hill. Noticing the smoke coming out of the chimney and light shining from the cabin windows, they hurried toward the cabin.

"Will Mother and Father let us keep Bray?" Mattie asked.

Evelyn Rose gave Mattie a light shove and told her, "That's a stupid name. Bray is what he does, not who he is."

"That's enough," Millie told them both. "Let's just wait and see if we can keep him."

Leading the way with a limp and a huge catfish slung over her shoulder, Millie told her sisters not to worry about the donkey and just hurry. Almost home, Millie noticed both parents standing on the big rock porch, watching. Millie dropped the fish on the ground and told Father, "They'll explain." Looking at her Mother, she said, "I need to see you in my room."

Mother began cleaning Millie's wound and doctoring her rear end. Everyone could hear Millie when Mother poured some hard whiskey into the lanced wound. Bray even answered with his loud "Eeyore!"

The rest of the evening was filled with stories about the donkey and Millie's fish. Father cleaned the fish while Evelyn Rose and Mattie did the talking.

Chapter 44

Early the next morning before the sun had risen but light enough out to see, Mattie slipped out of her bed. "Hey! Where are you going?" Millie asked, causing Mattie to inhale a gasp of air.

Whispering, Mattie told her, "I'm just going to see if Bray is still here."

"Wait, I'll go with you," Millie said.

Lightly stepping out of her room, Evelyn Rose scared them both when she said, "That's still a stupid name. I'm coming too."

"Fine," Millie said, "but you don't have to scare us."

Evelyn Rose grinned mischievously and told her sisters, "Should have seen you two jump."

Creeping out of their room and into the gathering area, all three girls huddled at the window. "Let me see," said Mattie.

"Move over," Evelyn Rose told them both.

Millie pointed and said, "Look! He's still here."

Their three heads looked out the tiny window at the edge of the big rock porch. They could see Rusty curled up in a ball lying next to the donkey, who resembled a sleeping dog on the ground.

"He's here!" Mattie exclaimed.

"Who's here?" came Father's voice from behind them, scaring all three of them.

"You did that on purpose," Evelyn Rose said.

"And you didn't?" was his reply. He then asked Millie, "How's your wound?"

"A lot better," she replied, embarrassed. "Good thing Mother is a good nurse."

"The girls said you really did a dance after you slipped," he said with a chuckle.

Millie laughed at herself, asking her sisters, "Was it better than the outhouse dance?"

Both girls laughed and mimicked Millie's dance, rubbing their behinds.

"Okay, that's enough," Mother said from the hallway. "It's not near as funny when you're in that kind of pain." Looking at Millie, she told her, "You could have been in serious trouble if we hadn't cleaned your wound when we did."

Mother and Father scooted in toward the window and looked at the donkey. "What are we gonna do now with a stray donkey?" Mother asked.

Silence surrounded the small window as everyone knew the right answer to Mother's question.

Father sighed and then told everyone, "I need a couple new files for my saws, so I might as well go back to town and get them."

Turning her head from the window, Mattie moved next to her father and with a shaky voice asked, "Will you see if we can keep him?"

"I'll check at the livery stable and see if anyone's been talking about losing their donkey," Father told her. "Then I'll let the sheriff know we have a stray donkey staying with us. Never know, someone might be hurt, trapped, or even died in one of those shallow mining pits. The sheriff might want to—"

"Eeyore!" came the ear-shattering bray as all the girls jumped and screamed at the sound. Looking back out the window, they saw the giant ears behind the muzzle of a donkey as he tried to see into the window.

"He can't stay near the house!" Mother said while catching her breath as she put one hand on her belly and patted her chest with the other. "If he keeps that up, I'll have this baby a lot sooner than I really want."

"Okay," Father said, doing his best not to laugh. "Millie, you go ahead and water the sheep, and you girls take that thing."

"His name is Bray," Mattie said, letting her father know he has a name and is not a thing.

"Yes, and he sure can bray," he told her. "But you need to clean him up some. Try to keep him near the shed and be very careful. He's friendly enough, but you just never know what he'll do if he gets scared."

Evelyn Rose and Mattie both happily nodded their heads and hurried off to get into their clothes. Mother looked at Father with a crooked smile and said, "Roosters crowing and donkeys braying, what next?"

Father slipped on his boots, grabbed his hat, and gave his wife a laughing kiss as he opened the door and said, "I'll see if they have any elephants I can bring back with me."

Mother placed her hands on her hips and returned his laugh, "Hurry back. I'll have breakfast ready."

In the days ahead, the young donkey proved his worth. With a homemade pack saddle, he hauled equipment to and from the cutting sites. He did more than his share of pulling the smaller treetops to areas where firewood and fence rails could be cut. After a couple of weeks, Bray was just like one of the family. His habit was to always sleep at the front door with Rusty. Every morning right after the rooster crowed came the awful sound of "Eeyore!" It was so loud it would echo off both the southwest and northwest hills. Evelyn Rose and Mattie would ride him everywhere on the farm. Millie would even ride him at times to check on the sheep. The donkey didn't tolerate a bit in his mouth but learned to guide with a harness and reins.

Chapter 45

In late August, work was going so well that there was an overabundance of logs to be hauled to the mills. One Sunday afternoon on a ride home from church, Father asked everyone, "How would you all like to take a trip?"

"A trip!" Mattie yelled as she worked her way from the back of the wagon to stand behind her parents. "Where?"

Millie and Evelyn Rose turned so they could hear better. Ole Smokey took the lead as Mother and Father both turned toward the girls and said at the same time, "To our new home."

Mattie was ecstatic, but Evelyn Rose yelled out, "What about school?"

Millie gave a blank stare, not knowing what to think.

"We'd be back well before school starts," Mother explained.

"Yeah," Father agreed, "we'll only be gone about a week."

With a worried look, Evelyn Rose said, "No, if we move, how will I go to private school next year?"

"You and your fancy school," Mattie told her. "I want to move." She stuck her bottom lip out but quickly drew it back because of a stern look from her mother.

"Our new farm won't have anything to do with you going to a private school," Father quickly intervened before anyone could say anything more. "Those plans are still there. You'll either go from Farmington or from Bonne Terre if we move sooner. The school in New York isn't moving anywhere."

Evelyn Rose became silent trying to think of something else to say. Father lifted her chin with his finger and assured her it would be all right. Ready to turn back around, he glanced past Evelyn Rose and Mattie to see Millie in deep thought. "Time away will be fun," he told her. "Then after a week, you can tell me about those deep thoughts you're having."

She returned a smile his way and gave him an agreeable nod.

Turning around to guide Ole Smokey, Father saw he was doing fine on his own. Father sighed and asked his wife, "We will have fun, won't we?"

Mother leaned in close and slipped her arm through his. "Yes, we will!" she said positively. "We all deserve a break and some rest."

For the next few days, plans and preparations were made with the intention of leaving on Friday. Father took care of the business of the new farm and care of the homestead. Mother acquired wood crates to pack some freshly canned goods from the garden and some dried meat. Hopefully Father could shoot a couple of squirrels or maybe a turkey to feast on while away. Perhaps some fish could be caught from the lake or river to provide a good meal. Just in case, she crated up a couple of young hens hoping they would keep laying eggs on their journey.

Mr. Highley or his hired hands would keep an eye on the place while hauling the logs. Mrs. Bell would feed the chickens and the cow while keeping a close watch in and around the cabin.

"Twenty-four," Mrs. Bell said, "I promise I will count them every day," assuring Millie that the sheep were of the highest priority. "Just don't tell all my cattle friends I'm tending sheep," she quipped.

Realizing her joke didn't set very well with Millie, she quickly gave her a hug and said, "Don't you worry about a thing. I'll care for them just like my prized Herefords."

"I know you will," Millie told Mrs. Bell. "It's just that I know some people really hate sheep. I know you'd give them the best of care."

"See that corner up there," Tennessee said pointing just past the pond to the gap in the fence. "I'll be there every evening for the count."

"Thanks," Millie told her. "Twenty-seven."

"Millie!" Mother yelled. "They'll be fine."

With that, everyone chuckled, even though Millie was still a little leery to leave them.

Chapter 46

Early Friday morning before the sun was up, Millie shut the gate and made sure it was tied secured. While the wagon was still going, she raced past Rusty and Bray and leaped onto the wagon, landing directly between her sisters. Father yelled outs, "Everybody good?"

"Yeah, we're good. Let's go!" came the replies from the three girls.

Evelyn Rose and Mattie snuggled together on the soft blanket pallet Mother had made. Mother held her husband's arm with both hands and laid her head on his shoulder. He took a sip of coffee from the tin cup and told Ole Smoke in a soft tone, "Get up!"

Millie placed both hands on the back edge of the wagon and stiffened her arms as she looked past her dog and the trailing donkey. She smiled at the cabin, thinking what a great shepherd's house it was. Looking past the house and up the hill, Millie tried to count the white dots of sleeping sheep. To the left, she squinted her eyes trying to make out the pond. The water was black and still. The menacing sight sent a slight chill up her spine. Almost hypnotized, she thought how it looked like a cold, dark grave. She blinked and shook her head. Her eyes followed the low ridge line behind the pond to the gap in the fence where she saw the top of the giant oak that gave her a feeling of peace. To the east, the dark sky was becoming a soft blue just at the horizon. A few wispy clouds had soft pink edges indicating the sun would soon be up.

Without warning, but right on cue, Millie heard the rooster crow. Bray heard the crow and answered back with "Eeyore" that caused everyone to jump. Mother placed a hand on her belly and told her husband, "I'm telling you, if that donkey doesn't stop!"

Father laughed as did Millie. Evelyn Rose sat up next to her big sister and said, "So much for trying to go back to sleep."

Soon the road connected to another road that connected from town. The family settled in with other travelers heading north. Father explained this was the road they would be traveling until they reach the Bonne Terre area. "It's a lot safer this way, especially with the war still going on," he explained. "Same group that shot me when we were marching is still raiding in the area."

Evelyn Rose looked at Millie and asked, "Same ones that tried to hurt Millie?"

"Same ones," Father replied. "But he and several others aren't around anymore."

"He's not in jail?" Millie inquired.

Father turned around and assured Millie saying, "Not this one. He and several others were snuck out of town one night and taken to some big prison across the Mississippi into Illinois. That's where they'll be tried for their crimes."

"Why didn't they try him here?" Millie asked.

"Because of the Southern sympathizers," Father said. "Hildebrand's family and gang, called the Bushwhackers, would have been around Farmington causing all kinds of trouble."

"That's why we left early this morning," Mother said joining the conversation. "It's safer traveling in groups. The farther north we go, the more travelers will join us."

"Where is everyone going?" Evelyn Rose asked.

"Different places," Father told her. "Several go to town to get supplies. Some are doing business with the different lead mines, and some are on their way to Saint Louis."

"Will we be in danger?" Evelyn Rose inquired, causing Millie to sit up at the word *danger*.

Mother noticed Millie's concern and explained, "There's always danger, even in our everyday life. Your father cuts down trees for a living. You know how a snake can strike without notice. Or even Ole Smokey could get skittish from a bee and kick someone."

"Or you could sit on a catfish horn," Mattie said.

"That's right," Mother said. "It's just as safe here on the road as it is at home."

"Especially for weekend travelers," Father said.

"Why weekend?" Evelyn Rose asked.

"Because on the weekend, Federal troops patrol the major roads just for travelers," he explained. "During the week, they go out and try to catch the bad guys."

"Can I ride Bray for a while?" Mattie asked.

"It's still early," Mother told her. "Why don't we just rest a while longer, and after we stop for breakfast, you can. If it's okay with your father."

Mattie and Evelyn Rose laid back down, and Mother snuggled back in next to her husband. Millie gave a sharp whistle to Rusty and patted the hanging tailgate so he would jump up and ride next to her. Bray picked up the pace and walked next to the wagon. She petted the donkey's soft nose and decided to dig out one of Mother's carrots. Millie glanced back to make sure Mother didn't see her and then gave it to Bray. "Don't tell on me," she whispered to Rusty.

For the next couple of hours, the girls rested while Father kept Ole Smokey in pace with a few other travelers. Every so often, Bray would trot next to Ole Smokey and walked next to him. "He's just like a pet," Father told his wife, amazed at how the donkey took to the family.

"More like a guardian," Mother said. "With that sound he makes, a man would be crazy not to run."

A small creek provided a great place to stop for a while. Father unhooked Ole Smokey while Millie and Mother made a quick fire to cook breakfast. Pork fat was thrown in a big skillet. Then Mother started cracking the eggs they had gathered before leaving. Fried eggs were usually one of their favorite breakfasts, especially when she made fried bread in the skillet. Without much conversation, the family ate the quick meal. Father took his coffee and checked the wheels on the wagon. A simple routine check from front to back assured him so far everything was good.

"Do you know where we are at?" Evelyn Rose asked.

Father grabbed the map that he made from the map at Highley's livery stable. He got a little more coffee and sat next to the girls and said, "Well, let's see." He paused a few seconds, took his finger, and followed a line coming from Farmington and finally said, "We are right here."

Evelyn Rose gives him a blank look till he said, "This is the Flat River. Hear tell that during drought times, this river will dry up. But if you look here,"—he pointed farther up the map—"in about four miles, we'll come to a bigger river. That's the Big River, and it's the same one that the farm we're going to is on."

"Can we swim in it?" Mattie asked.

"Probably," Father told her. "But not today. We're in a bit of a hurry."

"Unless you accidentally fall down," Evelyn Rose said.

Mother quickly stood up from the fire, placed one hand on her hip while wagging a finger with the other, and said, "Don't be placing any ideas in anybody's head. We are on a schedule, and we need to keep to it."

Mattie hung her head but gave Evelyn Rose a little grin from the corner of her mouth.

"Mattie," Mother said, "look at me."

Mattie looked up and saw her mother's eyebrows raised. She scooted next to her father, and in a half whisper, asked, "Can I ride Bray when we leave?"

"If your mother says it's okay," Father replied.

"I'm sorry," Mattie told her mother. "I won't accidently fall in the river."

Mother smiled and said, "We'll see. Help me clean up and pack."

Father put the fire out. Packing was quick, hanging the utensils on the side of the wagon and putting the food in tins and then rolled up in wool blankets.

Father hitched up Ole Smokey while Millie put a halter and reins on Bray for Mattie to ride.

After a couple of safety checks, Father hopped on the wagon and flicked the reins. Ole Smokey shook his head a couple of times and began to move toward the small river.

Father turned and told Mattie to keep Bray close to the wagon.

Mattie raised her head, grinned, showing all her teeth, and nodded her head.

Rusty followed between the wagon and the donkey, watching for Millie to pat her leg and tell him to come up.

Time passed quickly as they watched the many travelers on the road. Millie and Evelyn Rose made their way to stand behind their parents. "Now we can see where we are going and who is coming," Evelyn Rose told them.

"Will Big River be as easy to cross as the Flat River?" Millie asked.

"No, it won't," Father told her. "The Flat River has a rock bed and is really solid. The Big River, if I remember correctly, has a lot of gravel and gravel bars. It would be easy for the wheels to sink. We'll have to get off and push," he explained.

"What if the water is over our heads?" Evelyn Rose asked.

"There are deep holes," Father told her, "but we'll cross in the shallows. The water is swifter in those places, but this time of year, it's only about six inches deep, if that. Once we start, we have to keep going or the water will wash out around the wheels, then we might be in trouble."

"Can we tie a rope to Bray?" Millie asked.

"Let's not worry about it now," Father said.

"Girls, you need to go sit back down," Mother told Millie and Evelyn Rose. "Save your strength. You might need it later since I can't help."

"Hey there!" Mattie yelled as she and Bray trotted up and passed the wagon.

"Where are you going?" Father hollered back.

"Don't know," she yelled. "I think Bray wants to walk next to Ole Smokey a while."

Just as Mattie said, Bray trotted on by and settled in next to Ole Smokey as if he was part of the team.

For the next few hours, Father led the family north past mining towns and farming communities. Meeting people traveling south, Father asked about the river crossing. Almost everyone said it was good crossing and that there were Federal troops there to give a hand if there was any trouble. However, there were a lot of people crossing, and the gravel might be getting softer, causing it to be harder for heavier loads.

"We can put the pack saddle on Bray," Father told everyone. "That'll lighten the load. "Mattie can lead Bray across. Millie, Evelyn Rose, and I will push, if you will take the reins," he told Mother.

Knowing his good intentions and the dangers in the river crossing, Mother simply agreed.

The Big River was not a wide or deep river but got its name for its length. The French settlement of Bonne Terre was almost an island because the river came close to surrounding the township and its surroundings. Horseshoe bends were commonplace, and if a person didn't stick to the roadways, they could find themselves crossing the same river several times in a short distance. Coming upon the river, Father explained to the family, "This is the same river that the farm we're going to is on."

"Why don't we just follow the river to it?" Evelyn Rose inquired.

"The way it winds," Father explained, "it'd take over a day to get there. We'll be there in a few hours if the crossing goes okay."

Topping the hill that overlooked the river basin, Father explained why this was the crossing place, pointing out bluffs just to the left of the river then bluffs to the right.

"Wow!" Mattie yelled out. "Look at all the people down there."

"There's a lot of soldiers in blue down there," Millie said while standing behind her parents.

"They're there to help out and protect travelers," Mother told her.

"I wish Cecil was down there," Millie softly said to her mother.

"I know," Mother replied as she patted Millie's hand when she placed it on her Mother's shoulder.

A young man in uniform rode up to the river crossing and instructed the travelers to fall in line and have a little patience. As the young soldier explained, his eyes glanced at Millie, and in an instance, he completely forgot what he was saying.

Millie met his gaze and gave him a smile when Father said, "What would you like for us to do?"

Keeping his eyes on Millie, the young man said, "My name is Jonathan."

Father looked at his wife and mouthed the words, "What?"

Mother laughed a little then told Millie, "You better sit down till we stop."

Still smiling, Millie said to the young man, "My name is Millie. We're traveling to a farm just east of the Bonne Terre area."

Father yelled at Ole Smokey to move up in line, which brought the soldier out of his stare, and he apologized, saying, "We'll get you across, sir, don't you worry none." Looking back at Millie, he asked, "How far east, ma'am?"

Evelyn Rose burst out laughing and said, "He called Millie 'ma'am.'"

Millie turned and gave Evelyn Rose a glare with gritted teeth and furled brow. She quickly looked back at the young man with a smile and told him, "Not too far. It's a farm on this very same river."

Standing up in his stirrups, he asked Father to move forward again. "On the road that goes to the French Village?" he inquired.

"That'd be the one," Father said.

"Yes," Millie answered.

Looking at Millie's father, the young soldier told him, "There's a lot of Bushwhackers in the Bonne Terre area, sir. If it would be all right with you, maybe I should ride out and check on you." Then he looked up at Millie and said, "And your family. If it'd be all right with you."

"We'll be fine," Father said.

"That would be very nice," Millie told the soldier.

Mother broke the silence and said, "That would be very kind of you."

"Yes, ma'am," he said to her. "Thank you, ma'am." He touched the brim of his hat to be courteous and then tipped his hat to Millie. He looked at Father and said "Sir" then rode back to the river.

Millie tiptoed as high as she could to watch the young soldier ride away until he glanced back, then she hunkered down behind her mother.

"What the heck was that all about?" Father asked while commanding Ole Smokey to get-up again.

Mother wrapped her arm around him and whispered, "We'll talk about that later, okay?"

Father rolled his eyes and shook his head in a questioning nod as Mother patted his arm.

After a short while, Father pulled Ole Smokey up to the water's edge. Mother, Millie, and Evelyn Rose got out of the wagon while Father awaited further instructions. An older man rode up and pointed to a wagon coming across the river and explained, "After they get across, we'll get you to the other side."

"Thank you," Father told him.

Mother and Millie got a hold of Bray. "You'll have to get off and walk Bray across," Mother told Mattie.

Millie jumped when she heard her name and turned to see Jonathan ride up next to her. Addressing them all, he asked, "Would you ladies like for me to give you a ride across?"

"No," Mother said. "The water's not deep at all. It would feel refreshing to wade across."

"Yes," Millie said. "I'd like that very much."

Mattie and Evelyn Rose stared as the young man dismounted and stood toe to toe with Millie. She looked up into a pair of deep-blue eyes that almost captured her breath. He looked down, staring into her chestnut-brown eyes, not paying attention to the world around him.

"Soldier!" an old man yelled.

Jonathan jerked around and saluted his commanding officer and said, "Yes, sir!"

The officer rode closer and asked Millie, "Is this soldier causing you any trouble, ma'am?"

"Oh, no," Millie said. "He was just being a gentleman and offering me a ride across the river."

He nodded and said, "Then let's get these people across and on their way." He looked at Evelyn Rose and Mattie and asked them, "Would you two young ladies like to ride across too?"

Evelyn Rose and Mattie stared at each other; hearing the word *ladies*, they turned, giggling, and took off running to their mother.

"Ready?" Jonathan asked. Millie felt as though she was floating up into the saddle as he lifted her up. He placed her sitting sidesaddle on top of the horse. Thinking he would be leading the horse across the river, Millie was surprised when he mounted the horse and sat behind her with his arms around her waist as he held the reins. "Are you okay?" he asked.

Millie nodded.

"You might want to hold on," he told her.

She took her arm and wrapped it around his waist. "That's fine," he said with a smile. "But I meant hold on to the saddle horn."

Millie blushed and dipped her head some. She slowly slid her fingers from his side and held on to the saddle. This time, he blushed as Millie looked up at his face. Jonathan coaxed the horse to begin crossing the river.

It didn't take long for Evelyn Rose and Mattie to get into the water. Evelyn Rose led Bray while Mattie walked behind with a hand on his rump. Father stood up and whispered, "Oh no. I might be in a little trouble."

Mother knew they were all tenderfoots, but no one thought about Father having a shorter leg. "It's not far," she whispered back. "Just lean against me."

The river at the crossing was only about six inches deep, but the water was swift. The worst part was the small smooth, round river gravel. The cool water felt wonderful, but the gravel made for some very difficult walking. Without warning, Mother leaned one way. Father did his best to right her, and just as he had warned, the gravel washed out from under his foot. Mother toppled, grabbing for her husband. She squealed as she sat flat in the water, dragging her husband right along with her.

"Hey!" Mattie yelled. "You said we couldn't get in the water!"

Evelyn Rose pointed and laughed at the pair as the officer in charge quickly comes to their rescue. "Are you two okay?" he questioned.

Trying to compose herself, Mother waved one hand indicating they didn't need any help.

"Those sharp rocks can be hard on a person's tender soles," he said. "Though it looks like you two might be enjoying the cool dip." He tipped his hat again and said as he rode away, "Most folks do the same thing. Take your time. Your wagon will be over there."

Soon Evelyn Rose and Mattie joined their parents in the fun of cooling off. Though the most embarrassing moment came when water was splashed on Bray. Everyone's attention was drawn to the family when the earsplitting "Eeyore!" came from the donkey, not once but three times. Laughter could be heard up and down both banks of the river.

Millie didn't know whether to be embarrassed or not until the young man she was riding with told her, "Looks like you have a fun family."

"For the most part," she said.

As the family came out on the north bank, Jonathan quickly dismounted and almost stepped on Rusty. "Is that your dog?" he said as he held both hands up to help Millie down.

She nodded her head as he slowly lowered Millie from the horse. She held close, wishing her feet would never touch the ground. He bent down to pet the dog, and Millie noticed Rusty's tail wagging fast with that silly grin. "I think he likes you," Millie said.

"I sure hope he does," came the young soldier's reply.

"Time to go," came a young voice from behind the pair.

Millie turned to see Evelyn Rose standing right behind her. Behind Evelyn Rose was Mattie sitting back up on Bray. Behind them was Mother being helped up onto the wagon by Father.

"Be okay if I come to check on your dog?" Jonathan asks. "You know, since we've become good friends."

"I think he would really like that," Millie replied. She turned back to Evelyn Rose and walked with her, leading the donkey back to the wagon. This time, she didn't jump on but turned and lifted herself up to sit on the tailgate.

Jonathan took his blue cavalry hat off. Sun-bleached blond hair fell over his face as he waved to Millie. He then flicked the reins across his horse's hip, causing him to rear up and jump into the river to head to the other side.

Millie took a deep breath while Evelyn Rose and Mattie watched in bewilderment. She patted her leg, and Rusty jumped on the wagon next to her.

Father looked at his wife and asked, "Can we go now?"

Mother slightly bowed her head and said, "Sure, unless you want to take another dip."

"No, I'm ready," he told her. With a slap of the reins, he yelled to Ole Smokey, "Get up!"

Mattie did the same, only with a light touch with her heels to Bray's flanks. The family headed north to the Bonne Terre area.

Time slowly went by as they rode and talked. Three hours into the ride from the river, Father informed everyone, "After this bend, we'll be at the settlement of Bonne Terre."

"Will we go through the town?" Evelyn Rose asked.

"Wish we could," Father told her. "I just don't know if we'll have the time."

"Aww, I wish we could," Mattie said. "I need to get off Bray. My rump is getting sore. Can we stop for a minute?" she asked.

Pulling on the reins, Father said "Whoa" to Ole Smokey to get him to stop.

Bray stopped as well, and Mattie gingerly slid off the donkey. She stretched, then with both hands, rubbed her rear end. "You're a good boy," she said while rubbing the donkey's giant head. Bray twitched his long floppy ears in approval while enjoying the attention. After getting in the wagon between Evelyn Rose and Millie, Mattie whispered, "He sure gives a rough ride, but don't tell him I said so."

Millie laughed at the comment, but Evelyn Rose just rolled her eyes and said, "You're silly."

Around the bend and down a small hill, they came to an intersection. Father explained, "To the left about a mile is the mining camp and the hospital where I stayed for a while. Straight ahead, fifty to sixty miles, is the big city of St. Louis." He pulled on the reins, and Ole Smokey turned right. "This is the way we are going," he told everyone. By this time, the three girls were standing behind and hanging onto the wagon seat. "Somewhere between one and two miles, we will be at the Big River again and the place where we might build a new home."

Mother held his arm with both hands as the excitement was building from everyone.

Father pointed out farms along the way, saying, "These might be our new neighbors. More crop farming here than at home, but there are some cattle farms too. Oh, yeah, and just on the other side of the river is a small dairy farm. The family that lives there milks their cows every morning. They haul the milk in containers into town to sell to miners and families that live there around the mines."

"Wonder how people will take to sheep in this area?" Millie asked.

"Not sure," Father said. "We'll have to build pens to keep them in till we can get fences around the farm. There is a lot of free range around here. We'll just have to keep them close."

"Free range?" Mille asked. "That's where we'd get in trouble."

"Don't worry though," Father told her. "There's enough grazing grass on this farm to feed what we have."

"Better you get there soon," Mother informed her husband. "Don't know who's hungrier, me or this little one," she said, rubbing her tummy.

"It's not just you," Evelyn Rose said.

Mattie joins in telling everyone, "Me too! I'm starving."

Father apologized and explained, "I've been pushing it just a bit so we would have time to set up in the daylight." He then suggested, "Why don't we open a jar of peaches for Mother until we get there."

Millie handed her father a jar of peaches. He opened them and handed them to his wife. She stuck a half-peeled peach with a knife and then passed the jar back to her husband. Father passed the jar around to the girls and then took a peach for himself.

"Oh no!" Mattie said, looking down at the floorboard where she dropped her peach.

"Don't worry, Mattie," Millie said. "I'll wash it off for you."

Drying the tears in her eyes, Mattie thanked her sister and enjoyed her peach with the rest of the family.

Chapter 47

Approaching the next bend is a rather large white clapboard house with a big white barn behind it. What surprised everyone was how close it was to the road. An older man and woman sat on the shaded front porch with a redbone coon dog lying at their feet. When the old dog spotted Rusty, his front legs pushed his chest and head up to get a better look while still sitting with his hind legs under him. A long, loud, friendly howl from the old dog greeted the passersby along with a friendly wave from the old man and woman.

"We're staying at the farm next to yours," Father yelled to them, returning the wave.

The old man got to his feet, causing his dog to hobble up on all fours. "I'll give you time to get there," he replied to Father, "then I'll mosey down the lane for a proper greeting. If you're up to it."

"That'll be fine," Father shouted back. He gave the reins a little flick, causing Ole Smokey to come to life and pick up the pace.

When the bend straightened out, Father told the family, "This here is the upper field. It's the largest with almost fifty acres." He pointed across the center of the field and said, "Just on the other side of the slope where you see the tops of those trees is right where the cabin is, sitting right next to a big spring-fed lake."

Everyone stared at how green the thick grass was. "Sure is lush pasture," Millie told her father.

Father nodded his head with a broad smile on his face and told her with pride, "That, young lady, is river bottomland, some of the best in the whole county."

"Look!" Mattie yelled, pointing down the road. "Look at the bridge and big bluffs on the other side."

Just as they got a really good view of the wooden bridge, Father turned Ole Smokey off the road, turning into a lane with a gate about thirty feet off the road. "This is it!" Father said. "When we go through this gate, prepare yourselves to be amazed!"

Millie rolled her eyes and said, "I'll get the gate." She jumped over the side boards, and Rusty ran under the wagon just to check where she was going. Millie looked at the turquoise-painted cast-iron gate and couldn't help but admire the craftsmanship. The gate was made of rods bent into an upside-down U about four feet tall inserted into holes in flat bars that stretched six feet each way from the center. Between each bent rod was a spear that looked like an arrowhead on top of the bars. The two gates were locked by a heavy rod in the center and was inserted in a pipe in the ground. When lifted by a handle, the two gates came apart and swung open. Millie turned around, giving Mother and Father a smile but had to laugh at her sisters with their heads stretched up over their parents, gazing wide-eyed in amazement. The gate was hinged on two large cast-iron posts attached to more turquoise cast-iron fencing that ran at a forty-five-degree angle back to the road.

Father pointed to the end post and said, "We'll start building our fence here and go straight to the house we just passed. This side over the hill will go all the way to the river."

"Lots of fence," Millie said. "How far to the cabin?"

"About a hundred yards through the gate and down that lane," he answered.

Millie walked back to Ole Smokey and said, "I'll just lead him down."

As she entered through the gate, the first thing she noticed was the big sycamore tree just to the left and the red gravel road as she neared the bend by the sycamore. "What is that?" she asked.

"They told us it's tiff rock from down around the Potosi area," Father explained. "It's crushed tiff rocks, and the people that own the lead mines use it for roads. They said it packs really tight and makes it easier to haul lead."

"Who are they?" Millie asked.

"I'll tell you tonight," Father told her. "Just keep your eyes peeled for what's coming up."

Millie led Ole Smokey on with Rusty at her heels and Bray right behind him. Just as soon as she rounded the corner, Millie let go of Ole Smokey and walked on in wonderment. "What are these trees?" she said.

"We told you," Mother said. "They're mimosa trees in full bloom."

"They're beautiful!" Evelyn Rose said.

"This is why we waited till now to bring you here," Mother said.

Mattie yelled, "Wait for me, Millie!" She hopped off the wagon to walk with Millie for the rest of the way. "Look down there," she said. "It's the cabin."

"Look out there!" Evelyn Rose shouted, pointing. "It's the lake, and it has a bridge that goes out to the center."

"It's really a dock," Father explained. "But isn't it something?"

As the family continued on, they stared at the big mimosa trees and how they grew completely over the lane, intertwining with the ones on the other side.

The cabin was a large one-room cabin with a flat roof that had just enough pitch so water wouldn't stand on it. Along the back wall was the cooking area. There was a nice cook stove and a metal sink right next to it. Behind the sink was a large two-piece window that could be raised to open. There were two doors with windows and an outer screened door. One door was on the front that looked up the lane, and the other door overlooked the lake. The kitchen area had a table and chairs. The living area had several chairs and a couple of couches that could be slept on as well. A small black woodstove was in the corner just behind the front door.

"It may be only one room," Father said, "but it's a good size."

"Look at all these dishes and drinking glasses," Millie said, showing her parents. "Do all these things come with the place?"

"That's what we've been told," Father told her.

Mother pointed out to Millie that the dishes and bowls were matching sets. She told her everything here was brought from New York.

"Who are these people?" Millie asked.

"The people who own this place live in New York City," Father explained. "There's two families, and they're supposed to be big stake holders in the mines. In the settlement, there is a big company house for the families to stay in, but this family bought this place as a get-away from all the business dealings, a place to come and relax."

"And they are going to sell it to us?" Millie asked.

"As a matter of fact, I've already put money down on the place," Father said. "The story is the wife had bad allergies and suffered greatly. So they made a trip to the county seat to have it surveyed and sold. The surveyor sent them to Mr. Highley, who wasn't interested but told them about us. Simply put, they liked your mother and me and made us a deal that was hard to turn down."

"Well, it's a good thing you're up and working or you would have lost your money," Millie said.

"Nope," Father explained. "There are other buyers."

"Come out here and look at this!" yelled Mattie.

"Sounds serious," Mother said. "We better go have a look."

"Millie," Father said as he held both her shoulders with his hands, "these people have been very kind and have said, if any of the family didn't like the place, they would give the money back."

Millie smiled and said, "Thanks." She then told her father, "Guess we better go see what Mattie has gotten into."

Millie and her parents went out the door that faced the lake, stopping for a moment to admire the size and clear water of the five-acre lake. The porch surrounded the cabin on three sides, the lakeside, front side, and back side. The cabin roof covered the porch. A gazebo was built between the cabin and lake.

As they rounded the corner, they found Evelyn Rose and Mattie hard at work on a pump handle. They were pumping away trying to get water to come out of the spigot.

"It's broke," Mattie said.

"Or the well is dry," Evelyn Rose added.

"Nope, you're both wrong," Father told them. "I'll be right back."

He ran back into the cabin and could be heard going through the cabinet drawers. "Here it is," Father yelled out. Back at the pump, he held up a pin with a locking wire.

"See this pin. You have to stick it through this hole right here," he said, placing it in a hole in the center of the handle that connected to a piston down in the well. "There," he said, "now try it."

Evelyn Rose and Mattie stood facing each other as they placed their hands on the handle. "It's hard to push," Mattie said. With a little muscle, they get the handle to go down, then up, then down and up a little faster each time. Crystal clear water started running out of the spigot.

"Oh, oh," Mother said. "Don't stop! Let me get the buckets from inside the house."

Father went with her to open the back window so the buckets of water could be placed on a shelf and slid through the open window to a counter next to the sink.

After the last bucket was filled, Mattie and Evelyn Rose stopped pumping. Before the water stopped, Mattie tilted her head sideways to get a quick drink. Evelyn Rose did the same thing. Looking at each other, waiting for the other's comment on the taste testing, Mattie finally said, "It's not bad."

"But it's not as good as our spring water," Evelyn Rose told everyone.

"No, it's not," Mattie agreed. "But it is good."

"It's well water," Mother explained. "It will be somewhat different. There is a spring that feeds the lake. It's not big, but it might taste better."

"I kinda like not having to go away from the house to get water," Millie told them. She then pointed toward the cedar trees, "Is that the outhouse?"

"Yes, it is," Father answered. "Why don't you go check it out if you need to?"

Mother and the girls went to check out the fancy outhouse. On the way, they could see that the outhouse was built on the same order as the cabin. It was made of flat boards painted white with the blue-green trimming that matched the iron gate.

"Two doors?" Mattie asked.

Evelyn Rose opened both doors and let out a low whistle. Turning to her mother, she said, "It's a two-seater."

Mattie looked up at the doors and held them both as the doors opened toward each other. "Wow!" she said. "Two holes. No more outhouse dancing."

"That's a good thing," Mother remarked. "Especially when there is snow on the ground."

"I suppose so," Mattie replied. "Since we usually go together, we can both sit and talk through the wall. It will work just fine. Now if you don't mind," she said as she went inside and latched the door.

Millie looked at her mother with a smile and said, "Don't mind if I do." She went into the other side and latched the door. "Can you hear me?" Millie asked.

Evelyn Rose laughed, and Mother said, "You two need to hurry before the dancing starts."

The rest of the evening was spent unpacking. Father secured the corral that was at the end of the lane just past the outhouse. Bray was put in with Ole Smokey just for the company. Father gave them both a little sweet feed, grass, and filled the trough with a couple of buckets of water.

Rusty was everywhere marking his territory and sniffing everything he came to.

After a quick, late dinner, everyone sat back and listened to the sounds of the dying day. Big bullfrogs made low croaking sounds, hopping on the moss after catching a dragonfly. Bass would splash the water trying to catch a helpless insect on the water surface. After the sun dipped beneath the edge of the earth and covered itself with a pink blanket, a crane swooped in from the river. It made a sound only a crane can make, that could cause even the dead in their graves to shiver.

"I don't like that," Mattie said.

"Why?" Father asked as she ran to get on his lap. "She's only calling her babies to her. She'll find them and tuck them into their nest so they'll be safe for the night. Just like we're doing."

Mattie pointed a finger in the air and said, "That makes sense. I don't like it when Mother makes me go to bed either."

Mother shook her head but let it go. She looked at Father signaling not to start a conversation about it as it was getting late.

"Well, it's been a long day," Father told everyone. "So what you say we turn in and get an early start discovering this place."

"I'd like to go to the river," Millie said.

"Can I go with you?" Evelyn Rose asked.

Millie nodded her head, and Mother said, "If you get up early, just remember this is a vacation. So don't argue and wake me up."

"Okay, okay," Millie said. "I usually slip out without making a sound."

"She's out," Father said, holding a sleeping Mattie.

"I'll go make her a pallet to sleep on," Mother said.

Evelyn Rose raised both hands in the air and stretched her back while whispering to Mother, "I'll help. It's hard to keep my eyes open too."

Father followed his wife into the cabin, holding Mattie very carefully so he didn't wake her. Evelyn Rose followed behind, yawning so hard her eyes watered. A pale light shone through the window. Millie sat back in a high-back chair and quietly told them, "I'll be in, in just a minute." Millie looked up and saw the first stars starting to appear. Rusty came up on the porch and curled up next to her feet. She rubbed his head a little and told him, "I bet you're tired too." He didn't raise his head but let out a puff of air that blew out his upper lip. "Me too," Millie said with a slow exhale. She watched the sky as it became darker, and more stars appeared.

Millie jerked and so did Rusty. "It's dark," she said and noticed the Big Dipper overhead, shining brightly. "I must have dozed off." She got out of the chair and went indoors. Rusty stayed right where he was, watching over the family from a new porch. The yellow-orange light coming through the window went out.

Chapter 48

Millie and Evelyn Rose slipped on their shoes and crept toward the side door that faced the lake. "Stay out of the river," Father said then settled in, getting a little more comfortable.

Mother stuck her head up and told the two girls, "Don't be gone long. We'll have breakfast soon."

Neither girl said a word as they went out the door. The lake was still and calm as if someone had taken their last breath. Mist was rising from the water as though its spirit was rising. The land sloped downward from the lake all the way to the river. The sky above was still black with plenty of stars shining. To the east, beyond the river, the color of the sky began to change from black to deep purple then blue followed by a tinge of pink. Below the colored skyline and in the tops of the trees was the fog line of the Big River. Hovering above the river but trapped in the leaves of the great cottonwood and sycamore trees, the fog would rise and lower as though the river had breath.

"Lots of fog," Millie said. "That means lots of humidity. We'll probably get our socks and shoes wet."

Evelyn Rose made a noisy groan and said, "I hate having wet feet. Why don't we take our socks off and put them on once we get to the woods?"

Millie agreed, so the two girls sat down. Rusty crawled out from under the table that was on the gazebo. "There you are," Millie said. He stuck his head under Millie's arm trying to get petted. She stopped with the shoes and gave Rusty a little attention before taking off her socks. "How was your first night away from home?" she asked the dog.

Millie and Evelyn Rose took off even though the sun hadn't come up yet. Rusty followed since he didn't know where he was or where he was going. The girls walked out on the dock. The dock was about four feet wide and went over the water about forty feet. It had a white painted railing on both sides. The lake was full, and the surface was about six inches away from the dock's wood planks. With each step, either frogs would hit the water or a fish would take off causing Rusty to run from side to side to see what was causing the splash. As the girls got to the end, they heard a noise in the cattails on the other side of the lake. Without warning, the giant mother crane took off, making its spine-chilling cry as it flapped its huge wings. The bird turned and glided into the mist of the river.

As they rounded the spillway, Millie pointed out a deer path that led from the bottomland to the upper field.

"That's not a sheep trail or a cow path," Evelyn Rose said. "But at least we won't get our feet and clothes soaking wet."

They kept walking until they came to another gate. This fence came from behind the lake and then on out to the road just to the side of the old bridge. "Looks like someone has kept animals in here," Millie said.

"How can you tell?" Evelyn Rose asked.

Millie explained to her sister as the two pulled the rails back to get through, "Down there is the river, and that," she said, motioning her hands through the air, "is all the bottomland. See how this strip of trees has old dirty leaves up in the branches?"

Evelyn Rose said "Wh-what?" as she picked at some of the leaves, finding them covered with dirt and sand.

"That's how high the river floods," Millie explained.

Evelyn Rose looked down the row of trees, noting the leaves were the same height all the way down. "You think maybe the owners let their horses graze in the upper field?" asked Evelyn Rose.

"Makes sense to me," Millie told her. "This fence goes all the way to the road, then to the main gate and back down on the other side of the lane past the cabin. I'd guess it then goes past the corral through the woods and behind the lake to here."

After stepping in a circle while Millie is tracing the direction of the fence, Evelyn Rose told her, "This might be a good place to keep your sheep."

Millie gave a straight-faced stare, showing no pleasure in her sister's suggestion, then turned to walk to the river.

"Wait for me!" cried Mattie from the dam.

"Oh, no," Evelyn Rose said to Millie. "Look who it is!"

Millie frowned a little and told her, "It's okay. We'll wait."

"Go back!" Evelyn Rose yelled to her little sister.

Mattie stopped halfway down the spillway and told them, "Mother said since I was up, I could come too!"

"It's fine," Millie told Mattie. Looking at Evelyn Rose, Millie said, "You shouldn't be mean like that."

Back at the cabin, Father started a fire in the cookstove while Mother poured some water in the coffeepot. "Now that we are alone," he said, "why don't you tell me what's going on with Millie?"

"It's really pretty simple, but I'm not sure you'll understand," she told him.

"All right then," he said. "When the coffee is done, we'll sit in these fancy high-back chairs on the porch. I'll listen while you explain."

Mother came out of the cabin holding two glass mugs filled with piping hot coffee along with a cloth towel filled with slices of sweet bread made a couple of days earlier just for the trip.

"You sure know how to spoil a feller," he said while taking a steaming cup of coffee.

Sitting in the other high-back chair and placing the bread on the table between them, she smiled and said, "And don't you forget it!"

Sipping coffee, eating sweet bread, watching fish hit the top of the water, and hearing the girls' voices from behind the dam, Father said, "This little vacation has come none too soon."

"I agree," Mother said. "It's like you're trying to make up for the time you were healing."

"It's just that it is a great gift," he told her. "Tennessee allowing us to log off her woods was a real blessing."

The quiet of an early morning lakeside cup of coffee breathed out tension and anxiety and even fear. After a few moments of silence and some sips of hot coffee, he finally said, "You're right. I needed to feel strong and in control."

His wife slipped her hand into his and looked him in the eyes. She said, "You are."

Halfway through the cup of coffee, he asked, "Are you gonna tell me about Millie?"

"Yes, but could you warm up my coffee?" she asked.

Returning with more hot coffee, he set both cups on the table between them and shooed a fly off the sweet bread. He sat back in the chair and said, "I really like these chairs. Can't say I've ever seen anything like them."

"People back east call them Adirondack chairs," his wife explained. "It's a place in New York. Not sure if it's in the mountains or near the ocean, but that is what they are called."

He glanced at her with a quizzical look.

"I saw them in a store catalog," she said. "The owners of this place were from New York, so they probably knew how to make them."

"Seems like all the rich people are from New York," Father said. "Doc, his wife and family are all from there."

She set her coffee down and softly said, "Are you going to listen?"

He bit his bottom lip and told her, "Sorry, go ahead and tell your story."

"Millie and Cecil have known each other almost all their lives," she explained. "Through church and school, they've been like sister and brother. Now that's not to say their feelings are genuine. It's only natural to have the feeling she had with all she's gone through. I mean, I care deeply for the boy. He saved her life."

"Yeah, I do too—" her husband said.

"Now just hear me out," she said, cutting him off. "I don't want to run off track on my train of thought."

"Sorry," he said. "Go ahead."

"It's just that Millie has never known anyone to hold a fancy to, till yesterday. I don't know how real the affection was, but…" She paused for a moment. He placed his coffee down and waited patiently for her to continue.

With a knot in her throat, she continued, "But I saw a look on her face that reminded me of how I felt when I met you."

The two were silent for a while. His eyes became moist as he thought of his wife and gazed out over the lake.

Mother broke the silence, saying, "I may be wrong, but I would never deny one of my girls of true love."

This time, he took her hand and told her, "You are so wise, and I am so afraid."

"You think?" Mother quipped. "You shouldn't be afraid. Millie is a very smart girl with all kinds of common sense. She's young, and she'll figure it out."

"I won't let her get hurt," he said.

"I know you won't," she said with a soft laugh. "Physically, I know you will protect her, but there is nothing you or I can do but pray and be an example to her."

"Look, there's the river," Evelyn Rose said.

"Yeah, and look at those trees," Millie told them. "Those have to be the biggest cottonwood trees there ever was."

The girls walk on toward the river in awe of the giant sycamores and cottonwoods growing along the waterway. A few yards from the river, they waded through a lush, dense green weed that grew about two feet tall in the sandy soil. Suddenly, without warning, all three girls started scratching and rubbing their legs.

"This is terrible," Evelyn Rose shouted.

"Millie, will you hold me?" Mattie begged.

Rubbing and scratching her own legs, Millie told her, "I can't. This weed is stinging my legs so bad I can't stand it. Let's run to the water."

Following Millie's path, the girls high-step as fast as they can to the gravel bar. Without missing a beat, they ran right out of their shoes and into the water, rubbing and splashing water on their clothes and bare legs until the pain subsided.

"Look at Rusty," Mattie said, pointing at the dog. "He's just sitting there watching us. Why didn't those weeds bother him?"

Millie clapped her hands and called the dog to her, telling Mattie, "Maybe he went around the patch of weeds or it doesn't go through his fur."

Acting as if nothing was wrong, he heeded her beckoning call and waded right in the river.

"Look how red my legs are," Evelyn Rose pointed out. "I'm not going back the same way."

"Me either," Mattie said.

Millie looked up and down the river and suggested, "Not sure where the river goes, but if we go up river, the bridge should be just around the bend. As long as it stays shallow, we should be okay."

After the misery and pain from the stinging plant subsided, Millie, Evelyn Rose, and Mattie explored the river. They skipped rocks across the river and investigated the places beavers had cut down trees and pretended to be the first explorers to discover a new waterway. They waded through deep pools of water and sometimes had to swim through them if deep. Rounding the bend of the river, they came upon a large boulder at the edge of the river. They climbed up the bank to reach the boulder. From there, they climbed up the back side of the boulder to its top, which was flat. The water below the rock was clear and about ten feet from the top of the rock.

Mattie looked at her big sisters and asked, "Are you going to jump?"

Millie looked at Evelyn Rose and said, "If I jump, will you?"

Evelyn Rose looked down at the water and said, "What if there is something in there?"

"You mean like a giant catfish that can swallow little girls?" Millie teased.

"No!" Evelyn Rose replied.

"I'm not jumping," Mattie said as she stood up and backed away from the edge.

"I'm just teasing," Millie said, laughing.

"I'm not afraid of a fish," Evelyn Rose said. "But there might be another rock or a log under the water."

"Could be," Millie said. "Maybe we ought to swim around it some and check."

Still standing away from the edge, Mattie said, "Good idea."

Millie and Evelyn Rose stood as Evelyn Rose said, "I agree." Then she and Mattie started to walk to the back side of the rock. They both froze when a loud splash came from the river. They turned, and Millie was gone!

"Millie!" Mattie yelled.

"It's plenty deep!" Millie hollered back. "Jump in!"

The two girls stood at the edge asking each other, "Are you gonna jump?"

"I don't know. Are you?" they asked back and forth.

Evelyn Rose finally said, "Yeah." She looked down at the water and at Millie treading water. She took a deep breath, jumped, and squealed on the way down.

When she returned to the surface of the water, Evelyn Rose quickly looked at Mattie and told her, "It's fine. Just jump."

Squeezing her knees together, Mattie squatted a bit, held her hands under her chin, and told her sisters, "I can't swim."

"You can too!" Evelyn Rose said.

"Besides, we're right here," Millie told her. "We'll help you. It's okay."

Mattie swallowed the lump in her throat, squeezed her eyes shut, opened them wide, and jumped.

She squealed while in the air, then splashed perfectly between Millie and Evelyn Rose. Within a heartbeat, her head bobbed above the water as she yelled, "I did it! I did it!"

The girls swam to the shallow side of the river and rested on the riverbank. They laughed and giggled, amazed that they all jumped off the rock into the river.

"I can't believe we did it!" Millie said, looking up at the top of the rock. "Look!" Millie said and pointed to the top of the rock. "Come on, Rusty!" she yelled. They all yelled trying to coax Rusty to jump off the rock.

Without thinking twice, Rusty barked then turned to go back the way he came. He jumped in the river from the bank and swam to the girls.

"He's either chicken or smarter than us," Evelyn Rose said.

"I can't believe I just did that," Mattie said again.

"Well, you did," Millie told her. "But I don't know if I'd say anything to Mother and Father about it."

"Why?" Mattie asked.

"We might not get to come back down here," Evelyn Rose told her.

"Yeah," Millie agreed then told them both, "let's wait until we are about to go home."

"Was it dangerous?" Mattie asked.

"Not really," Millie explained. "When we all swam to the bank, I went under a couple of times and could see it was deep enough and clear of the rocks. It's just the idea of jumping off a rock into a river. You know, like swallowing water and choking." Millie ruffled the top of Mattie's head then told her, "That's why you don't swim alone. Now let's go to the bridge."

The rest of the walk was from gravel bar through ripples then back across to another gravel bar. "There it is," said Evelyn Rose. "Looks like others come here by the path going up the bank."

"That rock might be a popular swimming hole," Millie said. Then she told them, "Stay in the center of the path. You see all them vines growing up the trees?"

"Is that poison ivy?" Evelyn Rose asked.

"Yes, it is," Millie replied.

The mudbank was slick and steep. Because it was well used, it almost looked like stairs going up to the road. Once the girls get to the top, they decide to walk on across and check out the wooden bridge. Large beams stretched across starting from the bank on their side of the river to two large rock pillars on this side. The bridge ended on the top of a bluff on the other side. Oak planks were laid out crossways from one beam to the other. On the sides were rails to keep travelers from going off the edge. Crossbeams were placed underneath the bridge to keep it steady.

Stopping midway on the bridge to see the river from above, the girls discovered schools of fish swimming in the exact spot where they had walked. They took turns throwing rocks at the fish and seeing how far they could hurl a rock down the river.

"Wonder why there wasn't a bridge like this one where we crossed the first time?" Evelyn Rose pondered.

"There was one," Millie said.

"I didn't see one," Mattie said as she threw another rock.

Then Millie explained, "Remember that soldier that gave me a ride across the river?"

"The one you kept making eyes at?" Evelyn Rose said.

"I did not!" Millie shouted back.

"Yes, you did," Mattie told her.

"Jonathan told me—" Millie started to explain.

"That's his name?" Evelyn Rose interrupted.

Millie looked at her sisters sternly with squinted eyes, "Just listen, will you? Like I said, Jonathan told me the bridge that was there was blown up by Southern sympathizers to stop supply runs by the Federal troops. He said the timber was being cut to build a new bridge."

Evelyn Rose became very serious when she asked, "Do you think it was the same ones that shot Father?"

"Probably so," Millie answered. "And that's why the soldiers are staying there to help build and protect it."

"Will they blow this one up?" Mattie asked.

"I would say probably not," Millie answered. "This bridge is out of the way and more for the people living around here."

"I hope you are right," Evelyn Rose said.

"Me too," said Mattie.

Millie looked toward the end of the bridge where Rusty was exploring. "About time we get back, don't you think?" Millie told her sisters.

"Yeah, I'm hungry," Evelyn Rose said.

"Me too!" Mattie exclaimed.

The three girls walked off the bridge. They traveled about a quarter of a mile until they reached their gate. They proceeded down the mimosa lane and arrived at the cabin. Mother and Father were sitting outside accompanied by who looked to be the old man they passed at the beginning of the farm.

"Aren't you the man"—Millie pointed in the direction of his house—"that lives up the road?" she asked as an old coon dog rounded the corner of the cabin. "Guess that answers my question," she quipped, looking at the old dog.

"Yes, I am," he said and introduced himself and his dog. "Sorry I didn't make it down here yesterday evening," he explained. "My missus tells me your journey was long, and you might be all tuckered out. So we thought we'd let you be. You young'uns been down yonder to the river?" he asked.

The girls looked down at their wet clothes and then at their parents. Mattie told the old man, "We went down just to see the river, but some weed made our legs burn something fierce."

"We had to do something to get it off," Evelyn Rose helps explained. "So we washed off in the river. It was terrible."

The old neighbor started laughing and slapped his knee. "That plant is called stinging nettle," he told them. "And it do sting."

"Since we were wet," Millie continued the story, "we just decided to swim. The water was cool and clear."

"We even—" Mattie started to say but was bumped with an elbow and given a look.

"You even what?" Mother asked.

"We even went on the bridge," she said and returned Millie's stare.

"If you stayed on the back in the woods, you girls would've found ya some pawpaws," the old man said. "They're ripe this time of year and really good."

Talking about food reminded Mattie the reason they hurried home. "Are we going to have breakfast soon?" she asked.

Mother smiled at her girls and replied, "I figured you girls would come home when your stomachs told you to."

Millie grinned sheepishly and told her, "I'm about starved to death."

"Okay," Mother said, "you girls come in and help while your father and our new neighbor talk over another cup of coffee."

Both men smiled at the sound of another fresh cup of coffee.

Evelyn Rose and Mattie helped their mother with breakfast. Millie brought out the fresh coffee to the men and poured one cup for herself. She stayed and listened to the old man's intriguing tales of the surrounding area and the river lore.

The old man told about the lane and how at one time, it was the Spanish pass from the Ste. Genevieve area to St. Louis and was actually called the St. Louis Road. He talks about all the Indian arrowheads that he had found in the fields. He couldn't swear to it, but believed this area once was an Indian campsite. He pointed to where he thought there might be Indian graves. His voice changed to a mysterious tone as he told about a young girl that took her own life just on the other side of the river. "Young girl," he said, "with coal-black hair. Think she was part Indian but can't say for sure."

"Why did she do it?" Millie asked.

"Legend is," the old man said, "that Mary—"

Millie interrupted him, asking, "*Mary*, you know her name?"

He looked down at his cup and swirled the coffee around then said, "Yes, that was her name, Mary."

The old man's thoughts drifted for just a few seconds until Millie softly said, "What happened?"

He cleared his throat, took another sip of coffee, and rubbed an itch just under his eyes. "Well, the way I heard it was, this young girl was in love with a man the family didn't like. So she'd run away. Folks found her a couple days later just on the other side of the river." After a pause and the last sip of his coffee, the old man took a deep breath and exhaled. Looking into the empty cup, he finished saying, "She was found sittin' on a stump, leaning over like she was praying, hands folded together and head looking down." A short pause, then he looked up to the heavens and said, "Froze to death."

Father looked at Millie in a way to suggest, "Don't ask any more questions."

"Guess I need to mosey on back," the old man said. "The missus will think I wandered off and fell in one of them sinkholes back there by the lane." He pointed his thumb over his shoulder and explained, "After you pass your holdin' pen, the old Spanish lane continues. Our property line's in the middle, but we always just left it as it is. Rumor has it that them mimosas were planted from the seed brought over from the Spanish homeland."

Mattie poked her head out the door and said, "Mother wants to know if you want to eat in here or out there."

"Will you eat with us?" Millie asked.

"No, no, best be going," the old man said. "Already had breakfast a long time ago. Thank ya anyway, and I do appreciate the coffee. If you make it up my way, I'll return the favor," he told them as he walked to the back of the cabin and headed toward his house.

"'Bye," Millie hollered. She then asked Father while looking at Mattie, "Be okay we eat on that outdoor table?"

"Sure," Father said. "Tell your mother, Mattie. Let's clean it off and pull some of the weeds away from it."

Millie started toward the gazebo but stopped to look at the old man walking past the holding pen. "Did you get the feeling that his tale was a little more personal than what he called rumors?" she asked Father.

Father shrugged, suggesting he wasn't quite sure what to think. He grabbed the small hand sickle and said, "Help me out over here."

"Sure, is something wrong?" she asked.

"No," he said. He took a few swipes at the weeds. He stopped and looked at Millie and told her, "You've always been a smart girl and have made wise choices." He swung the sickle as though he was angry and spoke just loud enough for her to hear, "I will always love you no matter what."

Millie raked the cut weeds while trying to make sense out of what Father just said. Was it something the old neighbor said or something that she said or did? Then it dawned on her, young girl, young soldier at river yesterday, parents, and the old man's story. She stopped raking and waited until Father looked up at her. "I love you too!" she said.

"Here we go," Mother said, coming out the door with a cloth in her hands. She walked to the edge of the porch, tossed the cloth to

Millie, and told her, "Spread that over the table please. Then you two can help carry the food out."

The midmorning breakfast was fit for royalty. Mother's fried bread with sweet fried apples on top was most everyone's favorite. Bacon and eggs were plenty along with new potatoes that were sliced and fried. A bowl of bacon gravy finished off the perfect breakfast.

"Oh, wait!" Mother said. "Would you mind bringing out that crock," she told her husband. "I'll get five glasses."

"What's in the crock?" Evelyn Rose asked.

"Fresh milk," Mother explained. "Brought to us by the new neighbors."

Enjoying the large breakfast, Mother let everyone know she's on vacation too, and for the rest of the day, they would have to fend for themselves.

Millie said she would catch some fish, and Father told everyone he was going to thin the squirrel population. Exploring the new farm, pawpaws, buckeyes, walnuts, and plums were added to the fish and squirrels. Mother couldn't help herself but to make pies for the late evening delights.

The neighbor on the other side of the road had a couple of young boys and one girl the same age as Evelyn Rose. New friends expanded the girls' exploring area. There was a cave to explore and more river to wade, which made the vacation more enjoyable.

Chapter 49

On Tuesday, Millie and her parents walked the three main fields to determine the grazing availability. The upper field was the largest. The field by the lake was half the size of the upper field. Father suggested it would be a good place for the sheep to winter. The last field, on the back of the farm next to the river, was the smallest. It was the perfect place to graze during the hottest times of the year.

"The really good thing is the spring," Millie told her parents. "Though it's in the middle of the woods and feeds the lake, it's a great place for the sheep to water. It had a lot of cedar cover for hard winters and the heat of the summer."

"You gotta admit," Father explained as he bent over and picked up a chunk of flint, "this is rich soil and it runs deep." Tossing the flint rock to the side, he said, "Nothing like that clay mud we have at home."

"Our homeland has done good providing for us," Millie said, a bit testy.

Joining in the conversation, Mother told Millie, "That's just it. We really have no land to call our home."

As Millie and her parents walked through the woods, the conversation shifted to one of very few words until the three come to the last field, the bottomland next to the river. Walking next to the strip of woods that separated the bottom from the field next to the lake, Father got excited and said, "One year without a terrible flood, a person could grow enough crops in this field that would amount to five years on any other land."

"So you're getting tired of cutting down trees," Millie said in a quiet voice.

Father squatted down on his heels and scooped up a handful of rich river soil. As he slowly sifted it through his fingers, he said, "My time of cutting down trees is coming to an end. God has blessed us with great oaks and opportunities, but the way my body feels, I believe He's telling me, 'Now it's time to plant.'"

"I know," Millie said as she put her hand on his shoulder. "I know."

Mother smiled at the two of them and suggested, "Why don't we go up and start staking out the house?"

Millie nodded while watching her father pull an odd-looking smooth stone out of the ground. "What do you have there?" she asked.

He held it up in the air so everyone could see and said, "Not sure. I guess it's just a smooth river rock."

Mother held her hand out, and he let her have it. "I don't believe so," she said. "I think I know what it is."

"Well, what is it?" Millie inquired.

Mother examined the size, top and bottom, then said, "I believe this is a medicine man's rock. It is the right size, and see how this side is worn out to make it concave. And the bottom is perfectly flat so it doesn't rock."

"How would you use that as a medicine man's rock?" Millie asked.

Mother explained further, "The medicine man would carry this in his pouch along with a bone or another rock. When someone needed medicine, he would put roots or herbs in the dipped-out part and grind it into powder. It's his medicine rock."

"How'd you know about that?" her husband questioned.

"When I was a child, I had a couple of friends that were Indians. They were Osage and lived just outside the Mine La Motte mining town. Every so often, a couple girls would come to school. They wanted to learn, but their parents sent them to beg."

"Real Indians?" Millie asked.

"Yes, they were," Mother said. "I would even go with my Aunt Mildred and try to get more kids to come to school. They lived in teepees and were really poor. Not sure, but I heard they stayed close by because some of the miners would trade their whiskey to them."

As the three walked on through the field toward the lane, Mother continued talking about her Indian friends. "It was really sad," she said, "because some miners would trade for late-night visits to the teepees. That would cause trouble. Eventually, the authorities made them all pack up and move farther west. Anyway, that's how I know about that kind of rock. The Indian girls' father was somewhat of a medicine man."

Father looked to the east and said, "That way is south toward our home, and that way would be east. Between Ste. Genevieve and Farmington would be the place you grew up. Maybe this is one of their rocks."

"Yeah," Millie said. "You did say you recognized it."

"Don't be silly," Mother told them both. She became quiet as they walked on.

As they came upon the lane, Father pointed out a place about one hundred fifty feet this side of the gate. Mimosa and cedar trees were on one side, and large sycamore trees were on the other side about fifty feet from the lane. "Good flat ground," he said. "It's cleared and no large rocks."

"So this is where you'd like to build the house?" Millie asked.

"Our home," Mother said.

"Yes," Father told her. "Our very own home, and there's water here. First things first," he said. "Some man from the mining company told the owners he'd put in a nice well, like the one down at the cabin."

Millie listened and watched Mother and Father lay out the house. She had to laugh when they squatted to pretend to sit at the table in their new kitchen. They pictured bedrooms for Evelyn Rose and Mattie, and one for the baby boy they were sure they were going to have. Mother then stood where the front door would be as Father stands and explains that a hall between the bedrooms would lead to the back door. Sticks were cut for markers. Mother held them while Father drove them in the ground with the medicine man's stone.

Millie eased away and sat under one of the big mimosa trees. From there, she watched her parents lay out their plans and then argue on how each thought the house plan should be. She soon noticed something she hadn't noticed in a long time. Her parents were genuinely happy.

After a while, Father looked at Millie and asked, "What do you think of our new home?"

Millie nodded her head and said, "Looks like a bunch of sticks fell out of the tree and stuck in the ground."

"Well, maybe if you come over here and let us explain, you'll change your thinking," Mother told her.

About that time, a loud "Eeyore" came from across the road. They all looked, and sure enough, it was Bray coming down the neighbor's lane with Evelyn Rose and Mattie riding on his back.

Millie let out one of her famous loud whistles. Both girls looked up and waved. From behind Bray came Rusty, who raced ahead of them to answer Millie's call.

Once everyone was together, Mother told them if they'd catch some fish, Father would clean them for supper.

"Hey!" Father said. "I want to do some fishing too."

"You can," she told him, placing her hands on her hips, "as soon as we finish getting this kitchen area worked out."

Her husband rubbed his chin and walked around a bit. He scratched his head as his wife walked behind him. Sticks were pulled up and driven in different areas. More figuring and few more sticks were added until they heard, "You gonna clean these?"

"Oh wow!" Father said. "Those are the biggest bluegill I've ever seen."

"The lake is full of them," Mattie said. "And I caught the most."

Mother and Father looked at each other, and he asked, "Are we done here?"

With a satisfied nod, Mother said, "I believe so. Let's draw it on paper while we eat."

That evening, the family ate bluegill, fried potatoes, and corn bread. Father leaned back, rubbed his stomach, and said, "I'm so full I think it's coming out my ears." Everyone chuckled, feeling the same way.

Mother cleared the table, and the girls all pitched in to clean up. Father got out some large sheets of paper he had brought along just for this occasion. Once he started sketching, the girls hurried as fast as they could with the dishes so they could watch the drawing.

"You girls need to feed Ole Smokey and Bray before you get too comfortable," Mother told them.

They promised they'd do it later. Father put his pencil down.

"Okay, we'll do it now," Evelyn Rose proclaimed.

Mother told them that while they were gone, she would make some apple dumplings if Father would get the fire going again. They hurriedly ran out to do their chores in anticipation of the apple dumplings and watching Father draw. Just as the seven apple dumplings were placed in the Dutch oven, the girls came rushing in to make sure they didn't miss anything.

"Is the fire ready?" Mother asked.

With a broad smile and a woodstove shovel in his hand, Father said, "Ready and waiting."

He placed the Dutch oven on the shovel. Mother opened the stove door while he placed the Dutch oven right in the middle of the fire. "There," he said.

"Perfect, we'll give them about half an hour or maybe a little more," Mother said. "That ought to be about right."

Everyone sat at the table to watch Father begin sketching out the plans for the new house. With anxious, intense stares at the drawing, the girls' movements shook the table.

"Girls, it's hard to draw a straight line with the table shaking."

"Why don't you get your elbows off the table. Your Father needs to do this," Mother told them.

"Is that what our house will look like?" Mattie asked.

"It sure is," Father replied. "I'll make some different drawings, and on our way home, we'll drop them off at that sawmill we passed on the way here. They'll tell me how much lumber we'll need and how much it will cost."

Evelyn Rose gave her father a questioning look and then asked, "You're not going to cut logs for this house?"

"No," he explained. "This house won't be a log cabin. This house will be like the homes you see in town, like Cecil's parents' house."

The girls became very quiet, thinking about what it would be like to live in a home other than a log cabin. They imagined what it will be like to have friends over and more than four walls.

Father looked up in the stillness and met the eyes of his wife as she stood holding a towel with a smile on her face. "Sure does smell good in here," he said.

"It smells like Christmastime," Mattie said.

"They should be about done," said Evelyn Rose. "I can hardly wait."

Millie looked at the drawing and asked her father, "Does my name there mean I'll have my own room?"

"Yep, that's your room," he told her. "At least until you're married. Then we plan to move the girls there, and the baby will have their room."

"But I wanted to have my own room," Evelyn Rose whined.

"Your room with Mattie is a whole lot bigger than what we have now," Father explained, pointing out the size. "Besides, if you go away to school, you'll want to share when you come home."

"You don't want to share a room with me?" Mattie sadly said. She perked up and said to Millie, "Maybe I can share your room. You won't mind. Will you?"

"Millie's getting married," Evelyn Rose reminded her father. "So Mattie can have her room."

Mother walked to the table balancing a plate of hot apple dumplings and said, "Make room so I can set these down, and don't touch them yet. They are really hot."

Everyone moved at the command. Without being told, Millie got plates while Father got the house prints out of the way. Evelyn Rose and Mattie argued over who was getting the forks. Mother settled it when she told Evelyn Rose she would bring the forks and Mattie could bring the big wooden spoon to dip the dumplings out.

After serving the dumplings, Father asked, "Do we all want to go outside and eat these?"

"If the mosquitos aren't too bad," Mother replied.

Due to a slight breeze, the mosquitos weren't bad, and the late evening snack was a real delight. Stars shone bright above and reflected on the lake. To the southwest, lightning could be seen in the distance.

"Heat lightning," Father said. "They'll be a warm front moving in soon."

"I guess the humidity will be going up. I knew this nice break in the weather wouldn't last long," Mother remarked. Her husband agreed, but the girls were enjoying the treat too much to care.

Chapter 50

The next morning brought a different story. There was rumbling off to the southwest and getting closer, and the air was heavy with warm moist air. Everything had a damp feel. The girls complained how frizzy their hair was, and father remarked how hard it was to draw the house plans.

"Maybe when the front moves through, the humidity will go down," Millie said.

"Don't count on it," Father informed her. "Coming out of the south generally means hot, sticky weather. Might ought to check on the animals. We're gonna get a storm soon."

Millie jumped at the chance to get out and do something. "I'll go with you," she told her father.

"Me too!" Mattie said excitedly.

"No, not you too," Mother informed her. "We're going to check on all the food and make sure lids are on tight."

"Aww," Mattie complained.

"I'll help," Evelyn Rose said, giving Mattie an evil grin.

"You both will," Mother told them. "And there will be no fussing."

"We better go," Father told Millie. "It's starting to get dark out there."

About that time, lightning hit. Everyone saw the flash but jumped when the thunder followed it. Mattie and Evelyn Rose screamed at the sound of a knock and seeing two dark figures standing at the door.

"Oh my," said a woman's voice from one of the figures. "We didn't mean to scare you."

Recognizing the old neighbor, Father apologized and invited the two in. "Millie and I will be back in a few minutes," he told them. "Just need to check on Ole Smokey and Bray before whatever is behind those dark clouds comes in."

The old man agreed then said, "We were halfway here when the lightning struck. We almost went back."

"But we thought you might want some company to wait the storm out," the old man's wife said. "I brought some plum butter and bread that was made this morning." She placed a basket on the table and then set out the goodies along with a bucket of fresh milk.

Millie glanced at her father and could almost see the lust for plum butter in his eyes as his tongue licked across his lips. "I'm ready if you are," she told him.

"Okay," he said. "We better hurry before the storm rolls in."

Millie rolled her eyes with a smile on her face as Mother invited the old couple into the cabin.

On the way back to the corral, Millie asked her father, "How is it you and I always get caught out in these storms?"

"Never gave it any thought," he said. "But now that you mention it, it does seem we're always out getting soaked to the bone."

Millie and Father noticed the treetops starting to sway, and he told her, "Just climb the gate while I get a little sweet feed for them."

Millie climbed into the corral to give Ole Smokey and Bray some soothing assurance that she was there, and all would be well. Father handed her about a quarter bucket of ground corn and oats all mixed with molasses, a real treat for any animal. She fed the pair while Father checked all the gates and posts just in case a skittish animal bumped into an unsecured fence.

"Look who's coming up the road," Millie cried out. "Come on, Rusty!" she called to her dog.

"Guess he wants to spend a bumpy night with his friends," Father said.

Millie gave the grinning dog a good rub behind both ears and told him, "Looks like your box is right where it was last night." She looked inside just to make sure no critters were trying to make it their home and told him, "You sure you don't want to come with me?"

Rusty scampered over to Bray and wove around the donkey's front feet. He then sat down between Bray and Ole Smokey. "Don't know that I've ever seen two animals become so close," Father said. "Especially since they're so different."

Millie laughed at the dog staring at her. She told her father, "Just hope that donkey doesn't interfere with his herding."

Thunder rumbled again, and Father gave Millie a head nod to go. In a flash, she stepped on the middle rail then side hopped over the fence. "Let's get some of that plum butter," she said.

"You just read my mind," Father shouted back through the wind.

As the warm front moved through from the south, the family and their new neighbors enjoyed the plum butter and warmed-up bread, especially with the fresh milk. The talk was of other neighbors, where the churches were, and the Big River schoolhouse, a mile or two down the road. The storm didn't amount to much. It was just enough rain to make it miserable. Fog rolled along with the cool waters from the Big River. As the temperature went down, the fog seemed to creep in toward the cabin. Talk turned to the war, and the family wished it hadn't. They found out the old neighbors were Confederates and had lost their only son at the very beginning of the war. After hearing that, Father's eyes darted from one daughter to the other. He would purse his lips out trying to make sure no one said anything.

After a moment of uneasy silence, the old woman reached out and caught Father's hand on the table. "You folks don't need to worry," she said. "We already know what happened to you and the heroism of your friend. At the beginning, we had hard feelings and a lot of hate. Hate for everyone. But when these so called Southern sympathizing Bushwhackers started raiding and killing in the cover of darkness, well, we just…" The old woman pauses for a moment and looks down at the hand she is holding. She gently squeezes his hand and said, "We just kinda compared the way our son died facing his enemy in an honorable way and how things around here came to be."

She smiled and continued, "Then the strangest thing happened. We started praying again. The madness at God started wearing off, and we'd pray together morning and night. One day, we got a knock on the front door. It was our son's wife, whom we hadn't seen since the funeral services. She told us how she hated too. She hated our son, the war, us, and like us, even God. She said she never wanted to see us again, until she too started feeling the presence of love. She then introduced us to our grandson." The old woman took a breath, but this time, Father held tight to her hand. "We knew right off who he was. Spitting image of the son we lost. I know there's a God in heaven, and He has perfect timing. The little man is four years old," she said while reaching out and patting the back of her husband's hand.

He smiled at her and said, "This war has done a terrible thing, and I hope it ends soon."

"How did you hear about the raid up north of here?" Father asked.

"News travels quickly out here," the old neighbor said. "You folks are known more for your sheep, and there's not many sheep men around here, especially one that has been shot by a bushwhacker. Why, everyone knows about you."

Millie and her parents become very quiet with grim expressions on their faces.

"Oh, don't you worry about your affection for one side or the other," the old woman said, seeing their reaction. "This war's gone on way too long, and any normal folk just want it to stop." She changed the subject and told them about their grandson and how they'd hoped he could fish in the small lake.

Mother changed the conversation, telling them about the girls and how they hoped to have a baby boy to add to the family soon.

As the fog crept farther in from the river, the old neighbors thought they should head home. Goodbyes were said, and invitations to visit each other were given as they walked the neighbors to the gate. The vacationing family returned to the cabin and took turns at the fancy two-holed outhouse.

As the late evening set in, the river fog crept closer to mingle with the smoke on the lake. Evelyn Rose and Mattie stayed indoors drawing their own house plans while Millie and her parents sat on the porch, watching the lake disappear behind a dingy white curtain. The silence within the fog brought on its own eeriness that seemed to scare the breath out of all living things. The croak of a bullfrog sounded like the voice of some demon dragon hunkered within the cattails on the far side of the lake. A splash was heard coming from the lake. The three strained to see the monster creep out on this side. Nothing happened, so Millie said, "Guess whatever it was went down in the dark depth of his lair and is waiting till we go to sleep."

Mother looked at her husband and said, "Now that sounds like something you'd say. She's a chip off the old block."

Father laughed and gave a wink to Millie.

Millie felt something cold and wet on her leg and jumped, startling her parents. She looked under her chair, feeling relieved that it was just Rusty. Rusty curled up under the chair and lay his head on his front legs. Millie looked at him with her head upside down between her legs and told him, "One of these days, you're gonna cause me to faint right in my tracks. Then what you gonna do?"

Millie and her parents tried to relax and play the guessing game of what made that sound. "Okay," Father said. "I think it's time we go inside. It's about time we get some shut-eye."

Millie got up and said, "Right behind ya." She slapped her leg and told Rusty, "You better come in too."

Chapter 51

After a muggy night of falling in and out of sleep, Millie woke to the sound of birds outside. Still dark, she knew morning was right behind the chirping birds. As was her habit, Millie slipped off her floor mat, pulled on her pants and shirt, and carried her shoes to the door. She gave her dog a hard look that told him to keep his nose to himself. Out of the cabin, Millie sat for a moment in the high-back Adirondack chair. It was still foggy and as still as death itself. She pondered what to do. Back at home, she would know exactly what to do, where to go, and the secure feeling she got when she was there. She sighed softly and mumbled to herself, "I miss the giant oak and the hills they cover. I miss my sheep."

At the word *sheep*, Rusty jumped off the porch and with a raised head, looked all over for the white critters. "Come on, boy," Millie said with a laugh. "Let's see if we can find the river in this wet smoke."

The pair hugged the shoreline of the lake till they get to the spillway. From there, they walked the path to the gate and wood line that separated the upper farm from the bottomlands. "This is the only thing that feels like home," she told herself. Past the pond, through the gap in the fence, and on to another place. Looking down at Rusty, she asked, "Now where?" Rusty licked his lips, and Millie replied, "Yes, I know you're hungry. Hey! Why don't we see if we can find some pawpaws the old man told us about."

Millie and Rusty blindly made their way through the fog and wet weeds until they heard the running water of the Big River. Instead of going straight to the river, she and Rusty went left to the back field then walked the creek between the two fields to the river.

"That's a lot better than going through the nasty stinging nettle," she told Rusty. "Don't you think?" He gave Millie that funny grin and waded into the water for a drink.

Climbing back up on the bank, Millie started making her way toward the bridge. Halfway there and directly across from the swimming rock, she found what she was looking for. "These must be pawpaws," she said, examining the texture, size, and color comparing them to the description given by the old neighbor. She found one that was soft, wiped the dampness off, and took a small bite like she would eat an apple. She rolled the fruit around in her mouth, testing its taste. "Not too bad," she told Rusty. "It's really sweet. I like it." The bites became bigger, and she learned quickly how to spit out the large slick seeds.

"Wooh!" Millie yelled as she took a couple of steps backward. "Where did you come from?" she said to the gray grinning critter with a pawpaw in its mouth. Millie pointed out the opossum to Rusty and told him, "The old man said we'd better be quick picking them or the opossum would eat 'em."

Rusty looked at the poor animal while Millie got ahold of its naked ratlike tail and pulled him out of the tree. "Hush, Rusty! He's not going to hurt you or me." The opossum tried to curl up, but Millie shook him back down, but he never let go of his treat. "Now, get back!" she said to the dog. "Watch this!" Millie told Rusty as she put the gray animal on the ground. He just lay on his side as though he was dead. Millie backed up and called her dog to her side. Holding on to Rusty, she said, "Now watch this." About a minute later, the opossum rolled over, got on his feet, and took off to his hiding place, never dropping his pawpaws.

"See," she told Rusty. "That's what you call 'playing opossum.' He just played dead, then when it was safe, he ran off," she explained to the dog.

Rusty tried to run after the opossum, but Millie wouldn't let him. "Stay here," she said. "I'm about ready to head back." With a snap of her fingers, Rusty obeyed. Millie picked the tenderest fruit and filled her shirttail full to take back to the rest of the family. She found herself looking for a place that would match the peace she felt under the oak tree from home.

The river was great, and the sycamore and cottonwoods were towering giants. She loved them all, but it did not tug at her heartstrings like the giant oak.

"Oh well," she said as she sighed and shrugged her shoulders. "Let's take these home, if we can find the bridge." Walking the woods made it easy to get to the road since she didn't have to climb the steep river bank. The river fog was starting to lift. Millie wished out loud for a breeze to completely get rid of the nasty stuff.

Millie heard a sound and stopped dead still. Seeing Rusty's ears perk up, she called him to her side. Millie squatted next to her dog and said, "Somebody's humming by the gate." Rusty wasn't growling, nor were his hackles raised. "Blasted fog!" she said. She got up and slowly walked toward the humming. A little over halfway, Millie put her hand down to stop Rusty. She squatted down again and whispered, "Can you see that man leaning against the gate?" Rusty stared at the figure, but still no growl or raised hackles.

The man was leaning on a part of the gate. She could tell he was looking downward by the downward tip of his big hat. He was looking and doing something with his hands. His horse was standing directly in front of him. Millie looked behind her then strained to see if she could hear anything down toward the cabin. Millie looked around for the best way to run if she needed to. "Okay, boy. I'm gonna trust you on this one." She stood tall and yelled, "Who goes there?"

The man almost fell off his perch and dropped whatever was in his hand. His horse was spooked and nearly ran off. "Don't shoot!" he yelled back. "I'm a friend."

Recognizing his voice, Millie yelled, "Jonathan!"

"Yeah, it's me," he said. "Is that you, Millie?"

Millie started walking toward the man she met at the river crossing. The closer she got, the harder it seemed to be able to breathe. Her feet became heavy as Rusty went on to greet the man. "You 'bout scared me half to death," she blurted out.

"I know," he said as she walked up next to him. He bent down and gave Rusty a scratch behind the ears and told her, "This fog causes all kinds of imagination. Kinda spooky one too. At first, I didn't know what you were, walking up from the river." He then asked, "What you got there?"

"Pawpaws," she said. "You want one?"

"Sure," he said. "Are they good and ripe?"

"I suppose," Millie told him. "The opossums like 'em." Then she asked, "Would you like to come down to the cabin? Everyone should be up by now."

"I'd like that," he answered.

Millie opened the gate, and as he walked his horse through, Jonathan asked, "Would you like a ride down the road?"

Millie's breath caught in her throat remembering the ride with the young soldier across the river, and she thought her heart might have skipped a beat. For some reason, and a surprise to her, she said, "Thanks for the offer, but I'd just as soon walk. The mimosas are really beautiful to walk under." After closing the gate, she nervously laughed and said, "I was told these trees came all the way from Spain. They owned all this land at one time, you know."

"Not really good on the history," he said, shyly confessing. "My schooling only lasted to where I could read and write and do a little math."

Millie cut him off as not to let him embarrass himself and said, "I know most boys don't even know that much. You must really be smart to be able to read and write." She quickly changed the subject and asked him, "Are you from around here?"

"From the big city of St. Louis," he told her. "Have you ever been there?"

"No, and I don't know if I ever want to," she said. "I've heard and read a lot of things about St. Louis. Mostly about how rich and how poor the people are. They say when it rains, the streets run black with soot."

Jonathan furled his eyebrows pondering what Millie had just said. "I suppose you're right, but I never thought of it like that," he said.

"So how do you view the big city?" she asked.

"Well," he told her, "I miss the markets and stores. The waterfront on the Ol' Mississippi and the big boats going up and down the river. Why, St. Louis is so big you couldn't walk all the streets in a day's time. There is transportation that will take you right to where you want to go. Most people don't even own a horse. There's no need for one."

"Sounds like a nice place to visit," Millie said. "But don't know that I'd want to stay very long."

Jonathan nodded his head in agreement. He then stopped when the cabin and lake come into view. "I know what you're saying," he told Millie. "I felt the same way when our troop was sent down here. I really didn't like it at all. Then I saw you."

Millie smiled and kept walking. She told him, "Maybe we'll have something other than pawpaws for breakfast."

Mattie was the first to see Millie and the man in blue walking down the red tiff-laden lane. "Evelyn Rose!" she squealed. "It's Millie's soldier friend from the river crossing."

Evelyn Rose and her father both jumped out of the chairs and away from the table. "He came?" she asked and immediately and excitedly said, "He came!"

From the cookstove, Mother cleared her throat, and her husband turned to look back. She stood there with one hand on her hip, holding a wooden spoon. She held up the other hand with her thumb and index finger together, making a motion as if to say "Calm down." He remembered her words telling him Millie would do the right thing, but his heart was telling him, "She's my daughter, and he's a stranger." Not to defy his wife, he said, "I'll just tell him where he can put his horse."

The day wasn't an easy one for anybody. Mother did her best to have Millie's help in the cooking area while Father showed Jonathan the plans for the house. Evelyn Rose and Mattie talked his ears off and even showed the city fellow how to bait a hook, catch bluegill, and even clean them. After a late dinner, Father suggested they all walk up the lane and visit with the neighbors.

For some reason, Millie felt as though the day dragged on for what seemed forever. Her thoughts weren't on the here and now. Everyone noticed she seemed to be a little distant. Mattie brought up Cecil, and that made everyone a little uncomfortable. Mother suggested to Evelyn Rose and Mattie that she would like to see the river, so Jonathan and Millie could be alone to talk things out. Father told them to be careful, but Mother told him, "You're coming with us."

"That's a good idea. With that rain last night, the river might be up some, so I better come along too," he muttered.

Jonathan became a little embarrassed and upset and told Millie, "I need to go. I best be on my way."

"Could you stay a few minutes and listen?" she asked.

He agreed, and Millie explained, "Cecil and me have been friends since I've known anyone. I never thought of him as anything but a friend. That was till he left and then my heart grew fond. That has been several months now." Millie hung her head and admitted, "No one's ever touched me till you did, and well, I'm sorry. I've never felt that way."

Jonathan raised his hand and touched Millie's cheek. "It's okay," he said. "I felt the same way, but this can't be. I know your Cecil. Everybody from here north knows him. He's a hero and—" Jonathan paused and took a deep breath, saying, "And he's my brother-in-arms."

Millie almost felt shame but then told Jonathan, "I won't be shamed, and nothing wrong has been done here. I don't even know how to tell you how I feel."

"Millie, this crazy war is almost over, and until it is..." He stared deep into her eyes and backed up a step. After a moment of silence, he told her, "I can only hold you in my heart."

She knew it was right, but that didn't help ease the pain as he walked to the corral. Millie hurriedly walked to the lake and on past the dam toward the river bottom where her day had begun. Feeling lost and discouraged, she looked for a place of comfort. "I need my oak tree!" she yelled at the sky. "I want to go home, where the acorns fall!"

Chapter 52

The rest of the day was spent clearing brush and driving stakes to lay out the home and each of its rooms. With so much brush, Father decided to have a bonfire. Evelyn Rose and Mattie picked up sticks and limbs to add to the brush pile. They even got Bray involved, having him pull and haul the bigger limbs that were farther away. The bigger the pile got, the harder the girls worked to make it higher. Father finally informed them that was enough, and now it was time to load the wagon for the trip home.

"Aww!" Mattie said. "I don't want to go home yet. Why can't we stay longer?"

"Because next week, you girls have to start getting ready for school!" Mother said enthusiastically.

Evelyn Rose shouted for joy while Mattie folded her arms and buried her face in them. "Hate school," she said through her folded arms.

"I'm not going either," Millie said.

In a huff, Mother asked, "Because of what happened today?"

Evelyn Rose couldn't believe what she was hearing while Mattie let everyone know that school was a waste of time, especially hers. "If Millie isn't going, I'm not either," she said.

Millie hushed Mattie and told her, "You have to go, so hush!" She turned to her mother, who had a very unpleasant look, and said, "No, not because of what happened today."

"Then why?" Mother asked.

Father gritted his teeth and through them told Evelyn Rose and Mattie, "Come on, girls. Help me get the wagon ready to be loaded."

"Wait just one minute!" Mother shouted with one hand raised in the air. "We're on vacation, and I really don't want to leave on a bad note. So let's not talk about school until we get back home. Okay?"

"Sounds good to me," Millie said.

Mattie scooted in next to Millie and said, "Me too!"

Evelyn Rose held her head up and smiled. Mother said, "Before we left to come here, I was informed that you"—she looked at Millie—"were going to be asked to help teach the younger children."

Millie's jaw dropped. Before she could say anything, Mother held her hands up and said, "But we're not going to talk about school until we get home."

With a smile as wide as her face, Mattie looked up at Millie then buttoned her lips when Millie looked back down at her. Not being able to contain herself, Mattie ran out the door and yelled, "Yee haw! Millie is going to be my teacher!"

That evening, just before dark, Father sent Evelyn Rose and Mattie to the old neighbors to see if they wanted to come to the bonfire.

The adults gathered around the fire, sipping on warm cider with cinnamon, and talked about raising the house and sheep farming. The children threw sticks in the fire, watching sparks rise high in the air. Millie sat off on a stump with Rusty, wanting to be alone. "We'll be home tomorrow," she told her faithful friend.

Chapter 53

The new day started early. Packing was easier since most of the food had been eaten. After a quick breakfast of scrambled eggs and flat bread, the family made their way down the lane. Millie opened the iron turquoise gate to let Ole Smokey bring the family through followed by Rusty and Bray. After securing the gate closed, she hopped on the back of the wagon. Rusty jumped up and sat at her side. Bray walked so close to the wagon Millie feared he would try to jump up by Rusty. He quickly sniffed his friend and snorted then backed off and followed.

As they approached the neighbors' house, they were standing next to the road. They wished them a safe trip home and said they couldn't wait till they were permanent neighbors. They handed them a small wooden box. Inside the box was a whole fried chicken and about a dozen buttered and salted warm roasting ears of corn. Mother said she'd warm it all up for dinner. Father gave them a wink and hinted the roasting ears may not all make it till dinner. After a few hugs, warm goodbyes, and a lot of waving, the vacationers were on their way again.

"Next stop," Father yelled, "sawmill, on the way home."

Millie laid back and watched the stars disappear, and the black sky began to turn blue. Evelyn Rose back-scooted in next to her side, and Rusty made his head a little more comfortable on her stomach.

Millie's eyes popped open when she heard Father yell, "Okay, everybody, we're here!"

"Here! Where!" Millie pondered until she heard the sound of a steam engine and a saw blade making its way through a tree. Father had stopped at a sawmill halfway to the town of Bonne Terre. The girls all watched as Father got out his house plans and explained the dimensions to a couple of men. After some discussing and writing on the plans, the men shook hands with Father, and the family was on their way again.

Millie and Evelyn Rose got behind Father so they could hear what was said and see where they were headed.

"This trail is a shortcut to the main St. Louis road," he explained. "Just a ways up here is the Big River Hills Schoolhouse, then we should come to the main road. Fellas back there said it would cut our drive in half to the river."

"Did he say how much it would cost to have the lumber for the house cut?" Mother asked.

"He sure did," he said with a broad smile. "This is the best part of stopping back there. They said if I allow them to select cut the farm, they'll trade me tree for tree. They'd cut everything I needed for free, and the only thing I'd have to pay for is hauling the lumber back to the farm."

Mattie, who was sitting between her parents, asked, "What does *select cut* mean?"

"That means the woods won't be cleared out," Father explained. "They'll just cut a tree here and there. You know, like we're doing on Mrs. Bell's place. Nothing will be done until I give him the final plans."

True to what they were told, Ole Smokey pulled the wagon past the Big River Hills Schoolhouse. Then not quite a mile farther, they come to the main road. "Soon we'll be at the river crossing," Father let everyone know.

Mattie had her father stop so she could ride Bray to the river. Evelyn Rose jumped in her spot between her parents. "After we cross the river," said Mother, "we'll find a place to eat this chicken and roasting ears."

The river crossing went just like the first time, only no one got wet. There was a different troop to help people across the river. Millie looked for Jonathan and was a little disappointed that he wasn't there, but glad at the same time. Her thoughts turned to Cecil, and her daydreams turned to being held in his arms. She was glad when she caught herself looking at the blue sky and whispering, "Watch over him and keep him safe."

Millie sat up and yelled, "Are we about ready to eat this chicken? I'm starved."

Mother looked at her husband with a half smile and told him, "A good appetite is a good sign."

Warmed-up chicken and corn on the cob seemed to put the whole family in a good mood. A little rest for Ole Smokey along with some feed and fresh water made for a little quicker step toward the homeward way. After the Flat River crossing, anxiousness set in on everyone. Talk of the sheep, chickens, and the thirst for Bessie's fresh milk had everyone longing for home. School finally became something good, and Father planned the next tree to cut.

"Since we didn't sell any sheep this year," Millie told her father, "we'll need to buy some hay."

Father bobbed his head yes and then said to Millie, "We'll have to put it in the Link barn since we now have chickens and a donkey to feed too."

"And another calf," Evelyn Rose said.

Without thinking, Father said, "We'll butcher him later this fall."

No one said a word. Even the sound of Ole Smokey's hooves on the hard-packed ground seemed to disappear.

Millie looked at Evelyn Rose and Mattie.

"What do you mean *butcher*?" Mattie asked.

"Mattie!" Evelyn Rose yelled.

Without hesitating, Millie explained, "You know, like we do with a knife to the fish before we eat them."

"Okay!" Mother yelled. "That's enough! You know better than that!"

"What?" Millie sarcastically asked. "Am I right?" she asked Father.

For the next few miles, there was a lot of discussion about the calf and the natural order of farm life. Chickens, sheep, fish, and even cows were on the menu of life, and that was the reason Mrs. Bell even gave them the calf. Soon Mother had Evelyn Rose and Mattie calmed down enough that the tears had dried up. As long as Millie didn't bring anything else up.

One more stop to give Ole Smokey a bit of a rest along with a good drink and just a little grazing provided a break for the last leg home.

"We'll soon be seeing the northwest hill," Father informed his family while helping his wife back on the wagon.

"We really made good time, don't you think?" she told her husband.

"Shortcut really helped," he said. "And if we hadn't stopped at the sawmill, we'd already be home."

Standing behind her parents, Evelyn Rose said, "Seems like we've been gone forever. I can't wait to go into town."

Hearing the word *town*, Mattie yelled, "I want to go to town too!"

"Calm down, you two," their mother told them. "We're not going till the first of next week. There should be a new shipment of shoes by then."

Mattie looked at both her feet and just said, "Ugh." She wiggled her toes and wished she didn't have to wear shoes, at least until it started to get cold.

School shoes brought on talk of school and getting back to school friends, home studies, and getting up early. Mattie was happy about Millie being her teacher until Mother informed the girls they'd have to leave a little earlier so Millie had time to prepare lessons.

"I got an idea," Mattie shouted. "Millie can leave early by herself. Then me and Evelyn Rose can ride Bray to school."

"Evelyn Rose and I," Millie corrected.

Turning to look back at all the girls, Mother gave them a warm-hearted smile. She told them, "Your father and I were talking the other day about that very thing. If we can build a sulky cart, it just might be a good thing. But that depends on two other things—"

"If Bray won't be stubborn," Mattie interrupted.

"No," Mother told her and then explained, "if no one has laid claim to a missing donkey *and* if there isn't any problem with the other kids. I understand some kids along the way may want a ride, and that'd be fine if their parents didn't mind. He will have to be left alone till after school, and then you would have to come straight home."

"Wow!" Mattie said. "This really is going to be the best year ever."

"Remember," Mother said with a pointed finger, "there is a lot of ifs here, so try not to get too excited."

Evelyn Rose and Mattie could hardly contain themselves while Millie just thought about taking a donkey to school.

"Just over the hill, and we'll see the Link farm," Father said. "Tell me what you think about moving and buying our very own new place," he asked the girls.

The girls stayed silent. Mother finally said, "Remember, as it is now, we don't really have a home we can call our very own."

The girls questioned moving to a new permanent place. They were concerned about a new school and leaving behind their old friends and neighbors.

As Ole Smokey topped the small knoll, there it was. They arrived at the small valley with a small cabin at the front with pasture land rising at its foothills and a large pond flanked by the southwest hill to the left and the northwest hill to the right. The sheep were gathered along the tree line of the northwest hill.

Breathing in the sight, Millie said to herself, "Now if that ain't what makes a soul feel better."

Bessie and her adopted calf had been let out to graze awhile in the small field near the cabin and the sheds. Chickens were in the penned area around their coop and looked as though they'd just been fed some cracked corn. Lush green grass ribboned its way from the spring all the way across the lowest part of the farm following the stream.

"Well," Father said, "what you all think?"

Mattie said in a soft voice, "We're home."

With a flick of the reins, Father directed Ole Smokey to start moving. When Ole Smokey caught sight of the homestead and the horse shed, it was hard to contain him. He quickly trotted to the gate. Millie jumped off the wagon and raced to the gate, closely followed by Mattie. Mattie jumped on the gate and rode it open. Ole Smokey snickered and started prancing in anticipation for his stall and a good rest.

"Go on," Millie told her father. "I'll close up and be right there."

Father pulled on the reins to keep Ole Smokey from veering off into the stall. "To the house!" he yelled at the horse.

"The girls and I will unload," Mother said. "You can take care of Ole Smokey. Millie can help if you need her."

"I will," he said, slipping off the harness. "But I'm sure she's gonna want to go up and check on her sheep."

Father walked Ole Smokey toward the stall, and with his head hanging low, Bray followed. Millie and Mattie met their father almost at the shed. Looking at Mattie, Father told her, "Your mother needs your help unloading the wagon. Let her know we will be along shortly."

Without hesitation, Mattie took off at a run toward the cabin. As she got there, Mother stepped out on the big flat rock porch and yelled, "Mrs. Bell left a note for us to come up for supper, if we're back in time."

Millie apologized to her father and explained, "I got to get the sheep down to water at the Link place. I don't want to miss out on one of her big juicy steaks."

"You go on," Father said. "I can handle this."

"Don't forget the chickens!" she yelled. With a loud whistle, she summoned Rusty, and the two headed up the northwest hill where the sheep were grazing in the cool shade.

The whole family got the chores done in no time. The wagon was unpacked, and most things were put away. Father got Ole Smokey fed and watered along with a quick brushing. Bessie was put up while the adopted calf stayed close by. The chickens were fed, and Father gathered what eggs were there and carried them in his hat. Millie and Rusty herded the sheep to the gap that led to the watering trough behind the Link's barn. Millie pumped as hard as she could to get plenty of water for twenty-seven patiently waiting sheep while Rusty made sure none wandered off.

With plenty of daylight left, the family gathered at the spring for a quick washup and dusted the day's journey off their clothes.

"Okay," Mother said, "let me look at you all." Satisfied with everyone's appearance, the family took off across the field toward the new logging road for the walk to Mrs. Tennessee Bell's home.

"Wait a minute," Mattie said. "How did Mrs. Bell know we'd be home?"

"Your father told her we would," Mother explained. "He even said we hoped to be early enough to take care of the animals, and if we weren't, we'd do it in the morning."

"Well, I, for one, missed Mrs. Bell," Evelyn Rose said.

Father patted Evelyn Rose on the back and said, "A neighbor like Mrs. Bell is really rare. I think we all missed her."

Mrs. Bell hadn't started the late supper, just in case her neighbors hadn't returned. Overjoyed for their return, she quickly cut the beef into steaks while her neighbors started the fire in her stove. Talking about the trip made the time fly quicker than the girls had hoped. The juicy steaks with buttered potatoes and plenty of beans seemed to disappear before their very eyes.

Though the coffee was hot and strong, Father told Mrs. Bell, "We do really have to eat and run. This day started way before daylight."

"Oh, don't you all fret yourselves none," Mrs. Bell said. "I see you got two little ones just about asleep on their feet. You better get them home before you have to carry them." Tennessee knelt down in front of the two sleepyheads and said, "I almost forgot. The other day I was coming back from your place through the woods, and I heard this sound behind me. The sun was down, but it was still light out. It was hard to see in the woods because of all the shadows. When I heard this sound, I jerked my head around, and there it was."

"There was what?" Evelyn Rose asked.

"The headless horseman," Tennessee said.

Mattie ran to her father as Tennessee quickly said, "That or a deer that just jumped up. Couldn't really say."

Millie laughed at the fright Mrs. Bell gave Evelyn Rose and Mattie. "You two get scared over anything," she told them.

Mother rolled her eyes and told Mrs. Bell, "I guess these two won't be falling asleep on us now." She gave Tennessee a hug and thanked her for supper then said, "We better go. The sun is down, but it's still light out."

Evelyn Rose's eyes got big, and Mattie's jaw dropped open as Mother started laughing. Mattie pulled her father through the door in order to get home before dark as goodbyes were said to Mrs. Bell. It was a quick walk through the woods, and by the time they all reached the big rock porch, the evening star was just showing over the southwest hill.

Hurried trips to the outhouse and a cold drink from the spring let the girls' parents know that it was time to be tucked into their own beds.

"My own bed," Mattie said, snuggling in at her end of the bed.

At the other end, Evelyn Rose just mumbled her good nights and then turns to face the wall.

Mother turned the oil lamp down, but not out so Millie could see when she turned in for the night. She made her way to the opened door to see Millie sitting with her head on her father's shoulder. They both looked comfortable but tired. Worn out herself, she sat on the other side of her husband and lay her head on the other shoulder. No one said a word. A three-quarter moon was making its way from town in the east and would probably be where the evening star is when morning came. At the corner of the cabin, Bray was down with his spindly legs tucked in next to his side. His huge head drooped almost to the ground while his long ears hung straight down. Under his chin was a curled up and tuckered out pup that for some reason had become best friends with the donkey.

"If that ain't the oddest pair I ever did see," Father told his two sleepy companions.

Millie leaned forward for a look-see and said, "They've been like that from the very first time they met."

Mother sat up straight then looked around her husband at Millie and told her, "I believe they might have something in common that causes them to like each other."

"What could that be?" Father asked.

"Well, I think," Mother explained, "both of them have suffered pain by an evil person. We know Rusty has by the young sympathizer who tried to kill him, and it wouldn't surprise me none if the owner of that donkey wasn't of the same caliber."

"Could be," said Millie. "But I know for sure there is a deep trust and bond that you don't see very often. Especially in animals."

Millie lay her head back on her father's shoulder, and her mother did the same. He took a deep breath of cool night air. Millie raised her eyes to look at Rusty curled up next to Bray and wondered to herself, *Maybe animals feel that same spirit I feel right now from my father.* She questioned that thought, then looked out over the field and noticed the pond and the cold silver reflection of the moon on its surface. For just a second, it caused her heart to feel as though it stopped and started again. She jerked when a cold shiver went down her spine.

"Hey, are you all right?" Father asked.

"Yes, I'm fine," she told him, trying to calm down. "I guess I'm just really, really tired."

"Me too," Mother said as she got up and pulled on her husband's arm. "What you say we all get some sleep."

Father stood and so did Millie. "I'm all for sleep," he said, "about twenty-four hours' worth."

Chapter 54

Lots of work had to be done to catch up from a lost week. The beginnings of the preparation for winter starts in the garden with the storing of potatoes and apples, to canning beans and other vegetables. Buying and trading for hay dropped the sheep herd down to twenty-four sheep. The use of the neighbor's barn for the winter, or until the farm sold, made the hay-storing easier. Father wished he'd planned a place to build a barn on the new farm.

During the next week, the girls worked hard in the garden to harvest most of the things they grew. They made a trip to town for the school supplies that would be needed. Millie and Mother would ride behind Bray on the homemade sulky. The trial run went well as long as Rusty went alongside the donkey. Father remedied this at home with carrots and apples. Rusty would be tied up while Bray would be led somewhere else. When they got there, Bray would be fed apples and carrots. On their Friday trip to town, Bray did exactly what the girls wanted him to do; and when they got to school, he was happy to be fed.

"That was easy," Evelyn Rose told her mother.

"Yes, it was," Mother said. "Just be sure he's fed his oats and hay too. We don't want him getting stubborn on us."

"Why?" Mattie asked.

"Because we'll have to walk like last year," Evelyn Rose remarked.

Evelyn Rose then told her mother and sisters goodbye as she left for her house-cleaning job.

"See you tomorrow!" yelled Mattie. "Wish I had a job like that," she said.

"Well, if Evelyn Rose does go off to school, maybe they will still need someone, and the doctor's wife could hire you," Mother said as she wiped Mattie's face and used her fingers like a comb to straighten her hair.

Mattie fidgeted some then stuck her bottom lip out.

"What?" Mother asked.

"We won't live here next year," Mattie pouted.

Mother made a funny face and apologized to Mattie. Not knowing what else to say, she asked, "How about we get a piece of hard candy down at the General Store?"

For the time being, Mattie was satisfied, but Millie wasn't happy. She knew the move was inevitable. She pondered, if she got married, would she live close to her parents or in the woods where Mrs. Bell said she would give them property? She frowned, thinking of being separated from her parents.

Her mother noticed her sadness and asked, "Is there something wrong?"

"Uh, no! I mean, no, nothing is wrong," she replied. To cover her thoughts, she said, "Just thinking about school and assisting the teacher. That'll be in just a couple of days."

Mother gave Millie a quizzical look, and Millie told her, "We better go." Looking at Mattie, she said, "She's about to come apart at the seams for that hard candy."

New shoes for all three girls was a must. As far as clothes, the usual was cloth sewn into simple dresses or hand-me-downs from last school year. But this year, Mother said there would be no patches sewn in. If they were too bad to be handed down, she would just make rags out of them. Mother met with some ladies from church to donate money for children whose families weren't as well off. Millie watched and listened to her mother say that since the folks were so kind and generous when her husband was down, that it was only fitting to help others now. The timber business was going great, and the Lord was blessing them with a healthy flock of sheep.

Listening to her mother caused Millie to reminisce about the past year. For the first time, at that moment, she realized their home was no more than a cabin, and it wasn't even theirs. Being in deep thought, she wandered away. She headed outside and just sat on the store's window stoop watching others and even saying hello to a few smiling people. She questioned why she was thinking the way she was.

"Are you all right?" came a voice from the doorway.

Millie jumped a little and said, "Sure, you just startled me a little."

"I'm sorry," Mother said. She then asked, "Are you ready to go home?"

Millie slightly smiled and nodded her head.

Mother politely hollered for Mattie and told her it's time to go. On the walk back to the schoolhouse, Mother and Millie walked arm in arm and without talking. Mattie followed closely, doing everything she could do not to bite the hard candy.

"I'm going to head home," Millie said to her mother when they get back to Ole Smokey and Bray.

"That's fine," Mother told her. "We'll be right behind you as soon as we pick up our things."

On the way back, Millie's mind raced with all kinds of thoughts. She asked herself, "Why am I even thinking these things?"

At home while taking the sheep to the watering trough, Millie saw Mother and Mattie at the gate. Mattie rode the gate open. She saw Millie and waved. "Come on, Rusty," Millie commanded the dog, waving her hand to herd the sheep.

That evening, no one could get a word in edgewise as Mattie was so excited for school to start. A person would have never thought she said she didn't like school and didn't want to go. Millie was in a particular mood and asked if she could be excused from the table to take an evening walk. Before anyone could answer, she got up and headed toward the door. As soon as she grabbed her staff, Rusty was on her heels before the door shut.

Mother eased out of her chair, went to the window, and watched her go up the hill. "I guess I'll go up in a few to make sure she's all right," Father said, still sitting at the table.

"Not this time," Mother said.

He looked at his wife and said, "Why not? We always have good talks."

Mother turned back to the window, watching Millie make her way closer to the pond, and said in a soft voice, "She's not your little girl anymore." She turned to see a concerned expression and a bit of hurt in his eyes, and she said with a smile, "It's time for a good mother-daughter talk."

"Oh, okay," Father said. "Be okay if me and Mattie walk the gap with you? I don't really like the idea of you going by yourself. You know, in your condition."

"That'll be fine," Mother told him with a hand on her hip. "But I'll come back with her."

"If you say so," Father said. "I'll be sitting on the porch watching for ya."

Millie and her mother sat together next to the giant oak. She asked questions while Mother explained about tomboys growing into womanhood. She told her daughter that not only does she change on the outside but the inside as well. Getting older, she will have many emotions and mood changes. They laughed and cried together as both felt better as long as they had each other to share their thoughts.

"You gonna be all right?" Mother asked.

"I'm fine," Millie said. "But I think I'd like to be alone for a while more."

Mother rolled to the side so she could push herself up. Millie helped her and told her, "I better walk back with you."

"Oh, no, that's okay. Your father is in the field pacing and waiting for me," Mother explained. "He wanted to come up here, but I told him that it was our time."

Millie gave her mother a hug and said, "I love you."

"I know you do," Mother replied. "And I love you too."

Millie watched Mother walk back toward the gap in the fence. Rusty watched and then followed her a little way. He stopped, turned his head, and looked back at Millie. She flipped her right hand to indicate that it was all right to leave her and walk with Mother back to the cabin. Millie whispered to herself, "You're a good dog."

Millie sat back down intending to feel the comfort of the big oak tree. She glanced toward the gap in the fence to see that Mother and Rusty were already gone. After the heart-to-heart talk with her mother, she did feel better. The solid, sturdy, grounded-by-centuries old oak tree against her back made her feel more at peace than anywhere else she could imagine. She admired the ancient mountains that had been dwindled down to mere Ozark hills with a valley in between. Behind the saddle that joined the two hills was the crimson hue of the setting sun. Wispy clouds reflected the warm glow against a deep-blue sky that indicated the old tale of a sailor's delight.

She leaned back and closed her eyes to listen to the sounds of the closing day. As a soft breeze blew against her face, she imagined that it was the breath of God blowing all her troubles away. Off to her left, a bob white called out and was quickly answered by another across the field in front of her. She smiled, knowing it's that time of year that quail start gathering up to form their covey.

At that thought, she wondered what the winter will bring. "Maybe I need to slice open a persimmon seed," she said out loud. "Let's see, knife, fork, spoon. Bitter cold, fair, or lots of snow to shovel." Millie smiled at the thought of winter. Winter was her favorite time of year. Although winters could be tough on farmers, she loved tending to the care of farm animals and was rarely indoors except to eat and sleep. "The challenge of surviving the harshness that the dead of winter brings may be why I like the cold," she told herself. She sat a while longer, hoping to see deer come out of the woods and feed in the field. The wispy silver-lined clouds give way to darkening clear skies. "I'll stay till the stars appear," she said as if she was speaking to them. Willing herself to stay put became easy when she found herself talking to God instead of herself.

This time of the year once the sun set, the temperature dropped in a hurry. She continued her conversation with the Creator, asking God almost the same questions she had for her mother. She laughed when the answers came to her as if He was repeating Mother's answers. "Maybe Mother had this same talk when she was my age," she said out loud as she noticed the Big Dipper just above the northwest hill. She traced the end of the cup out to the first star and said,

"North Star." Just as she saw the North Star, a barred owl over the pond started hooting for her little ones. Millie continued her talk with the Lord above and found herself praying for Cecil and an end to the war. She prayed for those who've lost loved ones and a people that's looking to be free. "Thanks," she said, looking up at the North Star. "I guess it's not all about me, is it?" She tightly squeezed her eyes shut and interlaced her fingers as tight as her eyes and told God He's been good to her and then said, "I love You. Amen."

Chapter 55

The next day, the girls got to wear their new clothes to church as did almost every school-age child there. As was every year, the church house was full the Sunday before school started. As usual, the preacher's sermon was about the importance of learning and going to school. After church, mothers were telling their children to not get their clothes dirty. Others were talking about Millie teaching the younger children this year.

The township of Farmington was growing as was the school. New children made for new school friends. Mattie and Evelyn Rose were well known since their sister was a teaching aide and more well-known because of Bray. Everyone loved Bray and wanted to feed him carrots and apples.

The leaves soon brought on the fall colors. The sumac and dogwood turned deep red, and the sassafras's orange color mixed in with yellow hickory, and the red and brown oak leaves made the Ozark Hills look like a painted picture.

Father continued to cut timber on the Bell farm, which made for good trading for hay. With Tennessee's barn full and the Link barn too, it was time to turn to harvesting the late crops. Father devoted all his time to help with the garden as Mother worked mostly in the house since she was within a couple of months of giving birth. Millie and Mattie helped their father dig potatoes and turnips. They picked the late season corn and put it in bins for the animals. Evelyn Rose helped her mother in the house. Between the ragweed and golden rod, she hated being outside this time of year.

"We'll have a killing frost soon," Mother told Evelyn Rose. "Then you won't have such bad hay fever."

Looking up with her watering eyes and red nose, she asked, "Why doesn't everyone have this condition?"

"You're just more sensitive to weeds than most," Mother explained. "My aunt was the same way. You probably get it from her."

Mother handed her some woody bark she had cut from a willow tree. "Now don't eat the bark, just chew on it and swallow the juice. You should feel better soon," she told Evelyn Rose.

Sure enough, by the time the rest of the family came in, Evelyn Rose wasn't whining about the pain and pressure in her head.

"Big day coming up," Father said as he set a tow sack full of potatoes on the floor.

Evelyn Rose and her mother pushed the table back to put the spuds under the floor in the half cellar. "Let's put these up, then we'll talk about your big day," Mother told him, giving her girls a wink.

"Fair enough," he replied in a bit of a grumpy tone. He dragged the burlap bag toward the trap door, reaches down with two hands, and pulls the heavy oak floor up to reveal the small but very important storage area. After maneuvering some of the other goods to make room for the new potatoes, he finally got everything situated. "There now," he said, "is everyone happy?"

With both hands on her hips, Mother told him, "Since you're already down there, could you put these beets behind the green beans?"

"Is that it?" Father asked.

His wife smiled and told him, "Come on out of there, and let's hear about this big day you got coming up."

After everything was put back in place, Father told the girls, "It's been several months now, and if everyone has kept their distance, there might be honey in that old tree."

"You mean where we took that swarm of bees?" Millie asked.

"That be the one," Father said with a resounding head nod. "From the size of that swarm, and if the queen stayed put, there should be quite a sum of honey in that tree."

"You will wait till I get home, won't you?" Millie asked.

"I'll have everything we need down by the creek," he told her. "When you get home, hurry on back, and I'll let you drill the hole in the tree."

Sure enough, by the time Millie and Mattie, who just had to tag along, got to the back field, Father had everything ready. A small fire close to the tree was burning so smoke could be made. Father had fashioned a table right next to the tree.

"The fire is your job," he told Mattie. He began explaining before the girls could ask a lot of questions. "We need to make smoke to keep the bees calm. Don't ask me how it works, it just does. Millie, you stand on the scaffold and drill a hole right up there where you see that mark."

Millie shook the table scaffold Father made and asked, "You think that's the right spot to make a hole?"

"I tapped on it," he told her. "It sounded right. A little above it, you can hear bees buzzing."

Millie got her pocketknife out of her pocket.

"Wait!" Father quickly said. "You don't need your knife. I got this."

He got a tool off the ground and held it out to Millie. "It's a brace and bit," he explained. He then showed her how to use it.

Being a quick learner, she made a hole. As soon as she pulled the bit out, bees followed right out the hole.

"Quick, Mattie, hand me that long stick!" Father commanded.

Mattie handed her father the six-foot-long pole that had coal oil-soaked rags tied around the end. He lit the rags, making sure there was no flame but only smoke coming from it. He then stuck it up where the bees were. "Smoke will calm them down," he told the girls. When the bees retreated inside the tree, Father handed Millie a little wood stick he had carved. "Stick that in the hole," he instructed.

Knowing the size of the bit, the stick he had whittled fit perfectly. "Now try it again," he said. "This time about ten inches down from the first hole."

Father gave the smoky rags back to Mattie and told her to put it next to the fire.

Millie started drilling again but first asked for another plug that she held between her teeth. This time, honey came out. She plugged the hole and drilled again to find the bottom of the honey supply. Twenty inches down then five inches back up proved to be the bottom of the hive. Father handed Millie a hollow stick, which she poked into the hole, and a spigot was made for the honey to drain out.

"We'll drain the honey out till it stops leaking out your second hole," he explained. "That way, there'll be plenty of honey for the bees to survive the winter." He asked Mattie for the smoke pole again then told her to hand the buckets to Millie so she could fill them up. In less than an hour, they had seven gallons of honey from the tree.

"We've not drained to the hole yet," Millie told them.

Mattie shrugged her shoulders and said, "That was the last bucket."

Father told her to take the spigot out and place the plug back in. Then he said, "I can't believe we got this much. We can sell this by the quart or trade what we don't need. If we don't have an early winter, we'll be able to do this again."

Nighttime settled in well before the honey was all in the house. Millie and her father had to make a second trip to get it all home. With sugar being scarce because of the war, honey was a priceless commodity.

Chapter 56

Fall closed in on the town of Farmington as the farmers prepared for winter. The colored leaves lost their grip and fell to the ground. Days became shorter, and clear mornings were dressed in white crystals of frost. Gray skies gave hope to children for the first snow and a glistening wonderland. The older folks felt dread as the freezing rain covered the land. Farmers knew and understood nature; underneath its beauty, there could be deadly consequences.

Millie, Evelyn Rose, and Mattie had plenty of chores to do once they got home from school. Father cut and split firewood from the leftover treetops to sell in town. Millie tended to the flock of sheep. Mattie's job was to keep care of the chickens and keep firewood stacked for cooking and heating. Evelyn Rose did the milking though, Mattie liked talking to Bessie, so she'd milk easier. She also made sure that Ole Smokey and Bray were fed. Mother stayed in the small cabin keeping clothes patched and sewing new ones. Mrs. Bell kept a close eye on her and was always there whenever her husband had to go to town. Tennessee would rather visit or be visited just to keep from going to town herself.

As Thanksgiving was soon to be celebrated, it made the family anxious for a new member of the family. A month or less, and they'd find out if it would be a boy or a fourth girl. At the Sunday church service, most people seemed more concerned about the new arrival than they did the community dinner for Thanksgiving. As with all new arrivals in the close-knit congregation, the women were always more than eager to help.

"Just as I Am" was sung, and the preacher finally said his closing prayer. Within a heartbeat of the "Amen," someone boldly asked, "What time we gonna eat on Thursday?"

The preacher held both hands up and with a bit of a red face, said, "I'm not sure, but I'll let whoever is in charge come on up so we can get all the particulars." As a couple of older ladies came forward with all the instructions, the man of the cloth told them, laughingly, "Not too long ladies, we've got today's meal to worry about."

Some laughed, but the two ladies gave a stern, serious look as the preacher, again with a red face, followed most of the men out the door. That caused more ladies to laugh as the older ladies continued with the plans for the big day.

Millie, Evelyn Rose, and Mattie were more than thrilled to have the extra time off from school due to the Thanksgiving holiday. Most of Evelyn Rose's free time was spent cleaning and helping the old doctor and his wife.

The morning of Thanksgiving started way before daybreak with a knock on the cabin door from Tennessee. The agreement was that Tennessee would help with food preparation while Millie and Father took care of her cattle. Millie always jumped at the chance to be outdoors rather than be in the kitchen. Mattie wanted to help her sister and father at the cattle farm, but she would rather be with Mrs. Bell. She had taken a liking to her and considered her closer than anyone would their own aunt. They were becoming quite a pair.

As soon as the cattle were fed in the barn, Millie and Father cut through the woods on the logging road, turned at the corner stump where Millie cut down her first tree, and made their way to the big oak tree at the edge of the back field.

"Go get 'em!" she told Rusty.

Without having to tell the dog twice, he was off in a flash. Once across the field and just past the creek near the woods, they heard Rusty's bark. "There they are," Millie told her father.

Watching from the big oak, Millie gave hand signals for Rusty to herd the sheep to the gap in the fence.

"What a magnificent animal that dog is!" Father said.

Millie laughed a little and told her father, "I've always kind of thought he knew how to count. No matter what, he has never left a sheep behind."

After Rusty got all the sheep through the gap, their habit was to go directly to the pond for a drink. The sheep were then herded to the holding pen next to the barn on the Link farm. Millie and Father stopped in the middle of the gap to admire the orange rays of light streaking across a violet-colored sky. The stars shone brightly above a clear, crisp heaven while the field below glistened with a heavy frost. Frosty breath came from each of the sheep as Millie whistled and yelled for Rusty to continue his drive. The white smoke tethered from the cabin's chimney high into the air. It was a good day for a church gathering on a Thanksgiving Day.

"Bet that smoke smells like pumpkin pie," Millie told her father. Not hearing his reply, Millie turned to see her father looking past the pond and up into the woods of the northwest hill. She started to ask what he was looking at but was greeted with a raised head with his index finger pointing up, slowly moving his hand to point in the direction he was looking. If it hadn't moved, Millie would have never seen the big buck coming down the hillside. He moved very casually out of the woods, keeping an eye on the sheep and the dog herding them away from the pond. The deer never saw the two people watch him while he watched the sheep. The big buck crept closer to the pond for a drink although he remained skittish at every step. Finally, at the water's edge, he got his head up high and stared right at Millie and Father. They both held their breath so not to scare him off but were greeted with a loud blowing whistle from a couple of does that had come out of the woods behind them. Two does along with three young ones bounded across the field with their white tails held high.

"Look," Father said. "He's going to chase them."

Millie turned just in time to see the magnificent antlered deer leap to clear the fence and make his chase for the does.

"He never knew we were here," Millie whispered to her father.

"Not this time of year," Father explained. "It's the deer rutting season, and bucks chase does the same way bulls chase cows."

Changing the subject as quickly as he could, he told Millie, "Look, Rusty has the sheep in the holding pen."

By the time Millie and Father got to the pen, the sheep had settled down, and Rusty was sitting on his haunches looking at them with his silly grin.

"Yes, you're a good boy!" Millie said with a scratch behind his ears. She closed the gate while Father used the pitchfork to throw out the hay from the barn. Millie pumped water into the trough and pointed out to her father that ice had formed around the edge of the water.

Father looked toward the town of Farmington in the east and noticed the sun rising above the treetops. "It'll melt in a little while," he said. "But when it gets really cold, we won't be able to water here." He then explained, "If water gets up in the spigot, the whole pump might freeze and bust."

Millie looked back up the hill toward the pond and said to her father as she watched the frosty breath drift in that direction, "I love this farm life no matter the time of year, except for chopping the ice on the pond so the sheep can get water." Her voice trailed off as she continued to speak, "It's always so dark there." She took a deep breath and made the pond disappear with cold smoke as she exhaled.

"What? What did you say?" Father asked.

Millie brought her attention back to her chores and pumped on the handle a little harder. "Nothing," she said. "It was nothing."

Millie and Father made their way back to the cabin and were almost knocked down by the smell when Millie opened the door. "Oh my!" she said. "That pumpkin pie smells so good!"

"I'm just about starved to death," Father said, giving Millie a little push so he could get by her. "Look at those sweet potatoes. Can I have some now?"

"Just one," Mother told him. "Along with your breakfast, if you can wait till I cook your eggs." Turning toward Millie, she asked, "How about you? You hungry?"

"I'm starved," she answered. "Will pie come with that?"

Mother placed both hands on her hips as Mrs. Bell started laughing and told Millie and Father, "Afraid not!"

"Is everything good for us to go?" Mrs. Bell asked, meaning, were all the chores done for the day.

Before opening the door, Father told her, "Cattle's good, sheep's good, even your hounds are good. I do believe we're ready."

Without comment, everyone was ready to help load the wagon as Ole Smokey was brought up to be hitched to the wagon. Evelyn Rose and Mattie let their father do the hitching while they helped carry the food. Mother finished Millie and Father's breakfast while Tennessee cleaned up as best she could.

Millie didn't run to open the gate because Mattie beat her to it. Though she did notice Mattie's run to the wagon, her jump, and spin to sit on the opened end of the wagon. Millie smiled and told Mattie, "I couldn't have done better myself."

"Better make room for Rusty," Mattie said as Rusty maneuvered under the gate and leaped between Mattie and Millie and made himself comfortable for the ride into town.

Though the sun was shining, the air was very crisp, and you could still see frosty breath anytime someone spoke. Ole Smokey looked like a steam engine as he trotted on down the road. Almost all the leaves were gone from the trees, which made the sun's warmth feel good on the still day. Leaves fluttered to the side as the wagon wheels rolled over them and exposed the hard-packed dirt they had blanketed. Houses normally unseen because of foliage now were well in view. Smoke rose from the chimneys high into the sky so that everyone would know the weather would be clear and fair.

Mattie gave Rusty a hug and told the dog, "I'm surprised you decided to come with us."

Millie overheard Mattie talking to the dog and asked her, "Why?"

"Because Bray got tied up in Ole Smokey's stall," she said as she placed a hand under the grinning dog's chin and called him precious.

Millie smiled at Rusty and told Mattie, "Maybe he decided he wants some undivided attention from a precious little girl."

Mattie snapped her head up and blushed at her big sister's comment. She gave Rusty a big hug. Through his fur, Millie heard Mattie say, "Thanks," unsure if it was meant for her or Rusty.

"Wow!" Evelyn Rose shouted as Ole Smokey rounded the last bend in the road. "Look at all the people!"

Father turned his head to see Evelyn Rose standing behind him just over his shoulder. "Difficult times draws folks closer to God," he told her. "This war is wearing thin on everyone."

Mother looked at them both and said, "You're right, and a beautiful day helped too."

Before Ole Smoke was unhitched, Father guided him to the front of the church so the wagon could be unloaded. He took Ole Smokey where he could be hobbled and out of the way. On the way back, he heard one of the women yell that dinner would be served in about an hour.

Millie stayed with her mother and Mrs. Bell while Mattie and Evelyn Rose gathered with some of their friends from school.

All the talk before dinner was about the fine day, how the harvest was, or the war. Seemed that all conversations ended with words about war. Just like the old couple who was going to be their neighbors in the Bonne Terre area, it wasn't about which side you were on or why. It was about when will it end and who wasn't coming home. Though tempers flared now and then, it was usually about how hard it was with the rationing of food staples and who got what or there was none to get.

"Time to gather round!" yelled one of the church ladies. "Come on, gather round!"

Some looked that way, but a lot of talk was still going on till the woman held up a cast-iron skillet lid and banged on it with a metal ladle. She waved everyone in when she had their attention. "Gather around please," she yelled one more time. The large group squeezed together, and when all was still, she welcomed everyone and wished them a happy Thanksgiving. She explained the table seating inside the church and wished they'd had it outside because of the beautiful day. "Allow the older folks to go first," she said. "Then those who are with child."

Millie and Father looked at each other as Mother said, "Oh no." They both looked at her, saw how red her face was, and they thought she would explode.

To make matters worse, Mattie ran up and yelled, "Oh good! We get to eat first!"

"No! We won't!" Mother told her with gritted teeth. "We'll just stay in line like everyone else, and I don't want to hear another word," she said to her family.

After a couple of seconds, and when Mother wasn't looking, Millie whispered to her father, "Just pray that woman doesn't call her out."

The church lady looked at Mother and started to wave her to the front of the line when she saw the embarrassment on Mother's face. She smiled at her and decided to let it be.

The smell inside the church was heavenly, and it was almost impossible to not try and sneak a bite. Just like the Fourth of July, there were rows of tables made of wood planks placed on top of sawhorses covered with tablecloths. The church pews were turned sideways, all running longways to the church. The ladies in charge had food that was brought from each family equally divided on each table. Whole turkeys with dressing were placed on each table.

"Try to get to the table with Mother's sweet potatoes," Father said.

Mother slipped one hand on her hip and whispered back, "You're sweet, but just try to get a table where we can all sit together."

"I'm about starved!" Evelyn Rose told her father. "Wish everyone would be quiet so the preacher would say his prayer."

"Have patience, young lady," her mother said, overhearing what was said.

Evelyn Rose looked around her father and told her mother, "Talk, talk, talk, yak, yak, yak!"

Father placed a finger on his lips to shush her when she looked toward the front of the church and realized she might have been a tad too loud. Feeling a little sheepish and red faced, she bowed her head just as the preacher indicated her to do.

The reverend's prayer was simple and to the point. The day, the gathering, and the great harvest were all mentioned. Thanks to the Lord were made for the nation and its faithful heritage. With a quiver in his voice, he remembered those who had gone off to war and those who had paid the ultimate price for their beliefs. After a pause and moment of silence, the preacher prayed for safe delivery for new life. Millie noticed her mother's knuckles turn a little white and a bit of a firmer grip on her hand, although she had a bit of a smile on her face. In an odd sort of way and right before his "Amen," the preacher spoke in a soft prophetic tone to bring comfort to those who would face a terrible winter.

Mrs. Bell commented that the preacher must have cut open a persimmon seed. This prompted small talk about the weather forecast, but it quickly changed to how good the food looked. Of all the holiday meals, Thanksgiving was the one that really raised the taste buds. The flavors of the fall harvest were like no other. Maybe that's the way God meant it to be, just so a man could add a little weight to himself and survive the winter. Turkey was always the choice meat with corn, squash, turnips, and green beans with bacon. Pumpkin pie was usually the favorite dessert, though hot apple pie with cinnamon and sugar sprinkled on top was cause for debate. Hot cider and coffee kept the adults at the table while the children would run around chasing one another.

The same church lady that announced the meal was again up and asking for everyone's attention. "If I could have everyone's attention," she politely yelled. "There are just a few things we need to quickly discuss before some of you good folks start heading home. Christmas will be here real soon, and for the next four weeks, we need to collect things for those who have fallen on hard times. We will be quilting blankets on Wednesdays before prayer meeting. So if you're willing to help, it'd be greatly appreciated. Men, sharpen your woodworking skills. It's always a favorite, you know. The hardware store has informed me that for every pair of socks bought, one will be donated as long as supplies last." Everyone looked toward Cecil's parents. When the crowd settled down, she asked, "Are there any questions?" No questions were asked as everyone had hoped. "Well then" she said as everyone began to mingle and search out the coffeepot, but stopped as she continued to say, "The church committee has discussed and thought it would be nice if we'd put on a Christmas play."

Everyone clapped and agreed it was about time one was put on. Looking around with a smile on her face and her hands folded together under her chin, the church lady said, looking at Millie, "Miss Millie, we would really like for you to help and play the part of Mary."

"Oh! I don't know!" Millie responded, but wasn't heard because of the thunderous applause and cheers. "*No,*" she quietly groaned to her mother.

"Better you than me," Mother whispered back to her. "That lady would probably want me to have the baby on stage."

Giving her mother a quizzical look, Millie said, "Mother!"

"Oh, please don't say no," the lady said. "Everyone just loves the donkey, and your family is the only ones who have sheep. You know, Jesus is the Lamb of God."

Doing everything she could to keep from rolling her eyes, Millie glanced at her sisters across from her. Their teeth were clinched in broad white smiles that silently screamed, "Please say yes."

"Sure, I guess," Millie told the lady, "but I'll have to have Evelyn Rose and Mattie in it too. They're better with Bray than I am. Mattie can handle sheep almost as well as I can."

The lady standing up front clapped her hands together under her chin again and said to another lady sitting next to her and asked, "Can we make a couple more shepherd outfits?"

Mattie was so excited she could hardly contain herself, but the look on Evelyn Rose's face was something quite different. Millie looked at her with a big clinched-white-teeth smile and said through them, "You happy now?"

"Well, now," the lady said, "we have one main character filled along with a couple of shepherds. This Sunday after the church service, if you would like a part, you can come see me or someone on the committee."

On the way home that evening, Mrs. Bell told Millie, "You'll make a good Mary being probably about the same age."

"Will I make a good shepherd?" Mattie asked Tennessee.

Looking at Mattie with one shoe untied and a smudge of dirt on her face, Tennessee told her, "I think you'll make the best shepherd that there ever could be."

That made Mattie's day, so on the rest of the ride home, she had a hundred more questions about shepherds and what it was like in Jesus's day.

Chapter 57

Early the next morning while Mother was making breakfast, she heard Rusty barking then someone holler for somebody inside. "Hello there in the house!" came the yell. "Your dog won't let me on the porch."

Mother went to the door and was bumped on the backside by Mattie before she could open it.

"Sorry," Mattie said. Then she squirmed under her mother's arm to open the door. There stood a boy about the age of thirteen with a terrified look on his face. Between him and the cabin were Rusty and Bray, both guarding the home.

Though Rusty was barking, his hackles were not raised, and his tail was wagging. Bray's ears were up and slightly pitched forward, indicating his curiosity and that he wasn't afraid of the boy.

"You're okay," Mattie told him. "Come on up."

Mother snapped her fingers at Rusty, and just like that, he quit barking and came to sit next to the big rock porch.

As the boy walked forward, Bray bowed his head for a pet. Mattie got the words out, "You better…" as the lad sidestepped away from the donkey. Before she could say another word, Bray let loose with one of his ear-shattering "Eeyores," causing the boy to run to the corner of the cabin.

Mattie ran out of the doorway and grabbed Bray's halter. "He just wanted you to pet him," she told the young lad. Then Rusty started barking, thinking the boy was wanting him to chase him.

"Rusty, stay!" Mother snapped at the dog. He came back to the porch, panting with his tongue out, and grinned.

"You're okay, son," Mother told him. "Won't you come on in and tell us what you're doing here."

He walked toward the porch and was met by Mattie. She grabbed the sleeve of his coat, pulled, and said, "Yeah, come on in."

Mattie couldn't take her eyes off the young boy as they entered the warm cabin. He was greeted with "I know who you are" from Evelyn Rose. "We're in the same class at school, when you come."

Before he could say anything, Mattie told him, "You're cute."

He looked at Evelyn Rose then at her mother as his face turned red, and he tried to say, "I, I got this telegram." He fumbled through his coat jacket looking for the telegram. Getting flustered because it wasn't in the pocket he searched, he said, "It's here somewhere."

Evelyn Rose walked toward him, and he backed up a couple of steps. She reached out to his side pocket and pulled out a folded piece of paper. "Is this it?" she said and handed it to him.

He opened one fold and tried to swallow, but for some reason, his Adam's apple wouldn't work, and he squeaked out Millie's name.

"Yep," Mother said. "That would be our Millie. If you'd like to have a seat, she should be here in just a few minutes."

"She better hurry," Mattie said to no one in particular.

Evelyn Rose walked to the table where the young boy sat, smiled, and asked, "Would you like something to eat?"

He tried to say "Yes" but was afraid his voice would squeak again, so he just nodded his head.

"Mattie," Mother said, "why don't you go on out and let Millie know she has a telegram here."

Without a second thought, Mattie grabbed her coat and ran out the door.

Evelyn Rose put bacon in a pan and asked the boy how he would like his eggs. Mother appeared stunned to see her daughter cooking for a stranger. "How about we put the eggs in all at once," Mother told the young cook. She then asked their guest, "You do like scrambled eggs, right?" knowing Evelyn Rose could scramble eggs easier than fry them. "We're having flapjacks too, if you'd like some?"

With that, the boy found his voice and told the girls' mother, "Oh, I love flapjacks. They're my favorite." He then glanced at Evelyn Rose and smiled nervously.

Out back standing at the outhouse door, with Rusty and Bray for company, Mattie knocked and said, "Millie?"

"What?" Millie answered.

"There's someone here to see you," Mattie told her big sister.

"Is that what Rusty was barking at?" she asked.

As Mattie did the two-step, she said, "Yeah."

"Well, who is it?" Millie asked, not really believing her.

"A boy from the telegraph office," Mattie told her. "He's got a telegram for you."

Bursting out the door with a new store catalog in her hand, Millie said, "Your turn." She handed it to Mattie and almost ran around the corner of the cabin.

As the young boy watched Evelyn Rose and her mother fix bacon, eggs and flapjacks, Millie burst through the door and, in a couple of giant steps, was in front of the boy. She politely told him her name and said, "Mattie said you have a letter for me."

Looking up from his seat at Millie, he reached in the pocket that Evelyn Rose found the telegram in and began to panic when it was not there. Turning his head and looking wide-eyed at Evelyn Rose, the poor boy noticed she was tapping the left side of her chest. He then jumped when he felt a hand reach into his coat pocket.

"Is this it?" Millie asked.

"Yes, ma'am," he told her then reached inside his coat and took out a small ledger that was tied around his neck along with a pencil.

Before he could say anything, Millie took both; and as she signed her name, she asked him, "How do you like school this year?"

At that moment, he recognized Millie as the teacher for the younger kids and told her as she walked away toward her room with the telegram in hand, "It's been really good so far." Millie disappeared into her room.

Watching and waiting for Millie to come back and say something, he heard from the cookstove a metal utensil bang against a cast-iron skillet. "Good answer," Evelyn Rose said with a smile when he jumped and looked at her.

Mother took the spoon from Evelyn Rose and asked, "Why don't you get your father at the shed and let him know breakfast is ready?"

Evelyn Rose dignified herself as she walked by the young boy and told him, "You can take your coat off. Be easier to eat." She stepped out onto the big rock porch and yelled loud enough that Mrs. Bell, if she was outside, could hear her. "Father! Breakfast is ready!" When she came back in, both the boy and her mother were staring at her. He was wide-eyed, and her mother had both hands on her hips.

In a few minutes, Mattie came back in. Millie came to the table, and Father came in with a bucket of fresh milk.

"Look, Father!" Mattie said. "We got a guest for breakfast."

Evelyn Rose sat next to him and scooted her chair closer to the young boy and said, "There, Mattie, now you can sit here."

That didn't make Mattie happy at all, so she took her chair and dragged it to the other side, telling Evelyn Rose, "I'll sit over here."

Evelyn Rose reached up and took his hat off, saying, "Shouldn't eat with your hat on, ya know."

"All right, girls!" Father told them as he sat down. "Why don't somebody introduce me to this fine young man and tell me what he is doing here before we have a blessing."

Mother introduced the young man and told why he was there. Millie held her telegram up to show her father and said, "It's from Cecil."

Evelyn Rose bounced her chair again to scoot a little closer to the boy while Mattie put some bacon on his plate.

"Is Cecil okay?" Father asked with concern.

As usual, Millie gave her simple answer and no more, "He's fine."

With that, Mother put the skillet of scrambled eggs on the table and went back to the stove. She got a tall stack of flapjacks and put it in the center of the table next to the eggs. Father passed out the drinking tins and sat back down himself.

"Okay," Mother told everyone, nodding to her husband to signal the start of the prayer.

As Father prayed, there's one more clunk as Evelyn Rose scooted her chair a little closer. Father paused for a second to indicate his disapproval then finished with his usual closing and "Amen." He gave Evelyn Rose a hard look that brought a giggle out of Mattie.

After a second helping of flapjacks and maple syrup, the young boy thanked the family for breakfast and said he really needed to get back to town. As he got his coat and hat on, so did Evelyn Rose and Mattie.

"Mattie!" Millie said. "Do you want to see this telegram I got?"

Continuing to put her coat on, Mattie told her older sister, "No, thanks."

Mother informed Mattie to take her coat off, that she needed to help clean off the table. Mattie slowly took off her coat as Evelyn Rose escorted the young boy out the door and walked him to the gate. The rest of the family did their best to explain to the hurt little girl that she's way too young to think about boys and that Evelyn Rose and the young boy were friends at school.

As Evelyn Rose and her new friend rounded the corner of the cabin, they were met by Rusty and Bray, who were eager to play. Rusty was happy to chase a stick, but Bray wanted something else. He kept trying to stick his muzzle in the boy's coat and would just about knock him down.

"What's he trying to do?" he asked Evelyn Rose. "Is he trying to eat my coat?"

"No," she explained. "We always carry pieces of carrots or apples so he'd take us to school and not be stubborn."

"But I don't have any," he told both. Then he showed the inside of his coat pocket to the donkey. "See, there's nothing there."

Evelyn Rose shoved Bray's head away from the boy's coat pocket and shooed him away. Getting the message, the donkey just stayed where he was as Evelyn Rose and her friend walked on to the gate followed by a dog with a stick in his mouth.

For a few minutes, she told him about the sheep farm and her father's timber business. He didn't say a lot but acted as though he enjoyed the brief visit. After a bit more talk, he said he really needed to get back and started to walk away. "We're having a play at church," she said. He stopped and turned to look back. "It's a Christmas play. I'm a shepherd. I wish you'd come see it."

"I'd have to come by myself," he told her.

"You can sit with me," Evelyn Rose replied.

"But you're in the play," he said.

Quick to answer, Evelyn Rose told him, "If you come, I'll sit with you, and we'll watch it together."

Getting a little red in the cheeks, he told her, "I'd like that." He then hustled away from embarrassment.

She yelled "'Bye!" and he turned without stopping, waved, and yelled "'Bye" back.

For the longest time, Evelyn Rose stood at the gate and watched down the road. Every so often, she smiled and let out a sigh. She paid no attention to the dog sitting at her feet with the stick in his mouth. Finally, she reached down and took the stick from Rusty. "Here you go, fella," she said and flung the stick toward the chicken coop. Then she skipped her way back to the cabin. She curtsied to Bray and went inside.

"There you are," Mother said. "I was afraid you might have frozen out there."

Seeing Mattie with a sour look on her face, Evelyn Rose asked, "Did Millie read her telegram?"

A curt "Yes" was all she said.

"Well, is anyone gonna tell me what it said?" Evelyn Rose asked.

From the back room, Millie yelled out, "Cecil's coming home!" Millie walked back in where everyone was and told them, "He hopes to be here for Christmas, but he's not sure. Then he asked if I'd let his parents know. So what's up with your friend?"

"I asked him to come see the Christmas play," Evelyn Rose said. "And if he does, I told him I'd sit with him."

Mattie jumped up and said, "But you're in the play."

"Not if he comes, so don't count on me," she said. To make Mattie feel better, she said, "Besides, Bray likes you better anyway."

"You know," Millie said, "I may have a big part as Mary, but I believe you and Bray will steal the show."

The smile on Mattie's face lit up the room. Just like that, the young boy was an afterthought as she asked Millie, "Would you mind if I used your tall herding staff in the play?"

Father sipped his coffee, leaned over, and whispered in his wife's ear, "Will it ever get any better?"

She laughed, patted her belly, and said, "Just wait till there are four girls."

Chapter 58

For the next few weeks, life on the farm went smoothly especially with the few extra acres for the sheep and the barn for storage. Timber business remained high because of the high demand for the Plank Road. Millie started enjoying her teacher's helper job and got into a routine where she could start advancing in her own studies. With help from her mother, Evelyn Rose was way ahead of the rest of the kids in her class. Learning just seemed to come so easy to her. Weekends were filled with cleaning for the old doctor's wife, and every chance she got, the doctor would let her read some of his medical books. She helped decorate the house for Christmas and would at times act as though she was part of the family when guests were there. She'd catch herself and have to tell herself, "I have my own family." This made her feel sorry for the doctor and wife as they had no children or family to keep them company. She was thankful for her own family and loved her sisters. It was late at night that she missed her family and wondered what it would be like if she went away for months to school. She was already missing her mother and the little sister or brother that would be a stranger to her.

Mattie liked school and had no trouble going. Taking Bray to school and having Millie as her teacher seemed to be the reason. She paid close attention when it came to animals. She would find animal pictures and then draw them. She became quite good. Millie recognized her talent, and whenever she caught her a bit lost, she would challenge her with a drawing. During recess, Mattie's friends would trade something with her for a drawing of their pets. Every so often, she would make a penny or two. Pencil and paper were hard to come by, and the war made them even more scarce. Mattie quickly learned to draw on slabs of wood using charcoal to draw with. This became her favorite way to draw, and it showed from head to toe. Sometimes her face would be as black as the charcoal she held in her hand. Lucky for her, she had a mother that understood and even encouraged her.

Mother encouraged all her girls; Millie in farming and Evelyn Rose in her studies and reading. Mattie took a lot of work keeping her shoes on and keeping her clean.

Millie worried about her mother and the baby that was soon to come. Just after Thanksgiving, winter rolled in ahead of time, and the temperatures dropped well below normal and made life a little more difficult. With Millie teaching, Mother would help her husband with the morning chores and fix dinner. Mrs. Bell would come by the cabin during the early evening to make sure her neighbor hadn't gone into labor.

Such was the life here and all over the country. Winter was rough and hard on people. The war made it worse. Everything was hard to get, and the news seemed never to be good. The Christmas season seemed to bring a glimmer of light in a dark and depressive time. Christmas brought people hope and a sign that days ahead would be better.

"Big day today," Millie told her family at the breakfast table.

Father put his fork down and rubbed his bad leg. Looking into his wife's eyes, he told Millie, "I don't think we'll be able to go to church today."

At the same time, all three girls looked at their mother and with intense concern, asked, "Mother?"

"Is it time?" Millie asked.

Mattie rushed over to her mother's side as Evelyn Rose stood up and told her, "Here, sit down. I'll get the biscuits out."

"Not for real sure just yet," Mother explained.

"What ya mean? You're not real sure?" Father asked, patting her hand as he sat next to her.

She patted her tummy and with a concerned look, said, "I've had false labor pains before, and these are really light. It might even be something I ate."

Millie looked at Mattie saying, "I've got to go to church today. It's the last Sunday before the play on Christmas Eve. We're having the rehearsal. Are you going with me?"

Mattie looked at her mother then back to Millie. "I'm going to stay here." Standing up and almost crying, she asked Millie, "Is that okay? I know what I'm supposed to do."

Everyone comforted Mattie by telling her, "It's fine."

"You can help me clean up some," Mother told her.

"It's okay," Millie told her. "I'll leave Bray here, and we'll just do without him. That way, Rusty and I can take the two sheep."

Millie's father looked at her, questioning that action.

"Don't worry," she told him, noticing his look. Mr. Highley said we could keep them in a stall at his livery stable. He'll even feed them."

"Well, I'll be," Father said in surprise.

"Yeah, I know," said Millie. "I think it's his way of helping the church at Christmastime."

"Well then, if you do that," Father said trying to figure out his day in order to stay close to home, "I'll have Evelyn Rose go and get Mrs. Bell. Mattie and I will try to get the sheep down here for water."

"Thank goodness," Millie said. "This cold weather has really made an early mess of things. The pond's already got"—she stopped to think—"I bet a little better than an inch of ice on it."

"Yes, and the pump at the Link farm is froze solid," Father said.

Breakfast was eaten, and more plans were discussed for the family and farm. Everyone jumped when Mother flinched, but she made light of it just being a muscle twitch.

Evelyn Rose hurried to get ready to go to Mrs. Bell's, figuring she would help her with her farm chores before coming to the cabin.

All dressed and standing at the door, Millie grabbed her staff. Rusty jumped, readying to go, knowing the cue. "Sure you don't need Rusty?" Millie asked Father.

"Don't worry about Mattie and me," he told Millie. "We'll be fine."

"Wait!" Evelyn Rose yelled from her room. She came out dressed for the outside and told Millie, "I'll walk with you to the gate."

Millie and Evelyn Rose left together. With a rope and small halter, the two girls secured the wooly white ewe and had no trouble leading her as long as her baby stayed in sight. Rusty did his job whether he needed to or not.

"Cecil was to be home soon," Millie told Evelyn Rose. "I hope it was last night, and he'll be in church this morning."

"Well, if he's not, don't wait too long for him," Evelyn Rose said. "We'll need you here at home."

After the gate was closed, the two girls shared their concerns for their mother and told each other to hurry but be careful. Evelyn Rose watched Millie head east toward town on Maple Road. One last wave, and she headed south on the lane leading to Tennessee Bell's farm. After a few minutes, she found herself facing the redbone hounds barking their warning as Mrs. Bell was standing in the doorway trying to figure out who was standing in her lane.

Evelyn Rose waved both hands over her head and yelled, "It's me, Mrs. Bell. It's me, Evelyn Rose!"

"I figured it was," she replied and yelled to the hounds, "You hounds, calm down! You know who that is!"

Evelyn Rose rushed on past the hounds and onto the porch. She explained what was going on at home, where Millie had gone, and why she was there.

"Have you eaten yet?" Tennessee asked.

"Yes, before I left," she replied.

"Good, I'm just about done, so come on in and have some warm coffee," Tennessee told Evelyn Rose as she invited her in.

They sat as Evelyn Rose went into more detail about her mother, and Tennessee reassured her that her mother was healthy and she knew what to do.

Chapter 59

Just outside of St. Louis, Cecil leaves the Jefferson Barracks on a borrowed horse from the Army stables. As with Missouri weather, a cold front from the north can mix with warm moisture out of the southern gulf area and cause freezing rain or sleet more than snow. Cold and freezing temperatures were already in place.

No stagecoaches would leave in this weather, and Cecil figured with just two weeks off, he'd better try on his own before it got worse and he'd not get another chance to come home. After a few hours of riding, the rain came and instantly stuck to whatever it landed on and froze. Though he planned on a two-day journey, he didn't figure the weather would be this nasty. Pushing on as best he could and not giving up, Cecil took one of the Army wool blankets and cut four one-foot squares off it. With a little bit of a struggle from his mare, he pried the steel shoes off and tied the blanket pieces onto the hooves. This made it better for the horse to balance and to be more sure-footed on the slick ice. There was nothing good about the situation except that he was headed home. The rain was blowing from the north, and he was headed south. Cecil prayed the freezing rain would stop.

Chapter 60

"Mattie," her father said, "I'm going out to take care of Ole Smokey and milk Bessie. If you don't mind, would you carry some wood in?"

"I don't mind at all," she told her father. "Do you want me to gather the eggs and feed the chickens?"

"I want you to just stay close," he explained. "I'll take care of the chickens. Holler for me if anything happens."

Mother turned from cleaning the dishes and told the two of them, "There's nothing going to happen for quite some time." She put the dripping dishrag down then put her hand on her hip and said, "If you want, I'll go out and keep you company while you take care of the livestock."

"No," Mattie said.

Holding a hand up to stop her, Father said, "No, no, you don't need to do that."

"I could use a little fresh air," Mother said.

"Good," Father told her. "You can hold the door open for Mattie when she brings the wood in." He looked at Mattie and told her, "Bring in a lot of wood. The skies aren't looking that good."

* * *

"Never took you for much of a coffee drinker," Tennessee said to Evelyn Rose.

Holding the cup in both hands in order to warm them, Evelyn Rose explained, "Millie's more the coffee drinker. I just like the warmth it gives my belly and hands."

"That's good," Mrs. Bell told her. "I heard tell if you drink too much at such a young age that stuff would stunt your growth." She smiled at Evelyn Rose before another bite and told her. "Don't know if I really believe that. Before the war broke out and coffee weren't scarce, my husband and I drank coffee all the time. Even before bedtime, and I'd sleep like a baby. You can tell," she said looking down at herself, "it didn't stunt my growth."

They both hee-hawed at the comment as Evelyn Rose raised her cup for another drink and said behind her cup, "I'm not going to say anything about that comment."

"You girls were raised right," Mrs. Bell said, offering more. "I don't think any of you would ever speak ill about anyone."

"No, thanks," Evelyn Rose told her. "I'm good. No more coffee for me."

"Well, just give me a bit of time to get dressed for this nasty weather," Tennessee said. "We'll get the necessities out of the way then head on down to your place."

Chapter 61

It was just the break that Cecil needed. He pulled his pistol out and fired from the top of the hill that overlooked the Meramec River. The helmsman snapped his head up and looked back to see a man leading his horse and very gingerly trying to make his way to his ferry boat. He stopped and waved to indicate he'd wait then laughed as Cecil slipped and fell on his rear.

"Sure do appreciate your patience, Mister," Cecil told the man at the helm. He then led his horse onto the flat barge-type boat as the helmsman's crew prepared to leave again.

After yelling out his usual instruction, the man told Cecil, "You did a wise thing tying those pieces on your horse's hooves. If your horse went down on that hill,"—he nodded to where Cecil fell—"he could've fell on you as slick as it is." He gave more instructions to the crew, and the ferry made a slight jerk as it began to move. As he walked away, the stranger gave a little nod at Cecil's boots and said, "Might not hurt to tie some on your own hooves."

Cecil tipped his hat and thanked the man for the advice, then as soon as the ferry smoothed out from taking off, he led his horse to the other end of the boat. He pulled his collar up as high as he could and pulled his hat down low. He did this not because of the bad weather but because he didn't want to talk to anyone. Most of the passengers looked as shady as he did. Besides, he didn't want to ride south with anyone else for fear of slowing him down. Getting at the front of the boat, he checked the horse's hooves, then he reached inside his coat to check for his pistol. So many things he learned while in army training proved to be worthwhile in situations other than war. He walked to the other side of his horse and looked under the brim of his hat at a couple of the other passengers.

Keeping his horse between him and them, Cecil rested his hands on the back side of his saddle, right next to the scabbard holding his rifle. Light rain continued to fall and froze to most things it hit. Watching the movements of others, Cecil told himself, "Ride hard for a couple of hours or as long as the horse can safely do so, maybe three or four hours. That should put some distance between them." He rubbed the old mare under her chin and told her, "Then we'll find some shelter and grab a bite to eat." He took a handful of sweet mule feed he had stuffed in his pockets and fed this to the mare. Cecil took a little of the cracked corn, oats, and molasses and tossed it into his own mouth. "That's not bad," he said. He glanced at the strangers moving his way as the ferry barge hit the bank. The old mare remained steady though Cecil had to grab her mane to keep his balance. Two of the ferry hands slid out a broad, reinforced plank that slid neatly in place on the ice-covered loading dock. As soon as the lock-down pins were in place, Cecil led his mare off the ferry.

A quick glance revealed two ominous characters close behind him. Feeling his heart in his chest beat a little harder, Cecil remained calm until he heard the cry of one of the men's horses and a string of curse words. Cecil turned to see that the lead horse had fallen on the dock, dragging his rider down with him. He patted his mare and told her, "They aren't going anywhere till they get some socks on that poor animal." Reaching solid ground, Cecil mounted, pulled his collar up again, and rode south.

Chapter 62

Looking to the north, Millie noticed the thick clouds rolling her way. Behind her, clouds were coming in from the southwest behind the hill that she wished they weren't coming. "Rain," she said out loud.

Rusty circled behind Millie and gave her a light bump as if he's herding her along too. "Okay, I know," she told him. She gave the leash a tug, and Rusty made the lamb move on down the road. "I sure hope it doesn't rain, as cold as it is." Rusty looked back at Millie as he heard her comment and slowed a bit to keep pace with her. "Much rather have snow," she continued to talk out loud. She looked back to the north and said a silent prayer. "Lord, let Cecil be ahead of that cold front."

Millie and Rusty continued to push the mother lamb and her baby toward town. They were soon joined by a couple of other churchgoers. They walked with Millie and were astonished at the way Rusty worked the sheep. They were amazed at how he obeyed Millie's hand signs. Millie bragged on him and told the stories of his young life. The more she talked, the more she admired and almost became melancholy at the thought of not loving him more than she did. "Yes, he's part of the family, all right," she told her fellow travelers. She thought about what family life would be like if he hadn't been pulled from under old man Link's back porch.

Once they arrived at the church, Millie switched the rope to the lamb and tied it to a tree, leaving its mother and Rusty, knowing both would stay close.

"Millie, come on in!" yelled Cecil's mother from the door of the church.

Millie looked back at the sentry guarding its two priceless possessions and almost laughed at the dog's prideful stance.

"Where's the rest of the family?" Cecil's mother asked.

Millie gave a brief account of the goings-on at the cabin and then asked, "Cecil hasn't made it yet?"

Taking Millie's staff and leaning it in the corner, she told Millie, "Haven't heard a word from him since he arrived in St. Louis. Thought he'd be here sometime late this evening."

"I noticed the clouds to the north," Millie said. "They didn't look good."

"We noticed too," Cecil's mother told her. "The stage was supposed to have left yesterday afternoon." She bit her bottom lip and said, "He'll be okay. Now tell me more about your mother."

Their talk was short as the music started to play, indicating services were getting ready to begin. As it goes, the rumor had reached all the way to the front from Millie's fellow travelers or someone overhearing her conversation with Cecil's mother.

"Is everything okay at home?" the preacher politely asked Millie.

"Just fine," she replied.

The same lady that seemed to oversee everything stood and asked, "Has there been any pains?"

Embarrassed to death, Millie replied, "Maybe."

Some low-keyed talk mumbled throughout the congregation until the preacher quickly held his hands up. When everyone was still, he told Millie, "We'll be sure and remember your mother and the rest of your family in prayer."

Millie thanked the pastor then looked down at her folded hands in her lap. Cecil's mother patted Millie's hands, assuring her it's okay and she was there for her. The small choir began singing a Christmas song as thoughts flooded in on Millie's mind.

We're so poor, she thought. *Poor, dirty sheep farmers.* She looked around and saw happy well-dressed folks tapping their feet in beat with the song. Though almost everyone was struggling because of the war, her thoughts were *Your father is a cripple and can't even walk* right. *It's a struggle to feed the mouths we have, and my mother is bringing another baby into the world. We live in a small cabin. My sisters and I share the same small room and can only get dressed one at a time. The only recognition I would ever have is my name carved along with my sisters' on our homemade bed.*

The opening song came to an end, and as the preacher made his way to his pulpit, Millie told herself, *I don't like sitting here all by myself. I really don't like everybody looking at me.* Millie was feeling melancholy and sorry for herself as she looked at the preacher as he prepared to speak.

In a still moment, he said, "As Mary was laying the baby in a lowly manger, the angels went to the shepherds first and rejoiced with them. They followed the star and came to the baby that the angels said would be the Savior of the whole world."

Millie took a deep breath and tried to swallow only to find her throat knotted up. The sermon continued to lift her spirits as Christmas sermons are usually about joy and peace, love and salvation. The next thing Millie knew, she was asking for forgiveness for thinking the thoughts she had.

The rest of the sermon, the preacher talked about the darkness of war and the darkness of sin of death and hate. Then he told how the baby Jesus gave us hope in all things and for all people. "So rejoice!" he shouted. "A Savior is born."

Right on cue, the choir sang again as the closing song brought cheer to Millie and the whole congregation. An altar call was made, and the closing prayer was said. The preacher prayed for Millie's mother and the whole family during this time.

Millie remembered what her mother had said during prayer, and prayed herself that things were well, even if Mother was just having gas.

"Will you come home with us?" Cecil's mother asked. "We'll have dinner and then come back for the final practice."

"Thank you kindly," Millie told her. "That'd be better than staying here or at Highley's Livery Stable."

Chapter 63

As Father made his way to the shed, he noticed the strong cold front right of the northwest hill. "It's already colder than normal," he said out loud. He stopped and buttoned the top button on his coat and pulled his collar up. He turned to look back to see if Mattie was getting the wood and noticed the dark heavy clouds coming from behind the southwest hill. He glanced past the hill to his right then back to the cabin. "Mm, mm, mm," he said as he noticed the smoke coming out of the chimney. "The air is so heavy and there's lots of humidity. The smoke is almost dropping to the ground," he told himself. He took a deep breath, rubbed his leg with both hands, and muttered, "You might want to hurry, we're in for some bad winter weather."

Mattie came to the side of the cabin and saw her father. They waved to each other as they went about their business. She gathered some wood, and Father headed to the sheds.

"Father's back there looking at the clouds," Mattie told her mother as she walked in the door.

"I noticed them too," Mother said. "I think this baby feels the pressure too."

"Are you all right?" Mattie asked, a little anxious.

"I'm fine," Mother told her. She walked over where Mattie was putting the wood. She explained to her youngest, "It is time, but we will be a while yet." Noticing the worried look on Mattie's face, Mother took one of Mattie's hands and gently pulled her to the table. She pulled two chairs together so they faced each other. "Sit," she said. Mattie sat in one chair, and Mother sat in the other. With a smile on her face, Mother told her daughter, "I've been through this before, you know. As a matter of fact, three times, and I've never had any problems. It does hurt some." She then explained the process of having a baby.

Mattie listened intently and was very concerned. Mother told her about some of the times the sheep had their babies and focused on some of the humorous moments, causing Mattie to laugh and relax some.

"I will need your help," Mother said.

Mattie's eyes grew big as she leaned toward her mother. "I get to help?" she asked.

"Yes, you do," Mother told her. "I'll need you to keep the fire going in the stove. You'll need to make sure water is boiling, and you need to listen and don't be asking lots of questions. Now this is really important," she said as she reached out to hold Mattie's hand. "I might groan or holler some and maybe cry, but don't get upset. It's only natural and helps the baby come into this world."

Mattie didn't quite know what to think about this but promised her mother that she would do whatever she could to help.

"Good," Mother told her. "Now let's get some more wood."

Mattie headed back out, and as she rounded the corner, she saw Father in the stall with Bessie. "Get the wood, get plenty of wood," she said to herself. "Then I'll get plenty of spring water."

After Father milked Bessie, he took the bucket of milk to the springhouse, not to keep it cool, but to keep it from freezing. On the way back, he glanced past the pond to see if the sheep had made their way closer. *Them blasted things will stay in the woods till somebody goes after them,* he thought as he made his way back to Ole Smokey. The horse was content not getting out if he had food and water. "Well, ole-timer," Father said to him, "enjoy your rest while you can, 'cause after this baby comes, we'll probably spend more time out and about. Them womenfolks won't want to stay in." He grabbed the currycomb and gave Ole Smokey a good once-over and a little more feed just for good measure. On his way to the chickens, he took another look up the field toward the pond and the gap in the fence. He shrugged his shoulders then looked on past the hill that was beyond the pond and the gap.

As cold as it had been, they kept the small door blocked off so the chickens would stay in the coop. Father got a bucket of cracked corn and opened the outside door and entered the dark chicken coop. He filled the two iron troughs with feed, picked up a third, knocked out the ice, and headed back out for water. After feeding and watering, he opens the wood planks on the wall to let light in for a while. He gathered the eggs and told the hens, "I'll be back later, girls. Enjoy the light and fresh air." Livestock was all fed and watered. Father walked all around the henhouse and sheds just to give them a once-over to make sure groundhogs, foxes, coons, or opossums couldn't find their way in. After all the chores were done, he looked back to the skies in the southwest and said to Bray, who had come looking for a handout, "Might not be a bad idea to head back after the sheep."

Bray threw his muzzle up and down on Father's coat looking for his treat. "Hey! Careful there!" he told the donkey. "I got eggs in these pockets. If you want something to eat, I'll give you some of Ole Smokey's feed." He gave Bray some feed as a light sprinkle started to fall. "You better stay close," Father told him. "It could get mighty slick."

Father went back to the cabin to rest his leg and warm up some before going after the sheep. "Is that all the wood you brought in?" he asked Mattie.

Mattie looked up from a drawing she was working on and told her father, "Yes, that's all that was split. The rest was too big for me to carry."

Mother was sitting in the living area sewing on one of the girl's dresses. She noticed her husband trying to decide what to do. "That cold front in the north looks to be a strong one," she said, thinking maybe now would be the time to chop some more wood.

"I know," he told her. "It's starting to rain some, and the skies to the southwest don't look good either." He studied the stove and firewood, then he looked back at his wife. "Guess I better get more wood split so we can bring it in and keep it dry."

She slightly arched her back, and with one hand, rubbed the lower part. With a little wink, she told him, "Yes, it's going to be a long day."

Evelyn Rose and Tennessee finally got out to feed the cows and take care of her morning chores. Evelyn Rose admired the way Mrs. Bell had the feeding situation set up. The bigger cows fed out of a long manger under a lean-to at the side of the barn. The calves and yearlings got to go under a board fence across the runway of the barn so they could eat inside without being knocked around by the bigger cattle. Evelyn Rose liked that but didn't like the mud at all. "Is it always muddy like this around your cattle?" she asked.

Tennessee gave her a cock-eyed grin and asked Evelyn Rose, "It's not muddy like this with the sheep?"

"Oh, no!" Evelyn Rose said. "Might be a little, but you definitely don't sink past your ankles like you are in those boots."

"Well, honey," she said with that same funny grin, "this might be some mud, but it's mostly manure. These cows poopy a little more than your sheep."

Evelyn Rose looked down at her shoes and made a face as though she had bitten into a green persimmon.

"It'll clean off on your walk home," Tennessee told her. "But till then, why don't you just take care of the babies inside."

Evelyn Rose ducked under the board that allowed only the calves to enter. As she entered the stall and got a whiff of the cow manure, she told herself, "I don't want to be a farmer." She tiptoed around the manure putting the hay in the feeding troughs. She made her way out for a breath of fresh air.

"We'll get some wood on the back porch before we go to your place," Tennessee told Evelyn Rose. "I just don't like the looks of those clouds."

"Father says we might be in for some bad weather," Evelyn Rose said as they both looked to the skies.

Mrs. Bell held her arm out and told Evelyn Rose, "Here, load me up then hold the door open for me."

After seven trips of arms loaded with wood, Tennessee told her, "I think that's enough." She looked at the pile then said, "More than enough, just the way I like it."

Evelyn Rose surveyed the amount of wood and said, "Looks like enough for a week when added to what you already have." She was glad she didn't have to carry it.

"Thanks," Tennessee told Evelyn Rose. "Now we'll feed the hounds and be on our way. Okay?"

"That's fine," Evelyn Rose replied.

As they started walking down the trail to Evelyn Rose's home, a light mist began to fall. "That's going to freeze on everything," Mrs. Bell told her neighbor.

CHAPTER 64

Millie told Cecil's family that they didn't have to wait for her. She would just go ahead and put the sheep and its lamb in the stall at Mr. Higley's livery stable. "I'll feed them some and make sure they'll be all right," Millie told Cecil's mother. "Then Rusty and I will be right there."

Cecil's brother and sister wanted to stay and help. Millie explained she really appreciated the offer, but the livery stable wasn't hers, and she didn't think Mr. Highley would want her to let anyone else there without his permission.

Cecil's father tipped his hat at Millie and said to his two children, "I'd hoped you two would have the same judgment about our store." He then told Millie, "We'll wait if you like."

"No, I'm fine," she said. "You can go on."

She slid open the big door just enough for the mother sheep to get through then turned and waved goodbye to Cecil's family.

"We'll have dinner ready when you get there," Cecil's mother yelled back.

Millie coaxed the lamb and its mother on into the barn. Her sheep weren't used to being under a roof. With a little help from Rusty, they made it in just fine. Almost every stall had a horse in it. Millie figured those were the ones put up for the weekend. Outside the stall, in one part of the barn, was where the horses were tied to a picket line. "Must be for the churchgoers," she guessed. "Here we go," she told the sheep. In the corner of the barn was a small empty stall with just enough light to let her know it was empty. "This must be it," she told them. Millie led them in and noticed fresh hay on the floor and a little grain in a box. "Thank you," she loudly whispered though Mr. Highley wasn't there.

Rusty sat on his haunches in the doorway as Millie tied the mother sheep to a post and left her just enough slack to move around in the small stall. She saw a bucket filled with water next to the wall and smiled. "You pretty well thought of everything," she said as if speaking to Mr. Highley.

Millie sat down and watched the lamb and its mother nibble at the grain. She began thinking about her mother but told herself not to worry. Mrs. Bell would be with her. She took a long, slow, deep breath with her eyes closed to calm herself down. Suddenly, she heard a voice say, "Your mother and baby brother will be fine." For a second, she thought she dozed off. She jumped and gasped for breath as she heard a voice and felt a hand on her shoulder. Rusty came up on all fours and growled. "Who's there?" she asked in a commanding voice. No one was there. Being a little spooked, Millie decided to leave.

"Come on, Rusty," she told her dog. As she walked to the big barn door, she stopped and recalled the same presence she felt at the same spot on the Fourth of July. As she did then, she now said a prayer for her mother.

She slid the barn door open just enough to squeeze through. "Oh my!" she said, holding her hand out in front of her, palms up. "It's starting to mist rain." Looking over at the jail then up and down the street, Millie wondered where everyone was. "Nasty weather, dinnertime on a Sunday, guess they're where I ought to be, inside eating," she said to herself. "Come on," she told Rusty as they turned east and walked toward Cecil's family's home.

Chapter 65

After what Cecil thought was four hours or more of steady, easy riding, he decided to give the old mare a bit of a rest. Looking at the clouds, he figured to be right on the fringe of the cold front. He was in freezing rain one minute then out of it the next. He hoped to make it to the Bonne Terre area sometime tonight. Off the road about a hundred yards, Cecil could see some thick woods with a grove of cedar trees. He got off the mare and after a rub on her muzzle, he said, "Let's get in those cedars and out of the cold wind and rain." He led the mare to the cedars, picking out rocky glades along the way so neither would leave any tracks. "Tricks of the trade, thanks to the Army," he told the mare.

Once there, Cecil looked around and thought, *Out of the wind and unseen from the road.* Pleased with the spot, he tied his slicker in the trees to make a roof for himself and the mare. He made a small fire and warmed up some beans with pork fat and a tin cup full of coffee. While that was cooking, he placed a feed bag over the mare's head. They both ate. Cecil enjoyed the hot coffee and warmth of the small fire. He lay on his wool blanket and scooted as close to the fire as he could get.

Cecil began thinking of home and the girl he left several months ago. Drifting off, he remembered his mother and his father. He smiled, thinking of the kiss Millie gave him just before marching off.

Cecil bolted straight up with his pistol drawn when he heard the horse nicker. He stayed low on one knee, holding his pistol straight out, looking under the cedars as far as he could. He spotted the trio and his heart instantly started hammering inside his chest as his thoughts turned to fresh meat. But it wasn't to be when the three white-tailed deer caught Cecil's scent and bounded off with white flags raised. He took a deep breath and looked down at the fire. He must have slept about an hour. He put a little more coffee in the tin cup with some water and let it simmer while he got things ready to keep traveling. He saddled his horse and gave her a little more feed. "You done good with that warning," he told the mare as he rubbed her neck.

    He straddled the fire to warm his legs and drink the last of his coffee. "Now I'm warm inside and out," he remarked to himself. He kicked the fire out and mounted his horse. He left the cedar grove and got back onto the road. He was soon reminded of the cold, windy mist blowing in from the north. He quickly threw his collar up and was thankful the wind was blowing on his back instead of his face. He gave the mare a pat and told her, "We'll take it slow till it gets dark."

Chapter 66

As Evelyn Rose and her neighbor walked the trail north, Tennessee made the comment, "Sounds like we're not the only ones stocking up on firewood."

Evelyn Rose blinked at the cold mist blowing in her face and tilted her ear toward the sound of someone chopping wood. "Yep," she said, "that's Father chopping. Mattie is supposed to be helping him carry it in the house."

Another hundred yards, and the small cabin came into view. Tennessee noticed the darker clouds to the southwest and thought to herself, *What a day to have a baby.*

As the two got closer, Evelyn Rose caught her father turn for another log and look their way. She waved one hand high in the air until her father returned the wave. Soon Evelyn Rose and Tennessee were through the gate and walking up to a fatigued and nervous man.

Tennessee noticed this and told him, "Let's go in and see how everyone is doing."

"I'll cut a little more and be in soon," he told Tennessee. He then asked Evelyn Rose, "How'd you like doing cattle chores?"

"I'll need boots if I ever do that again," she told her father.

Tennessee put a hand on the ax and said, "If we go in for some warm coffee, we'll tell ya all about it."

He let go, knowing he really had more than enough wood. He took a deep breath and bobbed his head up and down. "That sounds good," he said. "I think it's time. Will you stay?"

Tennessee smiled at Evelyn Rose and her father and told them both, "I wouldn't be anywhere else."

Evelyn Rose led the way in, but her father stopped before going through the doorway and pointed out what looked like a strong rain front coming in from the southwest. "It's cold enough to start freezing now," he told Tennessee. They both looked at the cold front coming in straight out of the north. He said, "We may not get any help from a doctor if we get what I think we will."

As they both went in, Tennessee asked, "When do you expect Millie back?"

"As soon as the play practice is over," Mattie said as she came running to give Tennessee a welcome hug. "I sure am glad to see you. Mother is in her room straightening up some."

"Is she feeling all right?" Mrs. Bell asked.

"She's feeling fine," Mattie said, "but I can tell the way she looks at Father that her pain isn't any gas pain."

"I'm sure," Tennessee said. "I'll just go back and check on her, if you don't mind," she said, looking at Mattie's father.

"No, no! Go ahead!" Evelyn Rose said.

Mattie, Evelyn Rose, and their father had a seat at the table. All three looked at one another wondering what to do and straining their ears to hear what was being said in the back room.

As Tennessee walked by the girls' room, she couldn't help but feel bad for them as the room was so small. She then wondered how it was that all three were so bright and had nothing but the most positive outlook on life. Tennessee walked to the back room and saw the girls' mother sitting on the edge of the bed with her back to the door. "Can I come in?" she asked.

"Well, yes," Mother said. "I was just resting a bit."

Tennessee walked in, though it's just a couple of steps. She sat in a chair in the corner and reached out to hold the hand of the expecting mother. "You doing okay?"

"Yes, I'm fine," Mother said. "I've never thought about it before, at least not seriously, but this place is really getting crowded. I hate to move, but you really should see the new place."

Mrs. Bell, sensing a little embarrassment about the cabin, told her neighbor, "It might be a little small, but it sure is a good home. I can't wait to come north for a visit."

"I remember when Mattie was born," she told Mrs. Bell, "I had these same kinds of feelings. These moody feelings. Don't know why, but I get these blues for just a while and have to force myself to tell everyone how happy I am. I just want to cry."

Mrs. Bell got up and sat next to her neighbor on the bed. They both laughed when they almost sunk to the floor and fell over. Mrs. Bell held her friend and told her, "You cry anytime you want. I'll be right here. Between me and this family or yours, we'll all help."

"You're such a good friend," she said as a light labor pain came on, and she tightly gripped Mrs. Bell's hand.

"Well, now," Tennessee said, "I would say it's time for you to just lay back and rest."

"But I'm fine," Mother said as the labor pain loosened its grip. "Besides, I'm hungry, and I need to eat to keep my strength up."

Tennessee's eyes widened as she clasped her hands together and said, "This is your lucky day. Tell you what,"—she forced the expecting mother to lay back—"I just happened to bring a fresh beef roast with me. Thought I'd make a stew while we wait on that little feller to make his entrance into this world."

"You're just too kind," Mother said as she relaxed on the bed.

"I'm sure your family will think that," Mrs. Bell told her, "but all you get is the broth."

"Just make sure there's some left for me when this whole ordeal is over," the woman in labor told her friend.

Tennessee stood and gave her a wink. "I will," she said as she pulled a curtain across the doorway. With nothing but her head poking through, she reminded the resting mother-to-be, "Just yell if you need anything."

When Tennessee got back with Evelyn Rose, Mattie, and their father, she found out the roast was already being cut up for stew. The girls' father had moved the table in order to get some vegetables.

"Here," he told Tennessee as he handed out some more potatoes and carrots. "Might as well throw in some of these dried peas and corn too." He handed her a jar of each. He smiled and whispered, "You don't know how much this means to us."

As he climbed out of the half cellar and placed the cover back, he told his daughters, "While you all do this, I guess I better get the sheep down here to water before it's too late."

"What do you mean *too late*," Mattie asked.

As he pulled the table back in place, Father told the girls, "It was freezing earlier, and the temperature keeps dropping. With that moisture coming from behind the southwest hill, its's likely to freeze up something fierce."

As Father got dressed to go back out, Mattie did everything she could to go with him. He insisted she stay and help fix the vittles. He was thinking how she would probably slow him down and with the wrong voice, keep the sheep too skittish to drive down the hill. Explaining the situation, Mattie relented to staying put and helping cook and fetch anything Mother needed. All bundled up, Father reached for Millie's walking staff.

"What's wrong?" Evelyn Rose asked.

As Father picked up his walking stick, he told Evelyn Rose, "I forgot Millie took her staff with her. Now I'll have to use this"—he held up his short cane—"to drive the sheep down. Better than nothing, I guess."

He opened the door and set out to leave. As his foot and walking stick hit the big flat rock porch, they came out from under him. With a hard thud, he landed squarely on his back. The breath in his lungs was instantly knocked out of him. For just a short minute, he thought he would never breathe again. He could only breathe out, and no matter how hard he tried, no air would come in. Just as the world around him started to spin and turn dark, a great wheeze and gush of air filled his lungs, and soon his breathing returned to normal. As he sat up, he realized that most everything was covered with ice. "Oh no," he said as he tried to get to his feet. With his walking stick, he banged on the door that he had just slammed shut.

"Father!" Mattie yelled as she opened the door. "Are you all right?"

"Get your sister," he told her. "I think I broke my ankle."

"Evelyn Rose! Mrs. Bell!" Mattie yelled. "Father's fallen, and he's hurt!"

As they rushed to help, Father held his hand up and said, "Watch out! It doesn't look like it, but the rock is completely covered with ice."

Everyone did their best to get Father up, but no one could stand up to help him. They sat in the threshold and dragged him into the cabin.

"You know," Mrs. Bell said, "if you weren't hurt, this would almost be comical."

The girls got their father's coat off as Mrs. Bell gingerly loosened the laces on his boot. Almost to the point of cutting the boot off, he put both hands on the floor and told Mrs. Bell to just hold the heel and toe of the boot. He scooted straight back and winced in pain as the foot slid out of the boot.

"Somebody close the door please," Mrs. Bell asked as she examined the injured foot. She pressed some and felt all around the ankle. "Does that hurt?" she asked.

"Yes, it does," he said. "But not as bad as I thought it would."

Evelyn Rose and Mattie watched as Mrs. Bell gently felt all around the ankle then up and down the foot and leg. Evelyn Rose asked, "Is it broke?"

Mrs. Bell closed her eyes and tilted her head as she concentrated on feeling all around the ankle. She pursed her lips then opened her eyes and explained, "I don't feel anything broke, but that doesn't mean there isn't."

"I read in a book in the doctor's library the foot has more bones in it than anywhere else," Evelyn Rose said.

Mattie squinted her eyes together at her sister as Tennessee gave her a smile.

"In the human body," Evelyn Rose said as if just talking to herself.

"Well, Dr. Evelyn Rose," Mattie said, "what do we do next?"

"Let's not say anything to your mother," Father told his girls. Then he asked Tennessee, "Can you all help me up?"

Evelyn Rose gave Mattie a smart look then told Father and Mrs. Bell, "I also read the best thing to do for a sprain is to keep your weight off it and keep the foot elevated. Later, you might want to wrap it real tight so you can walk some on it."

Father looked around the small room, and everyone could tell that he was thinking what to do. He looked very dejected.

The girls made their father a pallet to lay on close to the woodstove as Tennessee made the stew.

Plans were made not to tell Mother unless absolutely necessary. They'd wait till Millie got home and then discuss what to do about the sheep.

"Those sheep know her voice better than mine," Father said. "They'll follow her anywhere."

Chapter 67

"That was really good," Millie told Cecil's mother. "I really can't remember eating roast duck before."

Cecil's mother looked at her husband then back to Millie and explained with a bit of disappointment, "If he isn't working in the store, then he's out hunting duck or geese. It seems to be his passion."

"It's the challenge to hunt ducks," he said.

"No," his wife replied. "The challenge is in cooking them so they don't taste like liver."

Cecil's brother and sisters were all squirming to get next to Millie when one of the girls said, "I always give mine to the dog," thinking she was safe because of the guest.

For a span of time that seemed like eternity, not a single word was said. No one even moved. Then Cecil's Pa stated, "At least it's good for you and makes dessert a whole lot more anticipated."

No one really knew how to take that comment till Cecil's mother got up from her chair and gathered a few dishes. As he walked out of the dining area, she said, "So my desserts are only good when we eat your ducks."

The poor man's face turned red as he yelled at the shut kitchen door, "You took that the wrong way. I meant—" As his wife reentered the dining room with a large pie, he said, "Oh my!" He then told Millie, "I hope you come to visit more often."

Coffee, pie, and milk made for a great visit for everyone. They spoke of Christmas, the play, and Cecil coming home.

"We know he made it to St. Louis," Cecil's mother told Millie. "I just don't know how bad the weather is up north."

His Pa set the steaming cup of coffee down and said, "If the weather is anything like the looks of the front moving in, he'll have some trouble getting here. I bet it won't be by the coach."

Millie made a guess that it was getting close for play practice to get started. It was agreed that Cecil's brother and two sisters could go with Millie and help with the sheep.

"Make sure you come straight home as soon as play practice is over," Cecil's parents told their children from the porch of the house. "Millie, make them mind you."

She assured them that she would and yelled back, "They've always been good for me," referring to the time she had them as their teacher in school.

Millie got the sheep from the livery stable and headed to church from there. As the temperature continued to drop, the drizzle started sticking and freezing to everything it landed on. Black oak leaves that hung on to the branches all winter were beginning to be coated with ice. Not everyone showed up for play practice, which made it a little more difficult to get through. The baby lamb was a hit with everyone, especially the children. It became a prize if the children minded and did their part correctly. The lady directing the play would let them pet the lamb when they did a good job.

As with most winter storms, when the day ends, Mother Nature seems to kick up her heels. The preacher called practice off early and let everyone know the weather was turning worse. The lady that was running the play asked, "If possible, come a little early on Christmas Eve to help set up." She told Millie, "Mr. Highley will board the sheep so you won't have to take them home in such bad weather."

"I'll bring Bray for the play," Millie told her and the reverend as he walked up.

He put a hand on Millie's shoulder and told her, "I'd like to have a word of prayer for your mother and the baby."

Everyone gathered around and had another prayer, then wished her Godspeed and Merry Christmas.

As Millie and Rusty left, she wondered if anyone would come out to check on her mother. *Christmastime*, she thought to herself. Rusty looked up as if he heard her thoughts, so she told him, "Along with this terrible weather, I doubt it." The dog had a bad habit of bumping into Millie's feet, causing her to fall on the slick ice. The first time was a little funny, but after a couple more times, Millie shook her staff in Rusty's face and told him "No!"

The mist changed to a light rain, and the wind picked up as the two fronts collided. It was too dark to see. It was just like the hailstorm back in July. Rain was coming in one direction as the cold wind came in from the other. Though she was dressed for bad weather, the cold wind seemed to cut right through her clothes. Down she fell again. She yelled at the dog though it wasn't his fault this time. She got up and decided not to take any more steps. Instead, she kept her feet on the ground and slid in strides. "It's gonna take forever to get home like this," she said.

On little hills and the gullies, Millie would slide backward and had to get on her hands and knees to get up them. When she went down, she sat down and slid on her rear. Everything would be wet but in seconds would freeze. Her clothes were getting soaked and freezing stiff. Rain would hit the left side of her face while the wind would blow hard on her right side. Darkness crept in as the rain fell harder and the temperature continued to fall. Finally, Millie and Rusty arrived at the fork in the road. Off down the valley, she could see the small cabin and light coming from between the curtains. She shook a little knowing the wind would be making the curtains move back and forth on the frost-laden window panes. Seeing the smoke come out of the chimney seemed to warm her all the way up the hill though the smoke was blowing to the southwest hill and into the rain.

Millie snapped her head up out of her coat when thunder rumbles from that very direction. "That's odd," she told Rusty. Then quickly told him, "Stay back!" The dog did as she commanded, and they started their slide down the road toward the gate. Veering to the left and sliding sideways, Millie just let gravity take hold, waiting for the fence to stop her. As she neared the fence, she got to her knees hoping for some friction to slow her down. It didn't, and she began picking up speed. She needed to stop. If she slid under the fence and kept going, she would end up in the water from the spring. Using different parts of her body like a rudder, she aimed for a post. Rusty tried to keep up but veered farther to the left. There was nothing Millie could do but hope he'd stop before the stream.

Then a sudden thud. Millie yelled out when she heard a creak in her ribs and all the air was knocked from her lungs as she slammed into the fence post. She groaned from pain and flailed to grab the post and stop her slide. "Got it," she said out loud though the words sounded like someone had been underwater too long and was gasping for air. She struggled to her feet whimpering at every move from the pain in her ribs. Just as she got her bearings, and everything quit spinning, she heard Rusty squeal when he hit the water. When she cleared the tears out of her eyes, she could see Rusty shaking the water off his fur. Millie thought it would be funny if her ribs didn't hurt every time she breathed in.

Millie hung onto the fence and walked up toward the gate. Going this way, the wind hit her square in the face and was so cold it made breathing that much more difficult. In her peripheral vision, she could see Rusty slip-sliding his way to the door of the cabin. If her calculations were correct, she'd slow down and stop just about the woodpile. Almost to the cabin, she spotted Evelyn Rose coming around the corner with nary a coat, hat, or gloves on.

"Are you okay?" Evelyn Rose asked as she slid up to Millie.

Millie groaned and told her, "Don't pull on me. I think I've hurt my ribs, and I don't want to pull you down too." Then she asked, "Did Rusty make it in?" Before Evelyn Rose could answer, Millie quickly asked, "How's Mother?"

"Mrs. Bell is with Mother in her room," she told her. "And, yes, your wet dog is with Father by the woodstove."

Evelyn Rose let Millie hang on to her, and as the two girls shuffled their way to the front door, Millie asked, "Is Mother doing okay?"

They stopped and looked at each other. Evelyn Rose told her, "I think so, at least Mother and Mrs. Bell say everything is as it should be."

"Then what's wrong?" Millie questioned.

As they started shuffling again, Evelyn Rose told her, "I just don't remember Mother groaning like that when she had Mattie."

"That's because it was in the fall, and you were probably outside," Millie told her. "But she did groan a lot."

"Well, there's something else," Evelyn Rose said.

"What's that?" Millie asked.

"Father fell on the rock porch," she told her.

Millie's shoulders slumped, and with a very concerned look, she asked, "Is he hurt? Is he hurt?" Then demanded, "Tell me!"

"It's his ankle," she explained. "We don't think it's broke. Maybe just a bad sprain."

"Can he walk?" Millie inquired.

"Not yet," Evelyn Rose said. "It's pretty swollen."

For the first time, Millie looked over to the holding pen and noticed the sheep had not been brought down. She exhaled and slowly nodded her head then told Evelyn Rose, "I'll warm up some and get something to eat." Thunder rolled again and she continued, "Then I'll go up and get them."

"Do you have to?" Evelyn Rose asked.

"If I don't," Millie told her, "they'll get soaked, get down, and die. That wool will hold so much of this rain, and it'll freeze."

"I'll go with you and Rusty," Evelyn Rose told her as they started walking again.

Millie shrugged her shoulders a little then a little bit more and said as they continued to make their way to the front door, "I think my ribs are gonna be okay. The way they made that sound, I just knew I had broken one." She lowered her voice in a stern tone and told Evelyn Rose, "And no, Rusty is not going with me!"

"He's not?" Evelyn Rose asked in surprise.

"That dog had me down on my knees more than I care to count," Millie explained. "It's so slick, every time he'd bump me, down I would go. Besides, with this freezing rain and slick ground, Rusty wouldn't be able to herd the sheep."

Both girls carefully stepped up on the big rock porch. Evelyn Rose said just before opening the door, "Then I'll go with you."

Millie smiled and told her, "We'll see."

Joy resonated throughout the small cabin when Millie finally came in. The wood heat through the small cabin glowed warmth all the more. While Mrs. Bell served up some hot stew, Millie told them about her day at church and the evening with Cecil's family. Tennessee checked out Millie's ribs and had to agree with her that they were probably badly bruised. Mrs. Bell tightly wrapped her ribs for her journey after the sheep.

Hearing the word *sheep* brought Rusty straight up out of his warm, comfortable spot between the woodstove and the girls' father.

"You're not going this time," Millie told the poor dog, who seemed to understand. "It's just too slick, and I don't need you knocking me down any more. The sheep definitely don't need to panic on this slick stuff."

"I'm going with you," Evelyn Rose said though Millie already knew that.

Mattie jumped up from the table and made a direct demand at Evelyn Rose, "I am going too!" Rushing to her room so no one could say no, she got extra clothes on and continued telling anyone who'd listen. "You'll need my help, and I'll mind what you tell me. We'll make a good team and get the job done."

"Okay!" Millie and her father both said. "Just make sure you two don't get in your sister's way," Father told the two young helpers. He then looked up at Millie and apologized for not already having the sheep where they should be.

Millie smiled tight-lipped and told him, "As if you didn't have anything else to worry about."

"Go see your mother before you head back out," Father told her. "Never know, you might be a big sister again by the time you get them sheep to their pen."

On the way to check on her mother, Millie looked in her room and told Evelyn Rose and Mattie to put an extra pair of socks on over their shoes. "It's the only way we'll be able to walk up the hill," she said.

"Mother," Millie whispered.

"Come on in, Millie," Mother told her.

Mrs. Bell came through the curtain before Millie could go in. "Did you get enough to eat?" she asked Millie in passing.

"Yes, ma'am, I did!" Millie said. "That fresh beef was so good. Why, I feel like a new girl!"

"Good," Mrs. Bell said with a pat on Millie's arm. She held the curtain back for Millie to go on in and told her, "Be quick so your mother can rest, and you can hightail it back here when you get the flock put away."

"Well, you look mighty chipper," Millie said to her mother.

"I feel good," Mother said with a smile. "It's just really hard to get comfortable."

Millie could see the worry in her mother's eyes though there was a smile on her face. She decided to sit for a few minutes and hopefully calm both their nerves. She held Mother's hand in both of hers and told her, "Father's gonna be fine. A sprain hurt, but a good wrapping, and he'll get around fine as long as he stays off the ice." She held her mother's hand in her left and took her right thumb and gently made small circles on each finger, going from the palm to the tip of each finger. Every so often, Mother would wince in pain and tell Millie, "That hurts so good."

After a few more minutes, Mother patted Millie's hand and said, "You better go now."

"Yes, I know," Millie told her. "I should have been gone hours ago."

"Take your time and be safe," Mother said. "We're not going anywhere here."

Millie stood and smiled at her mother. She leaned down and kissed her on the forehead and said, "Give that to my little brother, if he gets here before I get back."

Millie slipped out of the room as she heard her mother say, "Don't worry. I will."

Millie finished getting dressed and sat on her sister's bed to pull a pair of wool socks over her shoes to help with walking on the ice. As she stood to leave, her hand touched the barrette on the windowsill. She picked up the silver shepherd's staff with the lamb on it, opened her coat, and placed it in her shirt pocket. "There," she said, "I'm ready to go."

Coming into the gathering room, Millie saw Evelyn Rose and Mattie dressed exactly as she had told them. Father held Rusty and tried to tell the girls how to walk on the ice. He apologized again for not being able to help.

The three girls went out and closed the door. Millie looked up into the sky as the rain fell and said, "Listen to that wind!"

Chapter 68

Pulling his collar up as far as he could, almost to the brim of his hat, Cecil looked up into the black wet sky and told the old mare, "Well, girl, I guess this is as far as we can go for now." He gently got off his horse and slapped up and down both legs to get his frozen pants to bend so he could walk. He gave the old mare a little treat out of his coat pocket, and as he placed his forehead on hers, he said, "We'll walk till we find some more cedars and try to get out of this godforsaken weather."

Knowing cedar groves were common in Missouri, Cecil walked due south on the main road until he could find some. Only problem was, it was so dark. The ground was so slick Cecil was afraid to take his eyes off the road, and when he did look up, everything was pitch-black. After traveling for another hour, he noticed small cedar saplings just off to the west side of the road. "We'll just go a little farther. Maybe we'll get lucky."

A few more yards, and his luck changed. He led the mare right into some of the thickest and biggest cedar trees he had seen in this part of Missouri. Just as before, Cecil wove his way in far enough so he could build a small fire and not be seen from the road. He again tied his rain slicker from one cedar to another to have a roof over himself and the horse. He scraped some cedar bark from the trees and put the tar-like pitch on dead limbs he found lying on the ground. Cecil knew cedar sap was some of the best fire starters. In no time, he had a nice fire going. Cedar burned quick, and Cecil had to find wood. There was plenty on the ground, but it was all wet and frozen solid to the ground. Walking under a dead cedar limb, Cecil's hat got knocked off. Upset that he could not find dry wood, he slapped at the limb, breaking it off and at the same time, knocking the ice off.

Continuing to knock the ice off the dead limbs, soon he had enough firewood to last the better part of the night. "Now for a dry place to sleep," he told himself. He took live cedar branches and knocked the ice off. He laid a wool blanket on top. This worked great for a makeshift bed. All settled in, Cecil took out the remaining jerky for himself and the mule feed in his saddlebag pack for the mare. Coffee was brewed as the late supper was being chewed on by both man and beast.

"Not sure where we are at," Cecil told the horse. "But one thing is for sure, one way or another, after a short rest, we'll get home tonght."

The old mare nickered, and Cecil replied, "Now I know we've gone a long way, but we haven't passed up our turnoff." He laughed, blew on his steaming coffee, and mumbles, "I hope not."

The food and warm fire caused Cecil's eyes to grow heavy. The warm coffee wasn't enough to keep him from nodding off. The singing wind above the treetops lured Cecil's mind into a place and time of days gone by. He dreamed of warm sunny days walking past a pond, then through a gap in the fence, holding her hand tight and never wanting to let go. He saw the shade and knew they would stop and rest under the ancient oak tree. Rest.

Chapter 69

"If it wasn't for the wind," Evelyn Rose said, "I don't think it would be so bad."

Millie pulled Mattie's scarf tight and wrapped it around her neck. "There," she said, "keep it tight so nothing goes down your neck." Looking into Mattie's eyes, Millie knew there was no place in the world her little sister would rather be than right there with her sisters.

After a few minutes of trying to walk on the icy terrain, they decided to lock arms to help support one another. Socks helped a lot, but what helped the most was having help getting back up when one of them fell. That little lift made it easier not to fall right back down. Every so often, the girls would look back at the cabin, but the freezing, blowing rain would hit the skin on their faces so hard and sting that they would have to turn right back around.

"It's so dark I can't see if light is shining through the window," Millie said. "It's as if this storm has eaten the whole light out of the world. There's not even a tree line to guide us."

"I can't even see where the two hills are," Evelyn Rose said. "The wind is blowing in blackness that's devouring everything."

"But just think," Mattie answered her two sisters, "when we go back, all we need to do is sit down and just slide toward home. We'll be there in no time at all."

Mattie's sisters laughed, and Millie said, "Leave it to Mattie to find something good in all this darkness."

Slowly the three girls inched their way until they come to the dam of the pond. Using the bushes at the bottom of the dam, they pulled themselves to the spillway and then to the pond side.

"Wow," Millie said. "It sure makes a big difference getting out of that wind."

Evelyn Rose pulled Millie close and asked her, "I don't ever remember the weather being this bad. Do you?"

"No, I don't," came Millie's reply.

"Do you think we can get the sheep down off this hill?" she asked.

Millie looked into the eyes of her sisters. Mattie stuck her head in close and said, "Now what are we going to do?"

Millie thought for a minute then finally said to Evelyn Rose, "No, we can't." She then told them both, "You two stay here. I'll find the sheep since we're here and just see how and where they are. When I get back, we'll slide our way back down the hill." She gave Mattie a little pinch on the nose and told her, "Don't go anywhere! Okay?"

"So we're not going to get the sheep home?" Mattie asked as she rubbed her tweaked nose.

"No, we're not," Millie answered. "I'm sorry, but we just can't."

Evelyn Rose gave Millie a surprised look at the strange words coming out of Millie's mouth. She couldn't remember Millie ever saying the word *can't*.

"I'll be back," Millie said. "You two stay right here!"

Millie turned and gauged where the gap in the fence should be and took off. Her plan was once through the gap, she would walk along the fence to the great oak. From there, she would go straight across the back field to the creek on the other side. After a short way up the cedars, hopefully, she would find the sheep. "They always go there in bad weather no matter if it's winter or summer," she muttered to herself.

"How long do you think Millie will be gone?" Mattie asked.

Evelyn Rose stuck her arm through Mattie's and pulled her in close so they could huddle their heads together. "If she doesn't fall and hurt herself again," she said, "it shouldn't be too long. The ground is flatter up here than what we just came up."

Bumping foreheads, Mattie said, "Does she know where the sheep are?"

When Evelyn Rose nodded her head, Mattie nodded hers right along with her. "She knows those sheep so well," she said. "I'll bet she'll walk right up to them. Then in no time at all, Millie will be right back."

Mattie looked into Evelyn Rose's eyes. Evelyn Rose could see the anxiety begin to turn into fear. She grabbed Mattie's coat by the shoulders and pulled her up. "What say we keep a sharp lookout for Millie," Evelyn Rose said. "In a little while, we'll start calling to her so she can follow our voices back to us."

"That's a great idea," Mattie told her as she turned and started to walk across the pond on the ice.

"Hey!" Evelyn Rose said. "I don't know if that's a good idea."

"It's a shortcut," Mattie yelled back to her sister.

About twenty feet out, Mattie stomped on the ice to show Evelyn Rose that it was safe. Yelling into the wind, she said as she continued to walk backward toward the center of the pond, "See, it's plenty thick," and waved Evelyn Rose to her in case she couldn't hear her words.

Evelyn Rose didn't think it was a good idea, but when she saw Mattie sliding and having fun, she decided to walk on out and join her. Getting to within ten feet of her spinning sister, she heard a creak in the ice. She instantly stopped in her tracks.

Mattie did the same and asked, "What was that sound?" Another pop, and a streaking crack goes across the pond. "That doesn't sound good," Mattie said as she reached for Evelyn Rose and slid toward her.

The two girls met in the center of the pond. Their combined weight was too much, and in the blink of an eye and before either could scream, they disappeared through the ice into the deepest part of the pond.

Millie had no trouble crossing the field from the oak. The land wasn't as steep, which made it much easier to walk. The closer she got to the valley, the less the wind blew though she could hear the wind howling from the pond as it blew over the trees. As she crossed the creek and entered the edge of the cedar thicket, Millie called out to the sheep. Not being able to see anything, she said out loud, "If it would just snow some, I'd be able to see the ground." She stopped to listen, but the only thing she heard were the tree limbs popping from the weight of the ice. She heard the wind blowing above the trees and then heard a bell ring. She called out again and then thought that perhaps she just imagined the bell.

"That's a bell!" Millie shouted when she heard it for the second time. Walking to the back side of the cedar thicket, she told herself, "Where else would they be but the warmest spot in this valley." Millie ducked and wove through the cedars, holding her arms in front of her face to keep from having a limb poke her in the eye. She heard a baa from one of the lambs and an answer from its mother. "There you are," she called out when she saw the white wool balls all huddled in one small space.

The closer she got, the more the sheep recognized her voice and let her know they wanted to be fed. Knowing she couldn't get them over the hill and down to the feed lot, she struggled with how to handle the situation. She sat down in the middle of the flock and chastised herself for even making the trip as there was absolutely nothing she could do. The sheep huddled together in a group around Millie. They began to lay down, lamb next to its mother, mother next to its sister, and before she knew it, they were all down and counted. "Twenty-two," Millie said and continued to talk softly to the flock. "I'm going to be a sister again," she said in a low calming tone. "Father hurt his ankle, or you guys would have already been home and fed. Mrs. Bell is with Mother to help with the delivery, and Rusty is with them. Couldn't bring him 'cause I didn't want any of you running on the ice. Nope, that wouldn't be good. Cecil's coming home for Christmas. He should have already been here, but as you all can tell, the weather isn't cooperating."

Millie reached inside her coat and took her shepherd's staff barrette out to show the sheep. "See this," she said, "he gave it to me just before he left." Millie looks at the silver shepherd's staff then took one hand and gently touched the curled-up sleeping lamb and remembered the sermon she had heard earlier. "Christmas is coming!" she said a little too loud. Some of the sheep looked her way and baaed but stayed right where they were. "Yep, in a couple of days, it will be Christmas, and hopefully a little better weather."

"If I leave, will you all stay here?" she asked. She then told them, "I promise I'll bring some feed to you first thing in the morning." Millie sat a little while longer listening to some of the sounds. Wind was making music in the treetops while limbs heavy with ice would break off and crash to the ground. Very slowly, she stood and carefully slid away from the settled flock. "Lord, please don't let me fall," she prayed. She continued to back up until the white balls of wool disappeared behind the cedar limbs and cold slick, icy blackness. Millie stopped to listen fearing that one sheep would break and try to follow her. None did, so she turned and followed the tree line from the valley to the fence that divided the two fields. Hearing a voice, she stopped, looked across the field, and smiled at the giant oak, figuring the wind blowing through the leafless branches was what she heard.

Once she got to the fence, Millie had something to hold on to. "At last, to the gap," she said, "then I'll get the girls at the pond, and we'll get home."

From the gap in the fence, Millie made a little left turn and started a slow slide toward the pond. The closer she got, the harder she looked at the pond side of the dam. "Hey!" she yelled. "Evelyn Rose! Mattie! Let's go home!"

Due to the changing temperature, snow began to fall. Walking along the bank, Millie strained her eyes looking through the snowflakes for the two girls huddled together against the dam. *Surely they didn't go back home,* she thought. *I haven't been gone that long.*

Almost to the spillway, Millie stopped. She noticed some long sliding tracks going out onto the pond. Then in her peripheral vision, she saw what she hadn't seen at first. Millie groaned in a low drawn-out "*Nooo!*" Refusing to believe what she thought, she screamed out, "Mattie! Evelyn Rose! Where are you?" As loud as she could holler, Millie called out for her sisters. She watched the ice as her mind started grasping the facts. Finally realizing what had happened, Millie forced her legs to move toward the break in the ice. She began to panic. "Please *no!*" she said out loud. "What do I do?" Easing to the edge of the hole, her mind ceased to make sense of anything as her body instinctively reacted, and she jumped in the water.

The cold water hit her like a sledgehammer as all the air from her lungs instantly escaped her body. Millie's feet hit bottom, and her reaction was to get air. She pushed off the bottom and threw her arms out to come back up. As she did, her left hand touched one of the girls. Millie's mind cried out as she tried to find the one she touched. *Air,* she thought. *I need air—now* was her thought as her hand touched the freezing air above the water. She slapped until she felt the broken edge of the ice while trying to get air into her lungs. Each time she tried, her throat would shut off, and no air would feed her starving lungs. The world around her began to spin and turn black. She heard a wheeze and realized it was her sucking in great gulps of air. The first thing Millie saw were her hands grasping the ice. They were shaking so hard she couldn't control them. "Go back down," she cried. "Find your sisters!" She gulped in air to go under the water but cried out again thinking something stabbed her in the side.

Struggling, she remembered sliding into the fence post and hearing the creak in her ribs. This time, Millie slowly inhaled until she filled her lungs full then slipped down under the water. Her mind raced although she thought of nothing while reaching out into the black cold abyss. Her lungs burned, and her side felt as though the knife in her side was being driven deeper. Millie broke the surface again. Gasping and crying out, "Try again! You have to!" Millie noticed the water splashing out onto the ice from her shaking so hard. *Take your coat off so you can move easier,* she thought. She removed her coat and went back under, feeling, searching, trying to see something or someone until she felt herself sucking in air again. Fatigued, freezing to death, and trying to figure out what to do, she inhaled again. Her strength didn't allow her much air, and she descended again. This time, her foot touched something. She turned to grab for what her foot hit. There she was, her sister.

Millie grabbed with all her strength and pulled her to her. She kicked to go up and reached with her other hand for the surface. She kicked again until she came up through the hole in the ice. Grabbing the edge with barely enough strength to hang on, Millie got her elbow over the edge to hold herself up. She pulled the lifeless body up, and Millie cried out, "*Nooo!*" As the water flowed off, it revealed the face of her youngest sister. "Mattie! Oh, my Mattie! Please, dear God, help me!" Millie struggled to hang on as she tried to get Mattie onto the ice, but each time she pulled and pushed, the weaker she got. Her shaking was so hard Millie lost her grip only to watch her baby sister slowly slip back into the dark watery grave.

Millie screamed, but no voice came from her. She cried without making a sound no matter how hard she tried. Her instinct was to get out of the water, but each time she tried, the water splashing onto the ice along with the new falling snow made it almost impossible until at last, she got her foot on top. With her elbow, her head, and one leg on the ice, with the remaining strength she had, Millie kicked with her leg that was in the water and rolled. She rolled again and again. The third time, she rolled away from the broken ice. Millie tried to stand, but her shaking body wouldn't let her. She cried for her sisters. She cried for the pain in her body, and she cried for the sheep she left behind until she decided to give up herself. Lying there, shaking and barely able to breathe, she relented and relaxed.

Somehow Millie found herself crawling toward the dam. She didn't know how, but a force pulled her off the pond and up to the top of the dam. She lifted her head and looked toward the cabin.

Millie swore she could feel the warmth coming from the yellow glow of the small window. Next to it, the cabin door opened, and the yellow glow spilled out onto the big flat rock porch. There in the doorway stood her mother, holding a small bundle with both arms close to her neck. Millie could hear her name coming up the hill being sung on the frigid north wind. She tried to answer. She felt warm and comfortable, but no response would come from her body. Not even a blink when a snowflake lightly landed on her eyelashes. Father stepped next to his wife and child as a man leading his horse came from the dark side of the house. Stepping next to the big rock porch, the man watched Millie's mother lift her hand in the direction of the pond.

Through the slow, soft falling flakes of snow, Millie knew who the man was when he dropped the reins and tried to run as best he could in her direction. Rusty burst through her mother's and father's legs to follow the man. She tried to say his name, but only her mind could shout, *Cecil!*

Her eyes faded, and her spirit slipped through her. A longing, loving smile crossed her face as she was carried away on the breeze among the snowflakes into the dark winter night.

Chapter 70

Two days later, on a blinding bright, sunny day, Mrs. Bell told Ole Smokey to get-up with a light flick of the reins. With a bit of a jerk, the old horse stepped gingerly with his wool-covered hooves and started his trek up the frozen hillside. Wrapped up tightly next to Tennessee, Mother and her new child turned to make sure none of the three coffins had slid in any way. Cecil's parents along with the old doctor and his wife were right there with hands on the coffins, assuring the girls' mother all was well.

Rusty lay his head on one of the coffins and watched Bray keep pace with Ole Smokey from a distance. Bray's head hung low. The sun reflected off his low head to reveal the burden of the cross he bore down his shoulders and along his back. What folks that could make it, followed slowly holding on to one another in silence. Up the hill they trekked, past the pond, through the gap in the fence, and down the fence row to the majestic bare and lonely oak tree. Cecil lay down his shovel when the town's sheriff tapped him with the back of his hand on his arm and nodded toward the small procession making their way toward them. Both men took a step back, causing Father to look up from the shallow graves he was still cleaning out as best he could. He looked in the direction of the men's stare to the approaching wagon.

Mrs. Bell brought Ole Smokey to a halt just a few feet from the three men.

With tears welling up in his eyes, Father started to get out of the grave. While still on his bad leg, he placed his hand on the edge of the grave to raise himself up, only to knock some loose dirt back in. He stared at it. Tears fell. He reached down to pick something up and cradled the object with both hands near his heart. He struggled to stand and grimaced, stepping out of the grave still clutching both hands to his chest. He walked over to the wagon where his wife sat watching him. Father looked back at the girls, imagining three angels watching their sheep. He then looked at his wife and new son and slowly brought his hand to hers and said, "This is where our girls will find their rest." His hands opened to reveal a single acorn as he said, "Here under the oak, where the acorns fall."

About the Author

William Shelton always had a big imagination and a knack for telling stories. From a young age he worked by his father's side on a cattle farm, which instilled in him a love for the outdoors. His love for the outdoors and his talent for story-telling came together in Where the Acorns Fall to become his first work as an author. He has four wonderful children and seven awesome grand-children, who have listened to many of his tales. He has worked as a machinist at the local glass plant for forty-two years, and currently resides in the town of Farmington, Missouri, along with his wife, Barb of forty-six years, and their cat, Rango.

CPSIA information can be obtained
at www.ICGtesting.com
Printed in the USA
LVHW090501301019
635802LV00001B/1/P

9 781644 629512